UNSELFING

MICHAELA HULSTYN

Unselfing

Global French Literature at the Limits of Consciousness

UNIVERSITY OF TORONTO PRESS
Toronto Buffalo London

© University of Toronto Press 2022
Toronto Buffalo London
utorontopress.com

ISBN 978-1-4875-4376-1 (cloth)   ISBN 978-1-4875-4377-8 (EPUB)
                                   ISBN 978-1-4875-4355-6 (PDF)

University of Toronto Romance Series

Library and Archives Canada Cataloguing in Publication

Title: Unselfing : global French literature at the limits of consciousness / Michaela
    Hulstyn.
Names: Hulstyn, Michaela, author.
Series: University of Toronto romance series.
Description: Series statement: University of Toronto romance series | Includes
    bibliographical references and index.
Identifiers: Canadiana (print) 20220160996 | Canadiana (ebook) 20220161062 | ISBN
    9781487543761 (cloth) | ISBN 9781487543778 (EPUB) | ISBN 9781487543556 (PDF)
Subjects: LCSH: French literature – 20th century – History and criticism. | LCSH:
    Self in literature. | LCSH: Altered states of consciousness in literature.
Classification: LCC PQ307.A65 H85 2022 | DDC 840.9/353 – dc23

We wish to acknowledge the land on which the University of Toronto Press
operates. This land is the traditional territory of the Wendat, the Anishnaabeg, the
Haudenosaunee, the Métis, and the Mississaugas of the Credit First Nation.

This book has been published with the help of grants from Florida State University
and Stanford University.

University of Toronto Press acknowledges the financial support of the Government
of Canada, the Canada Council for the Arts, and the Ontario Arts Council, an agency
of the Government of Ontario, for its publishing activities.

For Matthew

Contents

Acknowledgments

This book took a decade of thinking and research to take shape. It is daunting to attempt to express the fullness of my gratitude to those who have supported me over the last ten years, but I have done my best to make a start.

This project is first and foremost reflective of the supportive and foundational intellectual environment I found at Stanford at the beginning and end of the project. I am deeply grateful to Laura Wittman for her wisdom and warmth, on which I have drawn since the beginning. Joshua Landy has been an engaged reader as well as a steadfast advocate and friend through the book's writing. Amir Eshel encouraged me to pursue a research question that matters, which I have tried to do. Special thanks to Dan Edelstein, Elisabeth Mudimbe-Boyi, Alexander Key, and Marie-Pierre Ulloa for their feedback on the book's argument at various stages. I am grateful to Robert Pogue Harrison for inviting me to share my work from this book with the *Entitled Opinions* community. Coordinating the interdisciplinary workshop at the Center for the Explanation of Consciousness with Paul Skokowski and John Perry was generative for me and my thinking at an early stage.

My colleagues and students in Stanford's Structured Liberal Education program introduced me to perspectives, orientations, and questions that have helped me refine and develop a theory of unselfing. Thank you especially to Greg Watkins and Jeremy Sabol for your hilarity, friendship, and wisdom (not necessarily in that order). You inspire me to ask the right questions. Teaching in this program has shaped my thinking in ways I am only now starting to fully appreciate. Thank you to Marisa Galvez for having me back!

Heartfelt thanks to Ann Delehanty, Hugh Hochman, and Catherine Witt of Reed College for their tenacious support and feedback on the book and the proposal during my time in Portland and since. I miss you all dearly.

Thank you to my colleagues at Florida State, especially my faculty mentor Martin Munro, for helping to push the editing process forward. Special thanks to the stellar junior faculty in the French program – Michelle Bumatay, Jeannine Murray-Román, Vincent Joos – for your camaraderie and engagement with my work. Thank you to Beth Coggeshall and Matt Goldmark for the café writing fellowship, and to Pete Maiers for the pasta. Coffee and meals with you all kept me going in Tallahassee. Françoise Lionnet, Andrea Loselle, and Lia Brozgal were my first mentors in Francophone literature and literary theory at UCLA. Thank you for your early and formative investment in me as a scholar and a person.

I am grateful for the work of my editor, Mark Thompson, and the support of the University of Toronto Press in publishing my first book. The three anonymous reviewers made the book exceedingly better thanks to their suggestions, corrections, and constructive feedback. Thank you to the wonderful Aditi Kumar for the index.

Research for this project was supported by Stanford University, Reed College, and Florida State University. At FSU, the FYAP award, departmental funding, and support from the Winthrop-King Center made the completion and the subvention of the book possible. At Stanford, the Taube Center for Jewish Studies and the G.J. Lieberman fellowship supported this work. I am grateful to the librarians at my home institutions as well as at the BNF for their support in researching the manuscript. Without the work of FSU's Interlibrary Loan staff, I would not have finished the book in 2020–1.

Early drafts of two sections of the book have been previously published: a version of chapter 3 on Paul Valéry and Charlotte Delbo in *Modern Language Notes*, and an early draft of chapter 4 on Henri Michaux in an edited volume on *Altered Selves/Altered Self Experiences*. Many thanks to Alexander Gerner and Jorge Gonçalves for organizing the "Cognitive Foundations of the Self'" symposium at the Universidad Nova de Lisboa in 2013, which was the inspiration for the latter publication. I am grateful to the many scholars who have enriched this book through meetings of the Modern Language Association, the American Comparative Literature Association, and the 20th/21st Century French and Francophone Studies Association.

I owe so much to my wonderful and extended family for their love and support. I am especially grateful to my Dad for showing me the joy of lifelong study. Thank you to my siblings, Ryan, Shane, and Katie, for sharing your lives with me. I finished a full draft of the manuscript at the Angers's house, sitting at a little backyard table in the sun on Tacoma Circle. It hurts to not be able to send a copy of the book to Karen, who I know would have celebrated its arrival with champagne.

Thank you to my California friends who have become family. Lucy Alford and Liz Spragins provided invaluable feedback and fierce friendship through the peaks and valleys of writing. Beth Coggeshall has been a sounding board on writing and parenting for a long time. Thank you to Michelle Lamy and Trevor Stuart for your generosity of spirit (and for being our emergency contacts for so many years). UCLA gave me Monica Bartos and Ryan Collins who have been listening to me talk about this writing project for years. My Cleland Avenue community made it possible for me to finish the revisions on the book while working from home during a pandemic with one and then two small children. Thank you, McCaa Illencik! They say it takes a village, and I can't believe we found this one. Dylan Montanari, Lucy Alford, Erika Nadir, Michael Thomas, Liz Spragins, and Gregory Haake generously read final drafts of the book's chapters. Any remaining errors are my own, but if a comma is in the right place, it is almost certainly thanks to them. Thank you for your comments, your ideas, and your brilliance.

I was finishing the first version of the book the year that my daughter, Hadley, came into the world and submitted the final manuscript in the months following the birth of my son, Rowan. I would like to think that the ideas expressed here have been shaped by the perspective and great joy that being your mother has given me. I love you.

Finally, this book is dedicated to Matthew Callahan, who has helped my ideas take shape on napkins in car and train rides together, on notes in different journals, and in the margins of the texts that are forever scattered across our shared space. I see the book as the result of one long and wonderful conversation. You light the rooms in the house of my soul and make sure that I have saved my work. For everything, thank you.

UNSELFING

Introduction

"Je suis étant, et me voyant; me voyant me voir, et ainsi de suite."[1] [I am being and seeing myself; seeing me see myself, and so forth.][2] So murmurs Monsieur Teste as he drifts off to sleep, his pain finally abating. The protagonist of Paul Valéry's extended thought experiment on the relationship between body, mind, and world is comforted, at the end of the narrative, to feel that he has recovered the control of the self. Like the feel of the soft bedcovers on his aching body, it is soothing for Teste to articulate the feeling of self-consciousness. He sees that his thoughts are his own and that his mind belongs to him. He had lost that sense of control, albeit briefly, when his mind was held hostage by the acute pain that was radiating through his limbs. Teste experiences unselfing in the narrative when his meticulous self-science system is interrupted by foreign geometries of suffering. Valéry delivers this experience as the story of disruption; unselfing puts the ordinary operations of the self on hold, even for the most exceptional of self-observers.

While Valéry describes unselfing as a disruption, Abdelkebir Khatibi sees it in a different light. Unselfing in Khatibi is the site of fragmentation; he depicts a mental love life lived between French and Arabic as a series of vertiginous and destabilizing encounters. "Pour décrire cet état, il lui fallait – lui le récitant – tourner, mot après mot, avec sa langue étrangère, dans la pensée du tourbillon."[3] [To describe this state, he the narrator, had to spin, word by word, in his foreign language, in the thought of the whirlwind.][4] In this text, the flimsy illusion of stability is fragmented into language-specific selves as the narrator meditates on the relationships between cultures, bodies, and languages in the postcolonial Maghreb. Unselfing narratives – like Valéry's disruption and Khatibi's fragmentation – relate the transformations of the self when the comforting illusions of unity, stability, or control are lost or transcended. Alongside tales of disruption and fragmentation, unselfing writers convey stories of the mutation and destruction of the self. This book identifies and analyzes these four narrative models for unselfing that resound across French-language literature in the twentieth century.

What does it mean to be unselved? If its usual operations are altered, can the self still manage to consider the other? How does awareness of others function at the fringes of conscious experience? Some accounts suggest that unselfing is an orientation towards the Good and delivers moral clarity. These writers focus on the ways in which unselfing productively expands the self's awareness of the world. In these accounts, the reduction of the self is an achievement, if difficultly won. Other accounts describe unselfing as a painful experience of alienation. These writers reject the idea that lessening the self leads spontaneously and unproblematically to an ethical relationship with others. This book shows how unselfing texts offer compelling and competing answers to these questions by exploring the range of interpretations that ensue after the experience of unselfing is over.

My discussion tracks a constellation of writers across the twentieth-century Francosphère; I use this term and others, such as "global French," throughout the book in an attempt to capture the decentered and transcultural reach of this body of literature. Simone Weil writes from a position of exile during the German occupation of France; Charlotte Delbo records her memories of deportation and internment in the Nazi death camps; Hélène Cixous writes on growing up Jewish in French Algeria; Khatibi writes in French on postcolonial Morocco; the Belgian-born, naturalized-French writer Henri Michaux documents his mescaline experiments in France after traveling to India, China, and Japan; Yolande Mukagasana publishes from Belgium where she took refuge after fleeing the 1994 Rwandan genocide against the Tutsi. Valéry and Georges Bataille, whose texts cross disciplinary borders and resist easy classification, write from France. Following the larger reframing of French literary history within the "French Global" framework, I seek to engage French and Francophone thinkers in the same project, with the aim of shedding light on "cultural difference within and beyond the nation."[5]

Unselfing texts are also diverse and varied when it comes to form. They sit outside of traditional publishing categories and often question the referentiality of the writing subject. From Weil's pithy aphorisms to Bataille's dramatization of the self; from Delbo's haunting prose to Cixous's *scènes primitives*; from Valéry's minimalist narratives to Khatibi's *récit*; from Mukagasana's testimony to Michaux's marginalia, the writers of unselfing bridge the gaps between mysticism, experimentation, and testimony in their unselfing texts. Moreover, as these writers attempt to make sense of altered states of consciousness, they draw from diverse traditions in the process: Sufi mysticism, Neoplatonism, Christian soteriology, Hindu conceptions of actionless action, the Buddhist idea of nonself, and Daoist philosophies of flow, to name just a few influences. Searching for a language for the self's undoing, unselfing writers in the modern Francosphère develop a syncretic approach to philosophy and tradition, innovating genre in the process.

This body of literature reflects the collective desire to offer a philosophy of unselfing using individual experience as a starting point. However, writers disagree about what these experiences mean. These accounts reflect the deep tension between those who conceive of unselfing as a virtuous lessening of the self and those who critique it as a dangerous form of loss. Indeed, for writers who fall into the first category, the draw of unselfing is its intersubjective promise. Weil imagines unselfing as the highest expression of our humanity: "Il n'y a absolument aucun autre acte libre qui nous soit permis, sinon la destruction du *je*."[6] [There is absolutely no other free act which it is given us to accomplish – only the destruction of the "I."][7] According to this view, diminishing the self is required for virtue. Unselfing exposes ordinary selfish consciousness as a mere illusion. These accounts suggest that by throwing off the illusion of egocentrism, we can orient the self towards a more just vision of others and the world. In the same vein, accounts of self-effacement, fragmentation, and ego-destruction recount the triumphs of selflessness. Thinking of the self as a provisional amalgam of fragments might make it easier to appreciate the plurality of selves within others. According to Khatibi, we ought to lessen the self in order to meet the other in desire: "Un affaiblissement loyal exige de rencontrer l'autre et de le perdre en soi, immémorialement."[8] [A faithful weakening of the self requires meeting the other and immemorially losing the other within the self.][9]

And yet, other unselfing narratives explored in this book draw the subject of experience away from the world and into tenebrous inner caverns. Though unselfing might deliver self-knowledge and reveal hitherto unknown inner passageways, it might not deliver a more just vision of what lies beyond the self. Whereas Weil celebrates the subversive potential of an ethics grounded in the piercing of the self, Cixous laments the "cuttings" (*coupures*) that she experiences growing up Jewish in post-Vichy Algeria. The radical mutation of ordinary self-experience may push some who have suffered towards activism as it did for Mukagasana, but it might just as well serve to pull others away from the world. Delbo describes witnessing the pain of others in Auschwitz as a disruption of ordinary experience, one that puts life on hold and makes care for the other impossible.

What, then, binds these texts together? In short, these narratives are insider tales of the self's undoing. Unselfing texts attend to the self as an object of scientific, mystical, and legal significance in the twentieth century in light of the death of God. If not always produced as "streams" of consciousness, unselfing texts give readers a map of the rivulets that emerge in the courses between the mind, body, and world. In this sense, these texts are attempts to give voice to experience; they condense the boundlessness of consciousness into minimal narrative arcs. They evoke an expansive view of consciousness, seeking to build a bridge between altered states and rational accounts of the self. In this sense, they reflect William James's celebrated intuition that a total accounting of the mind must include all forms of consciousness, not just rationality.

Like the conversion model for unselfing, which implies the wholesale inscription of a new subject, the four stories on which this book is centered – disruption, mutation, fragmentation, and destruction – become narrative in the telling. The story of Paul's conversion on the road to Damascus illuminates the book's approach to the relationship between experience and narrative. As the story goes in Acts of the Apostles, Saul was traveling from Jerusalem to Damascus when he was blinded by a flash of light. Alain Badiou describes Paul's conversion as a "thunderbolt, a caesura, and not a dialectical reversal" which constitutes "a conscription instituting a new subject."[10] Paul experiences his conversion as a transformative event in his narrative self; what constituted Saul is replaced, suddenly and entirely, by a new reading of his past and new direction for his future. Paul's religious experience is distinct from the story of his conversion, which involves reflection, action, and communication.[11] While unselfing should be envisioned expansively as a transhistorical phenomenon, I argue that the unselfing text thrives in the modern period with what Charles Taylor calls the "retrieval of the lived experience or creative activity underlying our awareness of the world, which had been occluded or denatured by the regnant mechanistic control."[12] In this sense, the unselfing text is remarkable because it is both fringe – in that it delivers experiences that are singular, unusual, or exceptional – and global, in that it resounds across nations and cultures in the twentieth century.

The phenomenological tradition, in its foregrounding of the first-person nature of experience and exploration of the self in a literary mode shapes the writing of fringe experiences during this period. Chapter 1, "Towards a Cognitive-Phenomenological Approach to the Self," tracks the rise of the phenomenological method in global French thought and its relationship to the literature of unselfing. It develops a cognitive-phenomenological theory of the self by synthesizing the work of Paul Ricoeur, Daniel Kahneman, and Antonio Damasio, who each make the distinction between the experiencing self and the narrative self. The theoretical framework built in this chapter serves as an analytical vocabulary for parsing the layers of unselfing later in the book. The final section of the chapter discusses debates on the nature of the relationship between subjectivity and intersubjectivity in the phenomenological tradition as a means of introducing the central disagreements on unselfing's prosocial potential.

Chapter 2, "What Is Unselfing?," continues this discussion by analyzing how competing interpretations of unselfing in both philosophy and literature reveal a basic conflict in our understanding of the stakes in becoming less of a self. While some philosophers claim that reducing the claims of the self is a productive form of transcendence (Simone Weil, Iris Murdoch, Elaine Scarry), others argue that it is damaging form of loss (Nietzsche). As is the case in debates on the structure and meaning of empathy, determining the value of unselfing proves to be more complicated than many accounts suggest; in fact, unselfing yields an array of intersubjective outcomes, not all of them virtuous or desirable. The chapter argues for a structural understanding of unselfing that encompasses both the interpretation of unselfing as required for virtue on the one hand and as a threat to personhood on the other. It shows how the work of theorizing unselfing is characterized by philosophical syncretism as writers draw from Eastern and Western religious and philosophical traditions in the process. The concept of unselfing emerges in the twentieth-century Francosphère from three overlapping vocabularies across these traditions: the mystical, the experimental, and the testimonial.

Chapter 3, "Unselfing as Disruption: Self-Knowledge and Pain in Paul Valéry and Charlotte Delbo," analyzes the disruption model for unselfing. Both writers explore the alienating effects of suffering on consciousness and the feeling of empathy. Valéry's *Cycle Teste* explores the limits of conscious experience in a series of short stories, with Teste as its appropriately named protagonist. Delbo's memoir, now known as the *Auschwitz et après* volumes, recounts her experiences of deportation, internment, and, as the title of her work suggests, life after liberation.

The disruption of the self is a suspension of the ordinary course of affairs; it is a stopping or a pausing in space and time. Unselfing is presented as the painful disruption of the processes of a pure mind in Valéry and as strange mental interludes that are spent away from ordinary mental life in Delbo. Although Valéry is interested in intersubjectivity, he primarily sees the approach to the other as an epistemological vehicle for better understanding the self. Delbo reports that self-disruption relays "useless knowledge" for living and being with others. Delbo's experience of radical empathy – sharing in the death cry of a fellow detainee – takes us far from the triumphant vision of interpersonal exchange that Valéry imagined with his *Teste* case.

Chapter 4, "Unselfing as Mutation: Hallucination and the Remains in Henri Michaux and Yolande Mukagasana," examines the mutation model for unselfing. It focuses on the mescaline texts of Michaux, the Belgian-born experimental writer (*Misérable Miracle*, *L'Infini turbulent*, *Connaissance par les gouffres*, and *Les grandes épreuves de l'esprit*) and the testimonies of Mukagasana, survivor of the Rwandan genocide against the Tutsi (*La mort ne veut pas de moi*, *N'aie pas peur de savoir*). The mutation model represents unselfing as a radical and profound change in the self. Michaux describes the self as mutated by mescaline, which leads to the emergence of a newly illuminated state of consciousness. He sees altered states as a privileged view onto the workings of the mind as well as a means of human evolution. However, Michaux ultimately conceives of unselfing as an alienating process in terms of his relationship to others. Mukagasana's mutation into a *pietà* figure allows her to mitigate her experience of extreme violence and debilitating grief. She invokes language as a weapon against genocide and the rationale for the eventual reconstruction of the self as an activist. These texts present two competing methods for interpreting the mutation of the self during altered states.

Chapter 5, "Unselfing as Fragmentation: Languages of Alterity in Abdelkebir Khatibi and Hélène Cixous," turns to the fragmentation model for unselfing in the context of the postcolonial Maghreb. Fragmentation evokes both the affectively neutral division of a whole into composite fragments and the painful process of breaking or tearing of that whole. Drawing on recent research from cognitive psychology on the mental representations of gender and time for multilingual speakers, this chapter shows how these factors impact the hermeneutics of the self in Khatibi as caught between Arabic, French, and Darija in *Amour bilingue*. Meditating playfully on the fragmentation of the bilingual self in love allows Khatibi to rehabilitate the notion of plural subjectivity from the context of mental illness and harness its social potential. Khatibi represents bilingualism not as a hierarchy that signals colonial domination, but rather puts fragmentation in the service of what he calls the *Pensée autre*. In contrast to Khatibi, fragmentary unselfing is an alienating obstacle for Cixous in *Les Rêveries de la femme sauvage*. Her interpretation of unselfing runs counter to the vision of plurality that she championed in her earlier writings, which expressed the liberating potential of the fragmented self. The fragmentation model for unselfing reflects a consideration of the role that language, culture, and narrative memory play in the decolonization of conscious experience. These writers' accounts of unselfing illuminate the emancipatory possibilities of the fragmentation narrative, while also exploring self-unity as a source of alienation and longing.

Chapter 6, "Unselfing as Destruction: Decreation and Inner Experience in Simone Weil and Georges Bataille," examines the destruction model for unselfing. The notion of destruction as an attack, a defeat, or a ruin is distinct from the disruption model in its central metaphors. While disruption amounts to a pausing of the operations of the self, destruction narratives evoke the breakage and rupture with the self as a source of comfort and stability. This chapter considers Bataille's acute desire for the destruction of self-unity and contrasts it with Weil's attempts to diminish herself in order to share in the suffering of others. According to Bataille, the violent destruction of the self during inner experience serves to dramatize life and free the subject from "project." I put his meditation on images of suffering, an experimental gesture that deliberately eschews both Christian and existential ethical systems, into conversation with Weil's theorization of décréation, the passing into the uncreated. Weil believed that lessening the claims of the self would make her more focused on the needs of a world in which God seems most absent. This tension – between unselfing understood as a passage into nothingness on the one hand and into possibility on the other – is a central focus of the book.

This book intervenes in the space between Iris Murdoch's call for the unselfing of the relentless ego and Nietzsche's critique of the unselfing of the objective man. It seeks to account for the inherent ambiguities and inescapable contradictions at the heart of the phenomenon. Unselfing emerges from this study not as an orientation towards the Good or towards objectivity, but rather as a site of attention, a registration of a change in what Merleau-Ponty called the angle of perception. Valéry tells us that Monsieur Teste is *l'homme de l'attention*, and Weil wrote that "l'attention, à son plus haut degré, est la même chose que la prière."[13] [Attention, taken to its highest degree, is the same thing as prayer.][14] As the ordinary experience of selfhood unravels, unselfing texts reflect on the relationship between the self and other at the limits of consciousness. The writings that emerge from these trials have a theoretical value as well as a descriptive one; from these outposts of the self, writers begin to craft an ethics without the stable self at the center.

1 Towards a Cognitive-Phenomenological Approach to the Self

The fringe and unusual nature of unselfing experiences in the modern period prompt a reconsideration of familiar philosophical questions on the experience of being a self: Who am I? What makes me the same person throughout my life? What is the relationship between me as an individual and my shared experiences with the people around me? The phenomenological method offered new ways of approaching these questions in early twentieth-century France and would lastingly shape literary representations of the self. Moreover, the pursuit of phenomenology as a decidedly literary philosophy in France contributed to the blurring of disciplinary boundaries within the body of unselfing literature. Unselfing writers across the century engage the methods of the phenomenological tradition in novel and divergent ways.[1]

Phenomenology is broadly understood as the bracketing of the natural attitude and the exploration of the lifeworld of a human person by describing what it is like to be a self. One of the main claims of this book is that phenomenological approaches to unselfing effectively expose the coordinates of selfhood, making visible the usually obscure workings of body and mind. In particular, this tradition contributed to the shift from Cartesian dualism to embodiment in self-writing, a shift which is mirrored in contemporary cognitive science. Given that each literary case study analyzed in the book uses an idiosyncratic language for representing the self, often synthesizing multiple philosophical and religious traditions in the process, my introduction seeks to lay the groundwork for analyzing its coordinates in a consistent way. Before examining theories of unselfing in detail in chapter 2, this chapter develops a cognitive-phenomenological account of the self. This framework serves as an interpretive tool for unlocking the complexities of the self, especially in the moment of its breakdown. It offers a means of distinguishing between two imbricated temporalities of a being a self: the *experiencing self* (comprised of consciousness, agency, temperament, and perspective) and the *narrative self* (comprised of situation, narrative ordering, and projects). The set of coordinates bridges the gaps between phenomenological and cognitive models of the self in an effort to craft a theoretical structure sufficient for responding to the interpretive challenges that unselfing texts pose. Though the classical phenomenological tradition has been described as lacking when it comes to the theorization of the relationship between selves and others, contemporary phenomenological inquiry has focused much of its attention on social cognition. Moreover, an expanded global vision of phenomenology that includes decolonial and anticolonial thought may serve as a corrective to the solipsistic tendencies at the heart of the classical model. These directions in phenomenological inquiry are essential to understanding the embodied experiences of colonial and postcolonial situations, especially the lived experience of racism.

What is the self, then, according to this transnational phenomenological method? In a minimal sense, the phenomenological tradition has argued that to be a self is to have a unity of consciousness. A self has conscious experiences and ownership of them; I know that these thoughts belong to me in a special way. In a fuller sense, to be a self is to be the agent and actor of one's own life, to have a unique perspective and character that is not identical to that of another. Being a self also means thinking of oneself as extending through time, both back into the past and forward into the future through relationships and projects. At the same time, the mere fact of being a conscious agent of action, having a perspective and character, and conceiving of oneself in terms of autobiographical memories and future projects is distinct from communicating self-experience to others. Selves take on narrative shape, especially when they are presented to others for interpretation and recognition.[2] We often think of our lives in terms of narrative arcs, with downturns, upswings, and sometimes even chapters. This account of selfhood is known as the narrative self, which prioritizes the question of characterization over the question of diachronic identity. Answering the question "Who am I?" within this view involves not only making sense of the persistence of the self through time, but also understanding its values and commitments.[3] Any discussion of selfhood must take into consideration both the synchronic and the diachronic aspects of selfhood, as well as the inherently relational and social nature of being with others. A viable account of selfhood should capture what it is really like to be and act in the world, to experience love and alienation, joy and suffering, transcendence and immanence. As Marya Schechtman writes in *The Constitution of Selves*, "Philosophical discussion has yielded some extremely sophisticated theories of personal identity, but they do not seem to be about persons as we know them, nor do they capture the real-world implications of personal identity."[4] My approach to the self in this book attempts to center those real-world implications.

French Phenomenology: Consciousness, Embodiment, and the Self

The phenomenological method as a mode of introspection has had an enduring effect on the representation of self-consciousness in French literature. Classical phenomenology, the study of consciousness from the first-person perspective, is the foundation of Continental philosophical thought and has resurged in recent cognitive research on philosophy of mind and the social self. Introduced by Edmund Husserl (1895–1938) in the late nineteenth century, the movement would have a defining influence on twentieth-century French and Francophone literature.[5] What Husserl eventually articulated as "transcendental phenomenology" offered a radically new method for the exploration of consciousness and our conceptual systems. The phenomenological outlook attempts to give a rich descriptive account of phenomena as it is experienced by the conscious subject through an "anti-traditional style of philosophizing."[6] Instead of pursuing selves as substances, Husserl argued for understanding the first-person experience of the world as the given structure of consciousness. According to this view, consciousness is pre-reflective, meaning that prior to self-identification and self-narrative, consciousness *already* has an experiential quality to it. In fact, by the phenomenologist's light, it is defined precisely by that quality.

Though it remains indebted to the Cartesian tradition, the phenomenological attitude introduces an important departure from Descartes's sceptical method into French thought. While drawing on the Cartesian theme of doubt, phenomenologists deploy it as a tool, rather than adopting a purely sceptical attitude.[7] This method of philosophizing proposes the "bracketing" of the natural attitude – developed by Husserl as *epoché* – in place of the phenomenological one. This so-called natural attitude, or the default perspective, includes our most basic experiences with other people and the environment as well as our beliefs, including our overarching belief in the world as such. One singularity in our natural attitude towards the world is the first-person nature of experience. Robert Sokolowski writes, "If the world is the widest whole and the most encompassing context, the I is the center around which the widest whole, with all the things in it, is arranged."[8] In this sense, the self is not separate from the life-world, but implicated in it, just as the world is implicated in the self. The phenomenological approach brackets the natural attitude in order to approach it as it is experienced from the first-person perspective. "When we so bracket the world or some particular object, we do not turn it into a mere appearance, an illusion, a mere idea, or any other sort of merely subjective impression. Rather, we now consider it precisely as it is intended by an intentionality in the natural attitude."[9] In other words, putting the natural attitude about oneself into brackets allows the subject to contemplate it differently, and slowly. Moreover, the crafting of a textual self further facilitates this deceleration of consciousness and its eventual articulation in language. The writers of unselfing preserve the fine line between experience and the experiencer in their diverse attempts to adopt a descriptive method. Valéry's Monsieur Teste's simultaneous "being and seeing" himself, quoted at the start of this book neatly captures this sentiment.

The phenomenological approach focuses on the way in which perception belongs to the observer in a special way. Paul Ricoeur offers this as a solution to Hume's self-scepticism in *A Treatise of Human Nature* (1739). When Hume thinks about his experiences and cannot find a self among his perceptions and feelings ("I can never catch *myself* at any time without a perception"), Ricoeur points out that Hume misses the fact that these perceptions (of heat and cold, light and shade, love or hatred, pain or pleasure) *belong to him* in a particular way. *Someone* is there to observe these perceptions. Hume, Ricoeur observes, was taking stock of experiences that he had already identified as his own.[10] The self, by this understanding, is not something that can be captured (a transcendental condition) but is rather an immediate feature of experiential consciousness.[11] The act of writing the self, then, becomes an attempt to sketch out the contours of conscious life. As phenomenology comes to dominate French intellectual life in the twentieth century, self-narratives reflect the influence of the phenomenological method on literary production.[12] This has far-reaching consequences for the ways in which philosophers and writers begin to think about literature as a vehicle for articulating the shape of the conscious self.

Phenomenology as a philosophical movement was eventually carried forward by those who broke with Husserl's methodology. Indeed, Ricoeur once remarked that the history of phenomenology is the history of deviations from Husserl's thought, and Heidegger argued that there is no such thing as *the one* phenomenology.[13] Husserl's transcendental phenomenology still had a neo-Cartesian character to it, which Heidegger would reject.[14] Heidegger developed the phenomenological method in a poetic idiom in *Being and Time* (1927), but moved away from Husserl's emphasis on subjectivity and the bracketing of experience. Instead, Heidegger focused on *Dasein* [existence] in this work and emphasized the centrality of hermeneutics rather than intentionality, representation, or lived descriptions of objects. Heidegger would push phenomenology into existential territory – though he would later reject this label – by directing his philosophical method towards understanding modes of being in the world.

Phenomenological inquiry took on a distinctly French identity in the 1930s and distinguished itself from its German inheritance precisely by its literary character and expression. The movement was first received in France as a more radical Cartesianism, which Husserl deliberately emphasized in his 1929 Paris lectures.[15] In the *Cartesian Meditations*, Husserl defines the phenomenological reduction as a suspension of the natural attitude on the world (the noetic side) in order to analyze it (on the noematic side): "Accordingly, not only in respect of particulars, but also *universally*, the phenomenologically meditating Ego can become the 'non-participant onlooker' at himself."[16] Yet, Husserl's early work was not the object of French fascination until Sartre "naturalized and activated phenomenology on Husserlian grounds."[17] Instead, Scheler was the first of the major German phenomenologists to visit France in 1924.[18] Phenomenology developed in France in the early stages through both Husserl's students such as Jean Héring and Raymond Aron, and also by Emmanuel Levinas, who was a student of both Husserl and Heidegger and introduced their ideas to French audiences.

These early French phenomenologists deliberately crossed the borders between philosophy and literature. Merleau-Ponty made this connection directly when he emphasized the literary nature of phenomenological inquiry: "From now on, the tasks of literature and philosophy can no longer be separated."[19] In his account of the successful transplant of German phenomenology onto French soil, Herbert Spiegelberg writes, "What is obvious is that [the French] write in a much more literary vein, compared with the all too frequently plodding style of much German phenomenologizing."[20] The sense that French phenomenology was "literary" spread not only because of the literary output of philosophers like Gabriel Marcel or Sartre, but also thanks to works such as Proust's *In Search of Lost Time*, which famously foregrounds rich sensory descriptions of past experiences.

French phenomenology enjoyed a porous relationship with literature from the beginning; some phenomenological thinkers deployed literature in their philosophy (like Merleau-Ponty), while others pursued phenomenology through literary forms, such as Sartre and Beauvoir. Indeed, Sartre's *Being and Nothingness* is famous for its "literary" locutions. For example, Sartre memorably writes that

"Nothingness lies coiled in the heart of being – like a worm."[21] After the publication of these groundbreaking works on the subjective nature of lived experience, many writers would attempt to overcome Cartesian dualism by exploring the sensory experiences of the body. Moreover, France became the center of phenomenological thought despite the fact that few of the major philosophers who employed a phenomenological method identified themselves with this label, grouping themselves rather by concerns such as existentialism. French thinkers tended to overlook the discrepancies between philosophers such as Husserl, Heidegger, and Scheler, and constructed a more unified picture of the German phenomenological tradition than a close study of these individual thinkers might have yielded.[22] The development of French phenomenology can be divided into two overlapping phases: a receptive period where German thought is studied as an "exotic plant" and a productive period, exemplified by Sartre's publications in the mid-thirties.[23] At this transition point is Sartre's philosophical novel *Nausea* (1938), which delivers a phenomenological account of the world, and in which its protagonist, Antoine Roquentin, confronts his existential freedom. In the novel's most iconic episode, Roquentin relates his encounter with the brute facts of the world through the roots of a gnarled chestnut tree. It is only by recognizing that the objects surrounding him do not carry inherent meaning that he is able to create meaning in his own life. Sartre's novel presents readers with the notion that the self is not a substance that is fully constructed and known to the subject, but rather objectified and made manifest by perception and situations. The text's phenomenological method is grounded in reflective descriptions of experience.

Through his literary works, Sartre put the phenomenological method in the service of his existentialist project. This blurring of the disciplinary boundaries between philosophy and art would shape the ways in which writers approached the construction of the self in writing. After reading Heidegger's *Being and Time* while interned as a prisoner of war between 1940–1, Sartre wrote an existential account of consciousness in *Being and Nothingness,* much of which he had developed earlier in his *War Diaries*.[24] Sartre, like Hegel, would distinguish between being in-itself (*en soi*), the contingent givenness of the world, and being for-itself (*pour soi*) as human consciousness; he argues that humans beings integrate both in their experience of existence. (Sartre avoids ontological dualism by claiming that the for-itself (*pour soi*) is a gap or disruption in being, which effectively attaches him to the phenomenological tradition.[25]) One of Sartre's main claims is that humans are defined by the facticity, or the givens of experience, and yet cannot be defined only by these facts of their existence. We cannot pretend to be mere facticity, nor can we be pure transcendence and do anything we like, simply by wishing it into reality. He illustrates this concept in *Being and Nothingness* with the example of the café waiter's bad faith, whose quick movements betray an eagerness to negate his freedom to pursue transcendence: "there is no doubt that I *am* in a sense a café waiter – otherwise could I not just as well call myself a diplomat or a reporter? But if I am one, this can not be in the mode of being in-itself. I am a waiter in the mode of *being what I am not*."[26] This enduring distinction between facticity and transcendence, as I explore in this chapter's section on phenomenology and ethics, plays an essential role in the existential component of feminist and anticolonial thinking in their considerations of the way the self is both constrained by external forces and simultaneously capable of breaking free of those constraints.

Merleau-Ponty, the first phenomenological thinker to publish a work with *phénomenologie* in the title in France, would seek to advance the phenomenological movement as such in a way that Sartre did not. Unlike Sartre, Merleau-Ponty rejected the cogito as a starting point; he sought instead to further Husserl's late thinking expressed in his posthumous works.[27] Over the course of a long, tumultuous personal and philosophical relationship, Merleau-Ponty would contest many of the dominant elements of Sartre's existentialist phenomenology. For instance, he stressed the social nature of being, judging that *Being and Nothingness* offered a radically individualistic view of human existence at the expense of a dialectical relationship between subjects and objects. Moreover, in his break from Kantian idealism, Merleau-Ponty sought to orient philosophy towards the body and its role in grounding lived experiences. His work is a testament to the interdisciplinary legacy of phenomenology in that he was influenced by research in psychology and neurology; his most famous work, *Phenomenology of Perception* (1945), draws on Gestalt psychology in order to give an account of the nature of sensory perception. This focus on the body as the seat and center of cognitive perception is also essential for understanding the ways in which selves are crafted by embodied experiences such as racism and sexism.

This is especially salient when it comes to the literature and philosophy of decolonization in the global French world. Frantz Fanon crafted a new phenomenological method, one informed by psychiatry, psychoanalysis, psychology, and existentialism, which continues to set the terms for decolonial and postcolonial theory. Though he studied Husserl through Sartre and Merleau-Ponty, as well as through Karl Jaspers's phenomenological psychology, Fanon's method is original. (As Lewis

R. Gordon puts it, "Fanon's phenomenology is, then, *Fanonian* phenomenology."[28]) Fanon insisted on the direct psychic effects of colonialism throughout his life, writing on colonial disorders as part of his theorization of colonial racism. As Camille Robcis writes, "Colonialism was not simply an economic doctrine that encouraged the pillage of natural resources, a political justification for confiscating the rights of certain groups, or the social transformation of all pre-existing structures: it could literally render someone mad by hijacking their person, their being, and their sense of self."[29] His originality resides in the development of what he called sociogenic explanations, a form of existential phenomenological social analysis that recognizes both the impact of the social world and the emergence of meaning and human identities. Fanon's oeuvre thus focuses on how "individual situations relate to the development and preservation of social and political institutions."[30] Fanon gives a phenomenological account of racialization in *Black Skin, White Masks* (1952) that is essential to understanding the embodied nature of racialized lived experience. This work, which analyzes the psychological experience of anti-Black racism, charts the paradoxical nature of the felt negation of the interiority of Black subjects. Like Merleau-Ponty, Fanon's phenomenological method is centered on the embodied experiences that shape the understanding of the self in the world. In this work which Fanon wrote while completing his medical training, he analyzes racial alienation as a product of white supremacist notions of rationality. The subject of experience in this work is defined by a structural analysis of consciousness that "allowed Fanon to stress the importance of the social, the permeation of structural racism, and also the foundational role of alterity in the construction of the self."[31]

Phenomenology has proved to be a useful tool for building bridges between culturally distinct and transcultural philosophies. Paget Henry has recently emphasized the need to adopt a comparative cultural approach to phenomenology in his study of Africana phenomenology, which draws on the work of Du Bois, Fanon, and Gordon. Henry writes,

> By phenomenology, I mean the discursive practice through which self-reflective descriptions of the constituting activities of consciousness are produced after the "natural attitude" of everyday life has been bracketed by some ego-displacing technique. An Africana phenomenology would thus be the self-reflective descriptions of the constituting activities of the consciousness of Africana peoples, after the natural attitudes of Africana egos have been displaced by de-centering techniques practiced in these cultures.[32]

Phenomenology is rearticulated here as a transcultural site for the study of the philosophy of lived experience. In another account, Leela Gandhi discusses the emergence of a "global phenomenology" as the site for the articulation of the relationship between theory and practice in postcolonial studies. The three sections of her account – Transcendental Phenomenology (inspired by Husserl's call for the return to the theoretical attitude as a corrective for the crisis of imperialist Europe); Existential Phenomenology (theory's participation in the world as engaging the possibility to rise above facticity and circumstance à la Sartre); Spiritual Phenomenology (Gandhi and Ghosh's *karmayoga* as the irreducible unity of idea and action in true revolutionary thought) – illustrate together the legacy and future of phenomenology in articulating a space for reflection on the nature of subjectivity and intersubjective critique.[33] It is in the spirit of these new directions in phenomenological analysis – ones that preserve the "traditional" notion of phenomenological intentionality, while also investigating the missing piece of culture – that this study undertakes to analyze what can properly be called a comparative and global French phenomenology of selfhood.

Experiencing Self and Narrative Self

Contemporary interdisciplinary research on the self has recently put the phenomenological tradition into conversation with findings in cognitive science. This new interdisciplinary energy is, in a sense, a return to the original spirit of phenomenological inquiry as a new science of consciousness envisaged by Husserl. Though Merleau-Ponty once claimed that the phenomenological attitude was the "rejection" (*le désaveu*) of science, both Merleau-Ponty and Husserl actually saw it as "supporting and clarifying science" in its fullest sense.[34] Once scholars began to pursue the experiential realm with renewed interest, phenomenology emerges as a viable cognitive methodology. While the field was dominated in its early years by naturalism and behaviourism, cognitive phenomenologists pursue the qualia, or the *what-it-is-like* of conscious mental states, seeking to bring together research in cognitive science and the phenomenological tradition.[35] Embodied approaches to cognition have since come to the fore in contemporary approaches to the self.[36] This embodied approach rejects the mind-body dualism that nevertheless persists in some cognitive scientific disciplines.[37]

Drawing on contemporary psychological and cognitive accounts on self-experience and the phenomenological legacy in global French thought, this section proposes a comprehensive set of coordinates through which the ordinary experience of selfhood is constructed. My set of coordinates is informed by the classical and existential forms of phenomenology that dominated French thought in the twentieth century as well as new developments in cognitive phenomenology. It proposes the self as a feature of embodied consciousness; being a self means existing in a body, in time, and sharing that world with others. This cognitive philosophical approach draws from three thinkers – Paul Ricoeur (phenomenology/hermeneutics), Daniel Kahneman (psychology/economics), and Antonio Damasio (cognitive science/neuroscience) – who each make the productive distinction between what I will call the experiencing self and the narrative self. This framework informs the analysis of unselfing from both a synchronic and diachronic perspective in subsequent chapters; it allows readers to distinguish between what it is like to be unselved in the immediacy of the present and interpret the event in relation to the persistence of the self through time.

The distinction between the experiencing self and the narrative self lays bare the different temporalities of cognitive processes that are involved in being a self. While the experiencing self is shaped by the accumulated life of the subject, it attends primarily to the immediacy of the present moment. The narrative self, by way of contrast, is primarily a reflective one. It accounts for long-term autobiographical memories, and the sense of the self's extension into the future through projects. In his Gifford lectures, later published as *Oneself as Another* (1990), Ricoeur grapples with the centrality of narrative to a sense of self. Narratives, he argues, are a means of responding to the fundamental questions at the heart of being a self: "Who am I?" "What does it mean to be a self in and through time?" "How do I communicate that self to others?" Rejecting the idealism of the Cartesian cogito and the Kantian transcendental ego, Ricoeur pursued the self as a form of being in constant relationship with other people. This account of selfhood fundamentally links the narrative self with the notion of reciprocity, or the ethics of being a self among other selves. In these lectures, he proposes that the meaningful experience of being a self as an agent of action includes two kinds of identity: *idem* identity, or sameness, and *ipse* identity, which accounts for identity with change through time. This distinction accounts for the peculiar nature of feeling like a self; I have the sense that I am permanently the same as myself, though I acknowledge that I am different than the person that I was when I was a child, or even yesterday.

Daniel Kahneman makes a similar distinction between a synchronic-focused form of selfhood and a diachronic one. His work seeks to explain the ways in which cognitive biases shape our sense of ourselves and our ability to form judgments, make choices, and think rationally (which in his vocabulary means according to statistical reasoning). *Thinking Fast and Slow* (2011) argues that distinguishing between two systems of thinking allows us to understand how these modalities shape our sense of ourselves as beings in time.[38] Kahneman calls these two systems of selfhood the "experiencing self" and the "remembering self." These two systems of thinking about ourselves co-determine each of our individual self-experiences. Moreover, the distinction between the two effectively captures the ways in which selfhood functions as both a perceiving lens and a retrospective analyst. "The *experiencing self* is the one that answers the question: 'Does it hurt now?' The *remembering self* is the one that answers the question: 'How was it, on the whole?'[39] The experiencing self for Kahneman has a life made up of a series of moments, while the remembering self, in a "storytelling mode," attends to critical experiences: the beginning, highs and lows, and the end.[40] Kahneman demonstrates that humans are notoriously flawed when it comes to accurately reporting the duration of experiences like pain or pleasure. Instead, we retrospectively evaluate experiences based on their high and low points. He writes, "The remembering self, as I have described it, also tells stories and makes choices, and neither the stories nor the choices properly represent time."[41] Kahneman's account offers an important corrective to idea that memory functions as a tape-recorder, delivering a literal account of experience.[42] Instead, the "remembering self" attends selectively to the peaks and valleys of experience.

A third thinker, Antonio Damasio, also distinguishes between what he calls the "core self" and the "autobiographical self." Damasio takes aim at Cartesian dualism in his embodied theory of human consciousness. His recent work, *The Strange Order of Things* (2018), seeks to recover the centrality of feeling and emotions to conscious experience, while *Self Comes to Mind: Constructing the Conscious Brain* (2010) builds a theory of consciousness grounded in neuroanatomy. According to Damasio, the core self emits pulses of subjectivity, while the autobiographical self extends through time. Damasio explains that the core self is like a protagonist for experience, built on the foundation of a "protoself," the primordial feeling of being conscious and being in a body.[43] However, these unadorned representations of life in the brain are not enough to generate a complex feeling of selfhood. Something critical changes in the protoself that gives way to narrative: "within the narrative of the moment, it must *protagonize*." This (nonverbal) process creates and reveals the protagonist, generating answers, in Damasio's provocative framing, to questions that no one has posed. He illustrates his theory with the thought-experiment of a narrator shifting his attention from watching pelicans feeding their young to the sound of his ringing phone: "Out of this global-scale brain map, core self states emerge in pulselike fashion. But suddenly the phone rings, and the spell is broken. My head and eyes move reluctantly but inexorably to the receiver. I get up. And the whole cycle of conscious mind-making starts anew, now focused on the telephone. The pelicans are gone from my sight and from my mind; the telephone is in."[44]

The autobiographical self, then, occurs when these pulses of core self are momentarily linked in a larger-scale coherent pattern. Damasio explains the difference between the two using an internet metaphor; the core self is always online (with a sometimes-stronger, sometimes-weaker signal) while the autobiographical self has both an online and offline existence. The autobiographical self reconstructs and replays lived experiences both consciously and unconsciously, subtly rewriting the history of an individual in the moment. As such, autobiographical selves are not built on the sum of all conscious memories and planning for the future but are rather constructed from selected memories and key episodes of one's autobiography. "Not even Proust would have needed to draw on all of his richly detailed and long-ago past to construct a moment of full-fledged self-Proustiness."[45]

In his earlier work, *Descartes' Error: Emotion, Reason, and the Human Brain* (1994), Damasio presents a compelling outline of the main contours of the neural basis for the self that is useful for understanding altered states of selfhood. Damasio's neural self is based on two sets of representations: key events in an individual's autobiography, and grounded representations of an individual's body. Damasio adds a third-party neuron ensemble, which he calls the "convergence zone." This space reciprocally integrates and builds dispositional representations in the brain. The nonverbal neural self begets subjectivity (meta self-knowledge) via a process in which the brain builds representations of the self in the act of perceiving and responding to the world. Under ordinary circumstances, we remain blissfully unaware of the processes of self and subjectivity reconstruction, which are both constantly in a state of renewal. Damasio writes, "At each moment the state of the self is constructed, from the ground up. It is an evanescent reference state, so continuously and consistently *re*constructed that the owner never knows it is being *re*made unless something goes wrong in the remaking."[46] Damasio's language on the evanescent reconstruction of the self is particularly helpful for understanding accounts of altered states, which bring this "ground up" process to the forefront of consciousness.

The phenomenological-cognitive account of selfhood that follows attempts to retain this distinction between these two ways of being a self. It seeks to give an expansive account of the ways in which an experience of selfhood is defined precisely by both a perceptual level of conscious self-experience and a constructed narrative. These two interconnected selves – the experiencing self and the narrative self – are essential to understanding the cognitive experience of unselfing and the minimal narratives that writers use to give shape to their lives. There cannot be a narrative self without the materiality of the experiencing self. Likewise, if selfhood were dependent only on the experiencing self, then what we think of as selfhood would only amount to the felt representation of life. The unselfing experiences explored in this book affect both.

The Experiencing Self

The experiencing self is the complex lens through which the subject experiences the world. It is a synchronic form of self and is thus a present-focused temporal construction. The ocular metaphor of the lens is especially fitting when we think about lenses as transparent apparatuses that frame and filter. Under ordinary circumstances, it requires focused attention to properly identify the ways in which the experiencing self shapes our interpretation of phenomena. Though the experiencing self appears to be immutable, stable, and unified, it is in fact the product of lived experience and interactions with others and is subject to constant evolution and change.

Five functions characterize the experiencing self consciousness, ownership, agency, temperament, and perspective. The first two features, consciousness and ownership, remain unaffected by the unselfing experiences explored later in this book. Without consciousness, the narrative for experience could not exist. Michaux testifies to this when he differentiates between taking mescaline (which merely alters his perceiving lens) and overdosing on the drug. The overdose leaves no knowledge in its wake, and the experiencing self is unable to serve its function as witness during this particular experience.[47]

The second feature of the experiencing self, ownership, can be altered, but only by serious physical trauma or the onset of a psychological disorder. Ownership refers to the feature of selfhood that Ricoeur identified in his response to Hume, the notion that perceptions and feelings belong to the observer in a special way. The third feature, agency, refers to the sense of being the actor of one's life in a synchronic sense. Shaun Gallagher usefully explains the distinction between ownership and agency in the context of the philosophy of psychopathology. He discusses schizophrenia and other psychopathological conditions to support his argument that while ownership can persist without agency, agency cannot persist without ownership. For example, a person can know that he is experiencing alien thoughts without feeling that he is the originator of these thoughts, but he cannot feel he is the originator of an alien thought without knowing it is happening in his own mind.[48] Charlotte Delbo's debilitating thirst during her internment at Auschwitz strongly impairs her sense of agency but leaves ownership intact. The experience causes her to hallucinate and to question her existence, but she is haunted to know that she is the "owner" of these thoughts.

This leaves the features of temperament and perspective. Temperament refers to one's attitudinal outlook, which is built through a pattern of engagements with obstacles, pursuits, and other people. Antoine Compagnon, in a course on selfhood and writing uses "character" and "temperament" synonymously; it is temperament that provides even the most avowedly episodic lives with a sense of coherence. To illustrate this idea of narrative temperament, Compagnon uses Stendhal's discovery of his character in *The Life of Henri Brulard*, his unfinished autobiography written under a pseudonym. In this work, Stendhal's narrator realizes that his "manière d'aller à la chasse au bonheur" [way of hunting after happiness] has not changed in forty-two years.[49] Out of a juxtaposition of incoherent episodes emerges temperament as a telling pattern. The task of the autobiographer, forever *à la chasse*, is to identify the pattern that, once tracked down, makes up the subject's identity.[50] We find a similar theory of temperament in Proust. In his book on selfhood in Proust, Joshua Landy writes that the fact that temperament can often be faulty in evaluating external others tells us that our recurrent perceptions and attitudes about the world are perhaps more reliable sources of information about ourselves. Landy writes, "the very temperament that turns all love objects into what we want them (or fear them) to be, and thus prevents us from seeing them as they really are, also constitutes that which we really are at a fundamental level."[51] Temperament in this book is often affected by unselfing experiences, especially the ones that the subject identifies as negative or injurious. In chapter 3, I discuss the way in which Delbo's temperament (seeing oneself as a "kind of person") is altered by her experience of Auschwitz, a view that is encapsulated by the title of her first volume, *Aucun de nous ne reviendra* (*None of Us Will Return*). Whereas Delbo previously saw herself as the kind of person who would share rations with a fellow prisoner, her experience in the camps produces the painful realization that she is pushed, rather, towards self-preservation.

The final feature of the experiencing self is perspective, which refers to the sense of identity that filters one's observations of the world. Perspective, here, is more robust than the phenomenological "unity of consciousness," and instead should be understood as a highly individualized vantage point that perceives and processes all external phenomena. Perspective is the element of the experiencing self that is most affected by unselfing experiences. For example, chapter 3 analyzes how Valéry's Monsieur Teste describes a new perceptual awareness of his body. Teste's experience of the body in pain illuminates formerly invisible inner expanses, squashing his desire to be pure thought. Similarly, Michaux, studied in chapter 4, refers to a "lightning that lasts" after the mescaline has left his system. The impact of unselfing on perspective is especially important for Bataille and Weil, studied in chapter 6; the former uses the dramatic undoing of situational perspective to escape of the mundanity of utilitarian project, the latter as a route to spiritual transcendence.

Perspective is also shaped by lived experiences of what Albert Memmi terms "heterophobia," or the rejection of the other based on difference, an idea worth outlining here. In *Racism* (1982), Memmi seeks to navigate between a narrow and a broad definition of racism. His narrow definition is based on the valuation of biological differences and refusal of the other based on these valuations, while his broad definition entails the rejection of the other based on any perceived difference. This broad definition has an explanatory value when analyzing self-experiences in the contexts of oppression, colonialism, and genocide across the Francosphère. As Memmi underscores, the expression of difference proves to be a challenge within the context of French universalism, given the problem of "Jacobin myopia." Memmi remembers being troubled by his well-meaning friends' inability to acknowledge the reality and impact of difference in their antiracist organizing:

> They affirmed that differences did not exist, from which point everything else followed coherently. If all "men" were "cut from the same cloth," then nothing provided any ground for social inequality except violence and injustice. This generous *Jacobin myopia* derives from the history of the French nation itself, which, in order to constitute itself, fought hard against the particularism or desire for autonomy of certain provinces, at times with terrible excesses. Yet it accepted that leap, even if it were a denial of the real. But what if it were mistaken in its fundamental premises. Suppose difference existed – what would become of the Jacobin position, and in its wake, of *our* entire social philosophy?[52]

Despite the persistent myth of the universal subject in the French tradition, the lived experience of difference shapes the experiencing self for many writers and the exploitation of these differences is essential to understanding its contours. For example, in chapter 5 of this book, I discuss Cixous's reflections on the formative role that anti-Semitism plays in her early childhood, as well as the way that exclusion from Jewish, Arab, and Franco-European communities affects her experiencing self. As the child of a German Ashkenazi Jewish mother and Algerian Sephardic Jewish father in post-Vichy Algiers, this experience of "heterophobia" shapes her self-perspective.

The Narrative Self

The narrative self is reflective and autobiographical. It looks back to the past and forward to the future in order to assimilate the unselfing event into a long-term self-narrative. The narrative self constructs a story from the messiness and immediacy of lived experience; these stories are indicative of both conscious and unconscious processes, which bind together autobiographical events. Always subject to revision, it is both a reflection of the subject's perception of the past as well as future plans, projects, and horizons. The narrative self is not a record or a tape-recording of the sum experiences of a life. Rather, it is a series of formative episodes and important events that come to shape the diachronic sense of self.

This selective function introduces an inherent tension in the narrative self in that it brings up questions of authenticity, fabrication, and truth-telling. Some worry that life stories are falsifications because because they attend disproportionately to the peaks and valleys of experience. Should we think of narrative selves as the reflections of complex lives or as constraining templates? Sartre might say that the narrative self is an indication of bad faith; his café waiter plays too close to his internalized script and forgoes individual freedom in service of his identity as a waiter. At the same time, the narrative self need not be considered "false" simply because it is constructed. All self-stories are subject to narratological emplotment. Ricoeur writes that the human experience of time and act of constructing a narrative exists in a circular relation: "time becomes human to the extent that it is articulated through a narrative mode, and narrative attains its full meaning when it becomes a condition of temporal existence."[53] The unselfing text investigates the human relationship to time as writers construct narratives for unusual experiences of temporality. Time might be stolen for quick, private use while imprisoned in the Nazi camps, while taking mescaline slows time down to open a space for contemplation. The narrative emplotment of these unselfing experiences reveals the desire to take inhuman or otherwordly experience and make it human.

The narrative self is made up three features: situation, narrative ordering, and projects. Narrative selves are built on a foundation of "givens," or the material facts of our existence. By Sartre's formulation, this foundation consists of the language we speak, the family we are born into, and the sum of our previous choices leading to the present moment. Though not everyone conceives intuitively of their lives in terms of an overarching life story, most would be affected by a major change in their understanding of the facticity of their existence (and soap operas trade in these revelations!) However, we are not merely the facts of our existence; being a self means more than having a personal history, speaking a language, or being born into a culture. Sartre's provocation that we are "condemned to be free" evokes the idea that we are *not* identical with ourselves (we are both the facticity of our existence and the transcendence of it). At the same time, without an understanding of situation, theories of selfhood become unmoored from the materiality of lived experience and fail to account for the ways in which difference shape the narrative self.

Selves, by this understanding, are also interpreted as trajectories that proceed from a known past towards an imaginable future, in accordance with the subject's projects. Narrative ordering helps us to understand selves as agents of actions and what it means to lead a life, rather than have a history. Schectman calls this position a "hermeneutical narrative view" because it conceives of selves as self-interpreting beings who are agents of their lives. To meaningfully act as an agent of experience, one must be able to interpret their actions in context, through narrative.[54] Alisdair MacIntyre argues that in order to understand a person's actions we need to conceive of those actions at the intersection of their various self-stories. It is the ordering of intentions that creates a narrative. "Narrative history of a certain kind turns out to be the basic and essential genre for the characterization of human action."[55] Ricoeur builds on MacIntyre's account, arguing that we need to understand our lives as narrative if we are to conceive of ourselves as the agents of our actions. Narrative ordering is profoundly transformed by externally imposed events on the experience of human agency (deportation, the Hutu genocidal campaign, the legacy of French imperialism). It is also subject to change in self-inflicted contexts (mystical contemplation, drug experiments).

A sense of project, closely related to narrative ordering, refers to a sense of vocation, goal, or purpose that serves as a framework for the narrative self. This feature of selfhood also comes to be affected by unselfing. Delbo, Mukagasana, and Cixous find this aspect of selfhood dramatically altered by historical events and take on the project of bearing witness afterwards. While writers such as Michaux and Bataille explicitly attempt to escape the tyranny of project (a term the latter often decries in his work), others like Weil and Khatibi are fueled by their fidelity to a set of linked aims or aspirations. Whatever their position on project in general, unselfing experiences demand to be integrated into a writer's sense of purpose as an intellectual, artist, or activist. As with the experiencing self, heterophobia plays a major role in the construction of the narrative self. The French colonization of North Africa and the targeted killing of the Tutsi in Rwanda dramatically shape the narrative self, to draw from the examples studied here. Just as, for example, the lived experiences of racism, anti-Semitism, and misogyny shape the experiencing self in Cixous, the narrative self bears witness to oppression, especially during violent historical contexts of persecution, alienation, and dehumanization.

In sum, accounting for the many features of selfhood through the distinction between these two modalities illuminates the complexities of the unselfing text. Focusing on the experiencing self captures the first-person experience of the world; it encompasses the features of consciousness, agency, ownership, temperament, and perspective. Studying the narrative self affords a longer view on what it is like to be a self; it gives a sense of the subject's situation, narrative ordering of events, and projects. Both modalities are essential to understanding the self as an entity that frames our experiences in the current moment and stretches back and forward in time. Finally, both forms of selfhood are shaped by the intersubjective nature of existence, which historically poses a particular set of challenges to the classical phenomenological model. I address these challenges further in the following section.

Subjectivity and Intersubjectivity

Critics of classical phenomenology have long characterized it as lacking when it comes to accounting for the sharing of experience and the production of social meaning. Given that it foregrounds the bracketing of the natural attitude on the world and prolonged, slow, introspection of the first-person perspective, it is perhaps unsurprising that it has been met with charges of solipsism. Habermas famously took Husserl to task for his focus on subjectivity at the exclusion of the other, and Daniel Dennett dubbed it "lone wolf autophenomenology" for its lack of engagement with other minds.[56]

Though the Husserlian model is still met with charges of navel-gazing, it is hard to say the same for the French phenomenological tradition, especially when understood in a global frame. The first generations of French phenomenologists were public intellectuals who put phenomenology in service of social commitment and political movements. "Black Orpheus," Sartre's preface to Leopold Sédar-Senghor's *Anthologie de la nouvelle poésie nègre et malgache de langue française* (1948), became a milestone in the intellectual history of *négritude*; Sartre also wrote the influential preface to Fanon's *The Wretched of the Earth* (1961). His phenomenological theories of race, oppression, and free will contributed to decolonial activism in France with the waves of independence movements. Moreover, Sartre's essay *What Is Literature?* (1948) defined literary creation as essentially a project of political engagement, which has since shaped Francophone African aesthetics in the postcolonial context.[57] Beauvoir's landmark study, *The Second Sex* (1949), moved the existential model away from Sartre's abstractions and used existential theories to interrogate the lived experiences (situations) of women. The text puts the phenomenological method to work in explaining the relegation of women to the position of Object in the Western tradition. Though originally associated with the existentialists, Merleau-Ponty put Sartre's positions into question; his late work published posthumously in *The Visible and the Invisible* (1964) pursued a corrective for the intellectualist tendencies of the phenomenological position. Fanon built on Merleau-Ponty's focus on embodiment in his phenomenological account of anti-Black racism as a lived reality. Phenomenological inquiry in these contexts have foregrounded the ways in which the self exists for others, with others, and is constructed in the eyes of others through questions of "intersubjectivity," "empathy," and "relationality."

The nature of this relation, even within the phenomenological tradition, remains a source of contention, however. Is the problem of intersubjectivity an epistemic or an ontological one? Sartre pursued the question of the existence of others as a fundamental ontological problem. Sartre's *pour autrui*, being-for-others, suggests that the relation between selves and others is not, in fact, one of knowledge, but one of being.[58] The existentialists were naturally troubled by the inevitable conflict between individuals, if they are sites of radical freedom. Indeed, *Being and Nothingness* casts the relationship between consciousness of self and other as a struggle, "for which at the time Sartre did not seem to see any clear constructive solution."[59] In this work, Sartre theorizes a new type of being, *pour autrui*, as the embodied experience of the self in relation to the other. Being-for-itself (*pour soi*) finds itself objectified or alienated by the gaze of the other. Fanon also builds his account of racialization of self-experience on the internalization of the gaze of the other. *Black Skins, White Masks* articulates the ways in which Black subjects are simultaneous identified and denied their interiority by the white gaze. Fanon's paradigmatic example of this is his memory of being interpellated on the street by a white French child in Lyon. This episode motivates Fanon's theorization of the way racialized self-experience arises from social encounter.

Other strains of the phenomenological legacy in France have focused on the mutually constitutive role of subjectivity and intersubjectivity, particularly after the work of Emmanuel Levinas. Levinas reverses the ontology of the subject by claiming ethics as "first philosophy." His work eschews an ethics rooted in self-experience for one based on the responsibility that the other places upon the subject. In *Totality and Infinity* (1961), for example, he argues that the relationship between self and other is an asymmetrical one rather than an encounter between two parallel sites of subjectivity. Levinas claims that the needs of the other are already apparent on their face, which demands both apprehension and estimation. The face, to which he returns often throughout his career, remains paradoxical for its simultaneous vulnerability and moral imperative, specifically, "you shall not kill." Indeed, Levinas describes the "epiphany of the face" as the locus of ethical interdiction:

> There is here a relation not with a very great resistance, but with something absolutely *other*: the resistance of what has no resistance – the ethical resistance. The epiphany of the face brings forth the possibility of gauging the infinity of the temptation to murder, not only as a temptation to total destruction, but also as the purely ethical impossibility of this temptation and attempt. If the resistance to murder were not ethical but real, we would have a *perception* of it, with all that reverts to the subjective in perception. We would remain within the idealism of a *consciousness* of struggle, and not in relationship with the Other, a relationship that can turn into struggle, but already overflows the consciousness of struggle. The epiphany of the face is ethical.[60]

This passage highlights the importance of the physical encounter with the face in Levinas; it is through this encounter that he develops the pre-reflective nature of the responsibility to the other. Levinas argues that this encounter with the other introduces otherness within oneself. "The relation with the Other as a relation with his transcendence – the relation with the Other who puts into question the brutal spontaneity of one's immanent destiny – introduces into me what was not in me."[61]

The relationship between self and other in the phenomenological tradition has alternatively been pursued as a hermeneutical question. Ricoeur, in *Oneself as Another*, argues that the understanding of others necessarily passes through a process of self-understanding. He asserts that the hermeneutics of the self has three major features: first, the detour of reflection by way of analysis (we approach the self indirectly), second, the dialectic of selfhood and sameness (again, which he terms as the splitting of "même" into *idem* and *ipse)*, and third, the dialectic of the self and otherness. Although the self is never absent from its other, the hermeneutics of the self reaches its fullest realization in the dialectic between self and alterity, or outside otherness. He writes, "It remains, however, that this dialectic, the richest of all, as the title of the work recalls, will take on its fullest development only in the studies in the areas of ethics and morality. The *autonomy* of the self will appear then to be tightly bound up with *solicitude* for one's neighbor and with *justice* for each individual."[62]

In the Seventh Study of this work, which analyzes the ethical aim of the self, Ricoeur uses Aristotle's notion of living well in conjunction with MacIntyre's narrative unity of a life to declare that the subject of a narrative is the subject of ethical imputation. Self-esteem (*l'estime de soi*) and solicitude cannot be experienced (or reflected upon) without the other. The esteem for the other is then conceptualized as a parallel structure for self-recognition and self-esteem. Ricoeur concludes the section on living with and for others with the following: "Becoming in this way fundamentally equivalent are the esteem of the other *as oneself* and the esteem of *oneself as an other*."[63] In other words, the possibility of an ethical aim for the self hinges on the perception of the other as a parallel self as well as the estimation of that suffering and acting being.

This focus on the sovereignty of the first-person position also resounds in contemporary phenomenological discussions. In an attempt to rehabilitate the traditional model as a site for intersubjective understanding, Zahavi argues that a satisfactory phenomenological account of social cognition depends on the understanding of the self as first and foremost a question of first-person experience. He writes, "rather than impeding a satisfactory account of intersubjectivity, an emphasis on the inherent and essential individuation of experiential life must be seen as a prerequisite for getting the relation and difference between self and other right."[64] In an effort to account for the multiple phenomenological methodologies on otherness, we might productively follow Zahavi's lead and employ a broad term such as "social cognition" to indicate the multiple ways in which selves both theorize others and are socially mediated by engagements with others, always from the first-person conscious experience of the world. This theoretical concern should be emphasized because it is precisely the individuation of experiential life that is at stake in experiences of unselfing. Some of these accounts illustrate the strange overriding of the boundary between self and other; Delbo writes of the experience of screaming a fellow victim's scream, while Michaux describes the voice of another pushing through his throat.

The literary writers that make up this project grapple with the problem of social cognition in a philosophical way. These accounts of selfhood at the limits of ordinary conscious experience are thus both important philosophical interventions on questions that have a global resonance and also intimate perspectives on the particular. As a result, these accounts are exemplary limit cases that should be considered in discussions of intersubjectivity. The next chapter continues to explore the coordinates of selfhood that are affected by altered states of consciousness as well as the ethical stakes of unselfing experiences.

2 What Is Unselfing?

Imagine that you are looking out the window in a resentful state of preoccupation, brooding over someone who has done you wrong. Suddenly, you notice a kestrel hovering on the horizon, and everything is altered. Your vanity and damaged pride vanish, and nothing but the bird occupies your consciousness. What was once self-absorption is now openness; beauty offers the occasion to free the mind of its egotistical tendencies by bringing the world into focus. According to some thinkers, unselfing is synonymous with this opening of consciousness towards the world. Iris Murdoch illustrates the concept in *The Sovereignty of Good* (1971) with this example of the hovering kestrel. In her account of unselfing, which owes much to the work of Simone Weil, the experience that the bird makes possible is a moral achievement. It puts the self into contact with the reality and demands of others. Though the prefix "un-" suggests a total erasure of conscious experience, Murdoch's concept of unselfing is instead a purification of the self through the refocusing of attention.[1]

At the same time, consciousness can be "refocused" in a direction other than moral clarity. Dreams, trances and other hallucinatory states indicate qualitative shifts in consciousness that affect the self, but which are not necessarily morally significant. While philosophers like Murdoch argue that becoming less of a self will lead to a more just vision of the world, others characterize self-loss as the site of alienation and displacement. Nietzsche, for instance, argues that "unselfing" is synonymous not with virtuous transcendence, but rather with the "depersonalization of the spirit."[2] Unselfing by this understanding is a reduction of the individual to the status of instrument. The discrepancies in these two lines of thought – unselfing imagined as self-transcendence on the one hand and as self-loss on the other – underscore a basic conflict in our understanding of what is at stake in escaping the ordinary experience of selfhood. Given these theoretical tensions, how ought we think about the promise and peril of unselfing? Does undoing the ordinary experience of the self lead to a more just vision of others and the world? Or, on the contrary, does unselfing, in effecting the loss of the stable self, constitute an obstacle to moral action?

My study of unselfing seeks to carve out space for an expansive account of unselfing, one that lays bare the full range of its potential ethical implications. This move away from its moral framing (in Murdoch via Weil) entails attending closely to the structure of unselfing by examining how these experiences can disrupt, mutate, fragment, or destroy the experiencing self and the narrative self.[3] Separating the experiential aspect of unselfing from its interpretations allows for a rich study of the experience of selfhood during altered states of consciousness. This separation makes it possible to distinguish the phenomenology of unusual conscious experiences from claims about their moral, epistemological, and metaphysical value. Murdoch's version of unselfing might be productively and provocatively pursued outside of its moral framework by focusing on the ways in which altered states of consciousness undo the self's ordinary functions. The subsequent chapters catalogue a wide range of unselfing experiences, some which serve to shake the ego out of its complacency and put the self in contact with illusionless reality, and others that do not conform to this model. This analysis seeks to illuminate the diverse interpretations that can ensue from the self's unravelling.

As we undertake the work of separating the experience of unselfing from its interpretation along axes of value, new and difficult questions emerge. What happens to the relationship to the world when the self is transcended, lost, or otherwise altered? While we might think that reducing the sovereignty of the self would lead to a heightened awareness of others and even a heightened sense of compassion, this is not necessarily the case. The sheer variety of experiences that a descriptive accounting illuminates indicates that not every unselfing experience should be understood as a virtuous one, and that there is more at stake in unselfing than correcting self-absorption. Though some unselfing experiences can be understood as a productive refocusing of attention, others prove to be alienating and cordon the self off from the world. The range of narratives for unselfing in the twentieth-century Francosphère dismantles the notion that losing, piercing, or becoming less of a self will automatically lead to compassionate consciousness.

The first section of this chapter, "Unselfing across Traditions," outlines the major debates and competing accounts of unselfing that have influenced global French writers in the modern period. The theorizing of the concept is characterized by philosophical syncretism as writers make sense of unselfing by drawing from diverse religious and philosophical traditions. The second section, "From Altered States to Unselfing" outlines the relationship between unselfing and altered states of consciousness. In this section, I show how the concept of unselfing in the twentieth-century French-speaking world emerges in three overlapping vocabularies: the mystical, the experimental, and the testimonial. The third section of the chapter turns to the relationship between experiences of unselfing and their expression in narrative. This chapter demonstrates how philosophical disagreements on the meaning of unselfing runs parallel to current debates on the nature and value of empathetic response. Like empathy, I argue that the value of unselfing proves to be more ambiguous than many accounts suggest. The experience of reducing the sovereignty of the self yields an array of intersubjective outcomes, not all of them virtuous, desirable, or emancipatory.

The reader might understandably wonder why the book continues to engage with the moral account of unselfing at all. Murdoch and others seem to be using the term "unselfing" in one way, while I am pursuing it here in another. Murdoch's account is particularly compelling because although she critiques egotism for its distortions of reality, she does not dismiss selfhood as a myth, or suggest that it does not matter.[4] Rather, she decries the way that philosophy has dismantled the substantial picture of the self, making it "thin as a needle."[5] I agree with Murdoch that this razor-thin idea of the self does not seem to match the rich experience of being one. Dismissing the self as a myth forecloses the conception of inner life as the site of significant change, moral or otherwise. These insights are essential to understanding the many ways in which altered states can be the setting for action, not just contemplation. Moreover, Murdoch's account challenges readers to consider aesthetic experiences (in the natural world, in literature, in art) as central to our inner lives.[6] However, it takes discipline to deliberately expel the self; Murdoch describes the process of seeing justly as an "endless task."[7] Though one might very well contend that the range of experiences examined here cannot be considered unselfing without the moral framing of the concept, I argue that it is precisely the separation of the experience of unselfing from its interpretation in this project that allows us to understand more fully the diverse set of intersubjective encounters that ensue from the undoing of the self.

Some of the writers explored in the following chapters describe the intersubjective promise of unselfing, despite its accompanying risks and costs. Yolande Mukagasana's testimony frames the loss of the ordinary self as the site of radical compassion, despite the incredible suffering she experienced after the murder of her husband and children during the 1994 Rwandan genocide against the Tutsi. Similarly,

Abdelkebir Khatibi's framing of self-loss casts unselfing as the ludic occasion to cultivate other-feeling and other thought for complex and "foreign" others. On the other end of the spectrum, writer and survivor Charlotte Delbo writes of the radical empathy that ensues from the disruption of ordinary self-function in Auschwitz as devastating, particularly because her ordinary sense of agency as an actor in the world is missing. Others like Cixous write of unselfing as a dehumanizing and alienating experience. Still others, like Henri Michaux, write of the mutation of the self on mescaline as an experience that takes the experimenter further from the world, not closer to ontological others. Finally, some writers occupy a middle position between the one that envisions unselfing as the inevitable route to compassionate consciousness and the one that links unselfing to alienating intersubjective experiences. Valéry, for example, seems to think that studying the stranger within might be good practice for understanding others in turn. The range of these interpretations makes clear that the experience of overcoming the ordinary relationship between self and world is best understood by attending to its inherent ambiguities and contradictions.

Unselfing across Traditions

Accounts of unselfing across religious and philosophical traditions reflect the desire to make sense of the relationship between the all-encompassing nature of interiority and ethical action. Twentieth-century writers across the Francosphère draw from multiple traditions in their writings on unselfing, including Neoplatonism and Christian mysticism, as well as accounts of nonself, non-being, and non-action in Hinduism, Buddhism, and Daoism. As a result, these texts are reflective of an experimental and syncretic approach to the theorization of unselfing.

In her essay "Forms of the Implicit Love of God," Weil writes that the greatest source of human trouble is that looking at beauty and eating are not the same thing. Children feel this, she explains, when they look at a beautiful cake, "almost regretting that it should have to be eaten" and yet are unable to stop themselves from eating it. Vice, depravity, and crime, she continues, are nearly always "attempts to eat beauty, to eat what we should only look at."[8] Ridding the self of its egotism for Weil involves a paradoxical detachment and attention to the world; it is an attempt to avoid devouring its beauty. The inescapable and persistent experience of self-consciousness creates this falsifying veil that conceals the needs and demands of the world. Weil argues that one can only apprehend and appreciate the existence of others by piercing this veil of self-illusion.

Murdoch was an admirer of Weil and drew significantly on her work in developing the notion of unselfing. Like Weil, Murdoch conceives of selfish thinking as a veil that must be pierced from the outside. Both imagine unselfing (though Weil does not use that word) as the task of looking at the world without egotism and selfish desire.[9] Accordingly, Murdoch claims that beauty – in this case, the occasional beauty that is on offer in the natural world – allows for an escape from the solipsistic tunnel of the self.[10] Murdoch writes, "And of course this is something which we *may* also do deliberately: give attention to nature in order to clear our minds of selfish care."[11] By this thinking, unselfing is a moral good, but one that is occasional and unpredictable: "And if quality of consciousness matters, then anything which alters consciousness in the direction of unselfishness, objectivity, and realism is to be connected with virtue."[12] For Murdoch, it is through the formative experiences of aesthetic contemplation, directed attention on another person, or reflection on beauty in the world that one might orient oneself to unselfishness and objectivity.[13] The kestrel example reflects Murdoch's critique of dominant psychological and philosophical accounts of inner life.[14] What is missing from these interpretations of responsibility, freedom, or action is the sense that attention is distinct from merely looking at an object and can effectively be a significant moral activity. Against the existentialists, to whom she repeatedly responds, Murdoch's literary and philosophical texts are grounded in Platonic conceptions of the Good and a deep worry that images of it are mere illusions.[15]

Elaine Scarry continues this dialogue between Murdoch and Weil in her account of "radical decentering" in *On Beauty and Being Just* (1999). Scarry's version of unselfing is built on the notion that the perceptual experience of beauty entails an ethical appeal. She argues that beauty assists us in the work of addressing injustice, not only by requiring constant perceptual activity, but also because it serves as a form of instruction.[16] Like Murdoch, Scarry's account of what she calls "nonself-interestedness" and "unself-interestedness" stems from the appreciation of beauty as an altered state; it prompts readers to engage in thought experiments on beauty as a starting place for ethical education. Her account recalls Schopenhauer's theory of aesthetics as a reprieve from desire and care; during states of pure contemplation "we are, so to speak, rid of ourselves."[17] The following example illustrates how beauty can accidentally provoke these moments of awakening:

One walks down a street and suddenly sees a redbud tree – its tiny heart-shaped leaves climbing out all along its branches like children who haven't yet learned the spatial rules for which parts of the playground they can run on. It is as though one has just been beached, lifted out of one ontological state into another that is fragile and must be held onto lest one lose hold of a branch and fall back into the ocean.[18]

The beautiful as a "freely arriving perceptual event" ignites a desire for truth, setting forth the possibilities of both conviction and error with unparalleled "electric brightness."[19] The second part of Scarry's argument defines the relationship between beauty and justice as one between the beholder and the beheld, especially when beauty is pursued actively. The radical decentring of the self is made possible as "we willingly cede our ground to the thing that stands before us."[20] This decentring of the self also provokes a sort of altered state, which Scarry calls "an opiated adjacency."[21]

And yet, unselfing as a ceding of ground is interpreted by other thinkers as a site of alienation and displacement. In *Beyond Good and Evil*, Nietzsche rails against the celebration of the "objective spirit," which requires the lessening of the self in the pursuit of truth as an inherent value. He writes, "However gratefully we may welcome an *objective* spirit – and is there anyone who has never been morally sick of everything subjective and his accursed ipissimosity? – in the end we also have to learn caution against our gratitude and put a halt to the exaggerated manner in which the "unselfing" and depersonalization of the spirit is being celebrated nowadays as if it were the goal itself and redemption and transfiguration."[22] "Unselfing" (*Entselbstung*) in Nietzsche is an erasure of the self to the status of instrument. The objective person is too disinterested to judge or take sides in an argument: "he is no 'end in himself'"; "whatever still remains in him of a 'person' strikes him as accidental, often arbitrary"; "the objective man is an instrument"; he is "a man without substance and content, a 'selfless' man."[23] In Nietzsche, the objective person, in becoming less of themselves, risks becoming nothing but a mirror that reflects the stronger, subjective selves around them, or at least the illusion of those strong selves. (Murdoch might argue that these are alterations in the wrong "direction.") Whereas Weil, Murdoch, and Scarry will later see the potential for justice in the removing of the self from the centre of experience even without a metaphysical dimension, Nietzsche warns against the instrumentalization of the person inherent in the act of distancing.[24]

The notion of unselfing as self-reduction in Weil and Murdoch closely resembles the Christian model of the suffering self as a route to justice. (It is precisely this lessening of the self that Nietzsche constructed as the source of *ressentiment* in *The Genealogy of Morals*). By this account, one ought to reduce (John 3:30) or deny (Matthew 16:24) the life of the self in order to bring Christ and others into sharper focus.[25] Murdoch's thinking is shaped by Weil's Platonic-Christian notion of the process of stripping the ego bare of its attachments and consolations."[26]

At the same time, Murdoch finds herself at odds with the traditional Christian view of the self in that she shies away from the Christian notion of the beneficial role of suffering and seeks to engage fully with the reality of death. Unselfing as a reflexive process is nearly impossible to achieve in this context precisely because the distortions of the self are so tenacious and difficult to overthrow. Experiences at the limit of human consciousness – when the self is ultimately threatened – might be the only sure way to clear the mind of its egotism and in so doing, foster compassionate consciousness. David J. Gordon writes, "Renunciation for Murdoch is always of the 'self,' never of the body only; she seeks not meek powerlessness but non-power, the absence of a dangerous charisma or psychological power over others. But the real danger of physical death may be the only force strong enough to shake the complacent ego."[27] Indeed, Murdoch's unselfing moves away from the Christian image of redemptive suffering and towards a Buddhist image of nonself.

Whereas Christian selflessness emphasizes consolation through suffering and powerlessness, Buddhist teachings stress non-power over suffering and the "I" as an illusion. One of the paradigms of the *Samyutta Nikaya* is that existence is defined by impermanence (*anicca*), suffering (*dukkhā*), and non-self (*anattā*).[28] In the second discourse of the Buddha after enlightenment, the Buddha addresses a group of monks (*bhikkus*) and enumerates the five aggregates – form (the body), feeling, perceptions, mental formations, and consciousness (awareness) – in order to show that the self is not in control of any of these features. Because we cannot control the form of our bodies and cannot will ourselves out of affliction, form cannot be self.[29] He continues through the rest of the aggregates, showing that feelings, perceptions, mental formations, and consciousness are also nonself. The Buddha then shows that each of the five aggregates is also impermanent. He concludes: "This is not mine, this I am not, this is not myself."[30] The Buddha's teaching in this *sutta* appears to be that none of the five aggregates can be considered the defining feature of selfhood. Enlightened consciousness consists in detaching from the illusion that any of these features are the self.[31] While the illusion of selfhood in Western philosophy is framed in terms of synchronic and diachronic unity, wherein memory and imagination create the impression of a unified self, the illusion of selfhood in Buddhism is instead rooted in the mistaken impression of being ontologically separate and unique.[32]

Michaux's and Bataille's accounts of unselfing are both influenced by Buddhist conceptions of nonself. Michaux was interested in occupying the void, or the emptying out of the container of the self, and the self that persists through his mescaline experiments bears a similarity to the Buddhist notion of witness-consciousness.[33] Michaux writes consistently of his attempts to escape the impression of the bounded, personal self, while attending to the witness position through experience. The purpose of Buddhist practice is to "selectively whittle away" the self-created illusion that dupes us into thinking that we are bounded entities.[34] Michaux emphasizes this practice of moving away from the illusion as a voyage inward; he cites the following excerpts of sayings of the Buddha from the *Dhammapada* and the end of his travelogue, *Un barbare en Asie* (*A Barbarian in Asia*) (1933):

Et maintenant, dit Bouddha à ses disciples, au moment de mourir:

A l'avenir, soyez votre propre lumière, votre propre refuge.
Ne cherchez pas d'autre refuge.
N'allez en quête de refuge qu'auprès de vous-même.

Ne vous occupez pas des façons de penser des autres.
Tenez-vous bien dans votre île à vous.
COLLÉS À LA CONTEMPLATION.

And now, said the Buddha to his disciples at the moment of his death:

In the future, be your own light, your own refuge.
Do not seek any other refuge.
Seek only refuge within yourself.

Do not worry about the ways other people think.
Hold fast on your island.
CLINGING TO CONTEMPLATION.[35]

Likewise, Bataille's work (and praxis) was influenced by his study of Hinduism and Buddhism, though the influence of Eastern religions on his work has not been studied nearly as much as his relationship to Christian mysticism. Bataille was interested in Tibetan Buddhism (through Alexandra David-Néel), Hindu traditions such as yoga (via Mircea Eliade), and Tantra, as well as the Hindu saints (through the biographies of Romain Rolland).[36] Indeed Bataille's theory of the sacred, with its emphasis on transgression and sites of "effusion" is inflected by his understanding of Tibetan Buddhism, often through Nietzsche. What Bataille calls "sovereign moments" are produced from both ritualized and spontaneous experiences of excess including laughter, tears, intoxication, art forms, beauty, and the divine.[37] During these sovereign moments, the subject is able to exist outside of labour and servitude and thereby escape the constraints of project and utility under capitalism.[38] Bataille writes admiringly of Tibetan Buddhism in *La part maudite* (*The Accursed Share*) (1949) as a society that, in his view, is oriented to this economic theory of domination and expenditure. Though other religions have preached nonviolence and still engaged in bloody wars, Bataille claims that the Tibetan case demonstrates the ability to contain explosive violence by investing its vital and economic forces in monasticism, hence avoiding the disfiguring effects of activity and growth.[39]

Whereas Buddhism teaches *anatman* (Skt.)/*anatta* (Pali), or the nonself, Hinduism emphasizes *ātman* as the enduring and metaphysical connection between the individual and the universe. In Hindu philosophy and spirituality, the individual self is part of the universal soul; the concept of *ātman* expresses of the metaphysical persistence of the self at the core of humans and all living beings. Though different schools of Hinduism differ in the metaphysical accounts of the relationship between the appearance of reality, the self, and the universe, the Advaita Vedanta tradition holds that *ātman* refers to the true self and is identical to *brahman,* the unity and oneness of the universe. For the composers of the *Upanishads,* the late Vedic Sanskrit religious scriptures at the core of Hinduism, the self (ātman) "was not a personal 'self,' but lay beyond both body and mind as a transcendent, yet immanent reality that was a person's true nature."[40]

Weil was an engaged reader of the *Upanishads,* as well as the *Bhagavad-Gītā,* the most famous episode of the Indian epic, the *Mahābhārata.*[41] Her late notebooks bear witness to her fascination with the Indian account of the relationship between the individual self and the universal soul where she meditates on introspection and yoga as routes to self-knowledge and self-realization. "Qu'aucune activité – travail physique ou étude – ne soit un obstacle à voir *l'ātman* en toutes choses."[42] [May no activity, whether physical or study, be an obstacle to seeing *ātman* in all things.] Schopenhauer was also an admirer of the *Upanishads* (and later, Buddhism).[43] The *Upanishads* appealed to both Schopenhauer's and Weil's sense that the individual soul is part of a larger, universal reality and that the seeming separateness of the two is an illusion.

Francophone writers of unselfing also draw on Daoism (particularly through the *Daodejing,* the multi-authored text attributed to the figure

Laozi, and the *Zhuangzi*). Michaux, Weil, and Khatibi were all readers of Daoism and were inspired in different ways by the dissolution
of the individual in early Chinese thought. Brook Ziporyn explains
that while Western philosophy may be thought to proceed from the
atomistic assumption that all things are mutually exclusive, or at least
the assumption that all things (words, acts, peoples, societies, and
abstract entities) interact as physical objects or mathematical entities
do, the Chinese philosophical tradition places personal interactions
as the model for how things interact.[44] Michaux, Weil, Bataille, and
Khatibi were intrigued by the Chinese model of holism, emptiness,
and non-action and its implications for value theory, and seized on it in
their writings.[45] The nature mysticism of the *Daodejing* emphasizes that
the Dao is non-being (*wu*) and emphasizes the power of non-action
(*wuwei*), which is distinct from inaction. Chapter 43 of the *Daodejing*
begins with the image of water, the "softest thing" in the universe,
running over rock, the firmest, as an illustration of the value of *not*
taking action:
   The softest, most pliable thing in the world runs roughshod over the
firmest thing in the world.

> That which has no substance gets into that which has no spaces or cracks.
> I therefore know *that there is* benefit in taking no action.
> The *wordless* teaching, the benefit of taking no action –
> Few in the world can realize these![46]

Weil focuses on the power of inaction, which she identifies in the
Bhagavad-Gītā and the *Laozi* as a "kind of passive activity."[47] Similarly,
Michaux writes of Laozi as a "a man who knows" and who "speaks
the language of the obvious" in *Un Barbare en Asie*: "Annihiler son être
et son action, et l'univers vient à vous."[48] [Annihilate one's being and
one's action and the universe comes to you.] Khatibi's extended 1976
poem, *Le lutteur de classe à la manière taoïste* (*Class Warrior – Taoist Style*)
transgressively grapples with the limits of both action and inaction by
attempting to merge Marxism and Daoism. Sounding much like Weil
in her meditations on the contagious and corrosive properties of force,
Khatibi's poem asks:

> peux-tu défigurer l'ennemi de classe
> sans emprunter ses traces?[49]

> can you disfigure the class enemy
> without taking on his likeness?[50]

The poem grapples with the ramifications of anticolonial struggle on the sovereignty of the self. *Le lutteur de classe* stages the disfiguring nature of violence in the aftermath of independence movements in the Maghreb. David Fieni situates this poem "after the promises of national independence and Arab and Pan-African unity had begun to lose their luster, in the midst of the Moroccan *années de plomb*, which saw many of Khatibi's friends and fellow writers imprisoned and tortured for taking political stands."[51] The poem references straw dogs, which appear fleetingly in the *Laozi* (chapter 5) and in the *Zhuangzi* (Outer Chapters 14:4) in a more extended form. In the *Laozi,* Heaven and Earth and the Sage are "not humane," but rather see "ten thousand things and common people" as "straw dogs."[52] These sacrificial objects – the likenesses of dogs made from grass – are treated with respect and reverence during the rite itself but are discarded unceremoniously afterwards.[53] Khatibi writes,

> la souveraineté brûle
> l'ennemi de classe
> comme chien de paille[54]

> sovereignty burns
> the class warrior
> like a straw dog[55]

The class warrior is taken up and discarded like the sacrificial objects. In the style of a manifesto, the poem invites the reader to abandon institutions (familial, cultural, or otherwise) and points of origin in favour of the perspective of the "orphan sage" who stands outside these institutions.

> en parlant de son errance un sage antique a dit
> je ne sais si le vent me porte ou si je porte le vent
> médite ce point cristallin de l'être[56]

> while talking about his wandering an ancient sage said
> I don't know if the wind pushed me along or whether I pushed the wind
> meditate upon this crystalline point of being[57]

In this fragment of the poem, Khatibi's experimental writing reflects a Zhuangzian sensibility on the impermanence of the self and the desire to show its contingency. Here, the poem invites the reader to meditate on the point of being; like in the duck-rabbit illusion, the self alternately appears as subject and object depending on the way that it is considered.

Though the Zhuangzian theory of the self is the subject of much debate within studies of Daoist philosophy, the Inner Chapters reflect a form of selfhood that is subject to perpetual transformation.[58] The butterfly dream in chapter 2 of the *Zhuangzi* casts the self not only as an illusion that one ought to overcome, but also as subject to absorption into the whole of experience. In the passage, the dreamer is unsure from which identity the dream begins and ends.

> Once Zhuang Zhou dreamt he was a butterfly, fluttering about joyfully just as a butterfly would. He followed his whims exactly as he liked and knew nothing about Zhuang Zhou. Suddenly he awoke, and there he was, the startled Zhuang Zhou in the flesh. He did not know if Zhou had been dreaming he was a butterfly, or if a butterfly was now dreaming it was Zhou. Surely, Zhou and a butterfly count as two distinct identities! Such is what we call the transformation of one thing into another.[59]

The self is not exempt from the eternal transformation of the seasons or tides, the flow of one thing into another. In this example, the *Zhuangzi* invites a reflection on the uncertainty of the positioning of the self with respect to the cosmos. The *Zhuangzi* refers to the namelessness of the container we call self, again drawing on dream states to illustrate the ever-changing nature of perspective. "You temporarily get involved in something or other and proceed to call it 'myself' – but how can we know if what we call 'self' has any 'self' to it? You dream you are a bird and find yourself soaring in the heavens, you dream you are a fish and find yourself submerged in the depths. I cannot even know if what I'm saying now is a dream or not."[60] Michaux echoes this Zhuangzian attitude of detached indifference to the container of the self, especially in his mescaline texts, which imagine the body yielding to the flow of the universe instead of striving towards it.[61] The idea of the self in the *Zhuangzi* emerges as a shifting reference point; writers across the French-speaking world are drawn to this relativizing impulse that they recognized in Daoism.

There are evident correspondences between French-language accounts of unselfing and the conceptions of non-being, non-self, and non-action in Eastern philosophy and religion. At the same time, it must also be acknowledged that these twentieth-century cultural crossings and readings are also the site of tensions and discrepancies in their often Orientalizing interpretations. For example, though he ironically positions himself as the barbarian and seeks to voyage against the grain

of exoticism, Michaux's early travel writings are replete with gener-
alizations about "races" and "ethnicities" (terms he uses interchangeably).[62] His impulse to categorize and essentialize cultures sometimes
reverberates into his philosophy on selfhood.[63] Separately, while Weil's
transcultural thinking demonstrates an impressive reach across traditions, her work tends to elide the tensions or discrepancies between
sacred texts as she weaves together ancient Greek wisdom with Hindu
philosophy and Zen Buddhism. She often reads Eastern texts through a
Christian lens, writing in her "Spiritual Autobiography" that upon her
first reading, the *Bhagavad-Gītā* sounded Christian to her.[64]

Weil's cake passage on "eating beauty" from the beginning of this
discussion illustrates an essential distinction between Eastern conceptions of nonself and the theory of unselfing that persists through Murdoch's and Scarry's accounts. Weil's passage gestures to her personal
ascetic habits and trouble with materiality by equating the dynamics
of aesthetics with the dynamics of desire. This focus on beauty as an
occasion for losing the self continues in later iterations of the concept
of unselfing. Weil writes that humans suffer because of the divorce
between looking and consuming:

> La grande douleur de la vie humaine, c'est que regarder et manger soient
> deux opérations différentes. De l'autre côté du ciel seulement, dans le pays
> habité par Dieu, c'est une seule et même opération. Déjà les enfants, quand
> ils regardent longtemps un gâteau et le prennent presque à regret pour le
> manger, sans pouvoir pourtant s'en empêcher, éprouvent cette douleur.
> Peut-être les vices, les dépravations et les crimes sont-ils presque toujours
> ou même toujours dans leur essence des tentatives pour manger la beauté,
> manger ce qu'il faut seulement regarder. Ève avait commencé. Si elle a
> perdu l'humanité en mangeant un fruit, l'attitude inverse, regarder un
> fruit sans le manger, doit être ce qui sauve. "Deux compagnons ailés, dit
> une *Upanishad,* deux oiseaux sont sur une branche de l'arbre. L'un mange
> les fruits, l'autre les regarde." Ces deux oiseaux sont les deux parties de
> notre âme.[65]

> The great trouble in human life is that looking and eating are two differ-
> ent operations. Only beyond the sky, in the country inhabited by God, are
> they one and the same operation. Children feel this trouble already, when
> they look at a cake for a long time almost regretting that it should have to
> be eaten and yet are unable to help eating it. It may be that vice, deprav-
> ity, and crime are nearly always, or even perhaps always, in their essence,
> attempts to eat beauty, to eat what we should only look at. Eve began it. If
> she caused humanity to be lost by eating the fruit, the opposite attitude,

looking at the fruit without eating it, should be what is required to save it. "Two winged companions," says an Upanishad, "two birds are on the branch of a tree. One eats the fruit, the other looks at it." These two birds are the two parts of our soul.[66]

Weil weaves together the account of original sin with the Hindu account of the two birds, one waiting, one acting and consuming. For Weil, this is illustrative of the two parts of the soul: the consumptive and the contemplative. Evil and vice stem from the human inability to look without eating, the desire to be God and engage in both in one single operation. Both the *Upanishads* and Weil emphasize the need for non-action and detachment; but as Kapani notes, these are not the same forms of detachment from the activity of the world. The *Upanishads* advise seeing things as they are from an affectively neutral perspective, but Weil's notion of beauty is at odds with this account of looking.[67] Weil's account of unselfing unites the aesthetic with the ascetic; one ought to resist the desire to "eat beauty."

Returning to this example underscores that though many of these accounts are evidently influenced by Eastern philosophical accounts of nonself and nonaction, the philosophy of unselfing in the modern Francosphère cannot be traced to any single philosophical or cultural tradition. Rather, the writing of unselfing is the product of intellectual syncretism, experimentation with genre, and the primary role that the phenomenology of experience plays for these writers.

Unselfing and Empathy

The theoretical uncertainty that characterizes the interpretation of unselfing runs parallel to contemporary disagreements on the nature and meaning of empathic response. Tracing the fault lines of these ongoing debates on this intersubjective question sheds important light on the stakes of transcending or losing the ordinary experience of self. While some theorists argue that lessening the self leads to a heightened empathic response (and therefore availability to the other), others argue that the self is the basis for social emotion and action. Studying unselfing offers a new perspective on these debates in that this literature suggests that empathy is not necessarily a morally meaningful or prosocial emotion.

Derived from the German *Einfühlung* (feeling-into), "empathy" emerges as a more active version of the concept of "sympathy," popular during the Enlightenment. Robert Vischer used the term "empathy" in 1873 in the context of German aesthetics as a way of understanding how

viewers appreciate a work of art. The term was then taken over by Theodor Lipps "who introduced it into the field of social cognition and used
it to designate our basic capacity for understanding others as minded
creatures."[68] Edward B. Titchener, who was influenced by Lipps, shortly
thereafter translated *Einfühlung* as "empathy," and focused on the way
individuals process and understand the feelings of others. An important limitation of the social power of empathy in these early accounts
is the notion that we can only understand mental states of others that
we have personally held.[69] As empathy became part of popular psychological culture emerging in Vienna, London, and other cosmopolitan
centres, the concept of empathy came to mean an active orientation of
one's perspective towards the lives of others. The distinction between
sympathy and empathy has since been characterized as the difference
between feeling for others and feeling what (we believe) others feel.[70]
The empathy-altruism hypothesis places empathy on lofty ground,
claiming that empathic concern (defined as other-oriented emotional
response to someone in need) produces altruistic motivation to reduce
that need in others.[71] However, in an analysis of contemporary theories
of empathy, Heather Battaly shows that the idea that empathy means
caring for others (as opposed to merely sharing or imagining the feelings of others) exists primarily in the folk definition of the term. The
"caring" aspect of empathy – upon which rests its great hope and social
potential – is absent from most of its theoretical forms.[72]

Some recent volumes on empathy use its intellectual history as evidence for the link between the rise in individualism and empathy as a
route to altruism.[73] Jeremey Rifkin's *The Empathic Civilization: The Race
to Global Consciousness in a World in Crisis* for instance claims that empathy is on the rise, and that empathic feeling may mature in time to save
humanity from the climate crisis. Many phenomena count as empathy
in this account (the bond between infant and mother; the growing con-
nectedness of large groups of strangers on social media). By this reading, the concept of empathy is linked to the birth of psychology as a
discipline and the rise in the culture of individualism. "The awakening
sense of selfhood, brought on by the differentiation process, is crucial to
the development and extension of empathy."[74] Here, the concept of self
is the basis for other-feeling, not an obstacle to it.

Others claim that empathy is on the decline and reference the rise
in narcissism as evidence of a troubling "empathy deficit."[75] In *The
Dark Sides of Empathy*, Breithaupt claims that this decline in empathy
might not be such a bad thing. As in Rifkin, Breithaupt analyzes many
diverse phenomena as examples of empathy's "dark side," including
side-taking, identification with a benevolent helper figure (rather than

the person in need), empathetic sadism, and "vampiristic" empathy.[76] These disagreements on the power and meaning of empathy demonstrate how the concept has become the keystone of contemporary discourse on intersubjectivity even though it remains conceptually fuzzy.

Despite the ongoing investment in the notion of empathy's social potential, these competing interpretations of empathy underscore that it is not clear what it means to empathize with another person or whether empathy is a morally significant emotion. Dan Zahavi writes, "There is still no clear consensus about what precisely [empathy] is, and how it is related to and different from emotional contagion, motor mimicry, emotional sharing, imaginative projection, perspective taking, empathetic distress, and empathetic concern ... People disagree about the role of sharing and caring and imagination in empathy, just as they disagree about the relation between empathy and social cognition in general."[77] The existence of an empathetic response does not necessarily mean that empathy is morally significant, or equivalent with compassion.[78] When considering the relationship between altered states and unselfing, it is useful to distinguish between advanced or "mature" forms of empathy such as the inference of mental states and imaginative perspective-taking and so-called "low" forms of empathy, such as motor mimicry.

In their consideration of the gap between self and other, unselfing narratives also grapple with the philosophical difference between shared experiences of presence, and empathy as an act of imagination. Unselfing narratives offer conflicting and ambivalent accounts on the social power of lessening the claims of the self, and thus mirror the fundamental uncertainty at the heart of contemporary empathy theorizing.

This question of whether the self should be considered a parallel structure for interpreting the minds of others has also framed debates on the structure of what cognitive scientists call "theory of mind." The debate between "theory-theory" and "simulation theory" of mind underscores the difficulty of pinning down the nature of intersubjective experience within the cognitive model. It is framed on one side of the debate as using one's own experiences to construct theories about the mental states of others, and on the other, as co-experiencing, or feeling what others feel. What is consistent across the theory of mind discussion (and distinct from the focus on intersubjectivity as an ontological problem within the phenomenological tradition) is the idea that the first-person nature of experience is what makes it possible to interpret the minds of others.

In the fields of developmental and social psychology and social cognition, theory of mind refers to the ability to attribute mental states to others, and to interpret and explain the behaviour of others in terms of their intentions, desires, or beliefs. While theory theorists argue that humans make use of folk psychology in order to understand the mental states of others, simulation theorists argue that humans use their minds to imitate these mental states. On the theory-theory side, for example, Simon Baron-Cohen has argued that the theorization of other minds is made possible by the implicit development of "mind-reading" capabilities, while Alison Gopnik and Henry Wellman have argued that theory of mind is acquired explicitly, that is, in the same way scientific theories are acquired.[79] Gopnik explains:

> On this view children develop a succession of theories of the mind that they use to explain their experience and the behavior of themselves and others. Like scientific theories, these intuitive or naïve theories postulate abstract coherent mental entities and laws, and they provide predictions, interpretations, and explanations. The theories change as children confront counterevidence, gather new data, and perform experiments. One consequence of this view is that the philosophical doctrine of first-person authority is incorrect; our knowledge of our minds is as theoretical as our knowledge of the minds of others.[80]

This developmental view presents the idea that humans enhance their cognitive perspective-taking capacities as they encounter new and complex others. Andrew Meltzoff, another theory-theorist who collaborated with neuroscientist Jean Decety, argues that self-experience provides a "like-me" framework that can be used to interpret other people's experiences. He writes, "The primitive on which social cognition rests is the perceived 'like me' equivalence between self and other. This provides infants, even newborns, with a feeling of kinship with fellow humans, and it supports bidirectional learning from and about people."[81] By this understanding of the theorization of other minds, self-experience is flexible and a change in self-understanding can in turn change one's conception of others.

On the simulation side of the debate, Alvin Goldman has argued that we understand the mental states of others via conscious imagination, while Robert Gordon holds that it is rather through explicit, though non-inferential, processes.[82] The discovery of mirror neurons by Giacomo Rizzolatti and his team in the 1980s and 1990s brought public attention to the relationship between intersubjectivity and social cognition.[83] Mirror neurons fire both during the execution of an action, and when the action is observed being executed by someone else. Proponents of the controversial theory that mirror neurons are indicators of empathetic capacity suggest that we imagine others as parallel selves.

Marco Iacoboni for instance argues that the brain as a biological unit serves as the guarantor of this parallel between self and other: "It seems as if our brain is *built* for mirroring, and that only through mirroring – through the simulation in our brain of the felt experience of our minds – do we deeply understand what other people are thinking."[84] Vittorio Gallese crafts an empirically grounded perspective on *Einfühlung* in his work, arguing that we come to know the presence and experiences of others directly, rather than through cognitive operations.[85] Since the discovery of mirror neurons, a number of volumes have been produced claiming that the human brain is "hard-wired" for empathy, though these experiments and readings mostly rely on low-level instances of empathic feeling, such as mimicry and emotional contagion.[86]

Many researchers and philosophers have reached the conclusion that a hybrid of theory-theory and simulation-theory views are needed to fully explain the complexity of social cognition.[87] As Paul Armstrong puts it, when analyzed from a phenomenological perspective, theory of mind, simulation theory, and mirror neurons are all "attempts to explain the acts of doubling me and not me that human beings routinely, automatically engage in as they negotiate their way through a paradoxically intersubjective and solipsistic world."[88] When the phenomenological tradition investigates the ties between our subjective experience with the world and the problem of other minds, it continues to emphasize the gap between our self-knowledge, other-knowledge, and knowledge of the world. According to Zahavi, the phenomenologists got it right by respecting the "irreducible difference between our knowledge of external objects, our self-knowledge, and our knowledge of others."[89] We can empathize with the another person's pain, but we cannot feel it exactly as the other feels it since our approach is from a different angle. The subjective experience of the social world involves an inherent presentation of others, which paradoxically serves to emphasize our feeling of solipsism. Merleau-Ponty writes, "I perceive the other's grief or anger in his behavior, on his face and in his hands, without any borrowing from an 'inner' experience of suffering or of anger ... But ultimately the other's behavior and even the other's words are not the other himself. The other's grief or anger never has precisely the same sense for him and for me. For him, these are lived situations; for me they are appresented."[90] Altered states of consciousness change the "angle" from which we approach the experiences of others; the experience of the other as it presented to us can slip into lived situation wherein the experience of self and other are confused. Levinas's account of the responsibility to the other distinguishes between the immediacy of the face-to-face encounter (like the one that Merleau-Ponty describes above) from imagining the mental states of other people in an abstract way. Altered states sometimes orient the self towards the experiences and feelings of others by changing the angle of intersubjective perception; however, we must be careful to distinguish between a change in the angle of perception and the more robust idea of altruistic response or care.

The many debates surrounding the nature of intersubjectivity and its relationship to prosocial action is not only relevant to the study of the relationship between selves and ontological others, but also to the study of the relationships between readers and the fate of imaginary others, especially as dramatized in aesthetics. This is variously analyzed as a question of theory of mind (Zunshine), as a question of empathy (Nussbaum), and a question of embodied simulation (Gallese and Guerra).[91] A novel might function like Murdoch's kestrel or Scarry's redbud tree, serving to pull readers out of a state of self-absorption and towards justice, an aesthetic claim that each philosopher makes in her respective work.[92] But self-loss might not be accompanied by any prosocial response, given that the novel's very fictionality frees us from our ordinary sense of responsibility. This is one of Suzanne Keen's arguments in *Empathy and the Novel*; she writes, "empathetic reading experiences that confirm the empathy-altruism theory are exceptional, not routine."[93] If narratives do carry social power, this power is rooted in the many ways in which stories stage and explore the paradox of the alter ego.[94]

Despite the obvious resonances of these aesthetic questions with the study of altered states in narrative, my focus in this book is on the literature *of* unselfing rather than literature *as* a site of unselfing. In other words, I am specifically interested in the narratives that writers craft to describe the loss or transcendence of consciousness and its effect on intersubjectivity during unordinary self-experiences rather than the potentially disruptive effect that narratives can have on readers themselves. Moreover, the writers that make up this corpus are all invested in the representative quality of the text (though to different degrees). That is, each text is situated in a different position on the spectrum between fiction and (creative) nonfiction. Each unselfing narrative seeks to arrive at the representation of the reality selfhood during unordinary experiences and uses different tactics to arrive at those representations. For these reasons, I have left to the side the separate, though related, reader-response question on the degree to which fiction improves theory of mind or promotes empathy in my consideration of unselfing.

Accounts of unselfing reveal that diminishing the claims of the self only sometimes improves the self's vision of others. It is true that the reduction of the self *may* bring others into focus; however, only some unselfing narratives relate this transformation of the self as an automatic turn towards moral clarity. Indeed, in other accounts, a robust sense of self is necessary for intersubjective feeling to flourish in the first place. Thus, while some unselfing texts seek to communicate the experience of altered states as the route to unselfishness, others indicate that things are not quite so straightforward. This relationship – between altered states of consciousness and unselfing – is central to sketching out the fault lines in this theoretical divide. The next section turns to this relationship by foregrounding the phenomenology of altered states as a qualitative shift in consciousness that entails a special relationship to time.

From Altered States to Unselfing Narratives

Though writers disagree on the meaning of unselfing and what it reveals about the world, all describe it as an alteration of ordinary self-experience. In other words, all experiences of unselfing are examples of altered states (broadly understood), but not all altered states result in unselfing. Each account of unselfing studied in the following chapters focuses on a different altered state, from Valéry's "geometry of suffering" to Delbo's thirst, from Michaux's mind on mescaline to Weil's decreation.

   The category of altered states includes dreams, trances, ecstasy, and mystical states through which the subject evaluates the qualitative shift in mental functioning to a hitherto unexplored realm of consciousness. Altered states differ qualitatively from ordinary waking states of consciousness and are necessarily dependent on self-report and first-person accounts.[95] In this sense, the significance of the psychological experience of hallucination, mystical transcendence, or harrowing pain are subjective. Only some witnesses of terrible atrocities suffer from Post-Traumatic Stress Disorder, and psychedelic drugs do not affect "ordinary consciousness" in universally predictable ways. Altered states in this book are not studied as instances of psychopathology or given clinical diagnoses; rather, they exist as shifts from a shared (common-sense, developmentally appropriate, and culturally determined) understanding of the real to what some researchers call the "frontier zone" of consciousness.[96] They can be self-directed or induced externally; experienced spontaneously or directedly; they are alternately perceived to be "natural" or "unnatural" depending on whether or not they are induced by meditation, ritual, drugs, or circumstance. As such, these states introduce philosophical challenges to the concept and experience of being a self.[97]

Altered states of consciousness have historically posed a problem for self-unification within theories of selfhood. Locke, for example, worries about the persistence of the self through time, and especially through these troubling lapses in ordinary consciousness. In his account of personal identity, the self appropriates past actions which are linked together through time by a unity of consciousness: "For, since consciousness always accompanies thinking, and it is that which makes every one to be what he calls self, and thereby distinguishes himself from all other thinking things: in this alone consists personal identity, i.e., the sameness of a rational being; and as far as this consciousness can be extended backwards to any past action or thought, so far reaches the identity of that person."[98] If altered states are a rupture in accounted time, they create an obstacle for personal identity when understood as the "sameness of a rational being." When the self is defined as a unity of consciousness extending into the past, what happens when the subject cannot reliably account for all of it? Locke's solution to this problem in "Of Identity and Diversity" is the existence of an omniscient God who sees and thereby judges the entirety of the person's identity. His theory of the unity of consciousness that persists through altered states is built on this faith in a divine onlooker. We are held accountable for our actions on judgment day, "when every one shall 'receive according to his doings, the secrets of all hearts shall be laid open.' The sentence shall be justified by the consciousness all persons shall have, that they themselves, in what bodies soever they appear, or what substances soever that consciousness adheres to, are the same that committed those actions, and deserve that punishment for them."[99] This account importantly includes the parts of life during which the subject was not fully conscious, such as the time they spend asleep (or drunk).[100] Once God is no longer posited in the position of the ultimate witness figure and judge, altered states pose a special problem to the perceived sense of continuity of the self through time.

Unlike ordinary conscious experiences, altered states are subjective ruptures with habitual ways of being in the world and being with objects. This quality distinguishes altered states of consciousness from other experiences like habit, such as driving to work or practicing a craft. Consciousness wanders freely during habitual conscious activity and does not investigate itself as an object.[101] Instead of an immersive experience in habitual conscious activity, unselfing experiences might rather be conceived of as a *heightening* of the conscious awareness of the self through the experience of strangeness.[102] Like habit, altered states of consciousness bear a distinctive phenomenological signature, and are a special kind of "hitch" in it of themselves. Unselfing writers give detailed accounts of how it feels to be a self under these circumstances. Though their effects extend long after the moment is over, altered states necessarily have a limited duration in time. Murdoch can only hold the kestrel as an object of attention for so long before her focus breaks, or the bird flies away. Some thinkers are particularly focused on bridging the gap between altered states as discrete moments and making them become involuntary habit through practice. Murdoch writes that one must demystify the bridge between the occasional altered state and practiced habits of attention: "There is nothing odd or mystical about this, nor about the fact that our ability to act well 'when the time comes' depends partly, perhaps largely, upon the quality of our habitual objects of attention."[103]

In sum, altered states distort habitual and experiential relationships to objects and time. Time becomes achingly slow for Charlotte Delbo as she images rotting leaves coating her throat; mescaline makes the mind speed up to dizzying velocities for Henri Michaux. The hermeneutics of the first-person perspective is intensified as the subject interrogates its relationship to the phenomenal world. In this sense, altered states like thirst and hallucination defamiliarize the self. Writers articulate the strange phenomenology of these opiated states by attempting to sketch out the contours of these newly illuminated inner expanses. Unselfing texts are an exploration of the specific shape of the strange contours of the self; their writing allows them to be externalized and presented to others. At the same time, exploring the intersubjective dimensions of unselfing invites new questions on the relationship between altered states, the self, and the world.

The attempt to document the effect that altered states of consciousness have on the experience of being a self represents a philosophical effort to include other forms of consciousness in a global understanding of the mind. As William James memorably writes, "Rational consciousness is but one special type of consciousness, whilst all about it, parted from it by the flimsiest of screens, there lie potential forms of consciousness entirely different ... No account of the universe in its totality can be final which leaves these other forms of consciousness disregarded."[104] In James's psychological and philosophical account of religious experiences and mysticism, he articulates the need for a comprehensive theory of the mind that includes hitherto disregarded experiences like altered states. Witnesses to these often-overlooked states of consciousness seek to understand what happens to the self during unordinary conscious experiences, and how to approach the knowledge that ensues from them. The writers in this project seek to understand and document what happens to the unified self during altered states.

From the disparate sources discussed above, three main vocabularies emerge from of the spectrum of altered-self experiences in the twentieth-century Francosphère: the language of the mystical, the experimental, and the testimonial. The mystic's central worries about the self are communicated in relation to concepts like the ineffable, the transcendent, and the infinite; the experimenter speaks of testing, verification, and exploration of the limits of the self; the witness figure seeks to verify their account of unimaginable experience. Though each vocabulary is associated with linguistic and epistemological commitments, they are overlapping and interconnected in twentieth-century discourse as religion, science, and literature respond to the same philosophical questions on the nature of the self at the limits of experience.

Mystical, Experimental, Testimonial

The mystic explores the limits of selfhood through the languages of religion, spirituality, and the divine. The secularization at the heart of modernity intensifies the worry about the existence of the self during altered states of consciousness and places human consciousness at the centre of religious experiences.[105] As theologically grounded understandings of the self – that is, ones that posit God as an objective and omniscient observer – begin to erode, the human witness takes on the responsibility of observing all mental states. The human subject becomes invisible in the absence of God, who once provided the basis for establishing the identity of the self. According to Michel de Certeau, what is qualitatively different about modern (Western) mysticism in this context is that it represents the rejection of, rather than the adherence to, religious doctrine, as well as a turn towards scientific experimentation on the self. Tracing the turn to the sixteenth and seventeenth centuries de Certeau identifies the mystical tradition with the margins of theology as well as society. He writes,

In particular, from the time that European culture has ceased to define itself as Christian – that is, since the sixteenth or seventeenth century – one no longer designated as mystical that form of "wisdom" elevated by a full recognition of the mystery already lived and announced in common beliefs, but rather an experimental knowledge that slowly detached itself from traditional theology or church institutions, characterized by the consciousness … of fulfiling a passivity in which the self loses itself in God. In other words, what becomes mystical is that which diverges from normal or ordinary paths; that which is no longer inscribed within the social community of faith or religious references, but rather on the margins of an increasingly secularized society and a knowledge that defines its own scientific objects.[106]

The wisdom of altered states comes from the margins of experiences rather than from the doctrinal knowledge of institutions and traditions. The value and particularity of experimental knowledge emerges precisely in the fringes of conscious experience, which take writers outside of inscribed communities that were hitherto responsible for making sense of these experiences.

According to Thomas A. Carlson, twentieth century thought is marked by the persistent notion that our relationship with the world has been demystified not only by death of God, but also by the rationalized approach to reality exemplified by a technocratic society.[107] It is also framed by the advent of technological subjectivity within a culture of totalizing presence and mystical subjectivity informed by theology. With the rise in technological understanding of the human comes the parallel and progressive erasure of the God-concept in popular consciousness and culture. Thomas J.J. Altizer's reading of Nietzsche attempts to make sense of the simultaneous anonymity of God and the anonymity of the human: "The human subject who was 'the center of uniquely Western self-consciousness,' which comes to birth (with Paul and Augustine) as a unique, interior 'I' only in relation to the 'pure otherness' of its God, has been 'eroded under the impact of the modern realization of the death of God. Thence it has disappeared in our late modern imaginative and conceptual enactments and is now becoming truly invisible in a new mass consciousness and society.'"[108] The death of God entails the death of the unique, interior self, which understands itself in relation to the total otherness of God. The erosion of this form of subjectivity, which was formerly the centre of Western self-consciousness, is simultaneously compounded by the anonymity of the subject in the totalizing nature of an increasingly technological society wherein everything seems manifest. By this account, Carlson explains, the death of a transcendent God implies the parallel and simultaneous "death or dissolution of the interior self, and such a dissolution would be spoken most fully by the anonymity of modern mass culture."[109]

The mystical vocabulary for unselfing experiences is marked by the attempt to achieve enlightenment, variously understood, by altering the relationship between the self and reality in order to overcome the basic errors in the ordinary attitude to it. During the modern period, "mysticism" begins to refer to religious experiences that involve a special kind of consciousness. What distinguishes mysticism from other forms of religiosity is the centrality of "infused contemplation" when compared to other religious experiences like grace.[110] Mysticism, understood experientially, is rooted in an "inner quest to still the conceptual and emotional apparatuses of the mind and the sense of self to sense reality without mediation."[111] Some writers integrate Western and Eastern mystical practices, embracing the *Laozi*'s call to "take emptiness to the limit" and "maintain tranquillity in the centre" in the attempt to be one with the Dao (the way).[112] This meditative practice of emptying is described in the *Zhuangzi* as "mind-fasting": "For the ears are halted at what they hear. The mind is halted at whatever verifies its preconceptions. But the vital energy (*qi*) is an emptiness, a waiting for the presence of beings. The Course alone is what gathers in this emptiness. And it is this emptiness that is the fasting of the mind."[113] Though each account of mysticism is shaped by local features, phenomenological accounts attempt to get beyond these features "by depicting their experiential characteristics presented to the subject while bracketing the questions of what is being experienced and whether the experience is veridical."[114] Modern mystics give accounts of this process, crafting new languages for communicating mystical experiences at a time when God seems most absent in the world.

The writers in this project who draw on the language of mysticism (Valéry, Bataille, Weil, Khatibi) replace traditional theological vocabularies with individual, experiential expressions of experience. In her correspondence with Gustave Thibon, Weil likens the process of writing the unwritten, mystical, text as one of translation. She writes, "À mon avis, la vraie manière d'écrire est d'écrire comme on traduit. Quand on traduit un texte écrit en une langue étrangère, on ne cherche pas à ajouter; on met au contraire un scrupule religieux à ne rien ajouter. C'est ainsi qu'il faut essayer de traduire un texte non-écrit."[115] [In my opinion, the true manner of writing is to write as one translates. When we translate a written text in a foreign language, we do not try to add to it; on the contrary, we put a religious scruple on adding nothing. This is how we must try to translate an unwritten text.] Valéry has been categorized as a *mystique-sans-Dieu*, while Khatibi's work manipulates sacred and mystical texts in his exploration of the relationships between self and other in the context of the multilingualism and multiculturalism of the Maghreb. Sartre dismissed Bataille as a "nouveau mystique" for his voyage into inner experience (a label that Bataille himself rejected). Moreover, writers like Valéry and Khatibi use their texts as testing grounds for articulating the conscious experience of pain and pleasure, respectively. Both experiences serve to root the mind in the body, illustrating the futile nature of any dualist theories of consciousness that attempt to keep them apart.

Like mystical experiences brought on by meditation or prayer, experimental accounts of altered states probe the relationship between the self, world, and the infinite. However, unlike their mystical counterparts, these vocabularies explore these relationships in at least two ways: through the languages of uncharted scientific tests on the physical body (Valéry, Michaux) and experiment textually with innovative forms (Delbo, Cixous, Khatibi).

At the end of the eighteenth century, William Blake's *The Marriage of Heaven and Hell* articulates a revolutionary hope for escaping the solipsism of an ordinary experience of the world. Blake's notion of our impoverished relationship to consciousness continues to reverberate in experimental discourses on the self, body, and mind. He writes, "If the doors of perception were cleansed every thing would appear to man as it is: Infinite. For man has closed himself up, till he sees all things thro' narrow chinks of his cavern."[116] Indeed, the notion of "cleansing" the doors of perception would become synonymous with the convergence of post-war mysticism and psychedelic drug use. Aldous Huxley was inspired by Blake's contribution to theology, philosophy, and art, and named his 1954 book, *The Doors of Perception* and his 1956 essay, *Heaven and Hell,* after the Romantic poet. Huxley's writings renewed the interest in the relationship between altered states of consciousness and drugs as routes for revelation.[117] Indeed, Bataille quotes Blake's *The Marriage of Heaven and Hell* in the epigraph to *La part maudite* with the line "Exuberance is beauty." Like mystical experiences, chemically induced states can be indicative of a practiced attempt to destabilize the ordinary relationship to the self. Though some of Michaux's contemporaries were inspired by shamanistic rituals and consumed psychoactive substances to transcend the ordinary relationship to the self within sacred contexts, Michaux pursued them outside both their recreational and spiritual uses. Michaux attempts to use mescaline to force the mind to reveal itself. The documentation of his experiments demonstrates his attempt at crafting a language to communicate this new knowledge.

The act of writing the unselfing experience produces new experimental forms of writing between philosophy and literature. In seeking to give voice to experiences that are often characterized as unthinkable or unsayable, these texts explore literature as a flexible space for their articulation. At the boundaries of literature and philosophy, writers stretch the limits of genre in their hermeneutics of the self. For example, Delbo intersperses free-verse poetry throughout her fragmented narrative testimony in order to communicate the world of the camps.

Cixous experiments with the productive power of neologism and associative writing in order to explore the relationship between exile and self-understanding. The writing that results from these experimental poetics deliberately eschews ordinary categories of self-writing, which extends to the marketing and categorization of the work. Cixous's autobiographical text, *Rêveries de la femme sauvage* (2000) is categorized not as memoir or fiction, but rather as *scènes primitives*. Similarly, Khatibi explores the notion of *la bi-langue* in *Amour bilingue* (1983) in the form of a *récit*. The story slips back and forth from first-person phenomenological accounts of bilingual consciousness, the lyrical address of the monolingual lover ("tu"), and allegorical reverie, before careening back to the first person again. Bataille seeks to overcome his distaste for what he calls "project," the notion that the experience is in service of a larger goal or objective, in order to relate the immediacy of experience. These texts experiment with the writing of the subject of experience, using altered states as the basis for these new articulations.

Unlike practiced routes to alteration, testimonial accounts of experience seek to bear witness to painful altered states of consciousness. These painful states of self-alteration can lead to embodied states of alteration such as hallucination and lucid dreaming. Unlike many examples in the mystical and the experimental branch of altered states, however, the witness often experiences unselfing unwillingly. Twentieth-century writers explore what Leigh Gilmore calls "the limits of autobiography," as they navigate memories of the traumatic past in light of the evidentiary demands of both autobiographical writing and legal contexts.[118] Over the course of the twentieth century, experimental self-writing slowly and idiosyncratically undermines the conventions of traditional autobiography. Autobiography (as a Western mode of self-production that reaches back to the Enlightenment and features a representative "I" at the centre) is challenged by new autobiographical experiments. The proliferation of generic categories that attempt to capture these autobiographical efforts (creative non-fiction, life-writing, memoir, and autofiction), further testifies to the blurring of boundaries between disciplines and genres that characterizes this period.

The witness figure takes on a new significance within hotly contested debates in "trauma theory" as it became known in the 1990s. Informed by deconstruction and psychoanalysis, trauma theorists have focused their attentions on aspects of limit experiences that resist narrative and representation. Cathy Caruth, in her psycho-historical reading of Freud in *Unclaimed Experience: Trauma, Narrative and History* (1996), attributes the pathology of traumatic events to the structure of its experience and reception. An oft-quoted line from this text exhibits her emphasis on trauma's so-called paradoxical structure: "Traumatic experience suggests a certain empirical paradox: that the most direct seeing of a violent event may occur as an absolute inability to know it."[119] Trauma is also a paradox of time in Caruth's work. She argues that it is "not experienced as it occurs," and cannot be defined either as a product of the event or the distortion of the event in memory: "The pathology consists, rather, solely in the *structure of its experience* or reception: the event is not assimilated or experienced fully at the time, but only belatedly, in its repeated *possession* of the one who experiences it."[120] Others have similarly insisted on trauma as a crisis of truth and representation.[121] Ruth Leys offers a well-known critique of these accounts in *Trauma: A Genealogy* (2000), which investigates the ways in which dominant theories of trauma are "designed to preserve the truth of the trauma as the failure of representation," and thus continue to emphasize the idea that traumatic experience is fundamentally incomprehensible or unknowable.[122] The literal view of the encoding of traumatic experience – particularly the notion that the event is *not* recorded at the moment of experience – is evidently at odds with cognitive accounts of autobiographical memory as the re-expression of cortical patterns. These accounts emphasize the important role that memory distortions and errors play in our mental lives.[123] Moreover, while Caruth's Freudian theoretical framework stresses the crippling nature of melancholic memory as a defining feature of traumatic mourning and post-traumatic identity, Dominick LaCapra cautions against this tendency to convert trauma into an occasion for the sublime, "to transvalue it into a test of the self or the group and an entry into the extraordinary."[124]

Some unselfing testimonies present writing as a route to the resolution of painful experience, while others frame their experiences as ones that resist closure, a question that has divided critics. Judith Herman argues that the construction of narrative is an empowering and therapeutic response to suffering, one that must be oriented in time and history.[125] Mukagasana seems to fall under Herman's empowering understanding of narrative in her assumption of an authoritative and authorial stance in her memoir of the Rwandan genocide against the Tutsi. At the close of her testimonial text, she writes that her memories were fragments that she couldn't piece together. "Mes souvenirs étaient en morceaux, que je ne parvenais pas à rassembler. Lorsque j'ai pu raconter mon cauchemar, la vie d'avant est revenue."[126] [My memories were fragments that I couldn't piece back together. It was only when I was able to recount my nightmare that memories from before returned.][127] Others argue that the focus on acting out or replaying can risk aggravating the distressing aspects of pain instead of promoting healing or recovery.[128] The writing of painful experience can sometimes serve as a mere recording, rather than a move towards resolution. The writing process yields what Charlotte Delbo in her memoir on Auschwitz calls "useless knowledge."[129] As LaCapra emphasizes, we needn't think of the mitigation of trauma as an "all-or-nothing" choice between two extremes, with the illusion of total mastery, definitive closure, and radically positive transcendence of trauma on the one hand, and endless fragmentation, melancholia, aporia, with the acting-out of repetition compulsions on the other.[130] Unselfing narratives are evidence of the need to account for both in the consideration of the value of memory and writing in the processing of extreme pain and suffering. I approach the ethical question of the reception of these narratives by orienting my analysis on the writer's construction of self, using the coordinates of the experiencing self and the narrative self to read each instance of unselfing for the insights it affords. As in the consideration of the value of unselfing experience in reorienting the self towards others, it is important to consider the wide range of possible experiences that can ensue from painful experience rather than generalizing its effects according to either of the two extremes described by LaCapra above.

Moreover, in keeping with the cognitive-phenomenological commitments of the book, I have generally chosen to discuss "pain" and "suffering" rather than "trauma" as a means of circumventing its associations with aporetic crisis.[131] Although unselfing narratives are not literal recordings – they are crafted and often "literary" – this does not mean that they are markers of the impossibility of truth about experience.[132] Though writers use different narrative strategies to approach the representation of unnatural self-experience, unselfing narratives are nevertheless invitations to explore their phenomenology rather than evidence of their incomprehensibility.

Finally, the global framing of the book requires a careful consideration of the universal and local aspects of testimony on pain and suffering. While accounts of pain in European contexts are often studied as examples of trauma and analyzed for their contributions to theories of consciousness, suffering and genocide in the colonial and postcolonial world are often neglected within literary and theoretical discourse.[133] Whereas trauma theory often focuses on the impossibility of recording painful events, I seek to explore the imaginative work on offer in unselfing texts. In so doing, complex representations of traumatic historical events can be appreciated as contributions to the literary-philosophical discourse on altered states and unselfing.

In addition to experiences that can be identified as traumatic ones, this branch of altered states also includes thinkers such as Valéry and Bataille, who deliberately use the phenomenology of painful experience to explore the limits of the human. Bataille's *L'expérience intérieure* considers the relationships between self-knowledge, transgression, and the body. The text includes an infamous passage that explores his fascination and meditation on the photograph of a Chinese torture victim who communicates, through the photograph, the excessive nature of his pain. A full account of altered states must put Bataille's iconoclastic perspective on suffering in conversation with the other writers of this project who explore the role of pain in our understandings of the boundaries between self and other. This subject, which is explored more completely in chapter 6 on destructive unselfing, requires a careful attention to the ethics of these controversial representations of pain. Studying the phenomenon from a structural perspective brings to light the varieties of unselfing experiences.

To review, drawing on the vocabularies of the mystical, the experimental, and the testimonial, unselfing narratives recount the stories of temporary self-loss and return, blissful self-transcendence, partial self-transformation, painful self-disruption, disorienting self-mutation, liberating self-fragmentation, and radical self-destruction. These texts give narrative shape to the phenomenology of altered states of consciousness, allowing seemingly ineffable experiences it to be presented in language to others.[134]

Representation and Reality

These mystical, experimental, and testimonial texts occupy the liminal space between fiction and non-fiction because of the unordinary nature of the knowledge they seek to deliver. Unselfing texts across this spectrum are committed to the evocation of embodied consciousness in the wake of altered states. Stories of unselfing are crafted in the space between testimony and creation, but neither pole fully captures the complexity of the unselfing text. Nevertheless, some important distinctions can be made with respect to each text's referentiality to truth claims, which ought to be conceptualized on a spectrum from non-fiction to fiction rather than sorted according to a binary logic.

On one end of the spectrum, some unselfing texts can be identified as works of non-fiction in that they seek to bear witness to pain suffered, to remember victims of genocide, or to raise international visibility on disputed historical facts. While these accounts of unordinary experience often question the representative capacity of the text, they remain rooted in a material commitment to the representation of history. In this sense, "unstable" truth claims in the context of genocide literature evidently carry different political and ethical stakes than truth claims in the contexts of meditation or drug experimentation.

And yet, within the world of unselfing texts, the referentiality distinction (between truth and fiction) seems to be a problem of degree rather than a problem of kind.[135] As Merleau-Ponty declared, "From now on, the tasks of literature and philosophy can no longer be separated."[136] The challenge of separating fiction and truth has a long philosophical lineage, stretching back to Plato and Aristotle, but has recently been taken up again by memory scholars. Susan Suleiman argues that the distinction between fiction and historical narrative is not necessarily clear-cut in the memoir genre, especially in the context of life-altering experiences such as deportation or genocide. Memoirs of the Holocaust, she argues, make truth claims (to referentiality and verifiability), which separate them from the novel, but are also prone to error (given the fallibility of memory) and can resemble novelistic forms.[137] When considering Delbo and Mukagasana alongside other writers of unselfing who are likewise invested in articulating the nature and meaning of suffering, it is clear that both writers of fiction and non-fiction are aware of the power of literary writing to elevate, transform, or potentially disfigure the truth of lived experience. In one interview, Delbo compares her writing project on Auschwitz to the work of Balzac or Proust and argues that literature is not the avatar of reality, but rather a work of art, which is the creator of meaning.[138]

On the other end of the spectrum unselfing writers fictionalize their approach to consciousness and reality. These writers of unselfing use fiction as the route to the truth about consciousness in their inclusion of non-existent subjects, or subjects who do not refer (directly, perfectly, or exactly) to a real person in the world. The fictional in these specific contexts represents a means of expressing the nature of perception or attention during altered states. Two of the texts studied in this book stand out in this regard; Valéry's *La Soirée avec Monsieur Teste* is considered a fictional third-person narration (though the narrator features in the plot) while Khatibi's *Amour bilingue* oscillates experimentally between first, second, and third narrations. Nevertheless, I argue that both texts, alongside the others studied in the book, approach the representation of consciousness with the goal of illuminating the lived experience of the first-person perspective. As his name suggests, Monsieur Teste is Valéry's "test case" on the workings of the mind; Khatibi uses his *récit* to explore the nature of bilingual consciousness.

In a number of his texts, Bataille occupies a position somewhere in between these two ends of the spectrum; he references the real in order to challenge it, or as Amy Hollywood puts it, he "invokes the autobiographical subject only in order to subvert it."[139] By this reading, Bataille stages the interplay between autobiographical and fictional selves in order to capture their dissolution, which in turn prompts the training of the reader's own work of self-shattering.[140] Indeed, Bataille's *L'expérience intérieure* mixes the subjective with the objective, the rational with the emotional, the experimental with the mystical in his attempt to challenge the phenomenological model of self-reflexivity. At the same time, Bataille's text seeks to evoke the consciousness of ecstasy and self-destruction in language despite the inherent risks and limitations.

Since William James's use of the phrase "stream of consciousness" in the *Principles of Psychology* (1890), writers have used various techniques to represent the so-called stream in language. James uses the stream metaphor to emphasize that consciousness is continuous rather than the sum of discrete thoughts. James writes, "Consciousness, then, does not appear to itself chopped up in bits. Such words as 'chain' or 'train' do not describe it fitly as it presents itself in the first instance. It is nothing jointed; it flows. A 'river' or a 'stream' are the metaphors by which it is most naturally described. In talking of it hereafter, let us call it the stream of thought, of consciousness, or of subjective life."[141] In recent years, cognitive scientists have questioned the validity of the stream metaphor for consciousness and investigated whether perception is continuous or discrete. Evan Thompson, reading the experiments of the neuroscientist Francisco Varela alongside Abhidharma literature and William James, writes, "So is perceptual consciousness a 'stream'? Yes, in the sense that it seems to flow, but no, if 'flow' means 'uniformly and continuously.' Instead, the flow is rhythmic, with variable dynamic pulses."[142]

Though the stream-of-consciousness technique in literature is readily associated with modernism, writers have responded differently to the challenge of the representation of the psychological stream of consciousness; some see it as a means of evoking subjective realism. Charles Taylor argues that subjectivism and anti-subjectivism exist in productive tension with one another in modernist writing: "Twentieth-century art has gone more inward, has tended to explore, even to celebrate subjectivity; it has explored new recesses of feeling, entered the stream of consciousness, spawned schools of art rightly called 'expressionist.' But at the same time, at its greatest it has often involved a decentring of the subject: an art emphatically not conceived as self-expression, an art displacing the centre of interest onto language, or onto poetic transmutation itself, or even dissolving the self as usually conceived in favor of some new constellation."[143] These two modes cannot exist without one another. T.S. Eliot's call for the poet's "continual extinction of personality" or John Keats's invocation of the "no self" of the "chameleon poet" serve as foils to the inward turn of author-based subjectivism exemplified by "La Méthode de Saint-Beuve" later repudiated by Proust.[144] And yet, though modernist consciousness is often described as "decentred" given that it evokes "living on a transpersonal rhythm," Taylor argues that this effect is only achieved through the attention to the inner world of consciousness: "But for all that it remains inward."[145] The writing of unselfing reflects the ambiguities and contradictions of this inward turn, with writers such Khatibi emphasizing the transpersonal nature of consciousness, and others such as Bataille plumbing the depths of inner experience.

Moreover, unselfing texts demonstrate a need for flexibility in accounting for the use of diverse narrative techniques in the representation of (embodied) mind. As Dora Zhang argues, stream of consciousness is often and misleadingly used interchangeably with the technique of interior monologue (as exemplified by Joyce), even though practitioners of the stream-of-consciousness text (like Woolf) use a range of techniques.[146] Dorrit Cohn offers a typology of these techniques in her classical narratological account of consciousness in fiction, *Transparent Minds.* Cohn separates the approaches to consciousness in third-person texts by identifying techniques such as psycho-narration, quoted (interior) monologue, and narrated monologue (free indirect discourse) from techniques employed in first-person texts, such as autobiographical narrative, autobiographical monologue, memory narrative, and memory monologue.[147] Cognitive narratologists have since dismissed Cohn's "speech-category" approach in search of what Alan Palmer calls the "whole mind," an approach which accounts for all evidence of character consciousness in addition to speech categories.[148] And yet, the typology is useful in that it shows how unselfing texts resist classification according to any one category or technique. In their attempt to represent consciousness at the limits of experience, unselfing texts use multiple techniques to represent phenomena such as hallucinations, mystical communion, or pain that cut across Cohn's typology. Some writers shift perspective from one chapter to the next, while others incorporate free indirect discourse alongside memory narrative. Approaching the embodied mind in minimal self narratives calls out for phenomenological analysis because of these inherent contradictions and complications.[149]

This debate in narratology sheds light on the diversity of narrative techniques that unselfing writers employ to evoke the workings of consciousness, whether in nonfiction or fiction. Indeed, the experimentation of unselfing texts between genres such as memoir and *récit* reflect not only the attempt to translate subjective reality but also to respond to the specific challenge of rendering altered states in language. Thus, while I have argued in the first chapter that each unselfing text communicates the phenomenology of losing or transcending the self during altered states of consciousness (and that the phenomenological approach is uniquely attuned to the first-person perspective), I emphasize that unselfing texts make use of a variety of narrative techniques, which are not limited to first-person narration or interior monologue. The stakes of the structural identity of these minimal narratives are rooted in what Ricoeur calls "the temporal character of human existence," though each writer approaches its representation differently.[150]

A first group of writers tends towards minimalism in their representation of time, relying on fragmentary phrases (Michaux, Delbo) and aphorism (Weil). A second group of writers are sceptical about the deforming power of narrative when compared to the vitality and incommensurability of lived experience (Delbo, Bataille, Michaux), while a third group embraces it as one route to the expression of difficult truths of reality (Valéry, Mukagasana). A fourth group reinvents narrative genres and experiments with modernist techniques to reflect the psycho-realities of experiences (such as decolonial subjectivity) in new ways (Khatibi, Cixous). Despite these differences in their respective methodologies, each unselfing text is dedicated to the emplotment of experience in time. Unselfing experiences destabilize the subject's ordinary relationship to time and illuminate formerly obscured contours of the space of the self; these texts impose narrative shape on the formlessness of these unorthodox experiences.[151] As such, the unselfing text seeks to give voice to the embodied nature of self-alteration; it describes the effect of altered states on the mind and body.

As discussed in the previous chapter, twentieth-century unselfing narratives recount the ways in which experience alters the complex network of selfhood. They demonstrate the interrelated constructions of the experiencing self and the narrative self at the limits of conscious experience. Some texts are weighted towards features of the experiencing self, such as perspective and the immediacy of the self in the present, while others focus their attentions on features of the narrative self, such as project. In the modern Francosphère, unselfing writers engage with the methods of the phenomenological tradition in divergent ways. For example, in *L'expérience intérieure*, Bataille contests the phenomenological method as a dominant discourse, seeking to go to the limit of human experience at the same time that he gives a phenomenologically rich description of extasy experienced from the inside.

The following chapters focus on the four unselfing narratives – *disruption, mutation, fragmentation,* and *destruction* – that emerge from the unseating of identity and the uprooting of consciousness in the global French twentieth century. Some accounts deliver a vision of unselfing, that while difficult, unnatural, or painful, proves to be a means of fostering a just vision of others. Such writers share the powerful sense of the intersubjective promise of losing or transcending the self. Others write of the loss of agency as radical empathy in a dark and disturbing sense, or of a neutral distancing from social life. And some write in a modest, hopeful vein, occupying the middle ground between those who believe that unselfing is a form of compassionate consciousness and those who link unselfing to an alienating loss of self.

A descriptive and broadly ethical approach to unselfing reveals what a prescriptive and moralistic account cannot. The experience of reducing the sovereignty of the self, of tearing down the barrier between self and world yields a staggering array of intersubjective possibilities, ambiguities, and tensions. The unselfing text spans the varieties of altered-self experiences, which are sometimes experienced as a pleasurable, enlightening, or empirically useful interludes, and other times described as terrifying, damaging, or useless ones. This structural approach to unselfing makes it possible to study and organize what we might call, after James, the "varieties" of unselfing experiences at the crossroads of mysticism, experimentation, and witnessing. While some of these writers in the final category recount terrible horrors, writing of violence, genocide, and the loss of life, each nevertheless returns to tell the story. This return to the writerly position opens the possibility for the story's telling, for the text itself to emerge.

3 Unselfing as Disruption: Self-Knowledge and Pain in Paul Valéry and Charlotte Delbo

Suffering and misfortune reduce the demands of the mind to the point where all that's asked is the following: *Anything, so long as this comes to an end, or that doesn't happen!* But at this point, the mind is hardly mind any more. The pain speaks *without intermediary*. Thought is only its activity and echo.

Paul Valéry

Whether you return from war or from elsewhere
when it's an elsewhere
unimaginable to others
it is hard to come back

Charlotte Delbo

On one of the pages of his voluminous *Cahiers*, Paul Valéry notes that pain reduces the demands of the mind to the point that it is hardly a mind at all. Suffering takes hold of consciousness, speaks without intermediary, and even leaves thought behind. Pain introduces itself between the mind and body; the body in pain speaks directly, interrupting the ordinary experience of being a self. When pain speaks to the point where all that is asked is *anything, so long as this comes to an end,* the self is undone by the sheer anguish of suffering. The question then arises: how does the mind return after pain releases it from its clutches? When the body returns from the disruption of suffering – "whether you return from war or from elsewhere" – it is hard to come back, especially when that elsewhere is unimaginable to others. This is what Charlotte Delbo writes on the Nazi death camps, the elsewhere from which she herself returns. Though she never sought this knowledge – knowledge she would later call "useless" – Delbo returns from the camps with the responses to the questions on consciousness that Valéry was so keen to answer. Valéry's *La Soirée avec Monsieur Teste* (*The Evening with Monsieur Teste*) (1895) and Delbo's *Auschwitz et après* (*Auschwitz and After*) (1965–71) present the disruption narrative for communicating unselfing from the inside.

The first text, a thought experiment on the power of pain on a pure mind finds its unexpected counterpoint in the second, which gives an account of the deliberate and systematic reduction of human beings to mute cries. Valéry and Delbo use the experience of the self in pain to articulate the strange phenomenology of altered states. The disruption of ordinary self-experience, pursued in Valéry and suffered in Delbo, reveals to each writer the unexplored and unimagined functioning of human consciousness. These texts chart the inner experience of pain through the haunting silhouettes of otherworldly presences, the contours of terrifying dreamscapes, and the lingering shapes of unnatural silences. What is at stake for both Valéry and Delbo is the possibility of return, after suffering, to an ordinary experience of self. To study disruption in Valéry and Delbo at the same time is to seek to understand the shape of pain itself.

This chapter seeks to answer the question: what does pain reveal about the self? It situates the narrative of disruption within competing discourses on the value of painful experience and its eventual expression. It offers a comparative analysis of disruptive unselfing in Valéry and Delbo by examining their philosophies of pain. The conclusion analyzes the effect of disruptive unselfing on the approach to the other, positioning Delbo's scepticism against Valéry's intersubjective idealism. While Valéry as a "mystique sans Dieu" would attempt to renew an authentic sense of spirituality in seeking disruptive unselfing, Delbo puts words to what is referred to as the unimaginable self-loss that occurred in the Nazi camps. Their paths meet in their shared attempt to offer a philosophy of the limits of the human. While Valéry envisaged the communion between ontologically separate beings as an ideal, if difficult source of desire, Delbo describes the overriding of the boundary between self and other as the apex of an experience of agentless horror.

The French *dolorisme* movement, which championed the salutary effects of pain, considered this link between the role of suffering in understanding selves and others during the interwar period. According to Julien Teppe, one of the movement's leaders and author of *Apologie pour l'anormal* (1935) and *Dictature de la douleur* (1937), suffering is a virtue precisely because it annihilates the mind's control and disrupts usual self-function. In order to better understand the value of pain, Teppe started the *Revue doloriste* (a publication to which Valéry contributed). Like Valéry's note in the *Cahiers* quoted in the epigraph, Teppe writes that pain is capable of colonizing the body with total, annihilating force: "Pain, of all the psychological states, is the one which takes over the entire being, both the flesh and the spirit, with the greatest urgency and force. It is a disposition, which sweeps away, blots out, and annihilates all the rest. It does not allow for cheating or compromise. It is there and it is enough to eliminate the rest."[1] Teppe argues that the value of suffering is rooted *both* in its power to enhance self-apprehension and for the way it affects our relationships with others. Roselyne Rey writes, "This physical pain which takes over the entire being and liberates the individual from any earthly ties should in consequence make him more compassionate, in the term's truest sense, towards others and more lucid about himself."[2] In other words, pain illuminates the nature of the self and also makes the individual compassionate towards others precisely because it liberates them from earthly attachments. Physical pain is valuable in that it is revelatory of embodied human perception.

Some theorists of pain argue that experiencing pain and expressing it are evidence of the possibility of world-making and invention. Elaine Scarry echoes the sentiments of Valéry and Teppe in her account of pain's role in the acts of creating, imagining, and making, which serve to underline the union between mind and body. Scarry writes, "In the long run, we will see that the story of *physical pain* becomes as well a story about the expansive nature of human *sentience*, the felt-fact of aliveness that is often sheerly happy, just as the story of *expressing* physical pain eventually opens into the wider frame of *invention*."[3] The expression of pain in this account is equated with creative design. Although Valéry also articulates the intuition that painful experiences are valuable revelations, he is more sceptical when it comes to the shape of pain's expression. As we will see, Valéry indicates that expressing painful experience in narrative is fraught precisely because pain is *not* language.

Delbo writes of suffering as a limit to self-consciousness, much like Valéry. In the three texts that are now known and published together as *Auschwitz et après*, Delbo depicts the two years and three months she spent interned in Auschwitz-Birkenau, Raisko, and Ravensbrück before liberation and her return to France in June 1945. In these texts, Delbo describes suffering that not only disrupts self-function, but also destroys the boundary between the self and her fellow detainees. Her account of imposed unselfing motivates a careful reconsideration of Valéry's methods and the conclusions he draws from his experiments on pain and the self. Valéry and Delbo both seek to represent experiences that are enigmatic in their resistance to intellection and articulation in language; their phenomenological depictions of pain are attempts to bear witness to the limits of the human. While some philosophies of pain propose that reducing the claims of the self will result in a reorientation of the self towards the world and towards others, Delbo's work exposes radical empathy as an unwelcome state.

Both Valéry's writings on Monsieur Teste and Delbo's work on survival in Auschwitz present the phenomenological experience of pain. Both seek to achieve the transparency of consciousness by witnessing its processes from the inside. In Valéry's texts, Monsieur Teste bears witness to the way pain disrupts the individuality of his perspective and his attempt to maintain control over thought.[4] In addition to her perspective on the way suffering disrupts the experiencing self, Delbo also writes chillingly on the effect of pain on her sense of her own temperament. Both writers lament the difficulty of incorporating the disruptive event into the narrative self, or long-term self-narratives. For Valéry, this amounts to a reflection on the pain that comes from the disunity of the self; for Delbo, it is an attempt to put words to physical pain experienced. While the work of condensing experience into narrative is a deep source of discomfort for both writers, the disruption of the experiencing self is much more important than the narrative self for Valéry. Valéry's work on Monsieur Teste reveals his focused study on the nature of consciousness in the present. Delbo's work focuses more on the way the narrative self is disrupted by the time spent in the camps (the "elsewhere" from which she tries to return). Indeed, it is Delbo who pulls the reader's attention away from the event (Auschwitz) and towards a contemplation of its aftermath (*et après*).

Consciousness of pain in Valéry and Delbo not only introduces new questions into discourses on the nature of the self and its persistence through time, but also reveals a novel and unsettling perspective on empathy itself. Both writers explore the relationship between self and other in pain by tracking the dissolution of the boundaries between suffering selves and the fate of others. Although Delbo speaks eloquently of literature as a weapon with the power to combat oppression in interviews on the subject, her writing demonstrates a fundamental ambivalence on the value of expressing pain. She encapsulates the knowledge that comes from surviving the Nazi camps with the label, "Une connaissance inutile" ["Useless knowledge"] which serves as the title of one of the volumes of her memoir. Delbo's text challenges the notion that suffering has a redemptive quality to it and that "understanding" the pain of others has any value at all. Her writings on Auschwitz suggest that suffering results in a total loss of rational control that makes an ordinary sense of compassion impossible. Delbo's work challenges Valéry's notion that "going to the last point" of human consciousness will be revelatory in the way that Valéry and other philosophers of unselfing have hoped. The reality of unselfing when experienced under duress in Delbo compels us to question the possibilities that Valéry associates with it. When read together, these works prompt readers to consider what it means to fully share the feelings of others and whether we should desire that at all.

Monsieur Teste and the Disrupted Self

In his prolific and heterogenous writings, Paul Valéry (1871–1945) sought to disrupt ordinary self-function in order to access and articulate the relationship between the human and the unknown. His search for the limit of human consciousness through intense and habitual contemplation reflects a larger interest in tracking the functioning of the human mind. This attempt to achieve self-alteration in pursuit of revelation was a once a hallmark of mysticism. If Valéry was a mystic, however, his practice was a secular one; he was a "mystique sans Dieu."[5] As Michel de Certeau emphasizes in his *Encyclopædia Universalis* entry on modern mysticism, this secular understanding of "mystical" entails a novel turn towards experimental knowledge that fulfils a passivity in which the self loses itself in God. "In other words, what becomes mystical is that which diverges from normal or ordinary paths; that which is no longer inscribed within the social community of faith or religious references, but rather on the margins of an increasingly secularized society and a knowledge that defines its own scientific objects."[6] Modern mystics emerge on the outskirts of recognizable religious dogma; these figures are defined by the unconventional epistemological groundings of their self-experiments and the new objects of their attention. This experimental mysticism was also intensified by the rise of individual spiritual practices after Nietzsche's critique of religion and European moral consciousness. Judith Robinson-Valéry writes, "This science of pure consciousness will be at the same time *Ars Magna*: the art of taking charge of oneself existentially under the heavens voided by 'the death of God,' an art of constructing and inventing oneself, which would be in the plenary sense an original form of spirituality."[7] Valéry's experimental praxis thus unites his spiritual and secular sensibilities in his focus on new objects of both religious and scientific attention.

The self, when examined through this modern mystical perspective, takes on new meaning as both a spiritual and scientific object. The self in Valéry becomes an object of meditation both inside and outside of language. His reflections are explorations of the limits of human consciousness through the intense contemplation and dissection of the observer's life-experience. As Valéry once put it (in English), the goal of this intense and focused self-observation is "TO GO TO THE LAST POINT."[8] By this understanding, the pursuit of the last outpost of the observable self will allow not only for the articulation of hitherto undefined regions of consciousness, but also for an original form of spiritualism. The more than twenty thousand pages of the *Cahiers*, produced over a span of fifty years, are a testament to his abiding interest in the scope of perception.

While this totalizing pursuit of the mind certainly maps onto the Symbolist desire to translate the immediacy of man's inner life through art as a superior mode of knowledge, Valéry remained attracted to the promise of science in understanding the human. As Reino Virtanen argues, Valéry escapes the subjectivist idealism of the Symbolists by conceiving of the self and world as existing in a reciprocal relationship.[9] Although he is known as the disciple of Stéphane Mallarmé, he departs from his former master in his focus on the inner workings of the human. Whereas Mallarmé focused on *le Livre*, or the perfect work, Valéry was more interested in *l'homme*. In 1891 at the close of an interview with Jules Huret, Mallarmé formulated what would become one of his best-known declarations on aestheticism: "Le monde est fait pour aboutir à un beau livre." [The world is made to result in a beautiful book.] He would later modify the statement in an article in *Revue Blanche*: "Tout, au monde, existe pour aboutir à un livre."[10] [Everything in the world exists to result in a book.] Valéry differentiated his method from Mallarmé's with the following: "C'était bouleverser l'ordre établi et surtout le système Mallarmé qui faisait l'Œuvre – but d'univers. Et moi c'était l'homme."[11] [It amounted to disrupting the established order, and above all the system conceived by Mallarmé, which made of the Work the goal of the universe. My goal was the man.][12] In the pursuit of this goal, the self would become a subject of great importance. Valéry formulated the dialectical relationship between the self and the world as the "Corps-Esprit-Monde" (Body-Mind-World).[13]

Though he has been attached to many schools of thought due to the sheer magnitude of his writings in the *Cahiers*, Valéry is sometimes known as a constructivist, if one decides to associate him with any philosophical school at all. Valéry refused to frame his ideas in the form of a philosophy, sceptical as he was of the role of chance in empirical observations and its subjection to the constraints of language. According to Jacques Bouveresse, who calls Valéry an "antiphilosopher," Valéry would have detested the premise of a philosophical paper, which "would give the deceptive appearance of objective consistency to what was just the outcome of chances, accidents, individual automatisms, and various helter-skelter conditions and circumstances that answered only to some personal need."[14] However, Bouveresse argues that in another sense, he could be thought of as a full-fledged constructivist, "a man concerned first and foremost with building and the building of his own self, with accepting nothing that is merely 'given' and not produced by himself ..." This would be a radical attempt, Bouveresse writes, to combat the contingency of the circumstances which shape a person.[15] Valéry recognizes in constructivism the emphasis on process and making, especially in relation to consciousness.

In *La Soirée avec Monsieur Teste*, Valéry explores the limits of self-consciousness through the experience of pain. A play on the old French spelling of *tête*, or head, "Teste" is also a play on the Latin *testis*, or witness. "M. Teste est le témoin," [M. Teste is the witness] writes Valéry in *Pour un portrait de Monsieur Teste*.[16] "Teste" is also a cognate of the English word in the sense of "experiment" or "trial." Valéry once memorably claimed in the preface to the second English translation of *La Soirée* (1925) that this experimental character could not actually exist for more than a few quarters of an hour.[17] What makes him so incompatible with reality is his desire to be pure and constant thought, that is, an entirely rational self. The narrator describes Teste in this way: "Il était l'être absorbé dans sa variation, celui qui devient son système, celui qui se livre entier à la discipline effrayante de l'esprit libre."[18] [He was a man absorbed in his own variations, one who becomes his own system, who commits himself without reservation to the frightening discipline of the free mind.][19] Valéry echoes this description in the preface when he writes, "Sa vie intense et brève se dépense à surveiller le mécanisme par lequel les relations du connu et de l'inconnu sont instituées et organisées."[20] [His intense and brief life is spent surveying the mechanism by which the relations between the known and the unknown are established and organized.]

In this sense, Valéry's writings on first-person experience through the perspective of the Monsieur Teste character are ideal testing grounds for the phenomenological method. The character embodies the bracketing of the natural attitude on consciousness, demonstrating the discomfort, the difficulty, and the sheer boredom that ensues from constantly tracking his ordinary processes of mind. Indeed, Monsieur Teste is characterized by both the banality of his conscious experiences and also seems to transcend it in his hyper-awareness of each conscious state. For Husserl, this is the central feature of phenomenological reduction: suspending the natural attitude in order to analyze it so that "the phenomenologically meditating Ego can become the 'non-participant onlooker' at himself."[21] Yet, as Jed Deppman argues, Teste moves beyond the position of the disinterested Husserlian onlooker in studying his own consciousness and seeks to make a habit of his conscious processes. By this account, Teste is an embodiment of "automimetic conscious-ness," (a self that mimes itself) which seeks to represent man's think-ing himself to an absurd, unreachable degree.[22] Teste is meant to be an intellectual of self-perfection and self-control, forever "self-seeing/self-risking."[23] Teste would inspire the work of Merleau-Ponty, particularly in his investigation of the relationship between the field of sensation and inner space.[24] Through Teste, Valéry examines the positionality of reflective consciousness; the experimental character thus serves as an ideal simulation space for understanding the possibilities and the limits of self-experience.

In *La Soirée*, the experience of unselfing shuts down Teste's practice of self-surveillance. Indeed, pain is the ultimate limit to the phenomeno-logical machinery. In the notebook entry on the relationship between the mind and pain quoted in the epigraph, Valéry writes that suffer-ing reduces the claims of the mind to the point that pain overrides the thinking self:

> La douleur et le malheur diminuent les exigences de l'esprit jusqu'au point de les réduire à cette demande: *quoi que ce soit,* pourvu que ceci cesse, ou que cela n'arrive point ! Mais alors l'esprit n'est presque plus l'esprit. Le mal parle *sans intermédiaire.* La pensée n'est que son acte et son écho.[25]

> Suffering and misfortune reduce the demands of the mind to the point where all that's asked is the following: *Anything*, so long as this comes to an end, or that doesn't happen! But at this point, the mind is hardly mind any more. The pain speaks *without intermediary*. Thought is only its activ-ity and echo.[26]

Valéry describes pain as speaking for itself as it takes over the subject. Pain is both a limit to consciousness in the sense that it overrides think-ing and also represents a challenge to discourse. The fluid usage of terms in this passage – *la douleur* (pain/suffering), *le malheur* (anguish), *le mal* (pain/ache) – emphasizes the difficulty Valéry experiences in pinning down the phenomenological experience of pain with language as each term carries with it a different set of psychological and physical reso-nances. (Valéry uses both the terms *douleur* and *souffrance* in *La Soirée*.) Suffering enters at the end of this Teste narrative and leads the epony-mous character to an ecstatic revelation. The body in pain experiences the disruption of the experiencing self, which leads to a new frontier of self-knowledge that was not perceptible before the painful experience.

We enter into the original Teste narrative at the breaking point of the self-science system that fails when Monsieur Teste's body disrupts his mental control. Before the pain sets in, he claims to know every inch of his body, to have conquered it entirely: "Maintenant, je me sais par cœur. Le cœur aussi. Bah! toute la terre est marquée, tous les pavillons couvrent tous les territoires."[27] [Now I know myself by heart. My heart included. Bah! The whole earth is staked off, all the flags are flying over all territories.][28] The elderly man subsequently attempts to describe the sentiments he experiences intellectually – the feel of his sheets on his still body, the mechanics of lying in bed – but his speech is interrupted by his physical suffering. In this example of unselfing, Monsieur Teste's pain becomes a limit to his purely intellectual life and results in a crisis of the experiencing self. Suffering the self as a strange and foreign presence, he is confronted with uncharted inner expanses despite that, just moments ago, he was certain that he knew himself by heart.[29] He exclaims:

> Il y a de ces instants où mon corps s'illumine ... C'est très curieux. J'y vois tout à coup en moi ... je distingue les profondeurs des couches de ma chair; et je sens des zones de douleur, des anneaux, des pôles, des aigrettes de douleur. Voyez-vous ces figures vives? cette géométrie de ma souffrance? Il y a de ces éclairs qui ressemblent tout à fait à des idées. Ils font comprendre, – d'ici, jusque-là ... Et pourtant ils me laissent *incertain*. Incertain n'est pas le mot ... Quand *cela* va venir, je trouve en moi quelque chose de confus ou de diffus. Il se fait dans mon être des endroits ... brumeux, il y a des étendues qui font leur apparition.[30]

> At certain moments my body lights up ... This is very odd. Suddenly, I can see into myself ... I can make out the depths of the layers of my flesh; I feel zones of pain ... rings, poles, plumes of pain. Do you see these living forms, this geometry of my suffering? There are certain flashes that are exactly like ideas. They make me understand – from here, to there. Yet they leave me uncertain. "Uncertain" is not the word ... When *it* is coming on, I find something confused or diffused in me. Inside my *self* ... foggy places arise, there are open expanses that come into view.[31]

For a fleeting instant, the unity of the experiencing self is disrupted, which leads to a new awareness of certain flashes that are almost identical to ideas. Yet, Teste insists that this momentary knowledge is ephemeral. The return to normal self-function leaves him uncertain. In the place of the conquered territories, flags flying high, he senses the existence of a strange inner unknown. He tries to make the disruption last:

> Alors, je prends dans ma mémoire une question, un problème quelconque … Je m'y enfonce. Je compte des grains de sable … et, tant que je les vois … – Ma douleur grossissante me force à l'observer. J'y pense ! – je n'attends que mon cri … et dès que je l'ai entendu – l'*objet*, le terrible *objet*, devenant plus petit, et encore plus petit, se dérobe à ma vue intérieure.[32]

> Then I pick out a question from my memory, some problem or other … and plunge into it. I count grains of sand … and so long as I can see them … My increasing pain forces me to notice it. I think about it! Waiting only to hear my cry … and the moment I hear it, the *object*, the terrible *object*, smaller and still smaller, vanishes from my inner sight.[33]

When he counts the grains of sand, small markers of time, he is able to prolong this encounter, but ultimately cannot retain the momentary knowledge of the unknown. The object of attention eventually vanishes with Teste's cry. His sensorial perception of pain leads to a diffusion of fogginess, a glimpse of a veiled strangeness within, which retreats just as it is apprehended. Unselfing is understood as a disruption, valuable in that it reveals uncharted territories within the self. Yet, this state of painful illumination cannot last; it ultimately dissipates with a return to ordinary consciousness.

Pain and the imagination in this episode function as the other's missing counterpart, given that pain is objectless and passive (it is suffered) and imagination is only objects (it is impossible to imagine without imagining something). Scarry develops this theory of pain in *The Body in Pain*. She writes, "Pain only becomes an intentional state once it is brought into relation with the objectifying power of the imagination."[34] This is certainly the case in Valéry. In Valéry's text, suffering takes on spatial referents; it is expressed as depths, zones, and expanses. The painful experience climaxes with a cry when the object, the focus of Teste's attention, is lost. Eventually, Teste arrives at the conclusion that he should have been focusing on suffering all along, "Car, souffrir, c'est donner à quelque chose une attention suprême, et je suis un peu l'homme de l'attention."[35] [Because … to suffer is to give supreme attention to something, and I am somewhat a man of attention.][36]

Although the *Cycle Teste* is focused on Monsieur Teste's perceptive lens and the mechanism of the experiencing self, Valéry devotes his attention to the narrative self in select illuminating passages. Among his other startling intellectual qualities, Monsieur Teste's autobiographical memory is exceptionally well-developed. The narrator observes, "Sa mémoire me donna beaucoup à penser. Les traits par lesquels j'en pouvais juger, me firent imaginer une gymnastique intellectuelle sans exemple. Ce n'était pas chez lui une faculté excessive, – c'était une faculté éduquée ou transformée."[37] [His memory gave me much thought. The signs by which I could judge led me to imagine incomparable intellectual gymnastics. This was not, in him, an excessive trait but rather a trained and transformed faculty.][38] Having unburdened himself of books and papers twenty years before, Teste relies exclusively on his memory and is able to retain what he likes. "J'ai cherché un crible machinal."[39] [I have tried to invent a mechanical sieve.][40] Teste's memory has a meditational quality; it is practiced and selective. Moreover, his narrative self, under ordinary circumstances, retains more than the average mind; Daniel Kahneman writes that the narrative self attends to the peaks and valleys of experience and notoriously neglects the duration of feelings like pain and pleasure.[41] Monsieur Teste's entire existence is devoted to closing the gap between experience and memory through the careful study of his own consciousness. The narrator explains how he achieves this by differentiating Teste's methods from the way ordinary minds might try to imagine the sensations that an aeronaut experiences when traveling in a balloon:

> Certainement sa mémoire singulière devait presque uniquement lui retenir cette partie de nos impressions que notre imagination toute seule est impuissante à construire. Si nous imaginons un voyage en ballon, nous pouvons avec sagacité, avec puissance, *produire* beaucoup de sensations probables d'un aéronaute; mais il restera toujours quelque chose d'individuel à l'ascension réelle, dont la différence avec notre rêverie exprime la valeur des méthodes d'un Edmond Teste.[42]

> Certainly his singular memory must have retained for him almost solely those impressions which our imagination, by itself, is powerless to construct. If we imagine an ascent in a balloon, we may with shrewdness and force produce many of the probable sensations of an aeronaut; but there will always remain something peculiar to the real ascent, and that difference from what we imagine expresses the value of the methods of an Edmond Teste.[43]

Teste's mnemonic methods, the result of fixed practice and attention, allow him to retain impressions of lived experience, rather than imagining them in the natural attitude. This is the value of Teste's methods, according to the narrator. "Et je sentais qu'il était le maître de sa pensée:

j'écris là cette absurdité."[44] [And I felt that he was master of his thought: I record this absurdity here.][45]

Unselfing in this work undoes the mechanistic, highly advanced functioning of Teste's narrative self, if only momentarily. Before the pain sets in, Teste differentiates between the way that children discover their bodies for the first time, and the way the elderly know their bodies entirely. "Quand on est enfant on se *découvre,* on découvre lentement l'espace de son corps, on exprime la particularité de son corps par une série d'efforts, je suppose?"[46] [When we are children we *discover* ourselves, we learn little by little the extent of our body, we express our body's particularity by a series of movements, I suppose?][47] While the child still has much to learn about himself, there is nothing new for the elderly Teste to discover. This leads to the surprising discovery studied in the section above: unmapped territories of the body are illuminated during painful experiences. The unselfing experience also disrupts Teste's ability to make of his memory "un crible machinal." While Teste normally drifts off to sleep conjuring up only his most pleasant memories, the painful experience disrupts his ability to remain in control. "Autrefois, en m'assoupissant, je pensais à tous ceux qui m'avaient fait plaisir, figures, choses, minutes. Je les faisais venir pour que la pensée fût aussi douce que possible, facile comme le lit."[48] [In the past, whenever I drowsed I would think of all that had given me pleasure – faces, things, moments. I would bring them to mind so that thinking would be as pleasant as possible, smooth as the bed.][49] When his suffering sets in, his carefully constructed flow of pleasant memories is violently disrupted by his cry. Pain is the only thing Teste is unable to manipulate. "Que peut un homme? Je combats touts, – hors la souffrance de mon corps, au delà d'une certaine grandeur."[50] [What is a man's potential? I fight against everything – except the suffering of my body, beyond a certain intensity.][51]

However, Teste's temporary lapse in control of his narrative self does not last long. Soon after the disruptive event, he explains that long ago, he had already fully imagined his suffering before he became ill. "Sachez que j'avais prévu la maladie future. J'avais songé avec précision à ce dont tout le monde est sûr. Je crois que cette vue sur une portion évidente de l'avenir, devrait faire partie de l'éducation. Oui, j'avais prévu ce qui commence maintenant. C'était alors, une idée comme les autres. Ainsi j'ai pu la suivre."[52] [Let me tell you that I foresaw my future illness. I had thought with precision about something everyone else knows. I believe that such a look at an obvious portion of the future should be a part of one's education. Yes, I had forseen what is now beginning. At the time, it was an idea like any other. So I was able to pursue it.][53] The event takes its place among Teste's other practiced memories, becoming as familiar as the object of the mystic's intense contemplation. Dismissing the experience as an idea among many others – ideas that he predicts, imagines, and calls to mind with utmost certainty – Monsieur Teste returns to the comfortable position of self-monitoring and self-control. "Je suis étant, et me voyant; me voyant me voir, et ainsi de suite."[54] [I am being and seeing myself; seeing me see myself, and so forth."][55] Pain introduces a disruption to Teste's finely tuned self-observation vessel, but it is not long before he finds himself at the helm once again.

Delbo on Pain, Self, and Imagining

The difficulty of linking inner experience with outer reality that Valéry explores with Monsieur Teste is intensified in Delbo's writing on Auschwitz. Delbo repeatedly conveys the limitation of literature's figurative capacity when faced with her experience in the Nazi camps. The texts, which detail the two years and three months she spent as a political prisoner confront the reader's ability to imagine the unimaginable. Though sections of the manuscript for *Aucun de nous ne reviendra* (*None of Us Will Return*) were written just after the war in 1946–7, Delbo once stated that she waited twenty years to publish her memoir until it stood "the test of time."[56] This was in part a deliberate effort to bring attention to the Algerian struggle for independence. Michael Rothberg shows how Delbo's process of juxtaposing (without equating) Nazi crimes with colonialism appears in both her earliest work and in her last.[57] Indeed in *Aucun de nous*, which was first published by Gonthier in 1965, recollections of Auschwitz merge with references to the Algerian War. In 1970, Minuit published *Aucun de nous*, as well as *Une connaissance inutile* (*Useless Knowledge*) under the collection title, *Auschwitz et après* (*Auschwitz and After*), sections of which were written in 1946–7. *Mesure de nos jours* (*The Measure of Our Days*), the third volume, was published in 1971.

Delbo identifies the incompatibility of experience and its representation in these volumes. She details the unimaginable and indescribable nature of camps both in the narrative itself and in her regular addresses to readers who never lived through such experiences. Given Delbo's expression "il faut donner à voir" [they must be made to see], which she used frequently after the publication of her memoir, scholarship on Delbo has often focused on the role of visual imagining in her text. Rosette C. Lamont, who translated *Auschwitz et après* into English, remembers Delbo's keen sense of moral obligation to communicate the knowledge she had acquired: "Je veux donner à voir!' she kept on repeating."[58] Accordingly, Delbo's work has been character-ized as one whose task is to "faire voir, de donner à voir, à sentir"[59] [to make see, to show, to feel]. However, as Lawrence L. Langer explains, this expression, *donner à voir*, points more to the pursuit of a deep mean-ing of *voir*, than to a particularly visual mode of transmission: "The Holocaust experience is the gadfly of the modern imagination, chafing memory to pursue the true meaning of *voir*, 'see.'"[60] This more pro-found understanding of *voir*, which requires complex mental imagin-ing, cannot be achieved by the visual alone; it also requires a careful attention (in particular, to the sounds of experience) to fill the gaps left by superficial looking. In order to achieve this relationship with her reader, Delbo excavates the harrowing sensorium of inner experience.

This difficulty of presenting unimaginable experience accompanied by the insatiable need to *donner à voir* is thus intertwined with the ques-tion of truth-telling. In the quote that became her epigraph to the 1970 Minuit edition of *Aucun de nous*, Delbo expresses the difficulty of both categorizing the veracity of this work and constructing the narrative self across time. "Aujourd'hui, je ne suis pas sûre que ce que j'ai écrit soit vrai. Je suis sûre que c'est véridique."[61] [Today, I am not sure that what I wrote is true. I am certain it is truthful.][62] From this epigraph onward, Delbo indicates that her experience is one that is difficult to represent faithfully, even from the inside. As Delbo writes in a short prose poem in *Une connaissance inutile*,

> Aujourd'hui on sait
> Depuis quelques années on sait
> On sait que ce point sur la carte
> c'est Auschwitz
> On sait cela
> Et pour le reste on croit savoir.[63]

> Today people know
> have known for several years
> that this dot on the map
> is Auschwitz
> This much they know
> as for the rest
> they think they know.[64]

Readers may now know how to find Auschwitz on a map, but as for the rest of experience, they merely think they know (*on croit savoir*).

Testimony is meant to supplement this incomplete, cursory knowledge. At the same time, Delbo is aware that testimony is not always successful. This problem is only magnified as she approaches the question of communicating her experience to others. How can she relate such experiences to those who never lived them?

French philosopher Sarah Kofman writes of the terrible paradox that the Nazi death camps presented to survivors in *Paroles suffoquées* (*Smothered Words*) (1987). This work, which Kofman dedicates to her father who was deported and died in Auschwitz, offers an analysis of Robert Antelme's autobiographical account of deportation in *L'Espèce humaine* (*The Human Race*) (1978) and a commentary on the work of Maurice Blanchot. Kofman describes the survivor's compulsion to speak of experience without being able to do so adequately, or in a way that other people, namely non-survivors, would be able to understand. "How can one speak of the 'unimaginable' – that very quickly became unimaginable even for those who had lived through it – without having recourse to the imaginary?"[65] This "recourse to the imaginary" in the translation of experience is perceived as a falsification of that experience in is translation into discourse, one that comes at the cost of communication itself. Delbo's experience of detention in the Nazi camps dramatically disrupts her narrative self, the tenuous link between prewar life, deportation, and afterwards. She aims to present a literary account of Auschwitz that will deliver her experience in ways that the historical record and maps cannot. After the camps, she puts literary creation in service of a project to represent conscious experience for an audience who may know how to find Auschwitz on a map but lack meaningful knowledge of what happened there.

At certain moments in her memoir, Delbo seems to indicate that this project is destined to fail in that figurative language is not represented as immune to the violent forgetting imposed by Auschwitz. For example, *Mesure de nos jours*, opens with reflections on returning to life after the war when words have lost their meaning for thinking and reflecting. "Comment réfléchir quand on ne possède plus un mot, quand on a oublié tous les mots?"[66] [How can you think when you have no words at your disposal, when you've forgotten all the words?][67] Literary language – housed in the books that friends give her after her return remain unopened on her nightstand: "Quand enfin je me suis risquée à en prendre un, à l'ouvrir, à le regarder, il était si pauvre, si à côté que je l'ai remis sur sa pile. A côté. Oui tout était à côté. De quoi parlait-il ce livre? Je ne sais pas. Je sais que c'était à côté. A côté des choses, à côté de la vie, à côté de l'essentiel, à côté de la vérité."[68] [When finally I ventured to pick one up, open it, look through it, it was so poor, so beside the point, that I put it back on the pile. Beside the point. Yes, everything was beside the point. What was the book about? I do not know. I only know it was beside the point. Beside things, life, essentials, truth.][69] Literature seems impoverished, inessential, or inadequate when faced with the magnitude of her experience.

Likewise, in her memoir, vivid visual imagery of the world before deportation often clashes with the reality of the camps. In the final section of *Aucun de nous*, Delbo is haunted by visual memories of flowers blossoming, which remind her of springs past. She asks, "Pourquoi ai-je gardé la mémoire? Pourquoi cette injustice?"[70] [Why did I keep my memory? Why this injustice?][71] In the camp where nothing is green, vegetal, or living, words also become grey and barren.

> Tous les mots sont depuis longtemps décolorés
> Graminée – ombelle – source – une grappe de lilas – l'ondée – toutes les
>   images sont depuis longtemps livides.[72]

> Words lost their color long ago.
> Grasses – umbels – brook – a cluster of lilacs – spring showers – all vivid
>   images have grown livid long ago.[73]

Both the image of a verdant springtime and the words themselves, which once carried a synesthetic power are now empty and devoid of their signifying capacity. Their arrangement on the page, separated by long dashes, suggests a stark winter landscape rather than the burst of new life. Delbo writes, "Loin au-delà des barbelés, le printemps chante."[74] [Far beyond the barbed-wire enclosure, spring is singing.][75] Her visual imagination has become bloodless and drained in the confines of this colourless space.

> Ma mémoire est plus exsangue qu'une feuille d'automne
> Ma mémoire a oublié la rosée
> Ma mémoire a perdu sa sève. Ma mémoire a perdu tout son sang.[76]

> My memory is more bloodless than an autumn leaf.
> My memory has forgotten the dew.
> My memory is drained of its sap. My memory has bled to death.[77]

However, in her 1966 interview with Madeleine Chapsal, Delbo rejects the notion that the camp experience is ineffable, or that it remains outside the purview of literary expression: "Certains ont dit que la déportation ne pouvait pas entrer dans la littérature, que c'était trop terrible,

qu'on n'avait pas le droit d'y toucher ... Dire ça, c'est diminuer la littérature, je crois qu'elle est assez grande pour tout englober."[78] [Some
have said that deportation cannot enter into literature, that it was too
terrible, that one doesn't have the right to touch it ... Saying that dimin-
ishes literature, I think that it is sufficiently large to cover everything.]
For Delbo, literature is capable of representation, even when it comes
to the camps. Delbo's use of the verb "entendre" is telling; the double
meaning resounds when Delbo expresses that the burden of listening
is on the reader. Although she attempts to make her experience heard,
Delbo emphasizes that the goal is not *faire comprendre*. The kind of careful mental listening she requires of her reader may give way, in the end,
to an *entendement* that trumps the superficial *savoir* to which she alludes
in the poem on locating Auschwitz on a map.

Elsewhere, Delbo states directly that the power of her work comes
from its literary qualities. At a conference given in New York in 1972,
Delbo explains that her goal in writing about Auschwitz goes beyond
the desire to bear witness.

> Transformer en littérature la montée de la bourgeoisie au XIXe siècle, et
> voilà Balzac. Transformer en littérature la vanité et la médisance des gens
> du monde, et voilà Proust. Transformer en littérature Auschwitz, et voilà
> pour moi. La littérature n'est pas l'avatar, la métamorphose ultime d'un
> évènement ou d'un réel. Elle est infiniment plus que cela. Elle est réel et
> transcendance du réel. Elle est art, c'est-à-dire création: elle est sens et por-
> teur du sens.[79]

> Balzac transformed the rise of the bourgeoisie in the nineteenth century
> into literature. Proust transformed the vanity and the backbiting of soci-
> ety people into literature. For me, it's about transforming Auschwitz into
> literature. Literature is not the avatar, the ultimate metamorphosis of the
> event or a reality. It is infinitely more than that. Literature is the real and
> the transcendence of the real. It is art, that is to say, creation: it is meaning
> and carrier of meaning.

Literature of the camps delivers meaning and represents creative life
in the face of dehumanization. For Delbo, literature transforms reality such that it is able to communicate "the meaning" of the events it
represents. At the same time, these truths are not necessarily easy to
digest. In her 1966 interview for *L'Express* with Madeleine Chapsal,
Delbo stresses that in writing *Aucun de nous,* she was not trying to
deliver a version of her experience so that it would be easily absorbed
and understood.

D'abord, je n'ai rien à faire comprendre. Il me semble que j'ai écrit tout ce que j'avais à dire dans *Aucun de nous ne reviendra,* toute la réalité d'Auschwitz, telle que je l'ai ressentie. Tant pis pour les gens s'ils lisent ça comme un fait divers quelconque, tant pis pour eux et non pour moi s'ils n'entendent pas.[80]

First, there is nothing that I am trying to get people to understand. It seems to me that I wrote everything that I had to say in *None of Us Will Return,* the entire reality of Auschwitz, as I felt it. Too bad for people if they read this as some ordinary news item, too bad for them and not for me if they don't understand.

Given this framing, scholars have analyzed the relationship between bearing witness and the aesthetics of Delbo's literary project. Langer refers to the "deathlife" that prevailed in Auschwitz and the way in which Delbo attempts to find words and modify language to best communicate this otherworldly experience. He argues that the moral universe of the Holocaust poses a unique problem to literary representation: when readers imagine Milton's or Dante's versions of Hell wherein the guilty are punished for their sins, analogies like "Hell on earth" are doomed to fail. There is no justice, no *contrapasso* in the camps. Moreover, ordinary imagery lacks its evocative power when, confusingly, the sun in the camps is not a healing source of comfort, or the moon is no longer a symbol of romance. "Charlotte Delbo's ambition was to shape a language of fatal sensation, a synesthesia of atrocity which would lure her readers into the world of threatened annihilation and make them feel, and thus to begin to see, to cite our initial witness, "what Auschwitz really was."[81] Delbo also stuns her readers with this "synesthesia of atrocity" throughout the memoir in her account of the relationship between dreaming and suffering. Jason D. Tougaw writes, "Charlotte Delbo is particularly attentive to the aesthetic experience crafted through the accumulation of her words, which have the effect of engrossing readers in a linguistic world where, as in a waking dream, the rigid boundaries of thought dissolve."[82] In a textual world where "sensations supersede ideas," Delbo's readers are invited to enter into the sensorium and experience the strange and disturbing world of the Nazi camps. Thus, Delbo's project of representation is as much literary as political. She seeks to make the conscious experience of the Holocaust present for readers by crafting a language that matches it.

For example, in a section entitled "La nuit" the mud of the camps becomes an octopus, smothering the women in their pointless, forced labour. "Les pieuvres nous étreignaient de leurs muscles visqueux et nous ne dégagions un bras que pour être étranglées par un tentacule qui s'enroulait autour du cou, serrait les vertèbres, les serrait à les craquer, les vertèbres, la trachée, l'œsophage, le larynx, le pharynx et tous ces conduits qu'il y a dans le cou, les serrait à les briser."[83] [The octopi strangled us with their viscous muscles, and if we succeeded in freeing an arm it was only to be strangled by a tentacle coiling itself around our necks, tightening round our vertebrae, squeezing them until they cracked, the vertebrae, the trachea, the oesophagus the larynx, the pharynx, and all the canals in the throat, squeezing them to the breaking point.][84] The passage entraps the reader in its cascade of clauses and enumerations as the tentacles squeeze the neck and coils through its inner passageways: vertebrae, trachea, oesophagus, larynx, pharynx. The metaphor continues as the beast corners the women from all directions. To free their throats, the women fight with their arms, legs, waist; they are tempted to give up the endless struggle when, suddenly, the tension breaks.

> Les tentacules se déroulaient, déroulaient leur menace. La menace restait un long moment suspendue et nous étions là, hypnotisées, incapables de risquer une esquive en face de la bête qui s'abattait, s'entortillait, collait, broyait. Nous étions près de succomber quand nous avions soudain l'impression de nous éveiller. Ce ne sont pas des pieuvres, c'est la boue. Nous nageons dans la boue, une boue visqueuse avec les tentacules inépuisables de ses vagues. C'est une mer de boue dans laquelle nous devons nager, nager à force, nager à épuisement et nous essouffler à garder la tête au-dessus des tourbillons de fange.[85]

> The tentacles uncoiled, uncoiling their threat. The threat hung deferred for a long time while we stayed there, hypnotized, unable to risk a dodge for fear that the beast would fall upon us, winding itself about our flesh, glued to it, crushing our bones. We were about to succumb when, all of a sudden, we felt we were waking up. These are not octopi, it is mud. We swim in mud, a viscous slime with the inexhaustible tentacles of waves. It is a sea of mud in which we must swim, swim strongly, to the point of exhaustion, running out of breath as we keep our heads above eddies of mire.[86]

Delbo represents the temporary reprieve from the octopi as an uncoiling of the threat, when the immediacy of the assault on the body is accompanied by the epiphany of the passage: "c'est la boue." Delbo describes this realization as an awakening, which is as representational as it is instructive for the reader. She calls for the reader to awaken to reality of the camps by delivering these altered states of consciousness through the phenomenology of its nightmares.

The beast does not relent for long, and the narrator slips back into the nightmare as her comrade sinks and is swallowed up by the mud.

> Il faut la tirer, la remettre à flot de la boue, lâcher la trague, impossible de s'en débarrasser, elle est enchaînée à nos poignets, si solidement, si serrée que nous coulons toutes deux dans un corps à corps mortel, liées l'une à l'autre par la trague d'où les mottes versent, se confondant avec la boue que nous brassons dans une ultime tentative pour nous dégager et la trague est maintenant remplie d'yeux et de dents, d'yeux qui luisent, de dents qui ricanent et éclairent la boue comme des madrépores phospho-rescents une eau épaisse, et tous ces yeux et toutes ces dents flamboient et vocifèrent, dardant, mordant, dardant et mordant de toutes parts et hurlant: Schneller, schneller, weiter, weiter, et, quand nous donnons des coups de poing dans ces gueules toutes en dents et en yeux, les poings ne rencontrent que taies molles, éponges pourries.[87]

> We must pull her out, set her on course in the slime, yet we cannot let go of the barrow, impossible to get rid of it, it is chained fast to our wrists, so securely that both of us sink in a mortal embrace, tied to each other by the barrow spilling its clods which get mixed up with the mud we churn in an ultimate attempt to free ourselves and the barrow is now full of eyes and teeth, eyes that gleam, teeth that snicker and light up the mud as do phos-phorescent madrepores in the deep, and all these eyes and teeth flare up and vociferate, flashing, biting, stinging, and biting from every direction, and shrieking: Schneller, schneller, weiter, weiter, and when we punch these maws all teeth and eyes, our fists hit nothing but soft leucomas, rot-ting sponges.[88]

The stream of consciousness stretches on and on, reflecting the physical and mental pull of the wheelbarrow on the one hand and the respon-sibility to the drowning woman on the other. Delbo evokes the famil-iar nightmare of wanting to run but finding oneself rooted in place. Here, the women are urged to move faster and onward by the guards (*schneller/weiter*), but they cannot free themselves from the endless mire of mud and bodies. The monster is again evoked through repetition and enumeration as strange and haunting sea creatures (phosphores-cent madrepores) suddenly populate the barren landscape of the camp. The senselessness of the labour, the impossibility of escape, and the unrelenting threat of the monster's tentacles merge in Delbo's trans-mission of night, where the women struggle against the nightmare of death: "c'est le trou de la nuit ou un autre cauchemar, ou notre vraie mort, et nous nous débattons furieusement, nous nous débattons."[89] [it is the hole of the night where we struggle furiously, struggle against another nightmare, that of our real death.][90] Night does not end with daybreak, Delbo insists, as the passage oscillates between daylight nightmares of work and the mud and the nighttime horrors of dysentery and death rattles in the bunks. The chapter suddenly breaks into broken verse with the refrain "ce n'est pas la fin de la nuit" [it is not the end of night].[91] It is not the end of the nightmare for those who are delirious in the charnel house, for the rats devouring lips of the living, for the stars frozen above their heads. The night doesn't end, Delbo repeats, because as one nightmare congeals and the shadows slip away, another begins.

This need for new forms of representation is also reflected in the challenge of conveying experience in narrative. In Delbo, the narrative self struggles to craft a cohesive story out of a series of moments, much in the way that Kahneman describes.[92] *Auschwitz et après* contains many abrupt declarations that position Delbo in France after the war, which follow passages that narrate events that took place in the camps. These juxtapositions emphasize the abyss between narrative time (the camps) and writing time (after). Delbo decries the story ["l' histoire"] that her experience has become. She describes, at a distance, the skeletal woman ("un squelette de femme") who jumps around frenetically, trying to keep warm in the doorway of block 25. The narration breaks: "Et maintenant je suis dans un café à écrire cette histoire – car cela devient une histoire."[93] [Presently I am writing this story in a café – it is turning into a story.][94] The memory is suddenly interrupted by the intrusion of the narrator, who suspects that the story losing some of its veracity in the telling. The gap between the immediacy of the experiencing self and the long-term autobiography of the narrative self is flimsily bridged by the return of the "I." At the end of her account of watching the Nazis haul truckloads of women to the crematorium, she writes, "Et maintenant je suis dans un café à écrire ceci."[95] [And now I am sitting in a café, writing this text.][96] The word "ceci" categorizes the past, emphasizing the distance between the two narrative frames. There is the subject that lives the camp experience, and the subject writing in the café. The text's juxtapositions testify to the disruption of ordinary self-experience, defying the reader to cross with its narrator from one world to the next.

This is not only the case in the narrative sections of *Auschwitz et après*, but also in its poetic breaks. These sections force us to consider the role of form in Delbo's larger testimonial strategy. When the narrative breaks into free-verse, Adorno's infamous assertion that "to write poetry after

Auschwitz is barbaric" looms in the background.[97] Although this oft-cited quote has since been dismissed by other survivors, especially those who write, the idea that representing the death camps in a poetic mode somehow does violence to its integrity calls attention to the role of poetic form in Delbo's project.[98]

In the "O vous qui savez" poem from *Aucun de nous*, the text counteracts the larger thematic worry that (poetic, literary, figurative) language died in the camps. As I have argued elsewhere, Delbo relays the unimaginable in a testimonial strategy that privileges *entendement* (listening) over *savoir* (knowing) for communication of her experience to be successful.[99] Attending to the acoustic resonance of the poem, which repeatedly alternates the phrases "O vous qui savez/saviez-vous," illuminates the way in which Delbo's style counteracts the voiding of words of their representative capacity.[100] The apostrophe, "O vous" is repeated five times at the beginning of the poem, calling out to those who "know" about the camps in the same way that those in the poem from *Une connaissance inutile* "know" how to find Auschwitz on the map. Rather than creating a Romantic effect, the repeated apostrophe to those who know calls their knowing into question and serves as a challenge. In the absence of a formal rhyme scheme, the repetition of the verb *savoir* – conjugated as *vous savez/saviez-vous* – creates an unsettling rhythmic effect. The poem batters the reader with the repeated transformation of the declarative into the interrogative; those who "know" are repeatedly questioned. The uncomfortable juxtaposition between the two lines, "O vous qui savez/saviez-vous," which is not mitigated by punctuation to smooth out the reading, furthers the poem's disjointed effect. The fragments resound for the readers, haunting them with the "O" sound of lamentation. Her manipulation of sound serves to communicate an acoustic haunting, a sensation that others feared was an intransmissible experience.

The representational strategy behind Delbo's poetic interjections in *Auschwitz et après* can be aligned with her post-war philosophy, given that her testimony is meant to bear witness to the suffering of the self as well as groups of unequally afflicted others. *Auschwitz et après* speaks to the radical difference between Delbo's suffering as a non-Jewish political prisoner and the suffering of Jewish prisoners in the camps where she was detained. Rather than providing an imaginative diversion, one that temporarily puts testimony on hold, the poems offer an alternative entry point to the inner experience of seemingly unimaginable experience. In her 1975 interview with François Bott for *Le Monde* where she claims that literature is a weapon, she specifically asserts the power of poetic language. "Chacun témoigne avec ses armes … Je considère le langage de la poésie comme le plus efficace – car il remue le lecteur au plus secret de lui-même – et le plus dangereux pour les ennemis qu'il combat."[101] [Everyone testifies with their own weapons … I consider the language of poetry as the most effective – because it moves the reader on the deepest inner level – and is the most dangerous weapon against the enemies it combats.] In this sense, Delbo's descriptions of the disruptive effects of pain on the mind and body are reminiscent of the way in which suffering functions in Valéry. However, while suffering occupies a privileged position in Valéry's work in that it provides the occasion for new (if momentary) self-knowledge, painful experience in Delbo's memoir is a constant source of anguish. Pain disrupts the experiencing self, introducing strange foreign presences into the solitary individual perspective. In some extreme cases, unselfing produces a terrifying communion with ontological others.

In a segment of *Aucun de nous* entitled "La Soif," Delbo describes the debilitating desire for water and the way that thirst overwhelms all rational thought. As for Monsieur Teste, suffering in Delbo's testimony is experienced as a limit to the intellectual self. While Teste's bodily pain interrupts his life of pure reason, Delbo's pain intermittently disrupts her ability to retain a standard of human rationality in the face of the dehumanizing efforts of the SS. Delbo begins by contrasting the place that thirst occupies in the collective imagination, inspired by tales of adventure. She writes, "La soif, c'est le récit des explorateurs, vous savez, dans les livres de notre enfance. C'est dans le désert … Le chapitre pathétique du livre. À la fin du chapitre, la caravane du ravitaillement arrive, elle s'était égarée sur les pistes brouillées par la tempête. Les explorateurs crèvent les outres, ils boivent. Ils boivent et ils n'ont plus soif."[102] [Thirst is an explorer's tale, you know, in the books we read as children. It takes place in the desert … This is the pathetic chapter of the book. At the end of the chapter, a caravan bringing provisions appears; it had lost its way on trails erased by sand storms. The explorers pierce the goatskin bottles and they drink. They drink and their thirst is quenched.][103]

Delbo's depiction of thirst here evokes the idea that literary thirst is always accompanied by its eventual relief, which arrives in the form of the rescue caravan and the gourds filled with water. According to the theory of pain that Scarry outlines, the imagination creates sources of objectification during extreme pain as a "ground of last resort" when faced with a lack of mental imagery.[104] The caravan of gourds filled with water that Delbo imagines should ultimately serve to alleviate her thirst as an escape from objectlessness. However, Delbo quickly contrasts this image with her personal experience of thirst, which lacks the possibility of relief. She writes, "Mais la soif du marais est plus brûlante que celle du désert. La soif du marais dure des semaines. Les outres ne viennent jamais. La raison chancelle. La raison est terrassée par la soif. La raison résiste à tout, elle cède à la soif."[105] [But the thirst of the marsh is more searing than that of the desert. The marsh thirst lasts for weeks. The goatskin gourds never arrive. Reason begins to waiver. It is crushed by thirst. Reason is able to overcome most everything, but it succumbs to thirst.][106] The mind resists the crush of thirst, but succumbs, eventually. Delbo first offers the imagined caravan to her reader and then revokes it; the thirst of the marsh is not the thirst of the desert in the explorer's tale. The role of Delbo's caravan is twofold; it stands in for the suffering that ensues in the absence of water, but also denies the narrative's expiation of the pain she is presently recounting. Delbo's denial of the mental imagery that might have made the experience familiar to readers emphasizes the extent to which pain disrupts ordinary consciousness. Instead of objectification, the ground of last resort stretches on, thirst unquenched.

As the passage progresses, thirst continues to prevent the mind from remaining lucid. In the place of a rational head, disembodied lips mouth a mute dread. "Le matin au réveil, les lèvres parlent et aucun son ne sort des lèvres. L'angoisse s'empare de tout votre être, une angoisse aussi fulgurante que celle du rêve. Est-ce cela, d'être mort?"[107] [Upon awakening in the morning, lips move but no sound comes out. Anguish fills your whole being, an anguish as gripping as that of dreams. Is this what it means to be dead?][108] Consciousness of the painful experience is characterized by an oneiric silence that leads her to question her existence. Delbo forsakes the mental images of thirst quenched by a miraculous caravan in the explorer's tale and replaces them with opaque dreamlike states that are much more difficult for readers to imagine. She repeatedly describes thirst as the impossible awareness of being dead ("cette impression d'être morte, d'être morte et de le savoir") or of being insane ("Je sens grandir l'épouvante dans mes yeux jusqu'à la démence").[109] Pain releases the mind's control as the will collapses. During Delbo's experience of unselfing, thirst becomes primary and forces her to notice a horrible growing presence. The awareness of death expands at the expense of all else. While Teste's pain forces him to notice foggy inner regions, Delbo tastes rotting leaves ("feuilles pourries qui durcissent") as her dread grows.[110]

As for Teste, this disruption of the self cannot last. The growing inner presence and the rotting leaves disappear with the first taste of water. Delbo writes, "Je bois. Je bois et je suis mieux. La salive revient dans ma bouche. Les paroles reviennent à mes lèvres, mais je ne parle pas.

La vie revient. Je retrouve ma respiration, mon cœur. Je sais que je suis vivante. Je suce lentement ma salive. La lucidité revient, et le regard – et je vois la petite Aurore."[111] [I drink. I drink and I feel better. I have saliva in my mouth again. Words return to my lips but I do not speak. Sight returns to my eyes. Life returns. I rediscover my breathing, my heart. I know I am alive. Slowly I suck my saliva. Lucidity returns, and my sight – and I see little Aurore.][112] What Valéry calls *l'objet* retreats as the pain subsides and Delbo rediscovers the possibility of normal speech and sight. The dash sets off the act of seeing from the rest of the sentence as if to pause and cinematically shift the focus from interior to exterior. During the disruption of unselfing, this feeling for others was not possible. Aurore and her needs are only visible when Delbo returns to ordinary consciousness. As Aurore comes into view, Delbo easily recognizes the thirst of her fellow detainee, writing simply, "Elle a soif." [She is thirsty.][113] Like her lips, Aurore's are discoloured and she has a desperate look in her eyes. But unlike Delbo, Aurore does not have the strength to run down to the stream to steal a few sips of swamp water. Delbo senses the demand that the other woman places on her, but writes that she remains "insensitive" to it:

Chaque matin elle se met près de moi. Elle espère que je lui laisserai quelques gouttes au fond de ma gamelle. Pourquoi lui donnerai-je de mon eau? Aussi bien elle va mourir. Elle attend. Ses yeux implorent et je ne la regarde pas. Je sens sur moi ses yeux de soif, la douleur à ses yeux quand je remets la gamelle à ma ceinture. La vie revient en moi et j'ai honte. Et chaque matin je reste insensible à la supplication de son regard et de ses lèvres décolorées par la soif, et chaque matin j'ai honte après avoir bu.[114]

I see her and think: she might drink this water since she is going to die. She is waiting. Her eyes beg and I do not look at her. I feel upon me her thirsty gaze, the pain in her eyes when I hook my tin cup back on my belt. Life returns to me and I feel shame. And each morning I remain insensitive to the supplication of her eyes, her lips discolored by thirst, and each morning I feel ashamed after drinking.[115]

As the gripping inner anguish disappears, the awareness of death vanishes as well. Ordinary self-experience is re-established. The devastating effects of unselfing on Delbo's sense of her own temperament come into view. The illusion of being someone who shares her water with others evaporates in the excruciating experience of thirst; she feels ashamed to find that she someone who keeps her water for herself. If, as Compagnon argues, the notion of temperament provides even the most seemingly episodic lives with a sense of coherence, this disruption of Delbo's sense of herself is no small matter.[116] Though words return, and sight returns to her eyes, she recognizes, with horror, that Aurore had been invisible to her all along.

It is in the return to ordinary consciousness and not inside the experience of unselfing that Delbo regains the ability to recognize the pain of others. In the first section of *Mesure de nos jours,* Delbo compares the time in the camps as a disruption of her ordinary self, during which she did not feel herself exist. "Dire que j'avais froid comme lorsqu'on a la fièvre, dire que j'étais épuisée, c'est facile à advancer aujourd'hui en guise d'explication. Je ne sentais rien, je ne me sentais pas exister, je n'existais pas. Combien de temps suis-je restée ainsi en suspension d'existence? (J'ai retrouvé mes mots depuis, vous voyez.)"[117] [To say I was shivering with cold as when racked with a fever, that I was at the end of my tether, is easy to declare today in lieu of explanation. The truth of the matter is I felt nothing, did not feel myself existing, did not exist. How long did I remain thus, in a state of suspension? (As you can see, I have found my words since that time.)][118] The experience is cast as a suspension of herself, which makes her question her existence. It is in the long process of coming back, which follows the disruption of the self, that words for the experience return.

Disruptive Unselfing and the Limits of Empathy

Does pain make the person who suffers more attentive to the world because it reduces the claims of the self? Valéry and Delbo offer two different perspectives on this question. In a section of *Aucun de nous* entitled "Un jour" (One Day), Delbo describes the experience of watching an SS officer's dog attack an emaciated woman. As in Teste's painful moment before sleep and Delbo's description of her anguished thirst, suffering is accompanied here by an eerie, dreamlike silence. This silence is followed by a harrowing scream whose source cannot be identified. Delbo writes that she is not sure whether the scream is coming from the victim or the witnesses.

La femme crie. Un cri arraché. Un seul cri qui déchire l'immobilité de la plaine. Nous ne savons pas si le cri vient d'elle ou de nous, de sa gorge crevée ou de la nôtre. Je sens les crocs du chien à ma gorge. Je crie. Je hurle. Aucun son ne sort de moi. Le silence du rêve.[119]

The woman lets out a cry. A wrenched-out scream. A single scream tearing through the immobility of the plain. We do not know if the scream has

> been uttered by her or by us, whether it issued from her punctured throat or from ours. I feel the dog's fangs in my throat. I scream. I howl. Not a sound comes out of me. The silence of a dream.[120]

Sound is silenced in this scene. The strange cry is described as tearing through the immobility of the landscape, and yet the profound dreamlike silence persists. The text delivers the phenomenology of a seemingly impossible experience; although Delbo knows that it is the victim who is in pain, she feels that it is happening to her. She screams and howls, though she makes no sound. Notably, "leur gorge" [their throat] is singular in this passage, which stresses the collective nature of this feeling. This intersubjective experience at the limit of human consciousness is characterized by the audible scream of the victim merging with the silent screams of the witnesses. The individuality of the subject is transcended in this moment of unselfing as the women share one choked throat. In the place of declarations of individual suffering, the women scream together, their voices merging. The subject and the object of attention remain walled in the strange, silent world together in an instance of radical empathy. Delbo feels the puncture of the dog's fangs in her throat and hears herself screaming the victim's scream. The experience not only thrusts her into a state of heightened reflective consciousness (hearing oneself hearing), but also forces her to suffer another person's pain as if it were her own.

This instance of radical empathy in the communion between observers and victim offers an uncomfortable response to the commentary Paul Gifford offers about the possibility of real interpersonal exchange within Valéry's conception of the self. In a reflection on desire in Valéry's work, Gifford asks, "Does this reflexive and functional duality (self and self-as-other) however, give any acknowledgment to a human vocation for genuine exchange, real encounter?"[121] Despite Valéry's resistance to the need for others in the empire of the self, he saw inner dialogue as the enabling condition of interpersonal exchange. Valéry writes, "l'homme communique avec – soi, par les mêmes moyens qu'il a de communiquer avec l'autre. La conscience a besoin d'un autre fictif – d'une extériorité – elle se développe en développant cette altérité."[122] [man communicates with – himself, by the same means that he has to communicate with the other. Consciousness needs a fictitious other – an exteriority – it develops itself in developing this otherness.] Though Valéry distances himself from the need for alterity when it comes to self-consciousness with the word "fictif," he acknowledges that man's understanding of himself develops by way of this dialectic. Gifford writes, "Strategically, it offers a consonance-in-desire with the *vaulting dream* to which it beckons: that of a communion with a genuine – ontologically different – Other, realizing a supreme degree of exchange and intimacy."[123]

The communion with a "genuine ontologically different other" in Delbo's narrative ensues from the experience of watching a dog rip a woman apart. The heightened consciousness in the narrative indeed offers a "supreme degree of exchange and intimacy" as the witnesses share in the victim's pain. However, this episode is evidently far from a vaulting dream. For Delbo, sharing the experience of the death camps goes beyond a dialectical encounter with alterity, breaching the separation between "I" and "we." The result is a powerless state of communal feeling and the women are described as cries that cannot be heard: "Chacune est un cri matérialisé, un hurlement – qu'on n'entend pas … Pour l'éternité, des têtes rasées, pressées les unes contre les autres, qui éclatent de cris, des bouches tordues de cris qu'on n'entend pas, des mains agitées dans un cri muet."[124] [Each one is a materialized cry, a howl – unheard … For eternity, these shaven heads, squeezed against one another, bursting with shouts, mouths twisted by cries we do not hear, hands waving in a mute cry.][125] The guttural cries of the women resound – they react to the sight of their companions being gassed and then incinerated – but remain unheard by the ears because their vocal cords are said to be broken. Each victim's body cries out towards the potential listeners. In *Totalité et infini (Totality and Infinity)*, Levinas argues that the ethical relation grounds itself in the face to face encounter. By this account, the face of the other appeals to the subject as a relation with his transcendence.[126] In Delbo's text, the entire body of the other calls out to the witness, demanding ethical attention. Delbo represents the bodies of the condemned women as cries that call out to her, calls to which she cannot respond.

While both writers glimpse the otherness within the self through the disruptions of unselfing, only Valéry retains the hope that tracking inner alterity will lead to exchange, intimacy, or communication with ontological others. Delbo experiences the victim's pain as her own under extreme duress, and yet does not describe the conflict between self-interest and the interests of other persons as dissolved by extreme experience.[127] Rather, she indicates that *both* are experienced simultaneously. What ensues is not self-preservation in a strict sense, nor can it be called true compassion, as the Dolorists had hoped. Rather, disruptive unselfing experienced under duress offers an invasive and powerless encounter with the fate of others. As she witnesses the dog's attack, she feels the victim's pain as her own. While Delbo might be said to empathize in the passage on Aurore, in the sense that her experiences provoke a recognition of the pain the other is experiencing, what remains of her rational capacities push her not towards self-sacrifice, but towards survival. With the return of her lucidity comes the return of rational thinking and the ordinary function of the experiencing self. The narrative self registers the added shame, each morning after drinking, after screaming, for having survived. Delbo's experience of the Nazi camps presents radical empathy as a powerless state, not an expansive vision of feeling for others. In the place of Weil's piercing of the veil and Murdoch's escape from solipsism, Delbo account of unselfing takes the form of an eternal cry.

In both Valéry and Delbo, the disruption of the suffering self exposes unexplored contours of human consciousness. Valéry explores the inner expanses that are revealed by disruptive unselfing through the aches and pains of Monsieur Teste, the ones that illuminate the geometry of his suffering. Though pain is an obstacle to the totalizing self-science system, it is epistemologically valuable in that it illuminates an inner geometry that was not visible before the experience of suffering. Delbo describes the phenomenology of extreme thirst, which delivers the uncanny feeling of being insane, or even of being dead. Her synesthetic testimony complicates Valéry's thesis on self/other exchange in that it depicts the crossing of the boundary between self and other as an undesirable and powerless state. Whereas Valéry hoped that this exploration of inner alterity might, in turn, lead to the parallel and complementary understanding of others, Delbo's text suggests that in destroying the boundary between self and world, the knowledge of suffering may be useless, for relating to the world of the living, at least.

4 Unselfing as Mutation: Hallucination and the Remains in Henri Michaux and Yolande Mukagasana

But, someone will say, aren't these worlds without object, beyond an object, love without object, contemplation without object – aren't such worlds so much smoke, leaving behind even less than smoke?

A new expanse, a profoundly hollowed depth, which may afterward be partially filled, but not annulled, subsists after the experiment and perhaps forever, though not quite uniformly either.

Henri Michaux

In this imaginary world where I was just elevated like the Assumption of Mary, there is only one woman who brings a beautiful child into the world.

Yolande Mukagasana

What remains after a hallucinatory altered state of consciousness? Are visions mere illusions, leaving nothing behind in their wake? These are the questions – or rather, the counter arguments from an imaginary interlocutor – that Michaux anticipates in *Les grandes épreuves de l'esprit* (*The Major Ordeals of the Mind*) (1966). Michaux's book catalogues the author's experience of taking mescaline; it records the way the drug bends his perspective and accelerates his experience of lived time. No, Michaux responds. What remains after the experience is a profoundly hollowed depth, a new expanse in the self subsists after the experience is over and remains, perhaps forever. Yolande Mukagasana recounts another miraculous change in the self in a text that reckons with its author's unlikely physical and psychological survival. *La mort ne veut pas de moi* (*Not My Time to* Die) (1997) is a witness account of the 1994 genocide against the Tutsi in Rwanda.[1] This testimonial text wonders, desperately, what part of a mother survives after witnessing the murder of her children by tracing the mental landscape of this acute experience of suffering. In the imaginary world of her hallucinations, which are brought on by extreme fear, Mukagasana feels herself elevated like Mary in Assumption. The gap between self and the Marian image is closed; while hiding in cramped quarters, she has the uncanny sensation of giving birth to her murdered son again.

This chapter investigates the mutation model for unselfing through these two accounts: Michaux (1899–1984), the Belgian-born writer and graphic artist who documents his experiments with hallucinatory drugs, and Mukagasana (1954–), the Tutsi medical nurse and writer who bears witness to extreme suffering. From distant cultural contexts, Michaux and Mukagasana write the dramatic changes in their self-narratives as mutations of their ordinary experience of selfhood. Unlike the "caesura event" of canonical Pauline conversion, the mutation model for unselfing does not usher in instantiations of entirely new subjects.[2] Rather, the biological notion of mutation evokes the reconfiguration of unselfing that Michaux and Mukagasana build in their work. Mutation narratives tell the story of slow structural change in the self, involving the deletion, insertion, or reordering of its composite parts.

For Michaux, hallucinatory drugs allow for the illumination of formerly obscured contours of the self. Through his experimentation with form and his idiosyncratic approach to textual and graphic representation, Michaux presents an account of consciousness at the extreme limit of perception. Michaux's mescaline texts explore the drug's effect on the experiencing self and how it is affected by intentional chemical alterations of ordinary cognition. He details not only the effect that his experiments have on his sense of agency (his rational consciousness is changed by the experience), but also on his perspective; Michaux memorably describes unselfing as a "un éclair qui dure" [a lightning that lasts].[3] Michaux pursues his mescaline experiments as a modern mystic much in the way that Georges Bataille pursues inner experience. Like Bataille, Michaux rejects the notion of "project" – the deferral of living and action – in his experimentations on the self. He seeks to use the deliberate and extreme exploration of the mind to free the self from its constraints.

Mukagasana's Marian hallucinations, which cast the self as a holy figure of eternal, redemptive suffering, allows for a mental escape from persecution. Mukagasana draws on the Catholic imagery of the *pietà*, the Virgin Mary cradling the dead body of Jesus after the Crucifixion, to communicate her experience of losing her children. Through the transformative power of this hallucination, Mukagasana distances herself from her psychological distress and interprets it through the model.

Her account pursues the effects of unselfing on her sense of agency and perspective (which are dramatically altered by the emotion of fear), and temperament. The *pietà* image is instrumental to the reconstruction of her self-narrative after its violent mutation. When read together, Michaux's and Mukagasana's texts offer new perspectives on the phenomenology and ethics of intersubjective experience during altered states of consciousness. Whereas others remain mere shadows during Michaux's self-inflicted hallucinations, Mukagasana recounts an increase in her feeling for others; compassionate consciousness extends outward, even towards her attackers. Her consciousness of others extends beyond mere perspective-taking and motivates an ethics of care for others, both immediate and distant.

The first part of the chapter focuses on unselfing in Michaux by situating the mescaline texts within the artistic, philosophical, and spiritual discourses that influenced his work. It first outlines his scepticism about selfhood when understood as national, cultural, or even personal identity and then examines the way in which unselfing, as expressed through the mescaline texts, is represented as a mutation of the self. The section concludes with an analysis of the self-knowledge that ensues from the mescaline experiments, explaining Michaux's notion of "lightning that lasts." The second half of the chapter focuses on Mukagasana's unique presentation of first-person experience in her memoir of the 1994 genocide against the Tutsi. Mukagasana describes her transformation into a *pietà* figure during her harrowing survival and experience of extreme loss. This section analyzes the maternal aspects of the self's transformation in relation to suffering to explain how Mukagasana uses painful lived experience to orient herself towards others. Finally, the chapter brings Michaux and Mukagasana together in a comparative section to examine how experiencing unselfing as a mutation impacts each writer's understanding of alterity, empathy, and radical compassion.

Michaux and Unselfing

Henri Michaux began taking mescaline and tracking the mental ordeals that ensued in the middle of his life. In a decade of self-experiments that began in 1954 and continued through the 1960s, he sought to use the drug to move beyond his ordinary experience of consciousness and thereby access privileged insight into the depths of the human mind. Knowing that hallucinatory drugs had long been used as entheogens (psychoactive substances that served to occasion enlightening divine or mystical experiences), he became interested in the naturally occurring psychedelic derived from the peyote cactus. In linking the role that peyote played in religious ceremonies in Mexico and in South America to his experiments in his Paris apartment, Michaux's experiments can be understood as a renewal of a Decadent gesture that seeks to recover access to the divine in an exotic cultural Other. In the first of his mescaline texts, *Misérable miracle, la Mescaline* (1956), Michaux writes that indigenous tribes such as the Huichol and the Tarahumara "allaient à un dieu en allant au Peyotl," but other gods, like the god of the volcanoes or of fire for example, were not far off.[4] (They "sought a god seeking the Peyotl.")[5] Through the peyote-induced visions, these peoples are able to gain precious access to the divine, and thereby change their ordinary experience of phenomenal reality. However, modern Westerners, he claims, are too estranged from the gods to achieve this transcendence and only see "infinite cascades of relativity" when they take the same drugs:

> Quant à l'Occidental d'à présent, depuis longtemps incroyant aux dieux, et qui serait bien incapable d'imaginer une forme sous laquelle ils seraient susceptibles de lui apparaître, ce que son esprit saisit, seul dieu qu'il aperçoive encore et qu'il serait vain d'adorer, c'est l'infinie relativité, la cascade qui n'a pas de terminaison, la cascade des causes et des effets, ou plutôt des précédents ou des suivants, où tout est roue entraînante et *roue entraînée*.[6]

> As for the Westerner today, so long an unbeliever in the gods and now incapable of imagining a form in which they might appear to him, what his mind grasps, the only god he can still conceive, a god it would be vain to worship, is infinite relativity, the unending cascade, the cascade of causes and effects, or rather of what goes before and of what comes after, where everything is driving wheel and *follower wheel*.[7]

Worried by the problem of relativism – that his pursuit of higher realms of consciousness will be shaped by his situated position in history and culture – Michaux compares the outcome of his experiments with the religious discourse of the Huichol and the Tarahumara. This commentary reflects his successive attempts at descriptions of the spiritual, without having recourse to a pre-existing religious or cultural vocabulary, a cultural critique that becomes a framework for questioning the self.

The connection between hallucinogens, altered states, and the divine has long been of interest to the philosophy of consciousness. William James, in *The Varieties of Religious Experience* (1902), writes of the need to include altered states in a full accounting of consciousness after conducting his own nitrous oxide experiments James argues that normal waking consciousness is merely one kind of consciousness, which exists alongside other forms, parted by the "flimsiest of screens." Though we may go through life without knowing those other types of consciousnesses exist, drugs might be what is needed to reveal them to us in their completeness.[8] In this passage, James not only claims that altered states must be considered in a complete account of consciousness, but also argues that they carry with them important insights of scientific, and possibly metaphysical significance. Moreover, it is the experiment itself that imposed the "impression of its truth." While a term like "mind-altering" has become cliché in discussions of hallucinogens, especially as related to the psychedelic sixties, there have been surprisingly few studies of altered states of consciousness that engage in philosophical discussions of the self.[9] Michaux's accounts of the process of unselfing, as explored through his self-induced drug experiments constitute the attempt to give a full accounting for conscious experience, including the ones separated from rational consciousness. If James describes the boundary between normal consciousness and altered states as parted by the flimsiest of screens, Michaux attempts to remove the screen and achieve continuity between the rational observer and the seer.

Michaux's experimental process thus draws on the languages of modern mysticism as well as the rhetoric of documentation and testimony. Through both, Michaux affirms the special status of the witness figure, the one who lives and documents the altered self experience. Like Valéry's attempt to develop a secular mysticism, Michaux's mysticism *sans Dieu* also seeks to engage with mystical practices without completely abandoning rationality in the process. As a young person, Michaux contemplated entering the priesthood but decided to pursue medicine instead (though he eventually abandoned his studies). His desire to document experience in all its complexity speaks to the interdisciplinary nature of his methods and his process. Of Michaux's approach to writing *Misérable miracle*, biographer Jean-Pierre Martin writes, "This would be the only book of trembling, which through its documentary aspect, would give the impression of an experience captured on the spot."[10] Michaux sought to document the experience rigorously (that is, without cultural or personal biases,) crafting the reader's experience with the book in its marginalia, notes, and drawings. In this sense, Michaux is a forerunner for later, more extreme drug experiments, but sets himself apart from them in his somewhat surprising commitment to documentation and control, as well as his distaste for Freud (and for psychoanalysis in general). Michaux retains his commitment to be both the observer and the observed, which plays an essential role in his writings on unselfing.

Michaux's exploration into the world of mescaline was not only an exploration of the human mind, but also of the nature of the experimental text, expansively understood as words, signs, and drawings. Though he would eventually experiment with hashish, LSD, psilocybin, and mushrooms, he professed himself to a teetotaller of sorts in the postscript to *Misérable miracle* (a "buveur d'eau," [water-drinker type]), and justifies these drug experiments by situating them in relation to his other philosophical and aesthetic projects.[11] His experiments, thus, are not only focused on the inner space of experience, but also on its outer expression. In this sense, the experiments reflect his attempt to find a universal language for the contours of individual experience; he sought to use aesthetic experience to transcend ordinary waking consciousness in order to access untapped expanses of the mind. Michaux's unselfing texts thereby enter into a tradition of both Belgian and French avant-garde writers who positioned the poetic imagination as a site for revelation.[12] Richard Sieburth dubs him a "true technician of the sacred and perhaps the century's most genuine Surrealist."[13]

Indeed, Michaux shared the Surrealist desire to reduce the control of reason as a means of achieving insight on the self and the world beyond phenomenal reality. His psychedelic texts reflect the belief that curated conscious experiences would lead to privileged states of insight and that "art arises from the imagination as a revelation: a form of insight-oriented knowledge."[14] He discovered Lautréamont in 1922, a *poète maudit* claimed by the Belgian avant-garde over twenty years before the French, who would have an important influence on his work. This tension would prove important for Michaux in his attempts to validate his native Belgian tradition at the same time that he sought to distance himself from it.[15]

Decadent poetics also stimulated Michaux's interest in transcendence and the occult with Rimbaud embodying the figure of the poet-as-visionary. Of Rimbaud's influence on Michaux, Rigaud-Drayton writes, "Constructing the poet as a 'Seer,' like Rimbaud, [Michaux] conceived of poetry and painting as modalities of the visionary – and the unlapsed. Nature and its poetic, visionary language was to be found locked inside the self, as much as outside it."[16] Instead of turning outward towards the divine, Michaux's experiments invariably lead inward towards undiscovered visions. While there are important differences between Rimbaud's poetic visions and Michaux's mescaline experiments – the centrality of aesthetics for the former and the importance of objectivity for the latter – there are clear resonances between the two as well. Michaux's mystical explorations of the unknown recall Rimbaud's quest for insight by way of *le dérèglement de tous les sens*.[17]

Yet, Michaux refused to officially join the Surrealists, or any organized avant-garde collective of the period, preferring to undertake his experiments in a more individualistic mode.[18] Moreover, the mescaline writings are highly crafted texts, and thus far from Surrealist automatic writing or expressions of the revolutionary power of the avant-garde. In the forward to *Misérable miracle,* Michaux writes that the original text had to be rewritten from a hundred and fifty pages that were more tangible than legible.[19] In a nod to Baudelaire's explorations in *Les Paradis artificiels* (1860) at the end of the forward to this first work, Michaux stresses the immense cost of his experiments. He casts himself as a prisoner held hostage by his visions. Like Baudelaire's description of the effects of wine, hashish, and opium on the faculties of perception, Michaux would decry the potential for solipsism inherent in these altered states. Both Baudelaire and Michaux feared that the use of drugs represented a shortcut to revelation, and that what was revealed was only a distorted self-mirror, not a glimpse of the beyond. In a tone of modern disillusionment, however, he separates himself from Baudelaire in the epigraph to *Connaissance par les gouffres*; he would have drugs instruct rather than enchant: "Les drogues nous ennuient avec leur paradis. Qu'elles nous donnent plutôt un peu de savoir. Nous ne sommes pas un siècle à paradis."[20] [Drugs bore us with their paradises. Let them give us a little knowledge instead. Ours is not a century for paradise.]

By the time he started his own experiments, Michaux had also read Aldous Huxley's *The Doors of Perception* (1954), but felt that Huxley's approach was too moderate, both in the dosage of mescaline that Huxley was taking and in the level of self-alienation he was willing to risk.[21] His writings are also contemporaneous with Timothy Leary's infamous experiments at the Center for Personality Research at Harvard University in the early 1960s.[22] What distinguished Michaux from Huxley, Leary, and other experimenters of the period was his simultaneous commitment to the documenting his experience with lucidity and the aesthetic crafting of his project.

Whither the Self? Elusive Selfhood in Michaux

Before turning to mutative unselfing in Michaux's experiences with hallucinatory drugs, it is important to first establish Michaux's philosophy of selfhood under ordinary circumstances. Michaux pursued the escape of the self when faced with attempts to pin it down using language, ancestry, or literary influences as markers of the self. Though he was born in Namur, Belgium, Michaux emigrated to Paris in 1924, and would consistently seek to distance himself from his country of origin. He hated proper names, especially his own, for the way they conjure up a portrait of regional and familial banality.[23] His wide-reaching travels took him throughout the Americas, Asia, and Africa, which further contributed to his desire to shake off the misleading ties between nation, culture, and identity. One of his biographers writes of the warning signs that make anyone who attempts to record his life uneasy. "Not only has he always refused to entertain a facile relationship with his public, retreating behind the wall of imagination and slipping from the grasp in bristling metamorphoses, but he has never felt any solidarity with his own life."[24] Michaux entertained an aversion to public life and celebrity, refusing the French Grand Prix National des Lettres, and refusing to allow photographs of himself to circulate, or even biographical information to accompany his writings. Michaux's texts testify to the fear that he will "désolidarise" [break away] from his own autobiographical experiences.

Moreover, as a writer he often distances himself from the first-person narrators of his texts. The reader of Michaux's prolific and idiosyncratic oeuvre is struck by the slippery boundaries between truth and fiction. Through his travelogues, poetry, and stories, Michaux's first-person narrators constantly wonder about the constructed nature of reality itself. The absurd figures prominently in establishing this worry about the nature of reality. His writings on selfhood often evoke the divorce Camus once proclaimed between man and his life, the actor and his décor.[25] In Michaux's writing, the self is often described as an undifferentiated inner space without justification, identity, existential project, or even status in reality. Because of this, he and his narrators are often frustrated by the lack of ensemble in life, and the eternal documentation of the present.[26] Much like Monsieur Teste, who serves as a testing ground for Valéry's philosophy of the self, Michaux created a pen name character, appropriately called "Plume," who substantiates his ideas on consciousness and the self in writing. Plume is a pathetic character, who uses humour to deflect the menacing power and intimidation of others. Thus, before turning his attentions to the mind on mescaline, Michaux was already particularly attuned to the constructed nature of self-unification. He viewed disunified states of the self as more "natural" than what he calls ordinary states of "ego-dominion" in the mescaline texts.

Mutation as a "Major Ordeal of the Mind"

When he undertakes the project of documenting the mind on drugs, Michaux is most interested in the way it affects his perception of time and lived experience. The mescaline texts – *Misérable miracle* (*Miserable Miracle*) (1956), *L'Infini turbulent* (*Infinite Turbulence*) (1957), *Paix dans les brisements* (*Peace in the Breaking Flood*) (1959), *Connaissance par les gouffres* (*Knowledge through the Abyss*) (1961), and *Les grandes épreuves de l'esprit* (*The Major Ordeals of the Mind*) (1966) – represent a decade of efforts to plumb the realm beyond reality. During ordinary circumstances, the experiencing self is maintained artificially, in Michaux's vocabulary, by a minimal feeling of unification. The process of unselfing undoes the self's illusory power of unification, and with it the sense of being the agent of experience. Michaux seeks to relate the immediacy of his experiences; he often completed sketches and took notes while taking the drug. During altered states of selfhood, Michaux documents the phenomenology of the experience of unselfing and its effect on his experiencing self. He sceptically and provisionally constructs the narrative self within the context of his overarching desire to escape project, or what he understands as the aligning of the immediacy of the present with a trajectory or aspiration. "L'œuvre achevée, j'aurais peur qu'elle ne m'achève aussi et ne m'ensevelisse. S'en méfier."[27] [The work completed, I would be afraid that it would finish me off and bury me with it. Beware.] Michaux recasts these changes to his ordinary self-experience as productive if limited mutations; these small transformations occasion evolutions in the self but are never entirely finished or complete.

Understanding the effect of Michaux's experiments on his narrative self demands an attention to the crafting of the text; the construction of a narrative for self-experience occurs during the writing process and after the witness event. Michaux presents his experiments as productive mutations in his temporal and spatial self-experience, ones that help him flee from the artificial or constructed nature of reality. According to Michaux, the experiments lead to a mutation in the self that does not disappear once the substance has physically left his system. Coming down from the drug, he writes, "Au sortir de la Mescaline on sait mieux qu'aucun bouddhiste que tout n'est qu'apparence. Ce qui était avant, n'était qu'illusion de la santé. Ce qui a été pendant était illusion de la drogue. On est converti."[28] [Coming out of Mescaline you know better than any Buddhist that everything is nothing but appearance. What came before was only the illusion of health. What has just been was only the illusion of the drug. You are converted.][29]

Michaux's notion of the illusion of synchronic unity can be traced back to the influence of Eastern philosophy on his thinking and methods. François Trotet identifies Michaux's epistemological commitment to the apprehension of the "Reality of the Void" as the most significant marker of these influences; his work explores the nature of the void through the perception of physical reality, psychic reality, and spiritual reality.[30] Michaux stresses that disunity would be our natural mental state, if not for the illusion of the ego, which holds us under its tyrannical control. Drugs deliver a temporary reprieve from this illusion. He writes, "La drogue, qu'on s'en souvienne, est plus révélatrice que créatrice."[31] [The drug, let us remember, indicates, *reveals* more than it creates.][32] Of the return from one such mescaline trip he writes, "Maintenant revient le pragmatique, l'utile, l'adapté, l'harmonieux, revient l'ego, ses bornes, son autorité, son annexionnisme, son goût des propriétés, des prises, son plaisir de s'imposer, de faire tenir ensemble, de forcer coûte que coûte. Et cela paraît naturel!"[33] [Now the pragmatic returns, the useful, the adapted, the harmonious; the ego returns, with its limits, its authority, its annexationism, its possessiveness, its grasping, its delight in imposing, in amalgamating, in forcing at all costs. And it all seems natural!][34]

Moreover, the idea of "conversion" used above is not invoked in a canonical way. He does not become a new subject like Paul on the road to Damascus. Michaux does not indicate he is converted *to* a transcendent absolute, not even to the Buddhist doctrine that he references. Rather, he seems to mean there is no "going back" to one's former self once one has experienced the fragility of reality. Michaux's perspective is altered by these drug experiments. He writes, "une fois là, c'est comme un éclair dans une nuit sombre, tout illumination, mais c'est un éclair qui dure. Ce qui a précédé est oublié."[35] [once there, it is like lightning on a dark night, all illumination, but it is a lightning that lasts. What has preceded is forgotten.][36] On the theme of awakening to an experience of unity (l'Éveil) in Michaux, Trotet writes, "With the lucidity that characterizes his work, Michaux plunges into this dimension to the extreme point – the last region – where being awakens totally to itself."[37] Unselfing in Michaux's work is framed as a mutation; the momentary state of illumination yields knowledge that transforms the conscious self, making it impossible to return to its former shape.

Michaux's description of a terrifying overdose experience illustrates the difference between the effect of mutative unselfing on the experiencing self and experiences that annihilate it, wiping out consciousness entirely. Overdose does not lead to unselfing. Whereas his other accounts on mescaline chart the phenomenology of the altered state that he documents as an observer, the possibility of maintaining the witness position disappears when he accidentally overdoses on the drug. During his fourth mescaline experiment, which he describes in *Misérable miracle*, Michaux writes that the overdose experience causes him to fully "coincide" with himself. He writes, "Qu'avais-je fait? Plongeant, je m'étais rejoint, je crois en mon fond, et coïncidais avec moi, non plus observateur-voyeur, mais moi revenu à moi, et là-dessus en plein sur nous, le typhon."[38] [What had I done? Plunging, I had, I believe, rejoined myself in my depths and I now coincided with myself, no longer observer-voyeur, but myself reunited with myself – and with that, instantly the typhoon is upon us.][39] Overdose for Michaux is a cresting wave of self-sameness, which envelops him entirely. He has the sensation of drowning in a mescaline ocean, which pushes him down and further down, until there is no longer a margin between self and self-consciousness. This represents a different degree of self loss than Michaux had hitherto experienced; the overdose removes the methodological possibility of observation. In a footnote to this passage on the word "coincide," he writes, "Coïncider, qu'est-ce à dire? Dans ma vie j'essaie (voulant observer), d'approcher le plus possible de moi, mais sans coïncider, sans me laisser aller, sans me *donner*."[40] [To coincide, what does it mean? In life I try to approach as near to myself as possible (since I want to observe), without letting myself go, without *giving* myself.][41] During the overdose experiment he can no longer fulfil the witness-experimenter role. Michaux attempts to distance himself from recreational drug use with this caveat, and reminds us of an important feature of unselfing in the process: consciousness is never fully lost during unselfing experiences.

To return to the passage quoted in the epigraph to this chapter, Michaux represents the experience of unselfing as a change that illuminates a new inner expansion within the self. At the end of his last text on mescaline, Michaux responds to his inner sceptic by asserting the formal changes in the self that subsist. A "profoundly hollow depth" persists after the mescaline is gone and after the experiment is over. He writes,

Mais dira quelqu'un, ces mondes sans objet, au-delà d'un objet, amour sans objet, contemplation sans objet, n'est-ce pas de la fumée, dont il restera moins encore que de la fumée?

Une étendue nouvelle, un fond surcreusé, depuis en partie comblé, mais non annulé, subsiste après l'expérience et peut-être à jamais, non pas tout uniment non plus.[42]

But, someone will say, aren't these worlds without object, beyond an object, love without object, contemplation without object – aren't such worlds so much smoke, leaving behind even less than smoke?

A new expanse, a profoundly hollowed depth, which may afterward be partially filled, but not annulled, subsists after the experiment and perhaps forever, though not quite uniformly either.[43]

Michaux's response is cast in spatial terms here; "a new expanse" is opened up.[44] In other places in the text, he refers to this as "a zone" that is awakened for the first time. When he crafts a narrative for experience, unselfing for Michaux involves opening this new zone, the profoundly hollowed depth that was hitherto unavailable to consciousness.

What does Michaux mean above when he says that this expanse may be partially filled "but not annulled," that the depth persists but "not quite uniformly"? Despite their illuminating character, each of Michaux's hallucinatory visions involves a return to more ordinary (if transformed) state of consciousness. In other words, the unselfing experience here is not a full conversion from one complete self to another. Huston Smith writes of this transition from the state of psychedelic enlightenment to ordinary consciousness in an essay that first appeared in 1967: "What are the conditions that are needed for theophanies to take hold? The most important one is conviction, carrying over into the non-drug state, that the insights that emerge in the theophany are true ... Except in the tragic case of psychotics, however, this world eventually reasserts itself and its claims press hard upon us, which claims in our culture challenge the validity of pharmacological theophanies."[45] Michaux is wary of the epistemic implications of the return to the world, too. While the rare state that he reaches during the drug experiment may lead to valuable insight, he laments that it cannot be entirely maintained once the drugs are gone. Though the return to the ordinary state of agency ("ego-dominion" as Michaux would put it) is inevitable, he stresses that the expanse cannot be filled in, annulled, or otherwise voided.

Perhaps most importantly, however, Michaux notes that ego-dominion is more comfortable than the painful authenticity of illumination. Michaux compares his state of illumination to a mental "occupation." He writes, "Fini! Les heures de l'occupation sont passées. A présent il est seul en son cerveau. Admirable impression. Jouissance intime, de toutes peut-être la plus intime, si discrète pour être presque identique au 'moi' collant indissolublement à l'être en vie, et dont l'absence est une essentielle, indicible, incessante catastrophe."[46] [Finished! The hours of alien occupation are over. Now he is alone in his brain. A wonderful feeling.

Inner enjoyment of rights, perhaps the inmost of all, so private as to be virtually identical with the "self," clinging inseparably to the living being, and whose absence is a basic, inexpressible, unremitting catastrophe.][47]

Despite Michaux's insistence on the ephemeral and provisional nature of selfhood, this work suggests that even during extreme experiences of unselfing, someone is "there" to witness the unselfing event. A witness figure persists in order to resist total self-abandonment and to recount the experience upon his return. The witness position, made up of consciousness and ownership (features of the experiencing self), is never fully transcended during the disorienting experience of mutative unselfing. Rather, illuminated as if by lightning on a dark night, the structure of the self for Michaux is indelibly changed.

At certain moments in his mescaline texts, Michaux acknowledges his fears that there may be nothing objective to be gained from these voyages into the beyond, since the mind is suggestible. He worries that there is no absolute truth to be learned, that his current obsessions will be unduly elevated to providential visions.[48] Despite this lingering scepticism, however, Michaux does not relinquish his hope that altered states are privileged moments of self-awareness. In this sense, he attempts to both maintain his epistemic commitments as a scientific rationalist ("This book is an experiment," *Misérable Miracle* begins), while simultaneously attempting to cultivate an aesthetic experience of the sacred as the subject of his own experiment. What results is a vocabulary for communicating states of insight in an age of disillusionment. In the absence of an operative theological framework for visions into the unknown, Michaux attempts to keep track of the self that persists through altered states, while also noting its subtle evolutions. Given his understanding of the self as a witness figure living in an eternal succession of present moments, altered states of consciousness productively change his perception of time and space. Unselfing entails the mutation of this witness position.

Unselfing as a Pietà Mutation

Yolande Mukagasana, a nurse and survivor of the 1994 genocide against the Tutsi in Rwanda, recounts the encounter with the limits of conscious subjectivity as a mutation of the self in her 1997 book, *La mort ne veut pas de moi* (*Not My Time to Die*). Mukagasana's testimonial text was published at the very beginning of the insurgency (1997–2000) and just three years after the events described in the book. It is recognized as the first full-length testimony to be published by a Rwandan author.

Written with the assistance of Belgian journalist Patrick May, Muka-gasana recounts the death of her husband, Joseph, and her three chil-dren, Christian, Sandrine, and Nadine. While the temporal proximity of Mukagasana's first testimony to the described events and the framing of the narrative as an unembellished document should be understood as contributing to post-genocidal public discourses on justice and calls for national unity, the authorial voice of this original testimony is much less explicitly political than it is in her later accounts of the events.[49] *La mort ne veut pas de moi* recounts her experience of unselfing during otherworldly hallucinations as she flees the genocidal campaigns of the Interahamwe. In a short but powerful section of this work, Mukagas-ana describes the out-of-body hallucinations that she experiences while hiding from her attackers under a neighbour's kitchen sink. During this experience, she relays an account of the sensation of becoming the Vir-gin Mary and giving birth to her eldest child again, after her children's murder.

After the genocide, some Rwandans recorded their experiences by writing testimonies, though the primary vehicle for artistic and literary expression before 1994 was oral storytelling and poetry. Nicki Hitch-cott writes that Mukagasana was among the relatively high numbers of women who contributed to these immediate non-fiction accounts, which were followed by a male-dominated field of fiction.[50] Mukagas-ana's text also stands apart from the six high-profile fictional works produced as a result of the 2008 Fest'Africa inspired literary project, "Rwanda: Écrire par devoir de mémoire," in which mainly non-Rwandan African novelists were asked to write works of fiction to raise inter-national awareness about the genocide.[51] Unlike Charlotte Delbo, who frames her project of writing on Auschwitz as a literary one (chapter 3), Mukagasana stresses that her story is a work of testimony. Her text is first and foremost a document of lived experience, recounted stylisti-cally in a mix of dialogue and narration. Moreover, she emphasizes that she did not write the physical text herself, but rather recounted it to May, who then transcribed it for her. The *Avertissement au lecteur* reads: "Je suis une femme rwandaise. Je n'ai pas appris à déposer mes idées dans des livres. Je ne vis pas dans l'écrit. Je vis dans la parole. Mais j'ai rencontré un écrivain. Lui, racontera mon histoire."[52] [I am a Rwandan woman. I did not learn to leave my ideas in books. I do not live in the written word. I live in the spoken word. But I met a writer. He is the one who will tell my story.] This *Avertissement* is absent from the 2019 English translation, replaced by an Afterward in which Mukagasana stresses her authorial control over the manuscript. Zoe Norridge, the translator of the work describes the decision to cut the *Avertissement* in the note following the work: "Intriguingly, Yolande didn't identify with the note's account of a woman who lives in the spoken rather than the written word, nor did the idea that her only friend was her testimony still resonate. So she suggested cutting it out. She wrote the Afterward as a replacement, but one that we placed at the end rather than the beginning of the text so that her testimony takes center stage."[53]

At the time of the work's first publication, Mukagasana (and May) might have wanted to stress the non-literary nature of the text because of the charged nature of truth claims about genocidal conflicts and the threat of historical revisionism. In the Afterward to the English version, Mukagasana describes May's hesitancy at the beginning of their collaboration; May reportedly was advised to "be wary of Tutsi women, because they sometimes don't tell the truth."[54] As Hinton and O'Neil write, "The 'truth' of genocide, for example, often becomes a power-laden tool over which politicians, activists and the international community wrestle by asserting and contesting representations cobbled together from the often fragmented and clashing memories of survivors, perpetrators, witnesses, and bystanders."[55] A narrative that is presented as unadorned spoken truth ("Je ne vis pas dans l'écrit. Je vis dans la parole") is positioned to have more political purchase in the contested territory of international public discourse on genocide in Rwanda, particularly from women in this context.

Mukagasana published her second memoir, *N'aie pas peur de savoir* (*Don't Be Afraid to Know*) (1999) two years later, which takes aim at French complicity in the genocide. In the *Avertissement au lecteur* to this later work, Mukagasana accuses the French public of ignoring her original testimony. She writes, "Français, la France ne veut pas savoir. Mon premier livre sur le génocide rwandais, traduit en plusieurs langues, diffusé dans le monde entier, elle l'a boudé."[56] [The French, France does not want to know. My first book on the Rwandan genocide, which was translated into many languages and circulated around the entire world, France showed no interest in it.] From this accusation alone, it is clear that Mukagasana has assumed an authoritative voice that was absent from her first testimony. While May is listed as the collaborator of this second work and the author of the *Annexes*, there is no mention of him in the *Avertissement*. Although she begins with the caveat, "Je ne suis pas une intellectuelle et vous auriez beau jeu de me prendre à défaut avec des considérations politiciennes," [I am not an intellectual, and it would be all too easy for you to find me lacking in political considerations,] she concludes with a justification of her authoritative position: "Mais je connais ma souffrance. Je n'ai qu'une chose à vous dire: mes enfants sont morts et ce n'est pas sans cause. Lisez et jugez. Et que Dieu nous départage si nous ne trouvons pas le moyen de renouer le dialogue."[57] [But I know my suffering. I have but one thing to say to you: my children are dead, and not without cause. Read and judge. And may God be the judge if we cannot find a way to renew the dialogue.] Mukagasana would continue publishing on the 1994 genocide against the Tutsi; she collaborated on a controversial collection of photographs and testimonies that portrayed both victims and perpetrators with Alain Kazinierakis, *Les Blessures du silence* (*Wounds of Silence*, 2001), wrote a collection of stories, *De bouche à oreille* (*Word of Mouth*, 2003), and published a testimonial narrative on life after genocide, *L'Onu et le chagrin d'une négresse* (*The UN and a Negress's Shame*, 2014).[58]

In the last section of her second testimonial narrative, Mukagasana draws attention to the difference between the neutral testimonial voice that she used in the original volume, and her present engagement in politics in the name of justice. She describes her original collaboration with May in her first testimony, referring to him as "mon écrivain" [my writer]. Framing her recording of experience as a first step in her pursuit of justice, she writes, "J'ai raconté les souffrances et les humiliations que j'ai endurées. Maintenant, je passe à la vitesse supérieure. Je parle de justice. La justice! Parlons-en!"[59] [I recounted the sufferings and humiliations that I endured. Now I am shifting into a higher gear. I am talking about justice. Justice! Let's talk about it!] May assisted two other Tutsi survivors of the genocidal campaign in recording their stories; he wrote numerous articles and books on the genocide against the Tutsi and collaborated with Marie-Aimable Umurerwa on *Comme la langue entre les dents* (2000) and Pauline Kayitare on *Tu leur diras que tu es hutue* (2011).[60] Mukagasana's first document is the only text of this group that explicitly recounts the effect of violence on self-experience and the only text that recounts the experience of unselfing. Moreover, while *N'aie pas peur de savoir* references the eleven days that she spent hiding under her friend's sink, it leaves out the hallucinatory experience of unselfing that she details in the first. All references to taking on the position of the Virgin Mary, giving birth to her son a second time, and worries about losing her sense of sanity that will be discussed in the following pages are strikingly absent from Mukagasana's second memoir.

A comparative study of Michaux and Mukagasana demands careful attention to the differences between voluntary and involuntary unselfing and must acknowledge the obstacles to comparison at the outset.[61] One text deliberately travels inward, while the other propels outward: Michaux's writing project reflects the desire to plumb the depths of inner experience while Mukagasana seeks to bear witness to genocide in the context of international exile. Most importantly, Michaux details self-inflicted experiments while Mukagasana testifies to her unwilling suffering. And yet, both use the French language to capture the self at the fringes of conscious experience; both understand the relationship between experience, documentation, and its written expression as ongoing and never finished. Like Michaux, Mukagasana's testimonial text presents a subject whose self is mutated; it is reordered according to the logic that ensues from her hallucinatory visions. Mukagasana's description of the violent unmooring of the self is invaluable to understanding the full spectrum of unselfing experiences. Her writing project, which is motivated primarily by political rather than aesthetic objectives, demonstrates that the phenomenological framework extends beyond solipsistic discussions of subjectivity. Mukagasana's account of mutative unselfing presents the lifeworld of a person under extreme duress, which has had lasting consequences on the reception of her experience in the global French world.[62]

Mukagasana describes the loss of self-unity felt at the moment of the experience, and later gives shape to unselfing while constructing a long-term self-narrative. In chapter 11 of *La mort ne veut pas de moi*, just after she describes fleeing her home and taking refuge in churches and the homes of her neighbours after six weeks on the run, Mukagasana relates the effect of this experience of attention on her experiencing self. From the cramped space under a sink where she would remain for over a week, Mukagasana describes the strange and impossible sensation of giving birth to her eldest son again. This leads to an altered state of consciousness that Mukagasana describe as madness. She recounts the sensation of the unravelling of her agency; she wonders if she is losing her mind, fearing that she is becoming like her aunt who has lost all touch with reality since the beginning of the killings.

At the beginning of this passage, Mukagasana introduces and rationalizes her hallucinatory experience with a description of the physical sensations of her body. "Peut-être parce que ma position est inconfortable, je sens une espèce de déchirure dans le ventre. C'est comme si j'allais accoucher … je me mets avec obsession à me remémorer mon premier accouchement."[63] [Perhaps because I am in such an uncomfortable position, I feel a tearing in my stomach, as if I'm in labor … I set out obsessively to remember his birth.][64] She continues, describing obsessively looking back on this memory of labour and letting it remove her from the material world despite the dangers of getting caught. The present tearing sensation of her stomach becomes connected to her memory of giving birth. Mukagasana relates a detachment from the world and wants to scream that she capable of miracles: of giving birth to the same child twice, of defying death.[65] As the anguish of physical suffering is compounded with the memory of past pain, she transforms this suffering into the impossible maternal power to bring the same child into the world a second time.

Mukagasana's temporal shifts in this chapter of the text lift the narrative subject out of time. Three distinct time frames become confused: the narrative present/temporal past (hiding under the sink), the distant past (the memory of giving birth), and the narrative future/temporal present (the delivery of her story). While the past and present are assimilated in Mukagasana's depiction of altered self-experience, the representation of the future demonstrates the fundamental mutation of her perspective. The composite parts of the self are reordered in this episode, and a newly vigilant *justicière* emerges from the pain of the foetal position.

Mukagasana's perspective is altered as the distant past encroaches on the present as an escape from acute violence. While this transformation from crouching and hiding to birthing involves a sense of empowerment, Mukagasana asserts that this birth is a sinister one, twisted by the circumstances of genocide outside the imaginary world. Of this long and painful labour, she writes, "Mon fils ne montre aucune envie de venir voir comment est le monde, tout comme moi, courbaturée, entortillée, recroquevillée sous mon cher évier, je n'ai plus envie d'aller voir comment est le Rwanda."[66] [My son shows no desire to come out and see the world, just as I, aching, contorted, curled up under my dear sink, have no desire to leave and see what Rwanda is up to.][67] The past (the birth of her son) is crushed into present (the space under the sink), becoming shrivelled and twisted in the process. The ensuing birthing scene is thus an amalgam of the three temporalities, the site of a consciousness torn in multiple directions.

However, Mukagasana mobilizes her position as the witness figure to look towards future relief from the present pain she is suffering. Her temperament is shifted by the experience of unselfing as she becomes a zealous *justicière*. She vows to herself that someday she will write this down:

Que ceux qui n'auront pas la force de lire cela, que j'écrirai peut-être un jour, me dis-je, se dénoncent comme complices du génocide rwandais. Moi, Yolande Mukagasana, je déclare à la face de l'humanité que quiconque ne veut pas prendre connaissance du calvaire du peuple rwandais est complice des bourreaux. Le monde ne renoncera à être violent que lorsqu'il acceptera d'étudier son besoin de violence. Je ne veux ni terrifier ni apitoyer. Je veux témoigner.[68]

May those who do not have the strength to read it denounce themselves as complicit in the genocide against the Tutsi in Rwanda. I, Yolande Mukagasana, declare before humanity that whoever doesn't want to know about the ordeal of the Rwandan people shares in the guilt of the perpetrators. The world will not cease to be violent if it doesn't examine its need for violence. I will write this not to scare you or make you feel sorry for me. I want to bear witness.[69]

As in the case of Michaux, the language of testimony ("je veux témoigner") serves as the driving force for reconstruction of a unified perspective after the witness event. The entrance of the future tense ("j'écrirai un jour") into the narrative marks the mutation of the self; it is in reference to this planned recounting of her experience in the imagined future that Mukagasana is able to restate emphatically her subject identity ("Moi, Yolande Mukagasana"). Though the self is altered dramatically in the rebirth experience under the sink, it is ultimately reclaimed in the name of bearing witness to the injustice she suffers. Mukagasana understands unselfing to involve a return to a state of self-unification in her invocation of the future.

Mukagasana links the imagery of the Virgin Mary with her position as a witness and thereby gives new shape to her narrative self. As she looks towards the future and reconstructs herself as a figure of female resistance using the narrative of the Virgin Mary, she reconstructs her own experience of unselfing as a saintly mutation. For Mukagasana, understanding unselfing according to the model of ultimate maternal suffering further contributes to her eventual sense of self-reconstruction and political resistance. This reorienting of inner distress towards the suffering of others is what Catherine Gilbert (after the psychologists Ervin Staub and Johanna Vollhardt) has called a form of "altruism born of suffering" wherein those who have suffered extreme violence mobilize their personal experiences in order to mitigate the pain of others.[70] Mukagasana both documents her hallucinatory experience of becoming a Marian figure, and uses that transformation to explain her turn to the needs and suffering of others.

Marian imagery and iconography were omnipresent in late twentieth-century Rwanda and continue to be particularly salient in the Rwandan public imaginary. From the colonial period onward, Rwanda was considered "one of the most Catholic societies in Africa."[71] Justin Kalibwami writes that while Catholicism was imported as a colonial religion, it quickly took on a Rwandan specificity. He writes, "It is said that Rwandan Catholicism benefited from the support of the European colonial regimes (German, then Belgian); but its success was not limited to being accepted, founding solid institutions or on counting an important number of followers. After a relatively short time, it became practically a Rwandan religion."[72]

Moreover, the Virgin Mary occupied a privileged position in Rwanda after November 28, 1981, the first reported apparition by Alphonsine Mumureke at the College of Kibeho, Diocese of Butare. After two other students reportedly saw visions of the Virgin Mary from the same middle school in Kibeho in February and March of 1982, twenty thousand people completed the pilgrimage to Kibeho to witness the Marian apparitions by August of the same year.[73] By 1993, a provisional chapel (*dortoir des apparitions*) was built on the site. The Kibeho parish would later serve as "le théâtre d'un horrible génocide tutsi" [the theater of a horrible Tutsi genocide] in 1994, and would see the massacre of war refugees on "l'esplanade des apparitions" in April of 1995.[74] The Virgin Mary retained a privileged status throughout this period. Whereas the Bishop of Gikongoro would officially recognize the three original Marian apparitions in 2001, the visions of Jesus Christ, reported seven months after the Marian ones, were not recognized by the Catholic Church.[75] The authors of the chapel's pamphlet underscore the following: "To our knowledge, the Kibeho apparitions are the very first in Sub-Saharan Africa to be solemnly recognized by the Roman Catholic Church."[76]

Mukagasana is certainly not alone in turning to the Virgin Mary as an intercessor in seeking release from painful experience. However, her particular usage of the Marian figure in shaping her unselfing narrative of the experience is unique and unusual when considered within the three texts that Patrick May co-authored.[77] Mukagasana uses the *pietà* to understand her experience, substituting the death of her three children for the death of Christ. She writes, "J'ai l'impression d'être une de ces *pietà* vues dans les livres de religion, mais qui aurait eu trois enfants de douleur."[78] [I remember pictures of the Virgin Mary with her suffering son. I have not one but three children in pain.][79] This image of simultaneous joy-in-suffering continues to shape Mukagasana's experience as unselfing upsets former boundaries between elation and despair, sanity and madness, and reality and fantasy. In the passage where she recounts hiding under the neighbour's sink, Mukagasana writes, "Je suis ivre de bonheur et de tristesse en même temps. Mon bonheur est viscéral, je suis si triste que j'ai l'impression que je vais éprouver un orgasme de tristesse."[80] [I listen to them complacently, drunk with joy and grief intertwined. My happiness is visceral, I'm so sad I feel like I'm about to have an orgasm of sorrow.][81] This experience of rebirth exceeds ordinary categories of perception, overwhelming her in the moment with both joy and misery.

Mukagasana meditates on the transformative image of the *pietà* and mutates into this figure in order to mitigate the heights of her extreme grief. She describes the hallucination of the rebirth of her son: "Je crois reconnaître le premier cri de mon fils. Je suis heureuse. Je viens d'accoucher pour la seconde fois de mon enfant. Je suis devenue folle. Je pleure et je ris en même temps. Joseph se penche vers moi, m'embrasse avec ferveur. Mais non, c'est la cuvette de l'évier contre laquelle est collée ma joue."[82] [I think I recognize the first cry of my son and I'm happy; I've given birth to my child for a second time. I've gone mad. I cry and I laugh at the same time, in silence. Joseph bends over me, kisses me with passion. But no, it's the sink pressing against my cheek.][83] In this altered state, she mistakes the sink for Joseph, Mary's husband. This detail emphasizes the extent to which Mukagasana pursues the structure and content of the Marian narrative. More than a passing analogy, the saintly model shapes Mukagasana's experience of suffering as it allows her to embody the Marian position: "Dans ce monde imaginaire où je viens de m'élever comme une Vierge en assomption, il n'y a qu'une femme qui met au monde un bel enfant."[84] [In this world, where I've just risen like the Virgin Mary at the Assumption, there's only a woman bringing forth a beautiful child, a child who no more wants to be born than he wants to die today.][85] Mukagasana reconstitutes her theory of selfhood to account for the otherworldly experience of her hallucination.

This mutation of her ordinary self-experience according to Marian iconography serves to alleviate Mukagasana's suffering and provides the impetus for the reconstruction of the narrative self. Unlike Delbo's narrative of the caravan discussed in chapter 3, Mukagasana represents her imaginative imagery as successful in providing temporary relief from psychological anguish, at least in this account of the events. Mukagasana links this saintly model of suffering to the act of witnessing in her long-term narrative of selfhood. It is the act of recounting, of putting words to suffering, that provides the link between before and after for the witness. At the end of *La mort ne veut pas de moi*, Mukagasana writes, "Ma vie avant le génocide, c'est un peu comme *une vie antérieure*. Il n'y avait plus dans ma tête que le génocide. J'oubliais tout sauf le génocide. Mes souvenirs étaient en morceaux, que je ne parvenais pas à rassembler. Lorsque j'ai pu raconter mon cauchemar, la vie d'avant est revenue."[86] [My life before the genocide is a different, distinct life. There's nothing left in my mind apart from the genocide. I've forgotten everything except the genocide. My memories were fragments that I couldn't piece back together. It was only when I was able to recount my nightmare that memories from before returned.][87] Life returns with the re-linking of before and after in a coherent narrative, an affirmation of the survival of the witness throughout the violent suffering of unselfing, a process of narration that is never fully finished.

And yet, this episode is conspicuously absent from Mukagasana's 1999 account of her experience in *N'aie pas peur de savoir*. The revision of the events between texts might tell us more about the political climate in Rwanda during this period than the experience of unselfing.[88] The absence of the formative episode can perhaps be explained by the widespread backlash against the Catholic Church in Rwanda in the aftermath of the genocide against the Tutsi, not only for its failure to oppose the massacres, but also for actively contributing to the violence.[89] Unlike the genocide of the Jews in Europe during World War II, religious identity did not serve to mark the Tutsi as other; the genocide occurred within religious groups with church parishes killing fellow parishioners and in some cases their own pastor or priest.[90] Scholars have since debated the precise role that Christianity and the Christian church played in orchestrating or failing to stop the genocide. But the connection is clear for Mukagasana. In her second memoir, she explicitly mentions the individual clergyman who contacted her before the publication of her first book in 1997 in attempts to dissuade her from writing about her experiences:

> Et pourquoi ne veut-on pas que j'écrive sur le Rwanda? Parce que le rôle de l'Église catholique n'est pas des plus propres dans le génocide. Combien de prêtres ont-ils trahi et laissé tuer les Tutsi, parfois tué eux-mêmes? Ils sont en liberté, aujourd'hui, protégés dans des couvents. Il y en a en Belgique, en France, en Suisse.[91]

> And why don't they want me to write about Rwanda? Because the role of the Catholic Church is not one of the cleanest in the genocide. How many priests betrayed and let Tutsis be killed, sometimes killed themselves? They are free today, protected in convents. There are some in Belgium, in France, in Switzerland.

This passage leads directly into a long denunciation of the role that the French and Belgian military played in facilitating the genocide against the Tutsi. Mukagasana reflects on the scene under the sink, marking it as a formative event, but omits the Marian transformation. Upon being urged to write down her story for the first time by a friend, Mukagasana thinks back to the episode under the sink. She writes, "Écrire mon histoire? Oui, j'y pense depuis longtemps. Depuis que j'ai écrit ma lettre à Lise, de Bujumbura. Non, depuis que j'étais sous l'évier, chez Emmanuelle."[92] [Write down my story? Yes, I've been thinking about it for a long time. Ever since I wrote my letter to Lise, from Bujumbura. No, ever since I was under the sink, at Emmanuelle's house.] The formative moment of unselfing under the sink remains in the later work, if only through this trace.

Je est un autre: Mutation and Others

Both Michaux and Mukagasana envision the approach to the other as one that starts with self-experience. The former seems to get lost in the folds of inner self-strangeness, while the latter deliberately uses unselfing to move outward towards the fate of unfamiliar (and even murderous) others. Mukagasana's account embodies a theory of altruistic unselfing, wherein the anguished self is exposed, through painful witnessing, to the needs of others. She is ultimately transformed into a justice-seeking activist, while Michaux's mutative unselfing instead ensnares him in an inner labyrinth of the self. One of the central results of Michaux's mescaline experiments is the experience of the self-as-other. This recalls Rimbaud's formulation that *je est un autre*, which evokes the need for the derangement of the senses in order to access the unknown depths of the self.[93] In his last mescaline text, *Les grandes épreuves de l'esprit*, Michaux is disturbed by the experience of hearing another's voice as his own. He writes, "Une autre voix que la mienne se pousse dans ma voix, en traître. Je m'arrête. Étrange. Freinant. Décourageant. Avec un mot, qui n'était pas de moi, une voix, étrangère aussi, a voulu intervenir."[94] [Another voice than mine makes its way into my voice, a traitor. I stop. Strange. Dismaying. Discouraging. With a word, which was not mine, a voice, also alien, has tried to intervene.][95] A stranger's voice is described as intruding upon the sovereignty of the experiencing self. Throughout the mescaline texts, Michaux stresses his position as the witness figure whose autonomy and authority is never fully lost despite the incorporation of new self-knowledge. In this example, however, he describes the alienating sensation of another's voice pushing through his throat and is disturbed to feel the boundaries between self and other start to erode.

This guttural experience of otherness later becomes a marker for unselfing in the context of André Malraux's autobiographical essay, *Lazare* (1974). Malraux describes a strikingly similar experience of a stranger's voice pushing through his throat in his description of his near-death experience in a hospital in 1940. In this text, Malraux writes of what he calls the *je-sans-moi* experience. During his semi-conscious state, Malraux mediates on the Russian front, and writes that the *je-sans-moi* leads to a radical feeling of communion among soldiers during war.

> Les hommes entendent toujours leur voix avec la gorge, et celle des autres avec les oreilles. Si nous entendions soudain une autre voix que la nôtre avec la gorge, nous serions terrifiés. J'avais écrit que tout homme entend *sa vie* avec la gorge, celle des autres, avec les oreilles, sauf dans la fraternité ou l'amour.[96]

> Men always hear their voice through their throat and those of others through their ears. If all of a sudden we did hear a voice other than our own through our throat, we would be terrified. I had once written that every man hears *his life* with the throat, the life of others through the ears, except in fraternity or love.

Unlike Michaux, Malraux moves quickly from the phenomenology of the experience to the interpretation of the experience, using the sensation of unselfing as evidence of humanism; the life of others is ordinarily experienced through the ears except in deep intimacy. This leads Malraux to assert that unselfing in the context of war is invaluable in that it is life-affirming. It effectively creates a shared feeling of communion among those who suffer together. Malraux's description of the *je-sans-moi* experience would later inspire Jean-François Lyotard to theorize *stridence,* or the sound-feeling of one's own voice heard through the throat (as opposed to the voice of others, which one hears through the ears). Lyotard writes that the abyss between "moi et je-sans-moi" [the ego and the I-without-the-ego] is unsurpassable by outer others – except during experiences of love (as Malraux already asserted) or, Lyotard adds, dread.[97] It is only through these extreme experiences that the boundary between self and other can be transgressed.

Unselfing, as theorized by Malraux and later Lyotard, pushes the individual into charged relationships with others that can yield a profound and extreme experience of collective subjectivity. But for Michaux, unselfing has no such collective power. Indeed, at one point, Michaux goes as far to say that his experiments are of little use for relations with others, because they are incommunicable.[98] At the same time, he insists that the derangement of the senses is not about solipsistic escapism. He insists that proper self-experimentation demands a commitment to mental control throughout the process. In a long and tortured footnote, Michaux offers the following reflection:

> Que ceux qui prennent des produits pour s'adonner aux excitations collectives, trépignements, danses hystériques, bagarres ou viols, s'arrêtent

et ne se mettent pas à croire qu'il y a quelque chose ici pour eux. On ne parle pas la même langue. On ne va pas aux mêmes effets. Celui qui est incapable de retenir les actes, incapable de garder tout *dans le mental* est complètement à côté.

Le psychique contemplateur est "retranché."[99]

Those who take drugs in order to surrender themselves to collective release and emotional abandon need not read further. There is nothing here that is meant for them. We do not speak the same language. We do not look for the same effects. He who is incapable of keeping his actions under control, incapable of confining everything to the *mind*, has missed the point completely.

The observer of psychic occurrences has to be "entrenched."[100]

This passage illustrates Michaux's commitment to retaining a sense of rationality and control though the experiments. His commitment to "entrenchment" contributes to the production of a literary genre that might be capable of communicating the special knowledge that drug experiments afford. Throughout the mescaline texts, Michaux comments in the margins, adding footnotes and addressing the reader directly. In the text, he speaks as the experimental subject, and in the margins as the experimenter, never fully engaging with his passing observation on the uselessness of the experiments for relations with the world. In this sense, Michaux's ethics appear Zhuangzian. Xiaofan Amy Li argues that Michaux's ethics reflect the *Zhuangzi*'s view that ethics is cosmic rather than social; Michaux's central preoccupation seems to be integrating with the universe rather than acting as an individual agent. "Michaux values indifference because it retains him, as a locus of sensations, to the primordial experience of *un*differentiatedly existing in the world."[101]

Others appear as synecdochical in Michaux's mescaline texts; they flicker into consciousness in the form of hands, echoes, shadows. The flimsiness of others complicates his attempts to justify his drug experiments with the claim that they are not motivated by the escape from reality. While Malraux moves quickly from documentation to interpretation of the experience in his attempt to rescue Western consciousness from despair, Michaux's interpretation of unselfing remains much more ambivalent. The experience of the self-as-other, of another's voice pushing through his own throat, does not push Michaux towards connections with the outer world, as it does for Malraux. Although he engages with new inner expanses of the self, outer sources of otherness are but shadows in the mescaline texts. Michaux remains entrenched in the changing contours of his own mind.

Mukagasana shares Michaux's sense that the experience of unselfing is one that exposes the inner foreignness of the self. Like Michaux, she writes of the strange guttural nature of her experience of extreme otherness, referencing an inner humming as well as an oesophageal dread in *La mort ne veut pas de moi*. Describing her confinement under the sink, she writes, "Il y a en moi comme un détachement de ce monde. Tels ces saints qui sourient vers le ciel en se faisant trucider et que les missionnaires montraient à l'école sur des images pieuses aux teintes pastel, je chantonne intérieurement en me rappelant la naissance de mon fils."[102] [I feel myself detaching from this world, like the saints who smile up at the sky while being killed; those saints depicted in the pious pastel-colored pictures the missionaries showed us at school. I sing inside as I remember my son's arrival.][103] Mukagasana's astonishing response to extreme violence – "joy-in-suffering" – provokes this inner hum. She describes silently vomiting bile as she hears the men who are hunting her threaten to chain her to a tree and amputate her children before her eyes: "Je sens remonter quelque chose dans mon œsophage. C'est de la bile que je vomis en silence, elle coule sur ma joue puis dans mon cou."[104] [Bile rises and I vomit in silence, it runs down my cheek and my neck.][105]

Mukagasana represents the mutation of ordinary self-experience as leading automatically towards a heightened consciousness of others. From the position of a mother who has lost her children, she embraces the position of the suffering Mary. Mukagasana embraces the Marian narrative in both her reflections on the relationship between the experience of prolonged psychological distress and her sense of self, and later in her approach to the other. Directly after the passage where she describes vomiting bile out of extreme dread, she unexpectedly experiences pity for the individual men before her. Mukagasana extends care towards her aggressors – men who have just described their desire to torture her and her children – and condemns instead the international community for its failure to intervene. She declares that those who do not want to recognize the ordeal of the Rwandan people are complicit with the persecutors.[106]

Whereas Michaux seems to dissolve into the murky waters of inner experience, Mukagasana propels herself outward towards political contestation and a life of engagement. She adopts an increasingly global perspective when considering the personal violence she suffered, using her testimony as a conscience-raising tool for the international community. Repeatedly referring to herself as a "wounded mother" or a "mother who has lost her children," this mutation pushes her to enter into the realm of politics. She writes emphatically, "Je ne fais pas de politique.

C'est la mère meurtrie en moi qui m'oblige à emprunter aux politiciens leurs armes pour les retourner contre eux."[107] [I am not playing politics. It's the murdered mother in me that forces me to borrow the politicians' weapons and turn them back at them.] Gilbert writes, "For Mukagasana in particular, this 'survivor mission' is an ongoing duty in her life … It is therefore her duty both to help those in need and prevent the perpetuation of further violence."[108] Mukagasana considers what she calls paradox of the Christian West and her hatred of Western intellectuals who are moved by the suffering of Christ on the cross but not the reality of thousands of Rwandans. She writes, "Combien seraient capables de dire ce que je me sens capable de proférer aujourd'hui sous mon évier: il faut leur pardonner, car ils ne savent pas ce qu'ils font? C'est la seule phrase qui me reste ce matin de toute mon éducation chrétienne."[109] [How many of them would be capable of saying what I utter now, under this sink: forgive them, for they know not what they do? That's the only phrase that remains from all my Christian education.][110]

When examined together, Michaux's and Mukagasana's mutation narratives demonstrate the range of intersubjective experiences that ensue from a change in the experience being a self. Michaux's mutations invoke the integration of new knowledge into the self as a "lightning that lasts." While these experiments may be of little use for being with others, they bolster the status of the witness, the one who is there throughout the entirety of experience. Mukagasana's mutative unselfing represents a reorientation towards an expanding sphere of others. Whereas Michaux seeks to underline the authenticity of his experiments by avoiding its interpretation, Mukagasana's community consciousness becomes the very driver for documentation itself.

5 Unselfing as Fragmentation: Languages of Alterity in Abdelkebir Khatibi and Hélène Cixous

A thought that is not *minoritarian, marginal, fragmentary, and incomplete* is always a thought of ethnocide.

Abdelkebir Khatibi

The oldest of my oldest Algerian memories about the Plan to annihilate the Algerian being is a tale of a girl who gets cut in two.

Hélène Cixous

Fragmentation tears the self asunder. Its wholeness is divided as the self is broken into doubles, pieces, portions, or personas. This chapter explores the work of two Francophone contemporaries who develop the fragmentation model for unselfing: Abdelkebir Khatibi (1938–2009) and Hélène Cixous (1937–). Both Khatibi and Cixous contribute to the literature of altered states by writing on the dissolving boundaries of the self in love and in desire, the relationship between the human and the sacred, and self-estrangement stemming from the effects of French colonial rule in North Africa. This chapter offers new readings of these authors' contributions to the discourse on altered selves and the other in two works in particular: Khatibi's *Amour bilingue* (*Love in Two Languages*) (1983) and Cixous's *Les rêveries de la femme sauvage* (*Reveries of the Wild Woman*) (2000). The first text stages the consciousness of bilingualism as a ludic meditation on perspective and desire, while the second relates painful memories of childhood to tell the story of self-separation. Cixous and Khatibi use the narrative of fragmentation to tell the stories of unselfing in surprisingly divergent ways. On the one hand, Khatibi's *Amour bilingue* dwells in the pleasure of losing a sense of unified selfhood, as it allows for the rethinking not only of inner alterity in the sense of synchronic division, but also of alterity in the sense of intersubjective relationships. On the other hand, while Cixous celebrated the pleasures of synchronic self-division in her early writings, she interprets self-fragmentation in this later autobiographical text as a series of painful experiences. Khatibi celebrates the subversive potential of an ethics grounded in the splitting of the self while Cixous laments the *coupures* that result from inner division.

What might it mean to feel the wholeness of the self break into separate pieces, or to suddenly experience a sense of its composite nature? A short introduction to the development of the notion of split selves in psychology and philosophy is apposite here. Despite the celebration of the escape from the unified self by writers such as De Quincey and Baudelaire, the "split personality" has long been pathologized.[1] French psychologists at the turn of the century made a case for the scientific nature of fragmentation against the Kantian transcendentalist model, which was inherited by the German idealists. Along with others like Pierre Janet, Alfred Binet argued against the metaphysical single-self view in favour of a multiple-self model, citing Hippolyte Taine and Théodule-Armand Ribot in his justification for this psychological turn.[2] In *Les altérations de la personnalité* (*Alterations of Personality*) (1892), Binet quotes Taine's *De l'intelligence* (*On Intelligence*) in a passage on a dissociative patient with no conscious memory of what she has written on the page: "Certainement on constate ici un dédoublement du moi, la présence simultanée de deux séries parallèles et indépendantes, de deux centres d'action ou, si l'on veut, de deux personnes morales juxtaposées dans le même cerveau; chacune a une œuvre, et une œuvre différente, l'une sur la scène, l'autre dans la coulisse."[3] [We certainly find here a dual ego, the simultaneous presence of two parallel and independent series, of two centres of action, or, if you will, two moral persons side by side in the same brain, each having its work and each a different work – one on the stage and the other behind the scenes.][4] The term *dédoublement* is another way of indicating split or fissure, here into two sites of consciousness. Binet takes this idea of *dédoublement* as his starting point for a chapter on what he calls "simultaneous double consciousness," writing that he will undertake a study of the curious psychological situation of doubling.[5] While it seems to be theoretically possible to have a double self in this account, the person who is doubled has no conscious knowledge of it.

Freud's work on war neuroses offered a different interpretive model for theorizing the fragmentation of self-experience in the wake of World War I. In *Beyond the Pleasure Principle* (1920), Freud theorizes a split in the victim's conscious personality; the war neurosis is a subtype of traumatic neurosis, and its onset is a product of fright, or lack of preparation for a flooding of unbound stimuli and conflict.[6] Freud observes that victims of these traumatic neuroses were capable of interior monologues, which he saw as a threat to the stability of the ego. It is this fear of an enemy within (a nefarious fragment of the self) that distinguishes war neuroses from other traumatic neuroses. This work offered a model for the way psychoanalysts explained the "split" in their patients' personalities in the context of PTSD and beyond.[7]

Freudian psychoanalysis would be influential on both Khatibi's and Cixous's understanding of the splitting of the self. In his essay, "Frontiers between Psychoanalysis and Islam," Khatibi seeks to sketch out this space, focusing in particular on Freud's analysis of Islam as an "abbreviated repetition" of Judaism, which Khatibi interprets as a turn away from unifying theories of origin, name, and self.[8] Moreover, in her plays, essays, and novels, Cixous engages in a close intertextual relationship with Freud's writings on self-fragmentation and interrogates the relationship between psychoanalysis and literature.[9] By 2000 when she publishes Rêveries, this complex relationship with Freud is most apparent in her focus on dreams and "primal scenes." While Freud's account of synchronic division is perhaps the best-known, his model relies on the patient/observer distinction to bring the hidden frictions between these fragments to light.

The question of the splitting of the self also plays a major role in the decolonial philosophy of Frantz Fanon. Fanonian phenomenology unites discourses on psychopathology and inner division with social analysis of existential postcolonial situations, particularly anti-Black racism. Fragmentation, framed as double consciousness in the context of the postcolonial subjectivity, comes to evoke the process of racialization under colonial rule. Paget Henry writes, "In Fanon's view, internalizing the colonial experience divided the Afro-Caribbean psyche, leaving it with a Duboisian 'double consciousness' of itself."[10] In Peau noir, masques blancs (Black Skin, White Masks) (1952), Fanon argues that settler colonialism superimposes one psychological reality onto another, which the colonial subject experiences as a psychic doubling. The Black man is torn between two systems of reference (African/European) and experiences the perpetual and inescapable experience of seeing himself through his own eyes and through the eyes of the white man, who only sees one reality. Fanon writes that the Black man must thus not only be (Black), but be (Black) in relation to whiteness:

Le Noir n'a pas de résistance ontologique aux yeux du Blanc. Les nègres, du jour au lendemain ont eu deux systèmes de référence par rapport

auxquels il leur a fallu se situer. Leur métaphysique, ou moins préten-
tieusement leurs coutumes et les instances auxquelles elles renvoyaient,
étaient abolies parce qu'elles se trouvaient en contradiction avec une civi-
lisation qu'ils ignoraient et qui leur en imposait.[11]

The Black man has no ontological resistance in the eyes of the white man.
From one day to the next, the Blacks have had to deal with two systems of
reference. Their metaphysics, or less pretentiously their customs and the
agencies to which they refer, were abolished because they were in contradiction with a new civilization that imposed its own.[12]

The doubling of the self in Fanon refers not only to what Binet via Taine
calls multiple "centres of action" but also the doubling of cultures and
customs, and, most importantly, doubling of "systems of reference." In
Fanon's account, the white subject only has to manage one perspective,
whereas the process of racialization leaves two that remain in contradiction with one another, and eventually lead to existential despair. In
Les damnés de la terre (Wretched of the Earth) (1961), Fanon calls for the
decolonization of the mind through the national liberation struggle that
entails both the rejection of the racialization of thought according to the
colonial imaginary and a rejection of the assimilation of the occupant's
culture.[13] This can only happen through the ending of European influence in the Maghreb. The European game is finished, "il faut trouver
autre chose" [we must find something else].[14]

Khatibi's and Cixous's texts enter into these disparate interdisciplinary discourses on the question of self-doubling in two separate (if
imbricated) moments of postcolonial theorizing in the Francophone
world. At the time of Amour bilingue's publication, Khatibi was focused
on reframing the search for "autre chose," to quote Fanon in the way
that Khatibi does at the beginning of Le Maghreb pluriel, which appeared
in the same year as Amour bilingue (1983). Like Fanon, Khatibi seeks to
free the Maghreb from the clutches European influence in this search for
"something different," but he enacts this in the form of a double critique
of both imperial discourse and the totalizing discourse that the Arab
world has produced about itself.[15] Both Khatibi and Cixous play with
the boundaries of genre, relying on the freedom that they find on offer
in creative non-fiction rather than realist testimony in their evocation
of the shifting sands of the self. This is a strategy sometimes associated
with women's life writing, especially in the desire to escape the unified
rational "I" at the heart of the autobiographical tradition.[16]

In these contexts, the notion of différance (particularly the division
that characterizes self-consciousness) offered the promise of the escape

from the reduction of identity to hopeless binaries and made possible a critique of culture as a monolith.[17] Khatibi and Cixous each engaged in long relationships and philosophical correspondences with Derrida, mutually influencing each other's theories on selfhood and otherness.[18] And while Robert C. Young argues that poststructuralism emerges as a response to the Algerian war, thereby uniting the aims of poststructuralism and postcolonial theory, the 1990s and 2000s marked a thematic return to the Maghreb in the writing of Derrida and Cixous.[19] Moreover, in 2008, Éditions de la Différance published the collected works of Khatibi with an introductory inscription text from Derrida. Though the intersections between the three writers are labyrinthine, perhaps the most resounding confluence lies in the sense that the boundary between literature and philosophy is elided in both Khatibi's and Cixous's work. Self-writing becomes a theory of consciousness for both Khatibi and Cixous, according to Derrida. He introduced Khatibi's writing as "à la fois une immense invention poétique et une puissante réflexion théorique" [both an immense poetic invention and a strong theoretical reflection] and once celebrated Cixous's trademark and paradoxical "hyperréalisme fictionnel" [fictional hyperrealism].[20] My chapter makes a new contribution to the extensive scholarly interventions on fragmentation in Khatibi and Cixous by focusing on the relationship between fragmented consciousness and phenomenological self experiences, rather than on the major investments of poststructuralist/postcolonial critique that have already been amply discussed elsewhere.

The next section explores fragmentary unselfing in Khatibi's work. Thinking about the loss of the unified *perspective* of the experiencing self as productive self-fragmentation allows Khatibi to rehabilitate the notion of plural subjectivity from the context of mental illness and harness its political potential.

Khatibi's Fragmentations

Possession metaphors for language have dominated literary debates in the Maghreb. Kateb Yacine, in the wake of the Algerian war, referred to the French language as his "war spoil" [*butin de guerre*] and the so-called "language debate" of postcolonial letters with Nguigi wa Thiong'o's paradigmatic call to decolonize the mind has centred language expression as a battleground site for this process. The Moroccan literary critic Abdelfattah Kilito, who publishes in both French and Arabic on Arabic literature, often writes of bilingualism using metaphors of possession and conquest. In a chapter on translation in *Thou Shalt Not Speak My Language*, Kilito asks, "Can one possesses two languages? Can one master them equally? We may not find the answer unless we ask another question: Can one possess any language?"[21]

Khatibi's experimental text *Amour bilingue* is a lyrical account of being bilingual in post-independence Morocco, one that is characterized by the constant oscillation between French and Arabic languages, and more importantly, the selves that emerge within and from the worlds built by them. With this experimental text on bilingual consciousness, Khatibi frames the multilingualism of the Maghreb in the decolonial era outside of the metaphors of conquest, possession, and warfare. *Amour bilingue* played a ground-breaking role on the Maghrebi literary scene by creating an imaginative space where thinking and being in two languages could be possible and even pleasurable. Réda Bensmaïa writes, "The originality at work here … stems from the fact that, for the first time in such a radical and concerted way, the question of belonging to (at least) two languages bursts theoretically and practically upon a space of writing that had previously been dominated by a Manichean vision of language and (cultural, ethnic, religious and national) identity."[22] Instead, the notion of bilingualism serves as a provocative shift in metaphor, demanding with it a transcultural literary theory that could accommodate writerly multilingual consciousness on the one hand and uneven readerly reception on the other. In other words, how can bilingual consciousness be expressed in a single tongue? Who would be the readers of such a text?

While the relationship between language and cultural identity in *Amour bilingue* has been carefully analyzed, the experience of bilingualism at the level of the individual in this work has yet to be fully explored. This section foregrounds the relationships between the phenomenological experiences of language, time, and agency that are most salient when we consider the structure of selfhood. Recent studies in cognitive psychology suggest that French and Arabic operate differently when presented with the same external reality. Calling upon this research on the effect of language on the perception of time and the gender of inanimate objects, I argue that the vertiginous episodes that Khatibi describes in the work should be understood as a staging of the mental experience of a life lived between French and Arabic perspectives. Switching back and forth between French and Arabic effectively creates schisms in the experiencing self, the perceiving lens for lived experience. It is the alternation between grammatical genders and reversals the directionality of time that produces the careening sensation of unselfing throughout the work.

Bilingual swaps effect a dizzying experience of unselfing in Khatibi's text, wherein multiple linguistic perspectives are ultimately understood to be integrated into a single person's self-experience. The persistent feeling of vertigo that the narrator describes is caused by his perpetual mental switching between language mindsets, which entail different ways of thinking about the self and thinking about others. The reversal of writing direction influences the narrator's perception of time, as he imagines time as moving first in one direction, and then the other. Moreover, the inversion of the grammatical genders of nouns – such as the sun and the moon associated with Genesis in the Bible and the Qur'an – leads to a series of magnetic attractions and repulsions. As the nouns switch grammatical genders in the narrator's consciousness, their associations are swapped as well. This gender flexibility contributes to the extended metaphor of androgyny in the work. Unselfing in *Amour bilingue* is written as a process of repeated self-fragmentation and reintegration, one that ultimately allows the subject to perceive the disparate parts of the self as participating in a successful gestalt, rather than a damaged schism. In addition to the social work that this achieves (the destruction of the Manichean vision of culture in the postcolonial Maghreb) this serves to recuperate the notion that the self is an amalgam of fragments from the association between *dédoublement* and mental disorder.

The formal qualities of Khatibi's text motivate a reading focused on the way bilingualism shapes individual self-conception. *Amour bilingue* is not quite a novel, not quite an autobiography. Khatibi labels it a "récit," [story]; it contains little character development or action, consisting rather of reflections and episodic events that are self-consciously perceived through a bilingual lens. The text, which is narrated by a nameless male protagonist, alternates between the third person and first person and addresses a nameless female lover in the second person. Khatibi's narrator indicates that he would also have us imagine bilingualism as a character of the story. "La bi-langue! La bi-langue! Elle-même un personnage de ce récit, poursuivant sa quête intercontinentale, au delà de mes traductions."[23] [The *bi-langue*! The *bi-langue*! Herself, a character in this story, on her intercontinental quest, beyond my translations.][24] The text renders these translations visible by engaging the reader in the phenomenology of bilingual consciousness.

In *Amour bilingue*, the narrator is perpetually engaged in self-translation in the attempt to present this consciousness to another person. The text is a complex exploration of the different permutations of bilingual experience when faced with one of the most challenging inter-subjective experiences: love. Given the shifts in pronouns and its experimentation with narration, this is not a phenomenological text in the classical sense. Rather, *Amour bilingue* reads like bilingual cognition on display;

it presents mental thought processes when processed through a bilingual perspective. The text suspends the natural attitude on the world in order to explore the experience of desire, attraction, and intimacy in bilingual terms.

Khatibi presents his readers with a bilingual narrator who imagines time as moving alternately from left to right (French) and from right to left (Arabic). As he attempts to represent time in absolute space, he experiences unselfing as a fragmentation of the experiencing self that is rooted in the recurrent reversals of the direction of time. If mental time-mapping is often determined by linguistic features (time-space metaphors) and non-linguistic features (writing direction and cultural attitudes towards the past), the loss of unified self-experience that Khatibi's narrator describes can be attributed to his mental flip-flopping from a French perspective to an Arabic one and back again.

At the nodal point in the triad of figures of the other – personified female bilingualism and the vague female lover – Khatibi's narrator mentally switches between Arabic (both Fusha and Darija) and French as he interprets these female others and the feelings of inner foreignness that love and difference inspires. In a passage of reflection and nostalgia on his shared moments with the lover, Khatibi casts the narrative self as a distortion of time, built from memories and the intrusion of the past on the present. Indeed, the narrator indicates that in the process of mentally conjuring up the time spent together, it was as if he were "multiplié par le désœuvrement du temps"[25] [multiplied by the idleness of time].[26] From this vertigo and lack of unity of consciousness emerges the fragmentation narrative for unselfing.

In writing about love in Morocco in 1983, Khatibi focused the decolonial energies of the independence movements of the past decades inward. Given that *Amour bilingue* first appeared in the same year as *Maghreb pluriel*, much of the scholarship on the bilingual text has focused on its relationship to the philosophy of decolonization and self-determination of the Maghreb expressed in the sociological text. Languages become symbolic in these readings: the French language stands for the enduring (neo)colonial and hegemonic power of France, and Arabic for the theological ideology of Arab nationalism. The Maghrebi subject of *Amour bilingue* is said to experience perpetual integration and disintegration as he navigates disparate cultural, political, and religious influences. The following quotation from James McGuire demonstrates the focus on Khatibi's work as a destabilizing force on "French French" as a symbolic cultural center: "The works of Khatibi exemplify the possibility of this sort of decentered writing. 'Le français de la France' becomes truly ex-centric in the sense that it is dislocated and rearticulated."[27]

While there are evident merits to this reading, the focus on decentring "Le français de la France" does not account for the phenomenological specificities at play in the experiences that comprise *Amour bilingue*, nor does it account for the non-symbolic encounters between the il/je and the tu of the novel, "encounters," to use a rather chaste term, that are very much physical. Much of *Amour bilingue* explores the dissolution of boundary between self in other through sexual pleasure. As Matt Reeck rightly notes of the experiential-focus of Khatibi's writing, "some works seem rooted in specific places and their histories, but many works, perhaps the strong majority, seem to be first and foremost not accounts of historical times and places but of the processes and experiences of the life of the body and mind."[28]

The specific ebb and flow between Fusha, Darija, and French in the narrator's mind offers an insight into how unselfing can be experienced as a fragmentation into language-specific selves. Khatibi characterizes Fusha, the standardized, formal register of Arabic as a written language rooted in his Qur'anic education, as separate in use and feel from the familiarity of Darija, the Moroccan vernacular Arabic, and French, which he reads, but rarely speaks at school as a child. Khatibi stresses the chasm between Fusha and the vernacular in his first autobiographical novel, *La Mémoire tatouée* (*Tattooed Memory*) (1971).[29] In this text, Khatibi relates becoming "triglottal" when he starts attending French school in 1945. He writes, "À l'école, un enseignement laïc, imposé à ma religion: je devins triglotte, lisant le français sans le parler, jouant avec quelques bribes de l'arabe écrit, et parlant le dialecte comme quotidien. Où, dans ce chassé-croisé, la cohérence et la continuité?"[30] [At school, a secularized instruction was imposed on my religion; I became trilingual, reading French without speaking it, playing with a few scraps of written Arabic, and speaking in dialect like usual. Where in these criss-crossings, coherence, and continuity?] The experience of being a self is characterized by discontiunity when it is torn between languages that have accompanying institutional spaces, spaces that do not overlap in the mental landscape of the past.

The particular relationship between colloquial Darija and French is framed in the following passage of *Amour bilingue*. Khatibi writes,

> Il se calma d'un coup, lorsqu'apparut le "mot" arabe *kalma* avec son équivalent savant *kalima* et toute la chaîne des diminutifs, calembours de son enfance: *klima* … La diglossie *kal(i)ma* revint sans que disparût ni s'effaçât le mot "mot." Tous deux s'observaient en lui, précédant l'émergence maintenant rapide de souvenirs, fragments de mots, onomatopées, phrases en guirlandes, enlaces à mort: indéchiffrables.[31]

He calmed down instantly when an Arabic word, *kalma*, appeared, *kalma* and its scholarly equivalent, *kalima*, and the whole string of its diminutives which had been the riddles of his childhood: *klima* ... The diglossal *kal(i)ma* appeared again without *mot's* having faded away or disappeared. Within him, both words were observing each other, preceding what had now become the rapid emergence of memories, fragments of words, onomatopoeias, garlands of phrases, intertwined to the death: undecipherable.[32]

In this passage, which obviously resists a smooth translation into English (or any single language, for that matter), Khatibi illustrates the mental gymnastics that take place when the narrator reflects on his bilingualism and its internal diglossia. On the surface, the chain of translations, transliterations and associations seem to "calm" the narrator, until we realize that "se calma" is another homonym of "kalma" the Darija word for "word." When he reflects on language, the play-on-words from his childhood come back to his consciousness in Arabic as he simultaneously registers the French term in a way that is distracting and disorienting. Thus, in addition to a historical-cultural allegory on the relationship between France and the Arabic-speaking Maghreb, Khatibi offers an account of the phenomenological relationship between the narrator's specific perspectives (French, Darija, Fusha) that jostle against one another in this text. *Amour bilingue* presents an account of selfhood that allows for the coexistence of fragments; a younger self that speaks in vernacular, conjured up alongside the French-speaking adult who arrives without displacing the learned Fusha-reader. This rich passage makes visible the transitory knotting together of these fragments in the stream of consciousness.

Debates in cognitive psychology on the way language and culture shapes thought allow us to bring the specific effect of bilingualism on fragmentary unselfing into focus. These debates are far from over, and the research summarized in the *Cambridge Handbook of Cognitive Linguistics* (2017), emphasizes that language is not the *only* feature that influences the way that speakers think about time.[33] However, since people use spatial expressions to talk about time, such as looking *forward* to retirement, and thinking *back* on childhood, experimental research has suggested that people activate these front-to-back spatial representations of time when processing language about temporal sequences.[34] This group of experiments demonstrates cross-linguistic differences when talking and thinking about the past and future motivated by differences in time-space metaphors.[35] In "How Languages Construct Time," Boroditsky writes that "people co-opt representations of the physical world (e.g., space) in order to mentally represent more abstract of intangible entities (e.g., time). This suggests that conceptions of time differ dramatically across cultures and languages and that the contingency of cultures assists in the construction of basic notions of time.[36] It appears that differences in basic spatial representations may have far-reaching consequences in many other knowledge domains in the cognitive system."[37] Another study shows that people access spatial representations of time automatically, even in non-linguistic contexts.[38]

Another group of experiments demonstrate that writing direction serves as a vector that organizes where things are perceived as beginning, and where things end. In fact, writing direction (as produced on calendars or timetables, for example) influences the way people think about time even if the directional metaphors themselves are absent from the language we use to evoke them.[39] (Though we say that "spring is *before* summer" in English, and not "spring is *to the left* of summer," we imagine spring to be situated to the left of summer when asked to represent it on the page). A French-speaking person generally imagines time as moving from left-to-right, with "earliness" being associated with the left, and lateness to the right; the reverse is true for an Arabic-speaking person. Arabic and French both use deictic motion verbs, which denote centres, or reference points, to describe time. Verbs such as *arriver /jaa'a* indicate both the directionality of time and the position of the observer. Time is understood, according to this model, to be moving from front to back towards the observer, who remains stationary. This is particularly germane when we consider two of the languages that interact in *Amour bilingue*, which move in opposite directions on the written page. For time to be understood to be consistently moving from front to back, the subject of *Amour bilingue* must conceptually pivot himself as the point of reference as he alternately imagines time to be moving from left-to-right (French) and right-to-left (Arabic).

A final set of experiments show that space-time mapping can sometimes contradict the metaphors that we find in language.[40] Though languages are not spoken orally from left to right or right to left, spatial conceptions of time can nevertheless reflect cultural attitudes about memory or the future. A 2014 study hypothesizes that the Moroccan participants' spatial conceptions of the past and future are based on cultural attitudes towards past and future; the researchers suggest that Darija speakers think of their past in front of them (the part of life that they can see) and their future behind them (the part of life that remains unknown). According to the Temporal Focus Hypothesis, those who devote special attention to the past should tend to imagine the past in front of them, "in the location where they could focus on the past literally with their eyes if past events were physical objects that could be seen," while people who "focus" on the future should instead imagine the future in front of their eyes.[41] According to this study, then, the cultural importance of the past is reflected in the mental mapping of time.

This experimental research provides novel insights into a work like *Amour bilingue* for the way it reinvigorates debates on the way the particular languages we speak shape our interactions with the world.[42] Two claims from this body of research will be central moving forward: First, a person's conception of time is influenced by the language that they speak, which means that conceptions of time differ greatly across different cultural groups.[43] Second, grammatical gender in language affects the way that people think about inanimate objects.[44] Khatibi draws on the variability of these same mental experiences in his work on the self in love. Indeed, Khatibi even describes the love-interest at one point in the text as transforming herself in "time's very instability."[45] In attending to the cultural and linguistic specificities of Arabic and French, the next section demonstrates how the destabilizing experience of bilingualism on the experiencing self is interpreted as a self-fragmentation.

Amour bilingue is a slender text, and the section breaks serve as some of its only signposts. The main narrated section (sandwiched between the epigraph and the epilogue) begins: "Les étés arrivaient avec fougue."[46] [Summers arrived in a blaze of energy.][47] Here is an example of a deictic motion verb: summer "arrives." If the observer remains stationary, he faces the front, the future, in French. A character in a comic book would face the right side of the page, with summer arrows arriving as the present moment moves over him from the right side of the page towards the past on the left side of the page. If one quickly switches into an Arabic mindset for time, it is suddenly as if the character is staring into the past. The summer (the present moment) is no longer arriving from front to back in a way that makes conceptual sense; rather, the character is now headed towards the past. Unmoored from linguistic directionality, the narrator lyrically describes the subsequent *fantasmagories marines*, which evoke swimming in the open ocean while remembering an erotic encounter with his lover. The lexical field parallels this unmooring from its reference point, conjuring up images of self-abandonment, being "adrift," and of limbs rolling over one another. Khatibi attempts to escape the influence of language on agency with these lyrical explorations. When his narrator tumbles in the waves as he imagines the erotic intertwining of bodies, he effects a pause in his perpetual practice of mental self-translation between his two languages. The imposition of memory (of pastness) marks this about-face in his mental perception of time.

Similarly, the final section, the epilogue, begins: "Le récit est tombé joyeusement en cet automne: les feuilles, les feuilles de papier, toute cette féerie très réelle de mon été."[48] [The story fell joyously that autumn: the leaves, the leaves of paper, that very real extravaganza of my summer.][49] The leaves of paper fall, signalling the end of the summer and the end of the narrative, the text's inscription coinciding with the end of the season. Khatibi also calls attention here to the directionality of page turning in French/Arabic. When a reader is finished with a text in French, the pages fall like autumn leaves; when a reader finishes a text in Arabic (looking at the back cover), the pages fall up instead of down. With the manipulation of these metaphors for the passage of time, Khatibi evokes the unmooring of the subject from its stable reference point. The events of the story fall from one direction and then another as the past encroaches on the present consciousness.

Thinking about cardinal directions in the work plays a central role in illustrating the narrator's experience of disorientation through embodied linguistic experience. Khatibi's narrator describes arriving at the airport and trying to read the word "South" written on a window, from the back.

> Permutation permanente. Il l'avait mieux compris à partir d'une petite désorientation, le jour où, attendant à Orly l'appel du départ, il n'arrivait pas à lire à travers la vitre le mot "Sud" vu de dos. En l'inversant, il s'aperçut qu'il l'avait lu de droite à gauche, comme dans l'alphabet arabe – sa première graphie. Il ne pouvait mettre ce mot à l'endroit qu'en passant par la direction de sa langue maternelle.[50]

> Permanent permutation. He understood this better thanks to a brief sense of disorientation he had experienced one day at Orly, waiting for a boarding call; he found himself unable to read the word South, seen backward, through a window. Turning it around, he realized he had read it from right to left, as if it were written in Arabic characters – his first written form. He could place the word only by going by way of his mother tongue.[51]

The narrator is disoriented as he mentally grapples with directionality: the word "South," which is written in French but refers to Arabic-speaking countries, shifts in writing direction (right to left, and left to right) in the narrator's mind as he tries to read the word from the back (and must therefore grapple with the sign's inversion). This episode at the airport demonstrates how Khatibi uses cardinal directions in the work to explain what episodes of mental disorientation are like. He refers to Arabic as his "first written form" and his "mother tongue."

Like in the time-space metaphor example, the past consciousness (of his Arabic instruction) intrudes upon his present consciousness. French and Arabic come to mind without any conscious effort as the fragments of the self displace one another as the default mode.

The mental mapping of space plays a central role in another episode that illustrates the loss of balance that the narrator experiences while contemplating the passage of time. As in the airport disorientation, concrete space and cardinal directions are also important in the scene. The narrator describes walking along the seashore, paying close attention to the direction of the wind and the waves. He writes, "Il marcha long-temps, seul, sur la plage. Un vent maritime le frappait latéralement … Plus il marchait, plus il prêtait une attention exagérée au mouvement du vent."[52] [He walked alone on the beach for a long time. A sea breeze struck him from the side … The longer he walked, the more he paid a heightened attention to the way the wind blew.][53] Suddenly, the sun sets before his eyes, an event marking the passage of time. This sets off a bout of vertigo as he experiences his body's typical "scansion – from language to language." He writes,

Alors qu'il regardait les vagues se fracasser contre la falaise, il comprit que le vent avait brutalement changé de direction. Il était face au vent, trans-porté par sa direction même, laquelle s'opposait à la sienne: comme si, tournant verticalement sur lui-même et marchant plus vite, il entrait dans le souffle du vent, sur ce sable glissant, sur la dureté de ce roc.[54]

As he watched the waves break against the cliff, he realized that the wind had brutally shifted. He was facing into the wind, carried in the direction it was blowing, which was different from the one in which he was walk-ing; it was as if, doing an about-face and walking more quickly, he entered into the wind's blast, on these sliding sands, on the hardness of this rock.[55]

Before the wind changed direction, it was hitting him laterally as he walked along the shore. This indicates that the wind must have been hitting him in the back when he turned to look at the setting sun. "Le soleil s'était couché devant ses yeux, tombant dans l'Océan."[56] [The sun had set in front of him, falling into the Ocean.][57] Now, however, the wind has turned to face him.

The volte-face of the wind signals the reversal of the directionality of time that is taking place in the narrator's consciousness as he watches day pass to night. While the sun rising in the East and setting in the West corresponds with a right to left trajectory of time that we find in Arabic, it does not match the left to right trajectory of time of French.[58]

Whereas the narrator *had* cried *Bahr! Bahr!* [Sea! Sea! (Arabic)] before the wind changes direction, he notices that it is the words *eau* [water] and *mer* [sea] that now "bathe" his mind.[59] The author's usage of the pluperfect ("il s'était écrié") marks the past-ness of his Arabic perspective, and the passage to a French perspective that motivates the sense of disorientation.

As in the airport episode, the narrator contemplates direction through his bilingual lens in the disorientation by the sea, but here as a reflection on the experience of time. This eventually leads him to the apex of his unselfing episode, as he feels as though he is losing himself in a process of infinite splintering and reversals. He writes, "Étrange illusion: il crut s'évanouir dans le coucher du soleil, tourner de l'autre côté de l'horizon. Puis, progressant dans l'invisible et glissant de cycle en cycle, il changea de vie et de mort. Debout. Statue de vent."[60] [Strange illusion: he thought he fainted as the sun set, he thought he sank below the horizon. Then proceeding in the invisible and sliding from cycle to cycle, he changed his life and his death. Upright. A statue of wind.][61] The experience of time moving first in one direction, then the reverse, causes the narrator to question his existence. He momentarily loses his cohesive sense of self, and feels it melt into the horizon. As he stands at the crossroads of two languages, two opposing vectors of time, he feels he is nothing more than an ephemeral statue of wind.

Arabic and French are both languages with grammatically gendered nouns. Another source of instability in the experience of bilingual consciousness can be traced back to the variability of the assigned grammatical gender of inanimate objects, something Jakobson observes as early as 1959. Jakobson writes of a Russian child's surprise at finding Death (feminine in Russian) to be depicted as an old man in a translation of German tales. "Even such a category as grammatical gender, often cited as merely formal, plays a great role in the mythological attitudes of a speech community."[62] While grammatical gender is semantically arbitrary (there is nothing inherently feminine or masculine about death) current research confirms Jakobson's idea that grammatical gender is meaningful to people's experience of the world.

In "Sex, Syntax and Semantics," Boroditsky, Schmidt, and Phillips demonstrate that "people's mental representations of objects are influenced by the grammatical genders assigned to these objects' names in their native language."[63] They write that grammatical gender affects meaning in at least two ways. One possibility is that in learning grammatical gender, children selectively focus on a property of the referent that helps them to categorize it as stereotypically masculine or feminine. "For example, if the word for 'sun' is masculine in one's language, one might try to remember this by conceiving of the sun in terms of what are perceived as stereotypically masculine properties like powerful and threatening. If the word for 'sun' is feminine, on the other hand, one might focus on its warming and nourishing qualities."[64] A second possibility relies on the concept of *thinking for speaking*. Arabic and French speakers mark objects with grammatical genders in order to speak correctly in the language. The task of referring to objects as masculine or feminine may lead people to attend to those stereotypical qualities, making those qualities more salient.[65]

The following passage from *Amour bilingue* illustrates the way in which the bilingual narrator experiences fragmentary unselfing through his relationship to gendered objects. The juxtaposition of these disparate mental states – the bilingual who frequently experiences inner fragmentation and the monolingual who romanticizes this breakage – while simultaneously calling up the collective consciousness of French imperialism in North Africa, should also be understood in an individual existential capacity when we consider the way that grammatical gender shapes the experience of reality. In *Amour bilingue*, Khatibi's narrator reflects on the gender of a given noun in French (the language in which the text is written) shifting to the transliterated word, and then the gender of the same noun in Arabic. For instance, Khatibi writes, "Il pensait au soleil, et déjà son nom, celui de la lune s'inversent – du féminin au masculin – dans sa double langue. Inversion qui fait tourner les mots avec les constellations, pour une étrange attraction de l'univers. En se disant cela, il croyait s'expliquer sa lancinance de l'androgynie, aimant, désaimant sous le coup des mêmes charmes."[66] [He thought of the sun and even in doing so its name, that of the moon, inverted itself – from feminine to masculine – in his double language. Inversion which makes words wheel with the constellations, making for a strange attraction of the universe. So saying, he believed he was explaining to himself his obsession with androgyny, attracted and repulsed by the same set of charms.][67] Here, the narrator refers to the differences in gender between Arabic and French when speaking about cosmic bodies. While "sun" (le soleil) is masculine and "moon" (la lune) is feminine in French, the reverse is true in Arabic.[68] "Sun" (al-shams) is feminine, and "moon" (al-qamar) is masculine. The passage also evokes the arbitrary linguistic feature that is marked on "sun and moon letters" in Arabic based on whether they assimilate the letter *lām* of the definite article, which are similar to elision rules in French. (The word *al-shams* assimilates the *lām*, while al-qamar does not). As the narrator sets out to think about the attraction between these cosmic bodies, the fragile unity of consciousness splinters into language-specific fragments, inverting their genders and inspiring an obsession with "androgyny" as a mythical absolute space.

The relationship between these cosmic bodies is staged in the Qur'an, passages of which Khatibi memorized as a child; in *La Mémoire tatouée*, Khatibi recounts his relationship to the tradition of memorized speech. "Arbre de mon enfance, le Coran dominait ma parole, alors que l'école, c'était une bibliothèque sans le Livre. Chant d'abord, le Coran s'apprend par cœur."[69] [As the pillar of my childhood, the Qur'an dominated my speech, whereas school was a library without the Book. Singing came first, the Qur'an is learned by heart.] The Surat Ash-Shams begins with an extended lyrical oath about the Sun; the first two lines describe the relationship between the sun and the moon:

> *wa-l-shamsi wa-duha* **ha**
> *wa-l-qamari idha ta la* **ha**

These lines could be translated as "By the sun and her brightness / And by the moon when he follows her." Not only do the nouns themselves have known grammatical genders to Arabic speakers, but also in this surah, the gender of the word "al-shams" is visible on the possessive pronouns which conclude each line in the form of suffixes: "her brightness" and "follow her." Michael Sells writes, "The word for sun (shams) is grammatically feminine in Arabic and takes the grammatically feminine pronoun *hā*. By making *hā* the key rhyme word throughout the first part of the Sura, the Qur'anic voice creates a partial personification. In other words, a 'gender figure' is produced. The 'her' is never fully personified as a woman, but is always on the verge of personification."[70]

While others have already analyzed the inversion of gender that takes place in this passage, it has been interpreted through a deconstructive lens as evidence of Khatibi's desire to demonstrate the contingency of concepts and the lack of cultural essences, especially in the Maghreb in the context of the fight for independence.[71] However, if we consider instead the way language is theorized to shape thought, it allows for a more specific analysis of the encounter between French and Arabic in Khatibi's work, especially when considering its representation of consciousness. Beyond an indicator of cultural contingency, this work allows us to enter the experiential realm of unselfing as fragmentation in the text. Considering the way in which language is theorized to shape thought allows for an engagement with the phenomenological *what-it-is-like* of selfhood at the crossroads of two languages, and brings into focus the mindset of a self who is trying to communicate intimately in his second language. In the text, French perspectives (the adult communicating in a professional context, the adult seducing a woman in their common language) exist alongside Arabic ones (the child speaking Darija to his mother, the adult reading the Qur'an). The narrator is unselved by his simple lovestruck reveries as reflections on the relationships between cosmic bodies illuminate his own experience of magnetism between human ones.

Under "the charms of language," the narrator experiences first the magnetic effect of attraction, and then demagnetization as the genders of the two nouns inverse their polarity. Indeed, he describes unselfing as he oscillates between his Arabic and French perspectives as the destabilization of the ordinary experience of unity. This sheds new light on Khatibi's *androgyne* metaphor in the passage on the sun and the moon. The term used in the passage can be understood not only to refer to the eternal movement of attraction and repulsion he imagines to be taking place between the two anthropomorphized cosmic bodies, but also to the inversion of grammatical gender that occurs as the narrator shifts between Arabic and French nouns. Thus, the magnetization and de-magnetization that occurs when switching from French to Arabic is accompanied, for the narrator, by a momentary loss of attractive force between biological "pairs": male and female, le soleil/la lune and al-qamar/al-shams. "Aimant," the present participle of the French verb "aimer," to love, intensifies the metaphor of physical magnetism between two bodies in the passage. The act of loving is lived through a fragmented lens for the narrator when these transmutations come into play. With the loss of stable grammatical gender comes the loss of the explanatory mental imagery that is central to the way he experiences the world. As nouns unhitch from their grammatical genders, the narrator considers his own attraction to the lover, recasting the experience of unselfing as a ludic – if disorienting – sense of self-fragmentation.

The revelation that the bilingual self is an amalgam of fragments, which are only provisionally stitched together by the illusion of unified consciousness, is reflected in Khatibi's understanding of the way the self engages with otherness. His notion of the *Pensée-autre* ("Other thought") seeks to underline the necessity of a planetary philosophy of insufficiency by attempting to escape the two competing and dominant metaphysical systems in the Maghreb: theocratic Islamic society and secular rationalism traced back to eighteenth-century Europe. In "Other Thought," the first essay of *Maghreb pluriel,* he argues for the double critique of these two systems that would lead to a "pensée planétaire et plurielle."[72] Khatibi writes "A thought that is not minoritarian, marginal, fragmentary, and incomplete is always a thought of ethnocide."[73] In his decolonial critique, Khatibi calls for a philosophy of plural thought that does not reduce others – both societies and individuals – to a sphere of self-sufficiency. Nasrin Qader explains, "'Pensée' and 'autre' are not two separate entities; rather, the two always belong together, are always drawn together without appropriating one under the dominion of the other."[74] The project of *Pensée-autre*, should then be understood as the attempt to imagine otherness as something other than an object. Qader continues, "'*Pensée-autre*' is plural thought (*pensée plurielle*), precisely because it is the thought of being in relation and thought in relation."[75] Achieving this being in relation is founded upon the possibility of understanding the fragmentary nature of the self.

From its first pages, *Amour bilingue* reflects this desire to make visible thinking and being in relation. This celebration is at once an ethics and an aesthetics.[76] Khatibi's work demonstrates the plurality within both language and tradition. The Arabic title of *Amour bilingue, Ishq al-lisnanayn,* ("love in two tongues") which is illustrated in calligraphy on the title page, requires its reader to reflect on the inner divisions between Sufi mysticism and orthodox Islam. The choice of the term *Ishq* (passionate love) in the place of *Hubb* points to a semantic dispute within Sufism that dates back to the tenth century.[77] Samia Mehrez ties Khatibi's usage of the dual form for "tongue" in the Arabic title in part to this inner division within Arabo-Islamic culture itself, that is, "the division between orthodox, institutional Islamic discourse and the popular mystical tradition which has always been marginalized."[78] Linking this semantic dispute to its content (desire, love), Khatibi stages amorous bilingual subjectivity as a parallel instantiation of minoritarian thought.

Khatibi's minoritarian, fragmentary thought, which is rooted in the *pensée-autre* recalls Valéry's desire for *un autre-fictif* with which he could come to understand the self, and which is examined in detail in chapter 3. Valéry imagined the self to communicate with itself in the same way that it communicates with the other; he theorizes that the self needs an encounter with alterity in order to develop.[79] The self and the self-as-other are thus tied together in a dialectic of desire. In a reflection on the role of desire in Valéry's work, Gifford questions whether the reflexive and functional duality (self and self-as-other) is actually tied to genuine exchange or real human encounter.[80] Despite Valéry's resistance to the need for others in his empire of the self, he saw this inner dialogue as the enabling condition of interpersonal exchange with real others.

It is here that Khatibi's work can be usefully distinguished from Valéry and other thinkers who have conceived of the other as a parallel self. Paul Ricœur in *Oneself as Another* exemplifies this account when he asserts that the hermeneutics of the self has three major features: first, the detour of reflection by way of analysis (approaching the self happens indirectly), second, the dialectic of selfhood and sameness (the splitting of "même" into *idem* and *ipse)*, and third, the dialectic of the self and otherness.[81] Ricoeur argues that although the self is never absent from its other, the hermeneutics of the self reaches its fullest realization in the dialectic between self and alterity, or outside otherness. By Ricoeur's account, the possibility of an ethical aim for the self depends on the perception of the other as a parallel self, and the estimation of that suffering and acting being.

Khatibi alters this dynamic; it is not in service of self-development or self-knowledge that we approach others. Rather, we ought to "weaken" the self in order to fully meet the other in a relationship of desire. In *Amour bilingue,* he writes, "Un affaiblissement loyal exige de rencontrer l'autre et de le perdre en soi, immémorialement."[82] [A faithful weakening must meet the other and immemorially lose the other in the self.][83] The encounter with the other is facilitated by this lessening of an ordinary experience of self-sovereignty. Understanding the self as a bundle of fragments facilitates an approach to ontological others. What Khatibi demonstrates in focusing on the pleasurable fragmentation of the self in love is that solicitude for the other might be better achieved not so much in conceiving of the other as a parallel entity, but rather as a provisional gathering of fragments. Khatibi harnesses the political potential of fragmentary unselfing in the service of *Pensée-autre*. Like Iris Murdoch and Simone Weil, Khatibi's account provocatively suggests that becoming less of a self by weakening its sovereignty and its frontiers leads to an illusionless experience of communion, and sometimes even ecstasy, with the other.

The next section contrasts this vision of ecstatic communion to the ways in which Cixous interprets unselfing as a fragmentation. While Khatibi celebrates self-fragmentation as a means of rethinking the relationship between self and otherness, Cixous despairs in her meditation on the pain that unselfing inflicts upon the subject of experience. For Cixous, the loss of the unity of the experiencing and the narrative self is a painful wound to self-consciousness. In contrast to the utopic vision of plural selfhood that she champions in her earlier writings on *écriture féminine* and Promethea, Cixous writes of fragmentary unselfing as a burden.

Cixous and Unselfing

One could argue that Hélène Cixous has been writing on becoming and unbecoming a self for decades, perhaps for her entire career. To cite only a few instantiations, she writes extensively about exceeding the poverty of individual experience in her work on the boundlessness of the self in kinship, relation, and connection; she explores the desire for a collective female subjectivity through the power of what she calls *écriture feminine*; she also penned a character called Promethea who enacts her vision of the feminine divine. These writings create a vision of the self as a powerfully disunified and changeable entity. During experiences of rapture and excess, the self defies the traps and constraints of the patriarchal economy.

Yet, at the transition between one century and the next, Cixous publishes a singular autobiographical work that foregrounds the lived experience of unselfing in a decidedly more melancholic register. *Les rêveries de la femme sauvage* (*Reveries of the Wild Woman*), which first appeared in 2000, has inspired new categorizations and even periodization of her work. Claire Boyle for instance, argues that a new autobiographical cycle begins with this text and another work from 2000, *Le jour où je n'étais pas là* (*The Day I Wasn't There*) as Cixous sets out to write her own "self-estrangement."[84] In 2000, Cixous presents unselfing using the language of separation, cutting, and alienation. The escape from self-unity, which was so often a source of power and pleasure in many of her earlier writings becomes a source of pain in *Rêveries*, to which she returns forty-five years after she left Algeria for France in 1955.

Indeed, the mourning, grief, and estrangement attached to the experience of unselfing in *Rêveries* seems to stand in contrast to her earlier philosophical and theological writings in which she embraces the self in difference as an escape from the painful strictures of unification. In her celebrated essay "La venue à l'écriture" (Coming to Writing) (1976), Cixous advances a notion of plural subjectivity, which is not unlike the revolutionary idea of subjective potential at the heart of Khatibi's *Pensée-autre* (*Other Thought*). She describes the potential for radical communion between distant women as a utopic fantasy, writing "Si tu les aimes, chaque femme s'ajoute à toi, et tu deviens *plufemme*."[85] [If you love them, each woman adds herself to you, and you become more-woman.][86] With this neologism, Cixous suggests that through the creative and ludic force of *écriture féminine,* the (woman) writer is able to embrace other experiences and escape the confines of a singular perspective. In so doing, she becomes a *plufemme*: a *more-than-one* woman, but also *no-longer-one*, in the sense of being no longer singular or unified.[87] She explicitly positions this possibility against the demands for identity, noncontradiction, and unity.[88]

In another work that explores her relationship to childhood and origins, *Photos de racines* (*Rootprints: Memory and Life Writing*) (1994), Cixous writes that "l'écriture me permet de jouir"[89] [writing allows me to *jouir*].[90] This text is co-written as a set of exchanges with Mireille

Calle-Gruber and includes excerpts from Cixous's notebooks. In *Photos de racines,* the act of constructing the self through the exploration of roots is represented as a pleasurable game, which Cixous designates with the verb *jouir* [to orgasm, to enjoy]. She plays extensively on the *je/jeu* (I/game) homophone; the narrative self is subject to pleasurable revisions as she writes and reconstructs the past. Writing and living are inextricably intertwined for Cixous. She explains: "si tu me dis, pourquoi tu écris? cela reviendrait presque à répondre: parce que je vis. C'est non-dissocié … vivre-écrire se sont confondus pour moi tout de suite."[91] [if you ask me: why do you write? It would almost come down to responding: because I live. It is non-dissociated … living-writing were mixed up for me right away.][92] With her teasing manipulation of syntax and experimentation with neologism, Cixous plays with and in language to present the unique perspective of the self.

In this context, Cixous theorizes that it is also pleasurable to dwell in what analytical philosophers call synchronic division. She writes, "Pure I, identical to I-self, does not exist. I is always in difference. I is the open set of the traces of an I by definition changing, mobile, because living-speaking-thinking-dreaming."[93] Instead of imagining the self as contained in one single "I," she sees each individual as a plurality, wherein *nous sommes* indicates both being (we are) and totality (sum).[94] With this wordplay, Cixous activates a sense of both amplification and collectivity, which requires knowledge of both French and English. The transfiguration of the self in Cixous's philosophy is not only rooted in gender difference, but also magnified by her deliberate play on her mobility between languages, literatures, and cultures and her sense of estrangement from them. Part of this play is inspired by her family tree and her family's relationship to Jewishness and exile (she once called herself a *juifemme*). Her ancestors on her father's side were Sephardic Jews who settled in Morocco after the expulsion of the Jews from Spain in 1492 and then Algeria, where Hélène Cixous was born. Her Ashkenazi mother was from Germany and fled during Hitler's rise to power, and spoke German at home; she held a French passport, which was revoked during the Vichy regime in Algeria. In this sense, Cixous is an emblematic writer of the Francosphère, whose manipulation of French evokes an estrangement from, rather than a belonging to the nation state. Cixous explains the difficulty of pinning down her biographical "origins": "I was born at/from the intersection of migrations and memories from the Occident and Orient, from the North and South. I was born a foreigner in 'France' in a said-to-be 'French' Algeria. I was born in not-France calling itself 'France.' To tell the truth we have to trap the appearances with quotation marks."[95]

Cixous, like Henri Michaux, is a writer who seeks to frustrate the reader's desire to read her work autobiographically. Part of this desire to frustrate the reader hails from the simplification of her heterogenous publications in North American academic contexts where she is known primarily as a feminist writer (though she is starting to be read as a "postcolonial" one). These labels, Cixous worries, are obstacles to knowledge and ultimately result in misunderstandings. Boyle argues that "the threat posed by false knowledge has influenced the development of Cixous's *oeuvre* away from the genre of autobiography (in which the conventional expectation is that the reader will gain more intimate knowledge of the autobiographical subject) whilst retaining autobiographical elements."[96] Indeed, Cixous scorns autobiography during this earlier period as a detestable literary genre, rather than a reliable source on a living person. Hélène Cixous isn't me, she insists in the essay "La venue à l'écriture"; rather, the "I" is crafted from the force and pain of others' voices, which she tries to make resound in her own writing.[97] Or, as she memorably decides in another work, "Quand je dis 'Je,' ce n'est jamais le sujet d'une autobiographie, mon je est libre."[98] [When I say "I," it is never the subject of an autobiography, my I is free.]

The sense that the self is not "one" is also rooted in Cixous's earlier work as a rewriting of the access to the divine. Writing against the Lacanian exclusion of the body from the realm of the Symbolic, Cixous continuously infuses her writing with the affects, needs, and pleasures of the felt experience of embodiment. Her attempt to inscribe *jouissance* into her writings on the self and the divine allows her to resist the way in which Lacan constructs the female self.[99] *Jouissance,* for Cixous, is a mental, physical, and spiritual experience of excess that borders on mystical communion and is akin to sexual rapture. The notion of *jouissance* in Cixous's writing is a powerful route to escaping the illusion of singularity. Cixous suggests that it is through this creative force that the feminine resists the demand for unity or a singular experience of identity.[100] Susan Sellers explains: "Depicted as beyond censorship, feminine writing is described as having the capacity to circumvent 'reason' labeled here as an 'enemy' of life. Drawing on the resources of the unconscious, in tune with the body's needs and pleasures, feminine writing is rooted in a liberating love."[101] Cixous's writing on the excesses of the self seeks to unite the experiences of the body and mind, a project rooted in desire and other-feeling.

Cixous writes about unselfing in *Le livre de Promethea* (*The Book of Promethea*) (1983) as a process that creates space for the other in the way it unsettles the self. She depicts feminine love and desire in this work as an experience of the divine. While this manifestation of love resembles Christian *agape*, the highest form of love that is rooted in charity, it also importantly also embraces the element of feminine multiplicity.[102] This understanding of the desiring self allows for living in the immediacy of the present in the absence of self-interest, which Cixous posits as the key to divinity. Promethea is perpetually unbound in acts of "unselfing the 'I'" as she explores the vulnerability or orienting the self towards the other.[103] Sarah Cornell writes, "This process of dispossession, of 'de-egoization,' of distancing from the self-centered ego, creates room for the other."[104] This vision of unselfing is close to Weil's and Murdoch's, wherein unselfing removes the selfishness of the ego, and orients the self towards others. Through Promethea, Cixous explores this experience of endless distancing from the ego as an experience of radical generosity of spirit. Focusing on unselfing, rather than the anxiety of the writing self, makes it possible to circumvent Cixous's worry about producing false autobiographical knowledge on the self. It is not so much a unified autobiographical self that is on offer in *Rêveries*, but rather a series of its undoings.

Cixous's choice of genre for *Rêveries*, like the subject of the text, suggests a return to origins and a new understanding of the process of fragmentation of the self. In this later text, self-splintering is explored in a melancholy light. Whereas Cixous writes of losing the self as an act of transformative generosity in her writings on *écriture féminine* and on the figure of Promethea, the experience of fragmentary unselfing in this later text is presented as an experience of alienation, cutting-off, and separation from the world. *Rêveries* is a work presented not as an autobiography, memoir, or novel, but published under the label of *Scènes primitives* (*Primal Scenes*). It relates Cixous's childhood experience of exile in Clos-Salembier (now El Madania), a municipality in Algiers Province. Rather than presenting events in chronological order, the childhood memories in the text are organized around events and characters from the past (the Bike, the Dog) that magnify in significance by this very process of remembering them. *Rêveries* oscillates between present conversations with her brother about their shared childhood and memories of the past. By experimenting with syntax and neologism in her characteristic style, Cixous explores the phenomenology of exile and alienation that characterizes these memories of her Algerian childhood.

The text considers the sense of exile that Cixous experiences in French Algeria as the child of a German Ashkenazi mother and Algerian Sephardic father. She writes of Jewish identity as a source of double alienation and rejection (and which Memmi theorizes as "heterophobia.")

While she experienced as a child, her Jewish heritage offered little ref-uge, causing "ces complications qui ont en commun des questions de porte, d'entrée, d'admissibilité"[105] [these complications which have in common some questions about doors, entries, admissibility].[106] Cixous writes that her mother felt little connection to her Jewish identity and "discovers" the Sephardic Jewish community upon her arrival Algeria.

Elle n'a d'ailleurs pas le sentiment d'appartenir à une communauté dont elle n'avait jamais entendu parler avant d'arriver en Algérie et si son beau-père n'avait pas été mort peu avant son arrivée elle n'aurait probablement pas épousé mon père qui n'aurait pas pu si facilement s'opposer au refus opposé par son père à un mariage avec une ashkénaze qui de son côté n'avait jamais entendu le mot sépharade avant d'arriver à Oran.[107]

Besides she doesn't have the feeling of belonging to a community she had never heard of before arriving in Algeria and if her father-in-law hadn't died shortly before she arrived she probably wouldn't have married my father who could not so easily have opposed his father's refusal to let him marry an Ashkenazi who had never heard the word Sephardi before com-ing to Oran.[108]

Moreover, Cixous's father reclaimed his Jewish identity in part as an act of resistance against the 1940 Vichy *Statut des juifs* ("en tant qu'antivichy"), which deprived the family of its French citizenship. Alison Rice analyzes the Vichy years and revocation of Cixous's citi-zenship as generative of her later philosophy of selfhood. She writes, "Growing up in Algeria was not incidental to the writings of Cix-ous, for it made her highly attentive to the traps of identity and the impossibility of 'self-sameness.' Witnessing the revocation and resto-ration of her French citizenship made her wary of national forms of self-identification."[109]

True to its title, *Rêveries* opens with a scrap of nocturnal dream writing, something composed in the middle of a hot July night. In the passage of self-citation, which is taken up repeatedly in the text, and eventually serves as its concluding line, Cixous contemplates the possibility of arriving in Algeria. She writes that the notion of arriving was a perpetually deferred dream, something that she never quite achieved. Now that the opportunity to return has presented itself, she must take it up and investigate the hid-den contours of memory to "explain" this gap to herself.

Tout le temps où je vivais en Algérie je rêvais d'arriver un jour en Algérie, j'aurais fait n'importe quoi pour y arriver, avais-je écrit, *je ne me suis jamais trouvée en Algérie, il faut maintenant précisément que je m'en explique, comment je voulais que la porte s'ouvre, maintenant et pas plus tard,* avais-je noté très vite, *dans la fièvre de la nuit de juillet, car c'est maintenant, et probablement pour des dizaines ou des centaines de raisons, qu'une porte vient de s'entrebâiller dans la galerie Oubli de ma mémoire, et pour la première fois, voici que j'ai la possibilité de retourner en Algérie, donc l'obligation ...*[110]

The whole time I was living in Algeria I would dream of one day arriving in Algeria, I would have done anything to get there, I had written, I never made it to Algeria, it is right now that I must explain what I mean by this, how I longed for the door to open, now not later, I had scribbled, in the fever of the July night, for it is now, and probably for dozens or hundreds of reasons that a door has cracked open in the Oblivion Wing of my memory, and now for the first time I may be able to return to Algeria, therefore I must ...

The original italics in the passage in French demonstrate the distance between Cixous citing her own feverish night writing and Cixous reading and commenting on this excerpt of found text. The passage comprises a mere half-page of notes of the missing five pages she (thinks that she) remembers having written. What could those missing pages have contained? The open question of arrival framed within the larger context of missing pieces and missing pages sets the tone for the rest of the work. The opening foregrounds the search for the self in relation to her Algerian origin story as a process that is never fully completed. Cixous gestures to the limitation of thinking of the self as a unified whole, a completed text, or a puzzle that could be solved. She emphasizes in this passage that she never "found herself" in Algeria (*je ne me suis jamais trouvée en Algérie*). The self, for Cixous, (in childhood, in Algeria, or otherwise) is not a discrete substance that could be lost or even recovered.

Instead, Cixous constructs a parallel between the anguish of searching for lost pages and the distress of never recovering a full understanding of the relationship between the past and the self. She frames this search for lost time as a disorder (*maladie algérie*), one whose grip threatens her with madness, and is filled with returns and reversals. In this sense, Cixous's opening enacts a similar gesture to Khatibi's opening of *Amour bilingue*. Both texts introduce nocturnal writing as a dream space of unreason and ludic possibility. Khatibi writes of *la bi-langue* in this opening passage at once as an opportunity, an inner chasm, and an amnesic energy, while Cixous presents night writing as an act of semi-conscious illumination and transcription. Both texts also stage writing as a perpetual series of beginnings. The first line of Khatibi's text begins with a parenthetical: "(Il partit, revint, repartit. Il décida de partir définitivement. Le récit devrait s'arrêter ici, le livre se fermer sur lui-même)." [(He left, he came back, he left again. He decided to leave for good. The story should stop here, the book close upon itself.)][111] The opening movement – leaving, coming back, leaving again – evokes the reversals inherent in the structure of the text. Likewise, Cixous's first and final line evoke the same dream of arriving in Algeria, which is never fully accomplished, and delivers the autobiographical subject back to the text's starting point. These openings frame the text as an ouroboros with a tail that arcs back to its own head. "Ce début du texte semblait dévorer le récitant, qui le lisait sans relâche." [The beginning of a text seemed to consume the storyteller, who read it ceaselessly.][112] With these structures, the texts foreground unselfing as a source of destabilization. Khatibi develops this idea in terms of vertigo with the *folie infinie* of the bilingual self, while Cixous writes destabilization as an Algerian malady that plagues her self-experience.

Cixous expresses unselfing as a fragmentation in this work, which begins with her most intimate childhood relationships and expands to include her fraught experiences with community and citizenship in colonial Algeria. The text examines each of these relations, radiating from the childhood familial self to larger and larger communities, which are experienced as sites of exclusion and loneliness. This section explores the way in which *Rêveries* presents Cixous's relationship with her brother, her traumatic relationship to the veiled girl whose death she witnesses as a child, and the overarching desire for a community in Algeria that could welcome her. Each site of self-separation evokes splitting and self-division through the experience of taking of sides and the loss of the fantasy of unity.

Fragmentary unselfing in *Rêveries* is presented first as gender difference experienced in childhood. Cixous is cut off from the inner life she once shared with her brother as he is granted a degree of freedom that remains foreign to her as they come of age together. The repeated references to self-division ("coupure") of the experiencing self point to the profound sense of estrangement she experiences. Until the family got a bicycle, which allowed her brother to leave home on his own, the two shared an intimate, and seemingly undifferentiated inner life. From that point forward, this shared existence is cut in two; she no longer looks through the world through a universal, undifferentiated lens, but rather understands that her perspective is solitary and also gendered. The bike, which allows her brother a sense of autonomy and mobility becomes the marker for the gender separation between the two siblings. Ironically, this vehicle for male freedom is a woman's bike, which enrages her 13-year-old brother. Cixous rarely rides the bike herself, and writes of the ensuing loss of the siblings' shared inner life as a violent separation.

In a passage on the impact of the bicycle on their relationship, Cixous writes, "Ce vélo nous a vraiment séparés, pensai-je, jusque-là nous ne faisions qu'un frère avec sœur intérieure et inversement maintenant je n'étais plus que sœur sans frère intérieur, et comme le dit mon frère je m'enfonçai de mon côté dans *mes rêveries solitaires*."[113] [That bike really drove a wedge between us, I thought, up to then we were just one brother with an internal sister and vice versa now I was nothing but a sister with no internal brother, and as my brother says I for my part burrowed deeper and deeper into *my solitary reveries*.][114] As in the passage examined later on her desire for community, Cixous expresses a deep longing for connection and a nostalgia for a missing and mythical shared origin. When she writes of this experience of isolation and alienation, she draws longingly on notions of kinship, community, and destiny. These themes are also present as she mourns the link between her and her brother. The seemingly banal event of getting a shared bike causes an alienating sense of fragmentation from the imagined whole, pushing her towards her solitary daydreaming and thereby distancing her from reality. She turns towards her "side" and feels alone in her reveries.

This sense of separation from those closest to her continues during adolescence, where the sense of alienation intensifies. Cixous writes of the loneliness she experienced at the lycée she attended in Algiers after her father's death. She writes, "À Alger je suis tombée dans l'Algériefrançaise, et c'était le Lycée contra lequel laquelle je ne pouvais rien faire. J'étais déjà coupée de mon frère, notre vie intérieure coupée en deux vies extérieures et coupée de moi-même."[115] [In Algiers I fell into FrenchAlgeria and that was the Lycée, my high school, against which I was powerless. I was already cut from my brother, our inner life cut into two outer lives, and cut off from myself.][116] Cixous writes here again of the lost communion between her and her brother, as well as the added estrangement she experiences from herself (*moi-même*). The text evokes a deep sense of exclusion and exile, which begins on the level of the family and expands to the nation.

Indeed, at the *lycée* in Algiers she grows acutely aware of her status as an outsider to the French from France, living in "l'Algériefrançaise." With this neologism, Cixous elides the space between Algeria and France in the unofficial colloquial expression, thereby evoking the parallel elision of autonomous identity in France's *départment*. Cixous attempts to physically push these entities together, and to overcome the artificiality of this division. At the same time, she is made suddenly aware that being Jewish from "L'Algériefrançaise" does not allow for a simple origin story and immediately requires more language and more explanation. Cixous expresses the self as cut up and cut off; the fragments are the fallout from her multilayered sense of exclusion from outside others and for the nostalgia for the connection with her brother that ends abruptly.

Cixous explores the result of this sense of inner separation on her perspective on reality. In a passage on the school for girls, which she attended in Oran, she explains that her father accidentally enroled her there without knowing that it was *ordinarement antisémite* [ordinarily anti-Semitic].[117] She locates the alienating aspect of fragmentary unselfing in the disorienting experience of unreality. Remembering these spaces brings on a bout of self-doubling in her consciousness:

> Dans la cour intérieure, des choses invisibles m'effleurent, dès que je suis seule je suis touchée par les fantômes, je suis doublée, double, tout est double, toutes les personnes qui s'assemblent et se séparent au Lycée sont doubles, et sont des doubles, toutes sont elles-mêmes et simultanément des figurantes. On joue une pièce. Un film est tourné.[118]

> Invisible things brush past me in the inner courtyard, as soon as I am alone I am touched by the ghosts, I am doubled, double, everything is double, all the people who come together and draw apart in the Lycée are double, are doubles, all of them at the same time themselves and a stand-in. The play begins. The film starts to roll.[119]

Like Michaux and Valéry, Cixous traces the inner space of experience during her reveries. In this passage, Cixous is sequestered in her loneliness (as in the earlier passage on her brother and the bike) but the sentiment here is amplified. She feels that everything she experiences is happening in an alternative reality, as if in a play, or a film. The "inner courtyard" is populated by ghosts; she is both herself and a double of her experience. Cixous's unselfing experiences are continually marked by these descriptions of separation, cutting, and doubling.

The most striking instance of fragmentary unselfing in Cixous occurs at the end of the text. The "coupure" motif resounds in this disturbing passage on witnessing; she writes that she is "cut off" [*coupée*] from the victim while simultaneously living with the girl's alien presence inside of her after her death. This event is emblematic of unselfing as fragmentation in Cixous's work as she witnesses the gruesome scene of a veiled girl being run over by the wheels of a carousel as a 7-year-old. In this episode, Cixous describes this experience of witnessing the young Algerian girl's death, which left her with the uncanny sensation of being cut in two. She emphasizes that this event is one of her first memories, an event of an original separation of self from self. "Le premier de mes premiers souvenirs ayant trait au Plan d'anéantissement de l'être algérien est une histoire de fille coupée en deux."[120] [The oldest of my oldest Algerian memories about the Plan to annihilate the Algerian being is a tale of a girl who gets cut in two.][121] She continues by describing the scene: "La jeune fille est entraînée dans le voile son corps est saisi comme une viande dans le moulin, elle ne peut pas le dégager."[122] [The girl is yanked after her veil her body is trapped like a piece of meat in a grinder, she can't extract it.][123] Seeing this accident results in the painful fragmentation of the experiencing self.

As she listens to the girl's haunting scream, Cixous feels herself split in two. Cixous writes, "Un affreux sentiment de délivrance me perce. J'ai l'existence coupée en deux."[124] [A dreadful feeling of release runs through me. My existence has been cut in two.][125] The spectacle puts tremendous demands on the subject: the girl's scream pulls her in and makes her feel that she has experienced the accident herself. However, there is a part of the self, the witnessing part, that can remain separate from the scene. Cixous explains, "C'est d'avoir vu et regardé le supplice que nul être humain ne devrait voir, dont nul être humain ne devrait détourner le regard, rivées que nous étions dans les wagonnets, l'une toute à la mort l'autre en dehors."[126] [It is from having seen and looked at the torture that no human being should have to see, that no human being should turn away from, riveted as we were in the little carriages, the one completely given over to death the other outside it.][127] The one/ the other pair here refers simultaneously to the split between Cixous and the veiled girl and the split Cixous experiences within herself. One part of Cixous is fixated on the death of the victim while the other part feels the shame of separation and individuation. By witnessing this event, Cixous feels torn between the orientation towards the death of the other and towards the life of the self.

In the section that immediately follows, she reflects on this self-doubling in a circuitous run-on sentence by way of prosaic enjambment. Omitting natural pauses, commas, and periods, she emits a long string of breathless text. Cixous writes that she carries the Algerian girl within her as a veiled other, a lingering presence that she has invariably tried to fight off throughout her life. The fate of the other girl is described in the following passage as something that has happened to her, the subject of experience.

C'est une tragédie qui est aussi une Ville, un pays, une histoire, l'histoire de celle que je ne suis pas, un voile nous sépare et pour cette raison même

je sens un voile tomber une buée rouge sur ma tête sur mes épaules,
effrayée de toutes mes forces je me débats mais je ne le nie pas, pour rien
au monde je ne le nierais pour rien au monde je ne le mettrais, et pour cette
raison même malgré moi je porte une jeune fille voilée que je ne suis pas,
j'ai en moi la fille coupée en deux le voile mortel la coupure parce que je
suis une fille témoin de la victime, coupée de la victime. Je rentre chez moi.
Je ne cours pas. J'ai le sentiment que *cela m'est arrivé*. Depuis l'accident
quelque chose en moi me reste voilé.[128]

It is a tragedy that is also a City, a country, a history, the history of the one
I am not, a veil keeps us apart and for this very reason I feel a veil alight
a red mist on my head on my shoulders, terrified I fight it off but I don't
deny it, nothing could make me deny it nothing could make me put it on,
and for this reason even in spite of myself I am the bearer of a girl in a veil
who is not me, I have within me a veiled girl cut in two the deadly veil
the cut because I am a girl the victim's witness, cut off from the victim. I
go home. I do not run. I feel that *that happened to me*. Since the accident
something inside me is veiled to me.[129]

Cixous describes her complicated relationship to the victim, a fragmentation of perspective that persists long after the screaming has ceased.
Although she is rationally aware of the distinction between the experience of the veiled girl and her own, the italics graphically emphasize
her personal relationship to the event. "I feel that *that happened to me.*"
The veiled girl becomes a piece of herself, one who asserts herself as a
light, and yet enduring presence. Afterwards, something inside her is
cut off, veiled, and held apart from the rest of the self. In this passage on
witnessing she writes that she is "cut off" from the victim while simultaneously living with the girl's alien presence inside of her after her
death. The theme of the pain of self-separation concretizes the amor-
phous sensation of alienation that resounds throughout the text.

Moreover, the unselfing that Cixous experiences in this exceptional
episode reflects her larger inability to integrate into post-Vichy Algiers.
She describes her "good luck" in avoiding integration into Algerian
society due to her position as a Jew: "À Oran nous avions eu la chance
mon frère et moi d'être entrés dehors, à l'école en carton, grâce à Vichy
nous étions passés à côté de l'internement dans *le plan d'effacement de
l'être algérien*, puisque nous étions nous-mêmes destinés à *l'effacement
de l'être juif*."[130] [In Oran we were fortunate my brother and I to have
entered outside, at the cardboard school, thanks to Vichy we avoided
internment *in the plan to efface the Algerian being*, since we ourselves were
destined to *the effacement of the Jewish being*.][131] She writes that she never

achieved integration into the Algerian society that was being made French, still a *départment* at this time, living instead at its fringes. The text sketches out layers of personal erasure; she avoids "Algerian" erasure at the hands of French empire because of her Jewishness, despite her ambivalent relationship to this site of exclusion.

And yet, she writes that she still desires to "arrive" in Algeria. Cixous uses the oft-quoted neologism *inséparabe* to convey the role that belonging plays in the construction of her narrative self. Estranged from her Jewish heritage and desiring, while not quite belonging to, the Arab communities surrounding her, Cixous lives painfully in this space between sides. The self is drawn to this other Algeria in desire and in love, but unlike Khatibi's vision of *Pensée-autre,* the self does not achieve plural thought or a disoriented orientalism. Instead, the relationship with the self is unliveable. She explores this in a paragraph-length burst:

Le plus insupportable c'est, par-dessus les combats et les humiliations, que nous étions assaillis au Clos-Salembier par les êtres mêmes que nous voulions aimer, dont nous étions lamentablement amoureux, auxquels nous étions liés pensions-nous par toutes les parentés et communautés d'origine, de destin, d'états d'esprit, de mémoire, de toucher, de goût, nos ennemis étaient nos amis, il y avait erreur et confusion de côtés de tous côtés je voulais être de leur côté mais c'était un désir de mon côté de leur côté le désir était sans côté, sans ici, c'était un brasier un buisson aux bras d'épines, je ne désirais que leur Ville et leur Algérie, je voulais à toutes forces y arriver je pouvais passer des heures accroupie à quelques mètres d'eux sans bouger, espérant démontrer mes bonnes intentions, une patience et un comportement que je n'eus jamais avec le camp des Français, dès qu'il y avait Français j'étais exultation arme où il y avait Arabes j'étais espoir et plaie. Moi, pensais-je je suis *inséparabe*. C'est une relation invivable avec soi-même.[132]

The most intolerable, above and beyond the battles and humiliations, is that we were assailed in the Clos-Salembier by those whom we wanted to love, with whom we were lamentably in love, to whom we were attached we thought by kinship and communities of origin, by destiny, by our manner of thinking, by memory, by touch, by taste, our enemies were our friends, there was error and confusion on the side on all the sides I wanted to be on their side but it was a desire on my side on their side the desire had no side, it had no here, it was burning coals a thornbush of arms, I only wanted their City and their Algeria, with all my strength I wanted to arrive there I could spend hours squatting a few yards away from them without moving, hoping to demonstrate my good-will, a kind of patience and behavior that I never had with the French camp, the minute there was French I was exultation arms where there were Arabs I was hope and wound. My, I thought I am *inseparab*. This is an unlivable relationship with oneself.[133]

Unlike her relationship to French Algeria (which pretends at autonomy and subjugates with violence and force), Cixous waits patiently and hopefully for entry to Arab Algeria. There is error and confusion (not to mention racism and misogyny, as she indicates earlier) from every angle. The word *côté* is repeated four times at the beginning of the passage. But there is also an ardent desire to be in community, calling upon shared attachments to ways of thinking, touching, and being. Unable to distance herself from this community that she covets from the outside, she feels that she is nevertheless inseparable from it.

While Cixous celebrates self-fragmentation and the escape from self-unity in her earlier writings, this notion of fragmented selves is presented as a source of suffering in her writings on Algeria. The tone of *Rêveries* is strikingly sombre when it relates the narrative of self-fragmentation: conjoined selves like the brother-sister pair individuate uncomfortably, and others like the witness-victim are painfully thrust together. This is particularly salient when compared to the fluid vision of plural subjectivity articulated in the context of Promethea, or *écriture féminine*. The dream of emancipatory plural subjectivity in Cixous's earlier writings is deflated by the shocks of unselfing that populate *Rêveries*. Occupied by ghostly doubles, the world of self-fragmentation in post-Vichy Algeria is defined by painful alienation in this work.

In this sense, Cixous's experience of fragmentary unselfing in *Rêveries* is closer to the sensation of radical and agentless empathy that Charlotte Delbo describes in her writings on Auschwitz than it is to Khatibi's theory of the *Pensée-autre*. Far from an exultant vision of plural subjectivity, Cixous's experience of unselfing is another cutting in a long set of associated splits that eventually get in the way of true intersubjective exchange. Whereas Khatibi in *Amour bilingue* writes of the fragments of the self as built on linguistic difference, and frames desire as the pleasurable attempt to cross over into the language of the other, borders in Cixous are not as easily traversed. The drama of side-taking is inherent in the relationship to being a self; this process is not ludic but rather "unliveable" for Cixous. These competing interpretations of the afterlife of fragmentation underscore the inherent ambiguities in the unselfing experience. For Khatibi, the splintering of the ordinary experience of selfhood paves the way to an ethical relation with the other; for Cixous, self-division is a painful turn away from the world.

6 Unselfing as Destruction: Decreation and Inner Experience in Simone Weil and Georges Bataille

We possess nothing in the world – a mere chance can strip us of everything – except the power to say "I." That is what we have to give to God – in other words, to destroy. There is absolutely no other free act which it is given us to accomplish – only the destruction of the "I."

Simone Weil

But in me everything begins again; nothing is ever risked. I destroy myself in the infinite possibility of my fellow beings: it annihilates the sense of this *self*. If I attain, an instant, the extreme limit of the "possible," shortly thereafter, I will flee, I will be *elsewhere*.

Georges Bataille

How can a self be destroyed in a way that leaves knowledge in its wake? What is the value of emptying the self? The promise of the passing into the uncreated? This final chapter investigates the destruction model for unselfing through these central questions in the work of Simone Weil (1909–1943) and Georges Bataille (1897–1962) by examining their theories of *décréation* and *expérience intérieure*, respectively. On the surface, these contemporaries seem to be antagonistically positioned in their pursuit of self-destruction, with Weil embodying the figure of the modern saint and Bataille serving as the philosopher of transgression. However, Weil and Bataille write of unselfing in strikingly compatible terms: both seek the last outpost of the self by attempting to obliterate its illusions during privileged states of consciousness. Despite that these two thinkers (who crossed paths in 1931) were mostly at odds in their visions of the world, both manipulate the discourse of self-sovereignty to alter it violently from within.[1] This chapter travels the forking paths to and from shared destruction in Weil and Bataille, focusing on their writings on the drama of inner experience.

Destruction as a narrative model stretches our interpretative categories and introduces new and difficult ethical questions on the survival of the self. The destruction of the self in Weil and Bataille cannot last indefinitely. Indeed, I have argued that it is the return to ordinary consciousness which allows for the possibility of storytelling, writing, and witnessing. Primo Levi develops this distinction between partial and total witnessing in his writing on Auschwitz. In his words, the "true witnesses" are those who were never able to return after the horrors of experience. In *The Drowned and the Saved*, he separates survivors who write from the *Muselmann* as the total witnesses to the Nazi death camps, who did not return because of their complete physiological and psychological collapse.

> I must repeat: we, the survivors, are not the true witnesses. This is an uncomfortable notion of which I have become conscious little by little, reading the memoirs of others and reading mine at a distance of years. We survivors are not only an exiguous but also an anomalous minority: we are those who by their prevarications or abilities or good luck did not touch bottom. Those who did so, those who saw the Gorgon, have not returned to tell about it, or have returned mute, but they are the "Muslims," the submerged, the complete witnesses, the ones whose deposition would have a general significance.[2]

The writing that survives experience only amounts to an "anomalous minority" or the unwritten and unthought testimony that remains unheard and unread. Those who experience total destruction cannot return to tell about it. Drawing on the testimonies of Jean Améry, Aldo Capri, Primo Levi and others, Agamben explicates the difficult term – *Muselmann* – in *Remnants of Auschwitz: The Witness and the Archive* as a figure of resignation and loss of all will and consciousness. He writes,

> The most likely explanation of the term can be found in the literal meaning of the Arabic word muslim: the one who submits unconditionally to the will of God. It is this meaning that lies at the origin of the legends concerning Islam's supposed fatalism, legends which are found in European culture starting with the Middle Ages (the deprecatory sense of the term is present in European languages, particularly in Italian). But while the muslim's resignation consists in the conviction that the will of Allah is at work every moment and in even the smallest events, the *Muselmann* of Auschwitz is instead defined by a loss of all will and consciousness.[3]

The notion that the survivors of the camps are not "complete witnesses" to the events experienced emphasizes the gap between those who write of unselfing, and those who never return to the subject position. In this sense, Weil and Bataille bear witness to the temporary annihilation of the self, but are not "complete witnesses." At the same time, both seem to be aware of the critical ethical territory that the notion of self-destruction occupies. Weil explains that while external (that is, imposed) destruction can be expiatory and even redemptive if associated with love, "La destruction purement extérieure du je est douleur quasi infernale."[4] [Purely external destruction of the "I" is quasi-infernal suffering.][5] Even so, both Weil and Bataille pursue the temporary destruction of the self as the route to undoing its illusions and delivering the self from the will (Weil) and discourse (Bataille).

Unselfing in both Weil and Bataille is pursued and framed in the language of mysticism, a fraught site of categorization for both thinkers. While Weil presents her mystical experiences of the divine as Christological interventions, she is more of a liminal figure than her canonical reputation might suggest. Alexander Irwin sets the record straight with the following: "Weil's thought is assuredly not for the tender-minded. Hers is a mysticism in which suffering and violence play central roles and whose ultimate aim is the brutal eradication of the human ego."[6] While Weil clearly positions herself in relation to Christian doctrine in her interpretation of experience, she also searches for an original vocabulary of immediacy to describe her encounter with the divine. Moreover, she struggles relentlessly to integrate the materiality of her body with selfhood and spiritual life. She also writes extensively on baptism and sacrament, though she was never baptized herself.

The contradictions and tensions in Bataille's "mysticism" has also been the subject of scandal and debate. Bataille emphasizes at the beginning of L'expérience intérieure that he approaches mysticism in an unconventional way in that he rejects domesticated religious experience and pursues inner experience *at the expense of* transcendence. Nontheless, Sartre famously dismissed him as a "nouveau mystique."[7] Studying unselfing in Weil and Bataille moves the discussion of their work away from the polarizing characterizations that have defined them and towards a new reading of their writings in light of philosophical discussions of the self. These texts on destructive unselfing are invested in epistemological questions (in that they interrogate the knowledge of self-experience) as well as metaphysical ones. I focus on their "mysticism" not as a dismissal of their thought as totalitarian or non-systematic (as in Sartre's critique of Bataille), but rather for the way they frame the individual experiences of suffering in relation to the sacred.

The first part of the chapter focuses on Weil's mystical experiences and her notions of decreation, affliction, and suffering. It argues that while Weil uses the concept of decreation to reframe self-destruction as a powerful moral force, she struggles to elucidate the definitive value of traditional units of ethical inquiry, such as the person and the human body. The second part of the chapter examines Bataille's acute desire for self-rupture when situated within his discourse of inner experience. Violent, destructive unselfing in Bataille serves to dramatize life and free the subject from what he derisively calls "project," at the same time that he insists that experience with non-knowledge does not "communicate."[8] I establish the links between Weil's and Bataille's thinking on habit and the fleeting nature of insight in their modern mystical experiments. The final section of the chapter considers the figure of the other in both of their writings as the site for the expansion of consciousness, first presenting Weil's understanding of destruction as a means of becoming less self-interested and more open to the needs of others. It compares this position to Bataille's meditation on images of human suffering as a transgressive gesture that deliberately eschews both Christian and existential ethics. For both Weil and Bataille, the reduction of the self changes the relationships between the self and world, and also entails ambiguous ethical consequences.

Simone Weil: Unselfing as Decreation

One of Weil's aims in theorizing the concept of decreation is to distinguish it from ordinary forms of destruction. She insists throughout her work that the two concepts are situated on opposing poles; decreation is the obverse of everyday destruction. She writes, "La destruction est l'extrême opposé de la dé-création. Essayer de concevoir cela clairement."[9] [Destruction is the extreme opposite of decreation. Try to see this clearly.] Whereas Bataille valorizes destruction as a rupture with knowledge and project, Weil seeks to reframe destruction through the notion of decreation as the route to the uncreated. Understanding Weil's reframing of destruction as meaningful decreation requires parsing the conceptual clarity that she demands between the two. Weil explains: "Décréation: faire passer du crée dans l'incrée. Destruction: faire passer du crée dans le néant. Ersatz coupable de la décréation."]¹⁰ [Decreation: to make something created pass into the uncreated. Destruction: to make something created pass into nothingness. A blameworthy substitute for decreation.]¹¹ Decreating the self, through affliction, whether it is through distress, poverty, labour, cruelty, torture, or disease, she argues, constitutes divine love. Suffering by these means does not reduce the self to nothingness, but rather makes it possible to enter into the realm of the uncreated and the possible.

My discussion of the concept draws on Weil's Marseille notebooks from 1942, which would eventually become her best-known work, *La pesanteur et la grâce* (*Gravity and Grace*). This celebrated 1947 volume, which was substantially edited and introduced by Gustave Thibon, introduced Weil to the likes of Camus, Ricoeur Girard, and Mauriac.[12] This section also examines the first-person accounts of Weil's mystical experiences primarily through "Lettre à Joë Bousquet" and "L'Amour de Dieu et le malheur" (The Love of God and Affliction), which were sent to her friend, Joseph-Marie Perrin, a Dominican priest. The latter text would eventually be published in the collection of writings *Attente de Dieu* (*Waiting for God*).[13] Both texts were both mailed just prior to Weil's trip to the United States in May 1942 and before her death the following year in London. By considering both the philosophies of unselfing in Weil's personal texts (notebooks and letters not originally meant for circulation) as well as her remarkable life, the conclusion attempts to account for the ethical concerns that stem from her relationship to the experience of suffering.

Weil's obsession with overthrowing the constraints of the ego in the pursuit of an illusionless experience of reality brings us back to the core inquiries articulated at the beginning of the book. It was Weil's notions of attunement and attention to the other as well as her commitment to escaping the illusions of the ego that motivated Iris Murdoch's account of unselfing. We remember that Murdoch emphasizes the need for a theology that could persist when God seems most absent from the world, a preoccupation she also inherited from Weil. Despite the profundity of her personal mystical experiences, Weil characterized her historical moment as one of divine absence, rooted in the separation of religion from the social and the real: "Depuis l'aube des temps historiques, jamais, sauf pendant une certaine période de l'Empire romain, le Christ n'a été aussi absent que maintenant. Les anciens auraient jugé monstrueuse cette séparation de la religion et de la vie sociale que même la plupart des chrétiens aujourd'hui trouvent naturelle."[14] [Since the beginning of historical time, never, except during a certain period of the Roman empire, was Christ as absent as he is now. The ancients would have seen this separation between religion and social life, which even most Christians today find natural, as monstrous.]

Nevertheless, Weil's philosophy of decreation stems from her formative visitations of the divine, which she expresses as experiences of Christ. In both her autobiographical and theoretical writings, Weil defines mystical experiences as short, ephemeral moments of divine presence that occur during great joy and great pain. These experiences have the power to destroy ordinary self-sovereignty in a transformative way. Weil, who was raised agnostic in an ethnically Jewish family insists in letters to both Père Perrin and Joë Bousquet that she had not read the canonical medieval mystics before her own experiences.[15] In the letter to Bousquet that dates from 1942, she describes her first mystical encounter in Christian terms of union and divine presence.[16]

> Pendant tout cela le mot même de Dieu n'avait aucune place en mes pensées. Il n'en a eu qu'à partir du jour, il y a environ trois ans et demi, où je n'ai pas pu la lui refuser. Dans un moment d'intense douleur physique, alors que je m'efforçais d'aimer, mais sans me croire le droit de donner un nom à cet amour, j'ai senti, sans y être aucunement préparée – car je n'avais jamais lu les mystiques – une présence plus personnelle, plus certaine, plus réelle que celle d'un être humain, inaccessible et aux sens et à l'imagination, analogue à l'amour qui transparaît à travers le plus tendre sourire d'un être aimé.[17]

> During all this time, the word God had no place at all in my thoughts. It never had, until the day – about three and a half years ago – when I could no longer keep it out. At a moment of intense physical pain, while I was making the effort to love, although believing I had no right to give any name to the love I felt, while completely unprepared for it (I had never read the mystics), a presence more personal, more certain, and more real than that of a human being; it was inaccessible both to sense and to imagination and it resembled the love that irradiates the tenderest smile of somebody one loves.[18]

Weil characterizes the divine as inconceivable and stresses that she was unprepared for this experience. A moment of physical weakness (an intense headache) occasions this unexpected vision of love. This autobiographical example has two features that will resound in Weil's theoretical accounts. First, the experience is transient and cannot last, like the smile from a loved one in Weil's analogy. The soul, she writes, can only live in God for short periods of time because it is poisoned by suffering.[19] Second, while this transformative experience is singular, unexpected, and miraculous, it stems from both intense bodily pain and "efforts" that continue after the experience is over (when God and Christ become mingled in her thoughts). These two features – the transiency of experience, the cultivation of habit from them – will also feature in her writing on destructive unselfing as decreation.

What exactly must be unselved in Weil's vision of decreation? An intuitive starting point in answering this question is the will. One of Weil's greatest ambitions was to erase her will, not only in the Schopenhauerian sense of endless and mindless striving, but all personal being, rooted in the past and the future.[20] Unlike the experience of dwelling on the past and harbouring the illusions that one has about the future, she argues that the experience of the present is a privileged moment of depersonalized innocence. She writes, "Si nous nous considérons à un moment déterminé – l'instant présent, coupé du passé et de l'avenir – nous sommes innocents. Nous ne pouvons être à cet instant que ce que nous sommes: tout progrès implique une durée."[21] [If we consider what we are at a definite moment – the present moment, cut off from the past and the future – we are innocent. We cannot at that instant be anything but what we are.][22] In this sense, Weil's overarching project of unselfing can be understood as the goal to reduce the conscious experience of the narrative self (the past, project, and plans for the future) to the lens and scale of the experiencing self (which lives in the immediacy of the present moment). This experiencing self, which is ordinarily shaped by features like perspective and agency, should be stripped of its uniqueness in favour of a universal conscious experience. Only then, she argues, is it possible to experience the uncreated in grace. The fullness of the cross, for Weil, is fully achieved in a human being who both destroys the "I" from within and experiences affliction from the outside in redemptive suffering. Thus, unselfing is written as destruction in Weil, but only when it is understood in this special way.

Weil theorizes the personalized self as a screen that shields a person from the intensity of God's attention. She writes, "Car si nous étions exposés au rayonnement direct de son amour, sans la protection de l'espace, du temps et de la matière, nous serions évaporés comme l'eau au soleil; il n'y aurait pas assez de je en nous pour abandonner le je par amour."[23] [For if we were exposed to the direct radiance of his love, without the protection of space, of time and of matter, we should be evaporated like water in the sun; there would not be enough "I" in us to make it possible to surrender the "I" for love's sake.][24] The self in Weil's work functions as a physical and spiritual envelope. When the envelope is pierced, the divine can enter, and the self can pass into the realm of the uncreated. Temporarily destroying the envelope of the self allows for this caesura in being.[25] Weil continues, "La nécessité est l'écran mis entre Dieu et nous pour que nous puissions être. C'est à nous de percer l'écran pour cesser d'être."[26] [Necessity is the screen set between God and us so that we can be. It is for us to pierce through the screen so that we cease to be.][27] Decreation is achieved by breaking through the human experience and thereby accessing the divine. She writes that we must give up the "I" in order to reach God: "Nous ne possédons rien au monde – car le hasard peut tout nous ôter – sinon le pouvoir de dire *je*. C'est cela qu'il faut donner à Dieu, c'est-à-dire détruire. Il n'y a absolument aucun autre acte libre qui nous soit permis, sinon la destruction du *je*."[28] [We possess nothing in the world – a mere chance can strip us of everything – except the power to say "I." That is what we have to give to God – in other words, to destroy. There is absolutely no other free act which it is given us to accomplish – only the destruction of the "I."][29]

Indeed, the destruction of the self is imperative, according to Weil. She writes, "Il faut se déraciner. Couper l'arbre et en faire une croix, et ensuite la porter tous les jours."[30] [It is necessary to uproot oneself. To cut down the tree and make of it a cross, and then to carry it every day.][31] The metaphor of the self as a tree here has different temporal implications than the self as envelope. While unselfing at the level of the experiencing self is described as fleeting and ephemeral, Weil describes this process of uprooting as something that must become habit. One must cultivate the wilful and teleological project of repeated self-destruction. Weil describes the transition from self-as-envelope to self-as-tree as an apprenticeship that one might take on as a craft that requires time and effort. Decreation means taking on this project in order to let the universe penetrate the human, a process that will inevitably be painful.

In the last years of her life, Weil became fascinated with the *Bhagavad-Gītā*, the teachings of the mystical *Upanishads*, and the *Dao* and used these texts to develop her understanding of decreation. Lakshmi Kapani writes that Weil understood the *Gītā's* prescription to act without attachment to either the fruits of one's actions, or attachment to the notion of non-action itself. Given her own philosophical and theological preoccupations, Weil was drawn to the *Gītā's* notion of action without desire, articulated through its moral pedagogy and its emphasis on intellectual and metaphysical awareness.[32] Her study of Daoism also illuminated and enhanced her understanding of *décréation* as a renunciation and a distancing of the self from one's actions while remaining intellectually and metaphysically engaged in the world. The appeal of these works for Weil was rooted in their emphasis on contradiction and renunciation as occasions for reflection and transcendence. In her forward to Weil's collected journals from September 1941–February 1942, Alyette Degrâces writes that Weil's double reading of the *Gītā* and the *Dao* led her to play the texts off one another and focus on their shared qualities (the presence of oppositions, non-action) rather than their divergences.[33]

Though Weil knew of the *Gītā* through her brother before her close study of the text, she describes her 1940 reading experience as a

spiritual awakening: "Chose singulière, c'est en lisant ces paroles mer-
veilleuses et d'un son tellement chrétien, mises dans la bouche d'une
incarnation de Dieu, que j'ai senti avec force que nous devons à la
vérité religieuse bien autre chose que l'adhésion accordée à un beau
poème, une espèce d'adhésion bien autrement catégorique."[34] [Strange
to say it was in reading those marvellous words, words with such a
Christian sound, put into the mouth of an incarnation of God, that
I came to feel strongly that we owe an allegiance to religious truth
which is quite different from the admiration we accord to a beautiful
poem; it is something far more categorical.][35] Instructed by her former
classmate and Orientalist René Daumal, Weil learned Sanskrit grammar during this period and followed the text in the original script. The
cover of her sixth journal is inscribed with the name *Krishna* in Devanagari (as well as citations of Aeschylus, excerpts of the Lord's prayer,
and the Pythagorean theorem).

The eighteen chapters of the *Bhagavad-Gītā* – the Lord's Song – from
the Sanskrit epic, the *Mahābhārata,* centre on the teachings of Krishna
(Vishnu, or an incarnation of the supernatural), who guides the warrior
Prince Arjuna to wisdom and right action. Set on a battlefield, the *Gītā*
both grapples with the destruction and atrocity of war and allegorizes
the inner struggle for ethical living. Throughout the dialogue, Krishna
emphasizes Arjuna's sacred duty (*dharma*) to use force to fight against
injustice, though Arjuna despairs at the prospect of further killing. Only
through truly unselfish action can Arjuna achieve transcendence, that
is, fulfil his duty and act without ego. Section 4.20 of the *Gītā* reads,
"Having relinquished [all] attachment to the fruit of actions, ever content and independent, though engaged in [right] action – he does not
act at all," and section 4.23 emphasizes that acting without attachment
is acting through God: "[For him whose] attachment is gone, [who is]
liberated, [whose] mind is established in knowledge [while] performing
action for sacrifice, [the consequence of karma] is entirely dissolved.[36]
Weil was struck by these contradictions in obligation and the need to
quiet the objections of the self when faced with the obligation to act
through God. She writes, "L'accomplissement pur et simple des actes
prescrits, ni plus ni moins, c'est-à-dire l'obéissance, est à l'âme ce que
l'immobilité est au corps. C'est là le sens de la *Gītā*."[37] [Obedience – no
more and no less than the pure and simple performance of prescribed
acts – is to the soul what stillness is to the body. This is the meaning of
the *Gītā*.] Her writings on the *Gītā* indicate a radical reorientation of her
thought on violence and struggle; in her commentary on the text, she
effectively moves away from pacifism and struggles to understand the
role of force in countering injustice.[38]

The notion of actionless action as acting through God becomes a refrain in Weil's journals where she repeatedly scribbled "l'action non-agissante."[39] Weil was taken by the idea of the *atman* (as the soul of the universe) and the *dharma* (the sacred obligation to the divine and to the universe) in her readings. Her ideas on the self were thus also influenced by the Hindu notion of the tripartite strands of *guna,* wherein the self is conceived as a dominant characteristic (*sattva*, or highest wisdom and harmony, *rajas*, or activity and action and attachment, and *tamas*, or ignorance, darkness, and lethargy). She emphasizes, however that one must detach from the self completely – even from *sattva* – to achieve decreation. "Se detacher des trois *guna* (même *sattva*), agir pour l'acte, non pour son fruit (même le fruit du perfectionnement intérieur)."[40] [Detach the self from the three *guna* (even *sattva*), act for the action, not for its fruit (even the fruit of interior perfection).] Weil writes that *sattva* is the tendency towards decreation. "Une créature raisonnable, c'est une créature qui contient en soi le germe, le principe, la vocation de la décréation. *Sattva* est cette tendance à la décréation. Création et décréation, comme force centrifuge et centripète."[41] [A reasonable creature is one who contains within the self the germ, the principle, the vocation of decreation. *Sattva* is this tendency towards decreation. Creation and decreation as centrifugal and centripetal force.]

Though she did not write a complete essay on the role of force in the *Gītā* as she did with other sacred and literary texts, Weil copied passages from the work in her notebooks (both in Devanagari and in French translation) along with her impressions and exegesis. Doering writes, "Weil perceived in the *Gītā's* message a mystical antidote for the contagious evil inherent in force, a validation of the message she had perceived both in the Gospels and in the *Iliad*."[42] The poem expanded her understanding of force (as both a social and natural phenomenon) and the possible routes to containing its spread. While Weil's understanding of force was in many ways synonymous with oppression and dehumanization in her study of the *Iliad*, her writings on force at the end of her life explore it as energy in its spiritual, physical, as well as psychic dimensions.[43]

Weil's obsession with actionless action (*action non-agissante*) also led her to the study of Daoism. In Marseille, Weil attended a lecture on Chinese art which cited Daoist philosophers and Zen Buddhism and thereafter embarked on her study of Laozi, Zhuangzi, and Lietzi.[44] She connected the crucifixion of Christ to the Daoist model of actionless obedience: "Cette espèce d'activité passive, la plus haute de toutes, est parfaitement décrite dans la *Bhagavad-Gîtâ* et dans Lao-tseu."[45] [This kind of passive activity, the highest of all, is perfectly described in the *Bhagavad-Gītā* and in

Lao-Tse.][46] Though she learned Sanskrit at the same time that she discovered Chinese philosophy, she approached the latter differently, "running" through Daoist thought and weaving insights (on the inversion of value, on water in movement, and on the Way as practice) into her thinking.[47] She writes, for instance, in her notebooks, "Je suis la Voie. Le Tao, l'action non agissante, est une forme équivalente."[48] [I am the Way. The Dao, actionless action, is an equivalent form.] Chinese philosophy appears throughout these later notebooks, but in a condensed form. These notes reflect her attempt to integrate Daoist teachings on perspective and passivity with her understandings of decreation.[49]

During this period, Weil also became attracted to Gnosticism through the works of the Cathars after her friend and eventual biographer Simone Pétrement recommended she explore the subject in 1939. Weil devoted two essays in the *Cahiers du Sud* to Catharism and the work of Déodat Roché, the Freemason and scholar of the Cathars. She describes her interest in the Cathars in a letter to Roché as more than historical or intellectual curiosity, but a source of joy to read that "Catharism may be regarded as Christian Pythagoreanism or Platonism."[50] While some critics have highlighted the Gnostic aspects of Weil's work, others have argued that Gnosticism in general and (Catharism in particular) are not necessarily helpful in understanding Weil.[51] If Weil can be called a gnostic, it is by virtue of her methods, not by the content of her thinking. Simone Kotva argues convincingly that Weil's sympathies with esoterica (wherein hiddenness and concealment are critical factors) are not deviations from, but rather a consequence of her way of thinking. "In Weil's work, occultism is thus signaled thematically, but it is perpetuated *methodologically* through her style of thinking."[52]

Weil's syncretic thinking and idiosyncratic methodology have frustrated some critics, while enchanting others through her astounding elisions. Indeed, her unusual integration of Greek philosophy, Hindu theology, Daoist teachings and, to a lesser extent, Gnosticism, during the last years of her life reflect her desire to pinpoint the resonances between sacred texts across traditions, not necessarily with the attention of an anthropologist or an intellectual historian, but with the sense that these texts offer vital responses to the ethical questions posed by war, suffering, and oppression. Françoise Meltzer writes, "Weil's writings are unnerving because they rigorously refuse to see the difference – in valence, disciplinary boundaries, even style, and certainly teleology – between philosophy, religion, and political activism."[53] Though Weil did not live long enough to convincingly develop the cross-cultural and transhistorical meditations of her last notebooks, her syncretic thinking seems to be the root of her originality as a radical thinker. Weil's refusal to separate the physical, political, and spiritual realms in her thinking is perhaps evidence of such: "Weil could show how the crystallization of spiritual force in mystical practice empowered the decreated, 'selfless' subject for courageous political engagement. On the other hand, she could argue that true mystical transformation not only revealed itself as compatible with political action, but positively demanded committed action and risk in the political sphere."[54]

Indeed, Weil emphasizes that unselfing is an embodied experience; it is as physical as it is spiritual. To illustrate this, she writes in her essay, "L'Amour de Dieu et le Malheur" (The Love of God and Affliction), "Avec la joie seule, nous ne pourrions pas plus devenir amis de Dieu que l'on ne devient capitaine seulement en étudiant des manuels de navigation. Le corps a part dans tout apprentissage."[55] [We could no more become friends of God through joy alone than one becomes a ship's captain by studying books on navigation. The body plays a part in all apprenticeships.][56] Painful experiences thus play a formative role in forging a relationship with God. When Weil describes the moment of unselfing as a spontaneous piercing of the self-envelope that allows for access to the divine, the violence of the puncture metaphor is intentional on both a spiritual and physical level. Weil describes joy and pain as "des dons également précieux" [two equally precious gifts] using the imagery of the Trinity to stand for joy, and of the Cross to stand for pain.[57]

Affliction in Weil's work is inseparable from physical suffering that uproots life in all its aspects (social, psychological, and physical). It produces a state of mind as acute "que si un condamné est contraint de regarder pendant des heures la guillotine qui va lui couper le cou."[58] [as that of a condemned man who is forced to look for hours at the guillotine that is going to cut off his head.][59] Sounding much like Bataille in his desire for self-destruction during inner experience, Weil writes, "Il ne faut pas être *moi*, mais il faut encore moins être *nous*."[60] [It is necessary not to be "myself," still less to be "ourselves."][61] She emphasizes the spiritual value of painful experiences in getting rid of the self; affliction provides a privileged route to spiritual apprehension. "Quoi qu'il arrive, comment pourrais-je jamais trouver le malheur trop grand, puisque la morsure du malheur et l'abaissement auquel il condamne permettent la connaissance de la misère humaine, connaissance qui est la porte de toute sagesse?"[62] [Whatever happens, how could I ever think an affliction too great, since the wound of an affliction and the abasement to which those whom it strikes are condemned opens to them the knowledge of human misery, knowledge which is the door of all wisdom?][63] The experience of affliction, though painful, indicates an adherence to the never-finished project of enlightenment. Each painful moment of decreation allows for eventual creation and participation in the universe.

While Weil emphasizes that pain and suffering are essential features of the process of unselfing, she stresses that not all pain is meaningful. She uses the metaphor of the boiling point of water to illustrate that some painful experiences do not cross the threshold into meaningful affliction. In other words, some experiences merely scald us: "Entre le malheur et tous les chagrins qui, même s'ils sont très violents, très profonds, très durables, sont autre chose que le malheur proprement dit, il y a à la fois continuité et séparation d'un seuil, comme pour la température d'ébullition de l'eau. Il y a une limite au-delà de laquelle se trouve le malheur et non en deçà."[64] [There is both continuity and the separation of a definite point of entry, as with the temperature at which water boils, between affliction itself and all the sorrows that, even though they may be very violent, very deep and very lasting, are not affliction in the strict sense. There is a limit; on the far side of it we have affliction but not on the near side.][65] This limit between meaningful and meaningless pain is subjective in the sense that the same event may sink one person into affliction, but not another. Unselfing requires crossing a personal threshold.

At the same time, Weil places three conflicting conditions on affliction as a universal value to be pursued. These tensions in Weil's philosophy reflects the difficultly in connecting inner experience to outer struggle, the *vita contemplativa* to the *vita activa* in the attempt to allow the universe to destroy the individual self. First, Weil writes that one must want to love during extreme affliction. She writes, "Le malheur rend Dieu absent pendant un temps, plus absent qu'un mort, plus absent que la lumière dans un cachot complètement ténébreux. Une sorte d'horreur submerge toute l'âme. Pendant cette absence il n'y a rien à aimer … Il faut que l'âme continue à aimer à vide, ou du moins à vouloir aimer, fût-ce avec une partie infinitésimale d'elle-même."[66] [Affliction makes God appear to be absent for a time, more absent than a dead man, more absent than light in utter darkness of a cell. A kind of horror submerges the whole soul. During this absence there is nothing to love … The soul has to go on loving in the emptiness, or at least go on wanting to love, though it may only be with an infinitesimal part of itself.][67] If the soul stops loving, even in the void, it falls into something close to hell. She explains that in understanding affliction as an orientation and not a state of the soul, man finds himself nailed to the universe in a meaningful way. This requires the person who undergoes extreme experience to exercise some agency for there to be value in affliction. Much in the way that Valéry, Michaux, and Bataille cling to the witness figure as the key to understanding self-experience, Weil expresses that there must be some part of the subject that remains throughout the extreme experience of decreation.

Second, Weil uses the metaphor of the threshold to explain how far one must go for the experience to be considered "affliction" at all. Decreation must be total for it to count as a valuable long-term life-orienting experience. She writes, "Si cruellement qu'un homme souffre, si une partie de son être est intacte, et s'il n'a pas pleinement conscience qu'elle a échappé par hasard et reste à tout moment exposé aux coups du hasard, il n'a aucune part à la Croix."[68] [No matter how acutely a man suffers, if a part of his being is intact, and if he is not fully aware that it escaped by chance, and remains at every moment exposed to strokes of chance, he has no part in the Cross.] In this example, unlike in the first, she seems to argue that nothing must remain of "being" during these altered states; one must go on loving in the void without a sense of the continuity of the self through time.

Finally, Weil writes that it is wrong to desire affliction and a perversion to do so. Affliction, contrary to Bataille's view, is suffered unwillingly, or it is not affliction at all.[69] In theorizing the value of unselfing, Weil struggles with the conflicting demands of subjectivity and objectivity that she alternately valorizes. On the one hand, the subject is required to retain a degree of agency that allows for the desire to love, and on the other, the subject should experience the brute materiality of life from the position of an adoring object. Moreover, though it plays a central role in Weil's philosophy, she maintains that affliction should never be desired directly.

For Weil, the power of affliction is that it ultimately reduces the "I" function to a two-fold obedience to the materiality of life and the divine inspiration of God. Of those who have accepted that the self is "un produit aussi fugitif et aussi automatique des circonstances extérieures que la forme d'une vague de la mer," [a product as ephemeral and as contingent on external circumstances as the vague form of the sea], she writes, "Il n'y a plus rien en eux qu'on puisse appeler leur volonté propre, leur personne, leur moi. Ils ne sont plus autre chose qu'une certaine intersection de la nature et de Dieu."[70] [There is nothing left in them that one could call their will, their person, their ego. They are no longer anything but an intersection of nature and God.] In this way, decreation through affliction is meant to function much like baptism, a connection that Weil makes in her work. "Dans l'ancien baptême par immersion, l'homme disparaissait sous l'eau; c'est se nier soi-même, avouer qu'on est seulement un fragment de la matière inerte

dont est faite la création. Il ne reparaissait que soulevé par un mouvement ascendant plus fort que la pesanteur, image de l'amour divin dans
l'homme."[71] [In the old baptism by immersion, man disappeared under
the water; it is to deny oneself, to avow that one is only a fragment of
inert matter of which creation is made. He only reappeared lifted by
an upward movement that is stronger than gravity, the image of divine
love in man.] While Weil acknowledges this parallel with baptism, she
stresses that the terrible presence of affliction is "plus mystérieux, plus
miraculeux encore qu'un sacrement"[72] [more mysterious, more miraculous than a sacrament]. This deviation from the Catholic tradition is
perhaps not so surprising when considering Weil's refusal to be baptized herself. Unselfing through affliction in Weil's work attempts to
allow for a conversion experience with agency, though she emphasizes
at the same time that affliction should not be pursued directly.[73]

The question, then, of communicating these experiences to others is
fraught when the threshold is personal and not universal, when the
loving self ought to continue without personality or being. While Weil
undertakes the process of unselfing precisely in order to orient herself
towards the world, she questions whether painful experience can be
communicated or shared with others. Moreover, she laments that the
suffering of others does not provoke the same anguish as the suffering of the self; it does not prompt the question: "Pourquoi les choses
sont-elles ainsi?" ["Why are things this way?"] She writes, "Le singulier
c'est que le malheur d'autrui, sauf quelquefois, non pas toujours, celui
d'êtres très proches, ne provoque pas cette question. Tout au plus on la
pose une fois distraitement. Mais celui qui entre dans le malheur, cette
question s'installe en lui et ne s'arrête plus de crier. Pourquoi. Pourquoi.
Pourquoi."[74] [The singular thing is that the affliction of others, (except
occasionally, but not always, for those that are very close to us) does not
provoke this question. At most one poses this question once, distract-
edly. But for whoever experiences affliction, this question takes hold
and will not stop crying out. Why? Why? Why?] One cannot escape the
first-person orientation of experience, even in extreme affliction. In this
aspect, unselfing in Weil's philosophy is distinct from popular accounts
of empathy wherein reducing the claims of the self leads automatically
to the consideration and care for the other.

In the same text, Weil goes as far as to write that true compassion for
the afflicted is impossible because of this problem of communication.
Affliction, which by her understanding is irreducible to other concepts
and thus cannot be explained to others, does not invite metaphorical
understanding.[75] For a thinker that seeks to reduce the claims of the
self and attune the soul to human misery, this seems to foreclose the

possibility of responding to the other. A solitary world emerges from this thinking, comprised of individuals who suffer and experience grace alone. The problem of consolation emerges from this lonely picture. In her correspondence with Bousquet, Weil indicates that the affliction of others should not necessarily be alleviated, a thought she finds painful to admit. "Je vais vous dire quelque chose de dur à penser, plus dur encore à dire, presque intolérablement dur à dire à ceux qu'on aime. Pour quiconque est dans le malheur le mal peut peut-être se définir comme étant tout ce qui procure une consolation."[76] [I am going to say something which is painful to think, more painful to say, and almost unbearably painful to say to those one loves. For anyone in affliction, evil can perhaps be defined as being everything that gives any consolation.][77] According to Weil, consolation may be evil because it forecloses potentially transformative pain.

Moreover, Weil writes that the great enigma of human life is affliction rather than suffering.[78] She writes that is not surprising that people are put in concentration camps, made destitute, or suffer chronic pain. "Mais il est étonnant que Dieu ait donné au malheur la puissance de saisir l'âme elle-même des innocents et de s'en emparer en maître souverain. Dans le meilleur des cas, celui que marque le malheur ne gardera que la moitié de son âme."[79] [But it is surprising that God should have given affliction the power to seize the very souls of the innocent and to take possession of them as their sovereign lord. At the very best, he who is branded by affliction will keep only half his soul.][80] In her development of the threshold metaphor (the limit that allows for the distinction between douleur and malheur), Weil suggests that the redemptive destruction of the self is a solitary process, one wherein the voices of others must be silenced. Destructive unselfing in Weil's philosophy of decreation is thus also often a distancing of the self from the world. Traditional units of ethical value like the body or the person seem to disappear in Weil's thinking on decreation, despite her instance that the embodied nature of the human is part of God's creation. In valorizing the piercing violence of affliction, Weil's prevailing desire for decreation may lead to the rejection of the shared, material world.

In her own short life, Weil suffered from severe self-starvation, which has been the subject of much discussion in relation to her philosophy of decreation. From a young age, she used suffering as a tool for revolt: she gave up sugar as a small child because soldiers at the front were going without, engaged in hard agricultural labour, defended the working classes in their strikes by reducing her income to the level of the unemployed (and giving away the rest), joined the efforts in the Spanish Civil War, went to London to fight in the resistance, and cut down her rations to those of occupied France. Weil also experienced terrible head-aches, writing about her suffering of chronic pain in her letters. She would sometimes feel as though she was losing track of reality because of them. In a 1941 letter to Thibon, she writes, "Je suis tombée dans une sorte de gouffre où j'ai perdu la notion de temps."[81] [I fell into a sort of chasm where I lost the notion of time.] On August 17, 1943, Weil was transported to the Ashford Sanatorium in Kent and died a week later. From the earliest reports of her passing, Weil's death has invited specu-lation, characterized by the interpretive tension between her choosing to die as an act of political resistance, or succumbing to an eating dis-order stemming from mental illness.[82] A September 1 article from the Evening Standard reports "She was found living in one room in Lon-don, where she had been starving herself so that she might send food to French prisoners of war."[83] Given her staggering ability to negate her own bodily needs, Weil scholars have struggled to differentiate her theory of decreation from the way she lived out it out. Thibon writes, "On the one hand there was a longing for absolute self-effacement, an unlimited opening to reality even under its harshest forms, and on the other, a terrible self-will at the very heart of the self-stripping; the inflexible desire that this stripping should be her own work and should be accomplished in her own way, the consuming temptation to verify everything from within and experience everything for herself."[84] When examined through this perspective, the questions sparked by her death are perhaps as difficult to resolve as the ones that characterized her life. As we will see with Bataille in turn, Weil clings to the praxis of unselfing on her own terms. In both her notion of loving through the void, and in her manipulation of suffering to both spiritual and political ends, Weil's thinking demonstrates the ethical tensions at the heart of unselfing. The tensions between her philosophy and life trouble the notion that empa-thy or altruism emerge automatically from the ruins of self-destruction. While becoming more selfless may make a person more empathic in the ways some recent accounts insist, it is not clear that they make the person available – mentally or physically – to the other. Weil's work on destruction should prompt us to question the idea that unselfing, even as a passionate devotion to selflessness, will lead unproblematically to care.

Bataille: Destructive Unselfing in Inner Experience

While Weil pursues decreation as a form of self-dissolution at a histori-cal moment when God seems absent from the world, Bataille offers *La Somme athéologique* (*Atheological Summa*) as a treatise on divine absence.

L'expérience intérieure (*Inner Experience*) (1943) was originally published as the first of its three volumes. The title references Aquinas's *Summa Theologiae*, a collection of Catholic teachings and guide to theology students on the cyclical relationship between God, Creation, Man, and Christ. Bataille seeks to understand the possibility of supplication and prayer without a divine object. Everything in *La Somme athéologique*, then, is confined to the realm of the human, rather than extending to the pursuit of the divine. Bataille, after Nietzsche, grapples with the contingency of individual existence given the absence of God.[85] What ensues is a text that pursues the limits of ordinary human experience in the interest of making and unmaking man. The first sentence of *L'expérience intérieure* reads, "J'entends par *expérience intérieure* ce que d'habitude on nomme *expérience mystique*: les états d'extase, de ravissement, au moins d'émotion méditée."[86] [By *inner experience* I understand that which one usually calls *mystical experience:* the states of ecstasy, rapture, at least of mediated emotion.][87]

In his attack on utilitarian purpose, Bataille opposes grasping knowledge with various means of experiencing the sacred.[88] Sexuality, sacrifice, and ecstasy are distinct means of destabilizing the social world and accessing the realm beyond the confines of liberal reason. Asserting that the mystics did not go far enough in their processes of self-abandonment, Bataille argues for a violent contestation of knowledge to proceed to the end of the possible. Man must abandon his desire to be everything, along with his notions of God and the promise of salvation. To reach the state of non-knowledge that he seeks, he must "risk" the self in the process. Amy Hollywood compares Bataille's meditation methods to those of the medieval Franciscan mystic Angela of Foligno, whose distinction between object-centred meditation and ecstasy in the void is replicated in Bataille's work. "Bataille's conception of the self-subverting nature of the divine suggests that there will be no place for a positive objective of meditation in his practice. But instead of rejecting such an object, Bataille reinterprets it, arguing that the object contemplated by the mystic is not a divine object of emulation but a projection of the self, a dramatization of the self's dissolution."[89] The destruction of the self ends in a fusion (communication) between the self and the other. Through altered states of consciousness (ecstasy, rapture, anguish), *L'expérience intérieure* presents another version of the destruction model for unselfing. This section explores the stakes of destructive unselfing in Bataille in the context of Bataille's desire to escape project. It examines how he seeks to temporarily destroy his sense of individuated perspective and remove his sense of agency. The conclusion explores the implications of inner experience on the relationship between self and world and self and others through Bataille's views on communication and communion.

Given his rejection of the mystical concept of divine insight, Bataille's destruction model for unselfing is far from Paul's transformation on the road to Damascus. He is aligned, however, with the Neoplatonic mystics, for whom the fervent desire to experience the metaphysical realm outside the self is tied to what Peter Tracey Connor calls the "linguistic predicament of the mystical text." Connor writes, "An acute awareness of this disturbance is especially pronounced in the Neoplatonic mystical tradition to which Bataille was irresistibly drawn: beginning with Plotinus, and continuing through Dionysius the Areopagite, Augustine, and Nicholas of Cusa, the 'crisis of discourse' that we like to see as specifically modern is carried through the ages into the Carmelite tradition and beyond."[90]

Even though Bataille clearly sought to separate it from mystical transcendence, inner experience shares many of the features of mysticism in its pursuit of the realm outside the self. Kevin Hart describes inner experience as a mystical gesture: "'Inner experience' is an experimental attempt to touch the indefinite reality that abides outside the self; when the attempt succeeds it is intensely pleasurable but also anguished (a taboo is violated) and strictly pointless (no knowledge of this Outside can be distilled)."[91] Like Michaux's mescaline texts, which are the subject of chapter 4, Bataille's writings reflect the desire to let experience lead the subject to uncharted territories. Bataille expresses this idea with the following:

> J'ai voulu que l'expérience conduise où elle menait, non la mener à quelque fin donnée d'avance. Et je dis aussitôt qu'elle ne mène à aucun havre (mais en un lieu d'égarement, de non-sens). J'ai voulu que le non-savoir en soit le principe – en quoi j'ai suivi avec une rigueur plus âpre une méthode où les chrétiens excellèrent (ils s'engagèrent aussi loin dans cette voie que le dogme le permit).[92]

> I wanted experience to lead where it would, not to lead it to some end point given in advance. And I say at once that it leads to no harbour (but to a place of bewilderment, of nonsense). I wanted non-knowledge to be its principle – for this reason I have followed with a keener discipline a method in which Christians excelled (they engaged themselves as far along this route as dogma would permit).[93]

Bataille emphasizes that inner experience can only be considered as such if it has no projected end point, no target or destination. He attempts to differentiate his pursuit of non-knowledge from mystical experience by emphasizing the naked, exploratory aspect of his methods.[94] Sartre took the to task for what he perceived as his desire to escape History and the totalitarian desire to be all. Hollywood writes, "Sartre recognizes – and is quietly appalled by – Bataille's 'fleshy promiscuity,' a mysticism not of the other world but of this one in all of its bodily particularity, and a conception of history as that which is irreducible to rational projects."[95]

It is in this vein that Bataille asserts his distaste for existentialist, rationalist "project," which gets in the way of experience. He envisioned action and discourse to be dependent on "project." Action is a deliberate delay of experience, whereas inner experience is pursued for its own sake and not another end. He writes, "L'expérience intérieure ne pouvant avoir de principe ni dans un dogme (attitude morale), ni dans la science (le savoir n'en peut être ni la fin ni l'origine), ni dans une recherche d'états enrichissants, (attitude esthétique, expérimentale), ne peut avoir d'autre souci ni d'autre fin qu'elle-même."[96] [Inner experience not being able to have principles either in a dogma (a moral attitude), or in science (knowledge can be neither its goal nor its origin), or in a search for enriching states (an experimental, aesthetic attitude), it cannot have any other concern nor other goal than itself.][97] He arrives at a principle of inner experience: the point is to emerge through "project" from the realm of "project."[98]

Bataille worries, however, that it may be impossible to avoid "project" altogether and also complete the manuscript at hand. "L'opposition à l'idée de projet – qui prend dans ce livre une part essentielle – est si nécessaire en moi qu'ayant écrit de cette introduction le plan détaillé, je ne puis m'y tenir."[99] [The opposition to the idea of project – which takes up an essential part of this book – is so necessary within me that having written the detailed plan for this introduction, I can no longer hold myself to it.][100] Bataille acknowledges that he cannot guarantee the homogeneity of his text because he has accepted that the foray into the unknown demands unequivocal sovereignty. Instead of charting out a planned destination for discourse, Bataille privileges the unexpected movements of experience. He wants experience to lead where it likes, we remember, not to some end point given in advance. Nevertheless, the problem of the "project" of completing the book, and of discourse itself, remains.

Thus, in his introductory discussion of his methods and evaluation of the finished text, he admits that only the second part, ("Le Supplice"), and the last part were written without "le louable souci de composer un livre"[101] [the laudable concern of writing a book].[102] He concludes the forward with the following: "Aux trois quarts achevé, j'abandonnai l'ouvrage où devait se trouver l'énigme résolue. J'écrivis *Le Supplice*, où l'homme attient l'extrême du possible."[103] [Three quarters finished, I abandoned the work in which the solved puzzle was to be found. I wrote *The Torment*, where man attains the extreme limit (*l'extrême*) of the possible.][104] For this reason, the remainder of this chapter focuses on the description of unselfing in "Le Supplice," which Bataille privileges for its escape of project and its proximity to unmediated experience. The following section parses Bataille's layers of the self in this section of the text.

Bataille actively aims to disrupt dominant discourses that give systematic and explanatory accounts of inner life, including philosophy, psychology, and psychoanalysis. He writes, "Le moi n'importe en rien"[105] [the self in no way matters].[106] Bataille envisions inner experience as a means of sketching out the layers of the self, an anguish-inducing process that is accompanied by what he calls the maladies of inner experience.[107] The first malady is that it is easy to mistake self-illumination for revelation: "Le ravissement n'est pas une fenêtre sur le dehors, sur l'au-delà, mais un miroir"[108] [Rapture is not a window looking out on the outside, on the beyond, but a mirror.][109] The second is that the subject can only emerge from "project" through "project," which he likens to the inanity of reason during pain or telling oneself that pain will lessen with time.

Moreover, it is difficult to pin down the self in *L'expérience intérieure* as Bataille's work already contains a rich spectrum of synchronic self-divisions. In "Le Supplice," Bataille opposes the infinite possibilities of man to a singular divine totality and relishes the anguish of a world without God. Two separate drives interact in this section. Bataille characterizes *ipse* as the wild, unknowable desire to be everything (which is opposed to the whole of the unknown) and *Je* as discontinuous, and therefore more like God.[110] Comparing his despair to God's despair in crucifying his son to save mankind, he asserts that "jamais rien n'est jamais joué"[111] [nothing is ever risked].[112] For man, there is no redemptive hope in sacrifice, only the possibility for a temporary disruption of stasis. The anguish that he experiences is the necessary result of his attempt to go to the end of the possible of the human, as he flees "l'horreur d'une réduction de l'Être à la totalité" [the horror of a reduction of Being to totality].[113] Subsequently in the text, Bataille returns to this scene wherein the subject (*Moi, je*) is filled with a sense of ecstasy as he stands atop various summits. He collapses after being thrown about amid dark nights of the soul that multiply and intertwine.[114] At the summit of this terrifying scene that ends in stopped motion, he asks himself, "Je suis?" [I am?] The subject unleashes a wild cry at the moment of climax, which conceivably serves as the response to the question posed immediately before.

In this scene, the "I" supplicates to God at the summit until the communicant *ipse* disrupts this pyramid as it flings itself into the abyss in its attempt to fuse with the whole. The result is a communication with the beyond: "Joie inhumaine, échevelée, de la *communication,* car désespoir, folie, amour, pas un point de l'espace vide qui ne soit désespoir, folie, amour et encore: rire, vertige, nausée, perte de soi jusqu'à la mort."[115] [Inhuman, disheveled joy of *communication* – for, despair, madness, love … not a point in empty space which is not despair, madness, love and even more: laughter, dizziness, vertigo, nausea, loss of self to the point of death.][116] Fleeing transcendence and the totality of being, the strident cry communicates the upending of the relationship between man and God, and subsequent interaction of *ipse* with the unknown.[117] The pineal eye, which is turned upward from the middle of the skull in *L'expérience intérieure* and associated with the blinding light of the sun, interrupts the "panoptical gaze of philosophy," according to Mark C. Taylor.[118] The attempt to go to the end of the possible of man yields this separation between *ipse* (wanting to be everything) and the "I" of experience.

My definition of the experiencing self maps onto a constellation of terms in Bataille's work that refer to the most basic level of unified first-person experience. The experiencing self refers to a subject position that Bataille alternatively calls "le sujet," "moi-même" or to which he refers with first-person pronouns in *L'expérience intérieure*. These terms – which relate the effect of experience on the experiencing self – are more robust forms of self than his terms *ipse* and *Je* which interact paradigmatically in the section described above. *Ipse* and *Je* bear more of a resemblance to Freud's Id and Ego than to the interconnected lens of the experiencing self, which offers a deep sense of synchronic unity. Unselfing in Bataille's inner experience is the violent destruction of the experiencing self, which results in the loss of the boundary between subject and object. This process also has a profound effect on perspective as the perceiving lens for phenomenological experience.

Though he shared the phenomenologists' desire to make knowledge an extension of inner experience, Bataille was critical of their methods. In this text he writes, "Mais cette *phénoménologie* donne à la connaissance la valeur d'une fin à laquelle on arrive par expérience. C'est un alliage boiteux: la part faite à l'expérience y est à la fois trop et pas assez grande."[119] [But this *phenomenology* lends to knowledge the value of a goal which one attains through experience. This is an ill-assorted match: the measure given to experience is at once too much and not great enough.][120] Phenomenology, he argues, does not allow for proceeding to the end of the possible when this means approaching the limit of knowledge. His text reflects the desire to upend Hegel's *Phenomenology of Spirit*, which Bataille calls a "philosophy of project" for its attempt to turn the unknown into the known. Bataille asks, what would it mean to conceive of sovereignty as arising from rupture, rather than discourse?

Bataille emphasizes the need for self-destruction to reach the end of the possible of man. In his discussion of the "maladies" of inner experience, he indicates that the subject requires an object point outside of itself for the purposes of self-projection. The paradox is that once the subject attempts projection, he automatically loses his place-holder subject position in the process. This is the only way that the subject can access any objective reality beyond the self, or "cross the threshold" in his terms.

> Dans la projection du point, les mouvements intérieurs ont le rôle de la loupe concentrant la lumière en un très petit foyer incendiaire. C'est seulement dans une telle concentration – au-delà d'elle-même – que l'existence a le loisir d'apercevoir, sous forme d'éclat intérieur, "ce qu'elle est," le mouvement de communication douloureuse qu'elle est, qui ne va pas moins du dedans au dehors que du dehors au dedans. Et sans doute c'est d'une projection arbitraire qu'il s'agit, mais ce qui apparaît de cette façon est l'objectivité profonde de l'existence, dès que celle-ci n'est plus un corpuscule tassé en lui-même, mais une vague de vie se perdant.[121]

> In the projection of the point, the inner movements have the role of the magnifying glass concentrating light into a very small incendiary site. It is only in such a concentration – beyond itself – that existence has the leisure of perceiving, in the form of an inner flash of light, "that which it is": the movement of painful communication which it is, which goes not less from within to without, than from without to within. And no doubt it is a question of an arbitrary projection of oneself, but what appears in this way is the profound objectivity of existence, from the moment that the latter is no longer a little entity turned in on itself, but a wave of life losing itself.[122]

During inner experience, the communicant is returned to the homogenous unity of things like particles in a wave. This ecstatic state characterizes the interaction with the abyss of non-knowledge. A fleeting apprehension of the unknown causes a violent destruction of the subject's agency, the goal of this mystical experience without God. The epiphany (the "éclat intérieur") cannot last, but nevertheless communicates insight into that which is.

Thus, unselfing as destruction offers the occasion to escape discourse and project in the pursuit of this experience of continuity. In the following passage from "Le Supplice," Bataille demonstrates how ecstasy provides an escape from the prison of "project" and knowledge. In this example, this break is first described as the rupture with these constraints. The subject expresses his desire to escape discourse and releases "un long cri intérieur, angoissé," [long, inner anguished cry]; "Et je sais qu'il suffit de briser le discours en moi, dès lors l'extase est là."[123] [And I know that it suffices to break discourse in me; from that moment on, ecstasy is there.][124] In what follows, the self is effectively broken open, and repeatedly described as an anguished and violent site of destruction. He writes, "Je suis *ouvert*, brèche béante, à l'inintelligible ciel et tout en moi se précipite, s'accorde dans un désaccord dernier, rupture de tout possible, baiser violent, rapt, perte dans l'entière absence du possible."[125] [I am *open*, yawning gap, to the unintelligible sky and everything in me rushes forth, is reconciled in a final irreconciliation.][126] This state is characterized by the sounds of mad laughter and the sentiments of rupture, loss, suffering, and indifference towards the self.

In the closing movement of this passage, Bataille describes the fusion of the self and the object on which it has projected itself. "Et surtout *plus d'objet*. L'extase n'est pas amour: l'amour est possession à laquelle est nécessaire l'objet, à la fois possesseur du sujet, possédé par lui. Il n'y a plus sujet=objet, mais 'brèche béante' entre l'un et l'autre et, dans la brèche, le sujet, l'objet sont dissous, il y a passage, communication, mais non de l'un à l'autre: *l'un* et *l'autre* ont perdu l'existence distincte."[127] [And above all *no more object*. Ecstasy is not love: love is possession for which the object is necessary, and at the same time possession of the subject, possessed by it. There is no longer subject–object, but a "yawning gap" between the one and the other and, in the gap, the subject, the object are dissolved; there is passage, communication, but not from one to the other: *the one* and *the other* have lost their separate existence.][128] Ultimate communication is achieved between the subject and object as they dissolve into one another and lose their sense of boundedness.

Bataille uses the narrative of destruction to describe the moment of unselfing, where the subject is annihilated and merges with the object of contemplation and supplication. Like Delbo's experience of debilitating thirst discussed in chapter 3, Bataille's attempt to reach the unknown leads to an oneiric state of consciousness that he situates between life and death. Ordinary selfhood is temporarily destroyed in the process, and images of breakage, rupture, and demolition fill the pages of the text.

Bataille uses the verbs *briser* [to break, to smash], *détruire* [to destroy, to ruin] and *déchirer* [to tear, to damage] to describe what happens to the self in inner experience throughout "Le Supplice." He writes, "Je reste là, quelques instants de plus, voulant forcer le sort, *et brisé*."[129] [I remain there, several moments longer, wanting to force destiny, *and broken*.][130] The term appears again in the poetic intervention at the end of the section.

Je hais
cette vie d'instrument,
je cherche une fêlure,
ma fêlure,
pour être brisé.[131]

I hate
this life of instrument,
I search for a fissure,
my fissure,
in order to be broken.[132]

During destructive unselfing, the self becomes as an open wound, or a yawning gap, and the subject seeks a fissure to break itself open. This state of destruction leads Bataille to the end of the possible.

From two very different points of departure – asceticism and decadence – Weil and Bataille emphasize that inner experience cannot be revolutionary without the destruction of the self. Although Weil's reputation as a modern saint might lead readers to believe that her unselfing is not as violent as Bataille's, she too exploits the potential of violent metaphors such as the nail and the cross and the piercing of the soul. Her texts are replete with images of annihilation, destruction and loss; she often uses *nier* [to deny] to express the reduction of the self to nothingness.[133] In "L'Amour de Dieu et le malheur" she discusses a sentiment that she attributes to the ancient Romans: the loss of "la moitié de son âme" [half of one's soul] that accompanies *le malheur*.[134] Weil even begins to sound like Bataille in the following description of the "pulverization" of the self: "Le malheur n'est pas un état d'âme. C'est une pulvérisation de l'âme par la brutalité mécanique des circonstances. La transmutation d'un homme à ses propres yeux, de l'état humain à l'état d'un ver à demi écrasé qui s'agite sur le sol, n'est pas une opération où même un perverti puisse se complaire."[135] [Affliction is not a state of the soul. It is a pulverization of the soul by the mechanical brutality of circumstance. The transformation of man in his own eyes from the human state to the state of a worm half crushed, wriggling on the ground is not an intervention in which even a depraved person could take pleasure.] Herein marks a major distinction between the two thinkers. Though there is transformative value in the reduction of the human to a wriggling worm, Weil insists that suffering should not be enjoyed. Whereas Weil uses decreation to distinguish between ordinary pain and true affliction, Bataille often depicts the power of destructive unselfing as rooted in pleasure.

This state of ecstasy and temporary destruction of the experiencing self cannot last, however, for Bataille any more than it can for Weil. His text also rails against the inescapable constraints of diachronic existence. After the destructive experience of unselfing, Bataille must account for the link between his former self and one that lives on after the experience, while maintaining his commitment to the claim that non-knowledge does not communicate. Using the metaphor of Ariadne's thread to account for the frail link between the past and present, he writes of the deep depression that occurs when it seems that the thread has been broken, and there is no hope for reconciliation.[136] Though he eschews autobiography in any traditional sense, Bataille writes that there is an unalienable part of the self that perseveres through the dark night of experience. He writes, "Il faut un courage singulier pour ne pas succomber à la dépression et continuer – au nom de quoi? Pourtant je continue, dans mon obscurité: l'homme continue en moi, en passé par là."[137] [A singular courage is necessary in order not to succumb to depression and to continue – in the name of what? Nevertheless I continue, in my darkness: man continues in me, goes through this.][138] In this passage, he goes on to differentiate between "l'homme" and "moi-même." In order to become man (or more) it is necessary for him to die to himself and give birth to himself. The man that continues in him provides the possibility for continuity but requires dramatic renewal (neutrally conveyed by both death and rebirth) if the reconciliation of the despairing "I" and the continuing "man" is to be successful.

For Bataille, the question of the persistence of the self through time and through experience is also a question of communication. How can the subject reconcile the experience of non-knowledge with knowledge? How can the writer transmit the foreign through the familiar? While he rejects the notion of mystical ineffability and seeks precisely to write the mad encounter with the unknown, the status of communication remains unstable in the work. In the section "L'Expérience seule auto-rité, seule valeur" (Experience: Sole Authority, Sole Value), he indicates that experience is not logically demonstrable, and that one must live it to know it. "Ces énoncés ont une obscure apparence théorique et je n'y vois aucun remède sinon de dire: 'il en faut saisir le sens du dedans.' Ils ne sont pas démontrables logiquement. Il faut *vivre* l'expérience."[139] [These statements have an obscure theoretical appearance, and I see no remedy for this other than to say: "One must grasp the meaning from the inside." They are not logically demonstrable. One must *live* experience.][140] Immediacy is necessary for the unselfing process.

When it comes to writing unselfing, however, Bataille is sceptical of narration, and of committing experience to time. Indeed, in the early section of the work, he identifies poetry as a conduit for the unknown. It is poetry, according to Bataille, that conveys the unknown through the familiar. He writes, "Si la poésie introduit l'étrange, elle le fait par la voie du familier. Le poétique est du familier se dissolvant dans l'étrange et nous-mêmes avec lui."[141] [If poetry introduces the strange, it does so by means of the familiar. The poetic is the familiar dissolving into the strange, and ourselves with it.][142] Like the divine, poetry allows man to appropriate what exceeds him without grasping it. This "perversion poétique des mots" [poetic perversion of words] allows for the destabilization of the authoritative structures of discourse.

However, in the next breath, Bataille assumes a more disparaging attitude towards poetic language vis à vis experience, asserting that it is "malgré tout la part restreinte" [despite everything the restricted part], linked to the realm of words, whereas the experience itself is linked to infinite possibilities.[143] Thus, Bataille's desire to communicate is consistently foiled by his reluctance to reify reality in language. He writes that poetry, in the end, is no less silence than language: "L'expérience ne peut être communiqué si des liens de silence, d'effacement, de distance, ne changent pas ceux qu'elle met en jeu."[144] [Experience cannot be communicated if the bonds of silence, of effacement, of distance, do not change those they put into play.][145] While on the one hand Bataille indicates that poetry is capable of communicating experience, he also sees it as a simultaneous concealment.[146] The bonds of silence, effacement, and distance must be manipulated in an unconventional way (poetic discourse) in order to convey experience that cannot be fully grasped. It is ultimately unclear in *L'expérience intérieure* whether any discourse (poetry included) can succeed in communicating the extreme limit. He writes, for instance, that Rimbaud's last poems do not constitute it. "Si Rimbaud atteignit l'extrême, il n'en atteignit la communication que par le moyen de son désespoir: il supprima la communication possible, il n'écrivit plus de poèmes."[147] [If Rimbaud reached the extreme limit, he only attained the communication of it by means of his despair: he suppressed possible communication, he no longer wrote poems.][148]

This sceptical voice struggles continuously with the burden of project in the work. Bataille shares with Michaux the desire to annotate and revise his book, calling "Le Supplice," as we remember, the only section written without the goal of writing it:

> A peu près chaque fois, si je tentais d'écrire un livre, la fatigue venait avant la fin. Je devenais étranger lentement au projet que j'avais formé. J'oublie ce qui m'enflammait la veille, changeant d'une heure à l'autre avec une lenteur somnolente. Je m'échappe à moi-même et mon livre m'échappe; il devient presque entier comme un nom oublié: j'ai la paresse de le chercher, mais l'obscur sentiment de l'oubli m'angoisse.
>
> Et si ce livre me ressemble? si la suite échappe au début; l'ignore ou le tient dans l'indifférence? étrange rhétorique! étrange moyen d'envahir l'impossible! Reniement, oublie, existence informe, armes équivoques ... la paresse elle-même utilisée comme énergie imbrisable.[149]

Almost every time, if I tried to write a book, fatigue would come before the end. I slowly became a stranger to the project which I had formulated. I would forget what enflamed me the day before, changing from one hour to the next with a drowsy slowness. I escape from myself and my book escapes me; it becomes almost completely like a forgotten name: I am too lazy to look for it but the obscure feeling of forget fills me with anguish.

And if this book resembles me? If the conclusion escapes from the beginning; is unaware of it or keeps it in indifference? Strange rhetoric! Strange way of invading the impossible! Denial, forgetting, existence without form, ambiguous weapons ... Laziness itself used as unbreakable energy.[150]

Bataille compares the narrative self, which persists through time, with the process of writing the book; both are hindered by the caprices of memory and the slowness of articulation when compared to the immediacy of lived experience. The difficulty in communicating experience is thus inextricably tied to the difficulty of articulating the self given the unreliability of memory and the delay of consciousness. The writing self can never catch up with the present. The ecstatic, broken subject at the moment of unselfing returns to tell the tale tired and forgetful. In this sense, the text is a reflection on the anguish of narrating experience. Like Valéry and Michaux, Bataille delights in the anguish and lucidity of the experiencing self, but experiences diachronic persistence as a nagging burden, experienced phenomenologically as sluggishness. Experience exceeds the writing project. From the vantage point of experience, destructive unselfing provides a temporary annihilation of project, which returns, to Bataille's dismay, when he sets out to write.

Bataille uses the notion of "communication" not only in his discussion of the way singular experiences are difficultly related to others, but also to describe the fusion of subject and object. This fusion occurs in the pinnacle rupture passage of "Le Supplice," examined in the section above on the destruction of the experiencing self. Bataille describes the difficulty of differentiating between himself and others during inner experience: "Je ne puis un instant cesser de me provoquer moi-même à l'extrême et ne puis faire de différence entre moi-même et ceux des autres avec lesquels je désire communiquer."[151] [I cannot for a moment cease to incite myself to attain the extreme limit, and cannot make a distinction between myself and those with whom I desire to communicate.][152] Indeed, the very promise of inner experience lies in the subject's dissolution into the object of attention. But what are the ethical consequences of this dissolution? At the close of "Le Supplice," Bataille claims that inner experience is characterized by the consciousness of others. It is defined by a loss of the self into the mass of unfamiliar being:

Mais l'expérience intérieure est conquête et comme telle *pour autrui*! Le sujet dans l'expérience s'égare, il se perd dans l'objet, qui lui-même se dissout. Il ne pourrait cependant se dissoudre à ce point si sa nature ne lui permettait ce changement; le sujet dans l'expérience en dépit de tout demeure: dans la mesure où ce n'est pas un enfant dans le drame, une mouche sur le nez, il est *conscience d'autrui* (je l'avais négligé l'autre fois).[153]

But inner experience is conquest and as such *for others!* The subject in experience loses its way, it loses itself in the object, which itself is dissolved. It could not, however, become dissolved to this point, if its nature didn't allow it this change; the subject in experience in spite of everything remains: to the extent that it is not a child in the drama, a fly on one's nose, it is *consciousness of others* (I had neglected this the other time).[154]

Bataille emphasizes that the subject is lost in the object at the same time as the object is dissolved into the subject. And yet, the subject in experience persists in the form of consciousness of others. This is what he "neglected" in his previous thinking about the self. In his commentary on this passage, Connor links the possibility of a new ethics in Bataille's work to the survival of this sliver of the self. "What Bataille had 'neglected' in his thinking of experience 'the other time' (i.e., earlier in the same book) was the necessity of an openness, on the part of the subject in inner experience, to others; a 'consciousness of others' that, even as it keeps open the possibility of communication (and community), loses itself in that communication."[155] Bataille returns again to this notion of the consciousness of others through the image of the fly: "Étant la mouche, l'enfant, il n'est plus exactement le sujet (il est dérisoire, à ses propres yeux dérisoire); se faisant *conscience d'autrui*, et comme l'était le chœur antique, le témoin, le vulgarisateur du drame, il se perd dans la communication humaine, en tant que sujet se jette hors de lui, s'abîme dans une foule indéfinie d'existences possibles."[156] [Being the fly, the child, it is no longer exactly the subject (it is laughable, in its own eyes laughable); making itself *consciousness of others* and, as the ancient chorus, the witness, the popularizer of the drama, it loses itself in human communication; as subject, it is thrown outside of itself, beyond itself; it ruins itself in an undefined throng of possible existences.][157] The self loses its discrete being and is thrown outside of itself into undifferentiation. Bataille's approach to the other does not begin with a focus on the self and the theorization of the other as a parallel entity, but rather consists of a consciousness of others that overwhelms the meditating subject, erasing the self in the process.

Bataille's unorthodox meditation practices trouble this claim on the centrality of the consciousness of others to the undertaking of inner experience. Bataille kept a photograph on his desk that was taken in China in 1910 of a prisoner suffering "the death of a hundred cuts" so that he could contemplate it daily.[158] In the following passage, he describes his practice of using this photograph as a focal point that helps him achieve self-rupture and transcend the self:

> De toute façon, nous ne pouvons projeter le point-objet que par le drame. J'ai eu recours à des images bouleversantes. En particulier, je fixais l'image photographique – ou parfois le souvenir que j'en ai – d'un Chinois qui dut être supplicié de mon vivant. De ce supplice, j'avais eu, autrefois, une suite de représentations successives. A la fin, le patient, la poitrine écorchée, se tordait, bras et jambes tranchés aux coudes et aux genoux. Les cheveux dressés sur la tête, hideux, hagard, zébré de sang, beau comme une guêpe.
>
> J'écris "beau"! ... quelque chose m'échappe, me fuit, la peur me dérobe à moi-même et, comme si j'avais voulu fixer le soleil, mes yeux glissent.[159]

> In any case, we can only project the object-point by drama. I had recourse to upsetting images. In particular, I would gaze at the photographic image – or sometimes the memory which I have of it – of a Chinese man who

must have been tortured in my lifetime. Of this torture, I had had in the past a series of successive representations. In the end, the patient writhed, his chest flayed, arms and legs cut off at the elbows and at the knees. His hair standing on end, hideous, haggard, striped with blood, beautiful as a wasp.

   I write "beautiful"! … something escapes me, flees from me, fear robs me of myself and, as if I had wanted to stare at the sun, my eyes rebel.[160]

Instead of the contemplation of the cross, Bataille uses images of human suffering. Especially when examining the photo for oneself, this last description is particularly hard to read. The victim, both hideous and beautiful in Bataille's estimation, allows him to escape the confines of ordinary self-experience, and reach new heights of ecstasy. In her interpretation of this passage, Susan Sontag credits Bataille's viewing practice for his ability to view pain as a method of transfiguration. "It is a view of suffering, of the pain of others, that is rooted in religious thinking, which links pain to sacrifice, sacrifice to exaltation – a view that could not be more alien to a modern sensibility, which regards suffering as something that is a mistake or an accident or a crime. Something to be fixed. Something to be refused. Something that makes one feel powerless."[161] Bataille writes that he loved the "young and seductive Chinese man" because he communicated the excessive nature of his pain to him: "il me communiquait sa douleur ou plutôt l'excès de sa douleur et c'était ce que justement je cherchais, non pour en jouir, mais pour ruiner en moi ce qui s'oppose à la ruine."[162] [he communicated his pain to me or perhaps the excessive nature of his pain, and it was precisely that which I was seeking, not so as to take pleasure in it, but in order to ruin in me that which is opposed to ruin.][163] Though his methods may be rooted in religious thinking, the trouble with this program of self-sacrifice is that Bataille seems to seek expiation through the pain of others.

   This objection is not new; Sartre lodged a similar critique of Bataille over the course of their disagreement on morality in the discussion that followed the 1944 Conference in what is now called "Discussion sur le péché" (Discussion on sin).[164] While Bataille claims that inner experience is essentially an other-focused process that results in the heightened consciousness of others (and sometimes the erasure of the boundary between selves and others) his instrumentalization of the Chinese torture victim suggests that it is ultimately a self-directed project, one wherein ontological others can be vehicles for self-annihilation. These challenges to Bataille's attempts to reimagine ethics are comparable to the tensions inherent in Weil's approach to suffering and the material world, despite her attempt to escape abstraction. Destructive unselfing might bring Bataille closer to imagining the pain of others, but it has little to do with altruism. Far from the contemporary vision of empathy as the radical route to intersubjective care, Weil and Bataille's excruciating experiences of destructive unselfing illustrate the insufficiency of empathy as a social concept.

Perhaps the most unexpected insight that emerges from a close study of Weil and Bataille together in the context of unselfing is that both philosophies of selfhood feature a minimal thread of continuity. This thread not only stiches the self together over time, but also holds the key to understanding both of their ethical intuitions. Weil describes this minimal degree of survival during destructive experience with the imagery of the soul "loving in the void." She writes, "Quand je souffre, je ne puis pas oublier que je suis, ni ne pas connaître que je ne suis rien."[165] [When I suffer, I cannot neither forget that I am, nor not know that I am nothing.] Bataille also references a threadbare awareness in the passage on the dissolution of the subject of experience into the object (il est *conscience d'autrui*). He calls this awareness Ariadne's thread, or a fly resting on one's nose; this awareness links past selves to the present and prevents the experiencing self from getting lost in the chaos of experience.

Both seek to make the fleeting experience of unselfing last: Weil through the inability to forget, and Bataille through this awareness of others. Bataille, like Weil emphasizes that he can only reach the extreme limit for a moment before the process must be started over again. Arrival is perpetually deferred, and inner experience requires continually putting into question of everything man knows of being.[166] Though the path will be feverish and painful, this journey must be repeated ceaselessly as the dramas of decreation and inner experience are dependent on the endless destruction of the self. Both Weil and Bataille realize that it is imperative not only to cultivate habit from singular experience, but also to do it *in their own way*. If either are to be successful in their attempts to revolutionize the social potential of the destruction of the self, it would depend precisely on the survival of a minimal thread of continuity of that self through the void.

Epilogue: Unselfing and Coming Home

Some nights she calls across the deaf ocean to no one
in particular. No answer. Her heart's double-vault
a muted hydra.
This hour a purge
of its own unselfing.
She must make a home of it.

Safiya Sinclair, "The Art of Unselfing"

A new time, a time which does not seem in the least inconceivable but, on the contrary, seems like true time rediscovered. The incommensurable is natural. It alone is natural. Strange as it may be, you have come home. Of this you are sure.

Henri Michaux, Miserable Mescaline

At various moments in history, philosophy has commanded us to achieve self-knowledge. The Delphic maxim "Know thyself" motivates philosophical inquiry for Plato's Socrates in the dialogues and those who know themselves attain "true wisdom" in the *Daodejing*. The writing of altered states reorients this injunction to make the unknown known. Though the matter of the self is far from obvious or given, unselfing texts suggest that we should focus instead on the ways in which the self comes undone. The unselfing text is a representation of the journey into the undiscovered: the goal is "to go to the last point" for Valéry and the "extreme limit of the possible" for Bataille.

This book has explored the ways in which such textual explorations are reflective of the long legacy of the phenomenological method in the global Francosphère, especially in the representation of the self as an immediate feature of consciousness. It bears repeating that while these writers are not phenomenologists *à la lettre* – Bataille, for instance, challenges the tradition directly – their accounts are insightful in a phenomenological sense because they foreground the *what-it-is-like* of experience from the inside. The unselfing text illuminates the formerly unidentified contours of the self during experiences as different as thirst, love, hallucination, pain, and ecstasy. Unselfing literature, in a first sense, evokes a voyage away from the familiar.

But could unselfing also be imagined as a homecoming? Altered states, while disorienting, naturalize the unfamiliar. Safiya Sinclair, quoted in the epigraph, offers the possibility of coming home in the loneliness of the self's undoing.[1] In the face of an unresponsive universe, the subject of the poem resolves to make a home in the emptying of time, the uprooting of consciousness, and the unmaking of identity. This idea resounds in the epigraph from Michaux's *Misérable miracle*, in which he describes settling into the uncertainty of unselfing. As his experience of time accelerates on the psychedelic drug, Michaux realizes that this experience of "true time" is natural. He writes that he now knows, as the Buddhists know, that his perception of reality is an illusion. Unselfing offers the chance to think expansively about the nature of the first-person experience of the world, and to transform ways of being selves against the threats of alienation or nonbeing. Strange as they may be, Michaux insists, these alterations can welcome us home.

Homecoming takes on another sense when considering the resonance of these narrative models across the global French world. While the texts studied in this book describe fringe experiences at the limits of consciousness, they also cover a vast expanse of geographical and cultural terrain. Establishing the unselfing canon has thus been a transcultural endeavour as the consilience of narratives across distant contexts serves as a challenge to the national literature model. From the conditions of exile and existential uprooting, it is perhaps unsurprising that these writers turn to literature as a means of pinning down the instability wrought by altered states. Writers use these marginal experiences to question their relationship to place, culture, and tradition. Cixous uses neologism to craft a space for the self as a Jewish woman in post-Vichy Algeria; writing becomes a refuge from an "unliveable" relationship to the self. Khatibi imagines bilingualism in the postcolonial Maghreb as a site of desire rather than warfare, one that requires him to abandon the idea of the unified self. Weil, who was once hailed as the "patron saint of all outsiders" by André Gide, and who died in exile from occupied France, writes movingly of the experience of rootlessness in *L'Enracinement* (*The Need for Roots*).[2] Like Delbo, Weil used her experience of exile to critique colonialism in the French empire.[3]

Mukagasana also writes from a position of displacement. She notes that when she first arrived in Belgium as a refugee, her testimony was her only friend. One of the guiding motivations for the new translation of her work was the "revulsion" at France's role in the genocide, which helped to shift the language of business and education in Rwanda from French to English. In some cases, the shocking nature of the revelations from these far-flung outposts of the self demand recognition. The communication of suffering might open a reader's eyes, forcing them to see the world as it is. Mukagasana memorably declares that whoever does not recognize what the Rwandan people have suffered is complicit with the persecutors. Delbo writes of the difficulty of "coming home" to oneself and to others after being liberated from the Nazi death camps. Whether you return from war or from elsewhere, Delbo writes, it is difficult to come back, especially if that elsewhere is unimaginable to others. Indeed, the failure to read without recognition in some of these contexts is conceived as both an imaginative and moral failing.

When compared with these writers, Valéry is perhaps more of an insider than the others alongside whom I have read him. And yet, in his celebrated forward to Montesquieu's *Lettres persanes,* Valéry writes that the answer to the text's central question "How can one be Persian?" lies in another question: "How can one be who one is?"[4] Thinking about the absurdity of the self when perceived through the eyes of the other turns insiders into outsiders, Valéry proposes. As an "anti-philosopher," Valéry continually contests conventional modes of thought. Like Valéry in the Teste cycle, Bataille's work investigates the possibility of a mysticism without God. His *Somme athéologique* exemplifies the heterodoxy of his writing on the sacred and his attempts to upend discourse, transgress limits, and escape project. Across these contexts, the act of writing offers a refuge for those who write the experience of the marginal.

This book has offered a typology of unselfing experiences, focusing on the nature of its shapeshifting, while also investigating the knowledge that unselfing delivers. While the conversion model for unselfing may be familiar to many readers, the book seeks to fill the gap in our language for other unselfing stories that take hold in the twentieth century. I have positioned four models (disruption, mutation, fragmentation, and destruction) as productive counterpoints to one another precisely because of what comparing them reveals. In some texts, escaping the selfish ego is what makes unselfish action possible; in others, compassion is impossible without the boundedness of individual experience. Studying the phenomenon in this structural way reveals the range of ethical interpretations that can ensue from unselfing: some see it as synonymous with transcendence while others caution against it as a debilitating form of self-loss.

One insight that emerges from a study of unselfing is the limitation of empathy as a social concept. As I write this epilogue at the start of another semester of pandemic teaching, this insight is timely. As the virus killed millions, filled hospitals, shut down schools, and changed nearly everything about the ways in which we live and work over the past two years, caregivers – most of them women – bore the brunt of the impact. An alarming number of women left the workforce to care for the most vulnerable members of our communities: children, the elderly, and the sick. As in other moments of political and social crisis, many have called for the cultivation of empathy, not only in response to the death and suffering caused by the virus, but also as a way of moralizing public health behavior.[5] And yet, in these calls, empathy is often conflated with compassion, altruism, or other forms of prosocial action. This underscores the lack of agreement – discussed in detail in chapter 2 – on what empathy is and the link between empathy and social cognition. What do we imagine that empathy can accomplish in the context of crisis? The literature of unselfing suggests that there is more to compassion than reduced self-interest and that we need more than empathy to ensure the welfare of the collective.

The theoretical uncertainties at the heart of unselfing run parallel to contemporary debates on the significance of empathy as an emotion. In these literary texts, reducing the sovereignty or control of the self sometimes delivers a new and better understanding of the experiences of others. Altered states can enact a special change in what Merleau-Ponty calls the "angle of perception," allowing the self to arrive at a better understanding of the thoughts, feelings, and beliefs of others. And yet, altering the angle of perception does not necessarily lead to compassionate action. Some accounts, as I have claimed, expose empathy as a powerless and alienating state. Chapter 3 argued that what Delbo experiences when she feels the scream of another woman piercing through her throat is a radical form of empathy. She senses another person's pain so deeply that it is as if the dog's fangs are at her own throat. And yet, radical empathy in her text makes acting or caring for others utterly impossible. Like the women around her who share in a collective scream, Delbo remains trapped, immobile, and powerless. My point is not that it is worthless to try to understand the thoughts, feelings, or beliefs of others. It is rather that encouraging the teaching of empathy during a global pandemic exacerbates the problem of approaching ethics from the standpoint of individual actors when we most urgently need to consider the fate of the collective.

Instead of calling for empathy, we might shift our focus to care. This concept, which has experienced a recent resurgence in feminist philosophy in North America and in France, refers to the maintenance of both biological and social life. The ethics of care centres on the need to recognize our collective vulnerability and interdependence against the neoliberal model of individualism and stresses the economic, political, and social value of caregiving. (Global phenomenology, with its focus on individuals as relational and embodied beings, may very well play a role in the future of the ethics of care.[6]) Describing the uncomfortable way in which the global pandemic has raised our awareness of our interconnectedness, Najat Vallaud-Belkacem and Sandra Laugier write, "The crisis became a crisis of collective conscience because it made it possible to realize that a society thought to be morally good was in reality built on this indifference to what makes life liveable. This is uncomfortable and this is what care teaches us."[7] An understanding of the varieties of unselfing experiences suggests that if what we are after is the health of the collective, it unwise to focus on the decentring of the self. We must respond instead to the acceleration of the care crises in our communities by attending to the structural inequalities that have engendered them. While cultivating empathy can be apolitical, the valuing of care requires taking a political stand.

In the end, a full picture of unselfing must account for the spectrum of experiences it encompasses. The danger in imagining any reduction of the self as the automatic reorientation of that self towards others is that it misses the complexity of unselfing experiences and conceals its inherent ambiguities. A full picture serves as a corrective to the view that unselfing will lead, as a matter of course, to the recognition of suffering or the care for the other. Though not necessarily desirable or morally meaningful, the evaporation of the stable, unified self illuminates new ways of understanding the individual in relation to the world. At stake in the unselfing writing project is the possibility of knowing the self through the lens of altered states and understanding the weight of this knowledge in sharing the world with others. This return to writing, after unselfing, might even offer a chance to make a home in it.

Notes

Introduction

1 Paul Valéry, *Œuvres*, eds. Jean Hytier and Agathe Rouart-Valéry, vol. 2 (Paris: Gallimard, 1957), 25.

2 Paul Valéry, "The Evening with Monsieur Teste," *Paul Valery, an Anthology*, selected by James R. Lawler from *The Collected Works of Paul Valery*, ed. Jackson Mathews (Princeton: Princeton University Press, 1977), 16.

3 Abdelkebir Khatibi, *Œuvres de Abdelkébir Khatibi*, vol. 1, *Romans et récits* (Paris: la Différence, 2008), 217.

4 Abdelkebir Khatibi, *Love in Two Languages*, trans. Richard Howard (Minneapolis: University of Minnesota Press, 1990), 17.

5 *French Global: A New Approach to Literary History*, Susan Suleiman and Christie McDonald, eds. (New York: Columbia University Press, 2010), x. Though I sometimes use the term "Francophone" as an adjective to indicate "French-speaking" in the text, I seek to differentiate my study from the colonial heritage and longstanding debates surrounding the politics and rhetoric of *la Francophonie*, which perpetuates the centre/periphery model. For a short overview of the "taxonomic uneasiness" inherent in the debates on globalizing French studies, see Charles Forsdick, "Between 'French' and 'Francophone': French Studies and the Postcolonial Turn," *French Studies* 59, no. 4 (October 2005): 523–30.

6 Simone Weil, *La pesanteur et la grâce* (Paris: Plon, 1948), 29.

7 Simone Weil, *Gravity and Grace*, trans. Emma Crawford and Mario von der Ruhr (New York: Routledge, 2002), 26.

8 Abdelkebir Khatibi, *Œuvres*, vol. 1, 264.

9 Abdelkebir Khatibi, *Love in Two Languages*, trans. Richard Howards (Minneapolis: University of Minneapolis Press), 90. Translation modified.

10 "Whenever Paul addresses his writings, he always draws attention to

the fact that he has been entitled to speak as a subject. And he *became* this subject. He became it suddenly, on the road to Damascus." Alain Badiou, *Saint Paul: The Foundation of Universalism* (Stanford: Stanford University Press, 2003), 17.

11 Colleen Shantz, *Paul in Ecstasy: The Neurobiology of the Apostle's Life and Thought* (Cambridge: Cambridge University Press, 2010).

12 Charles Taylor, *Sources of the Self* (Cambridge: Cambridge University Press, 1989), 460.

13 Valéry, *Œuvres*, vol. 2, 25.

14 Weil, *La pesanteur et la grâce*, 135. Weil, *Gravity and Grace*, 117.

1. Towards a Cognitive-Phenomenological Approach to the Self

1 For example, in *L'expérience intérieure*, analyzed in chapter 6, Bataille contests the phenomenological method as dominant discourse, seeking to go to the limit of human experience at the same time that he gives a rich description of extasy experienced from the inside.

2 Non-self theorists ("the self does not exist") and non-substantialist self theorists ("the self is consciousness, but not an agent of consciousness") reject the narrative concept of the self by critiquing the idea that there is an entity that is both the author and the protagonist of a life story. They sometimes argue that the narrative self is a fiction (if a useful one) that reflects a commitment to social values and social structures. See Mark Sidertis, Evan Thompson, and Dan Zahavi, Introduction to *Self, No Self?: Perspectives from Analytical, Phenomenological, and Indian Traditions* (Oxford: Oxford University Press, 2010), 7.

3 Though scepticism has long shaped the discussion of selfhood (with Hume in the Western tradition and the Buddhist tradition as paradigmatic examples), recent scholarship has attempted to refute the existence and the importance of the (narrative) self. Derek Parfit argues for the existence of non-identical time-slice personas and the idea that psychological continuity (provided that no one else is psychologically continuous with that person) is what matters, rather than identity. Galen Strawson's "pearl self" view indicates that the self only lasts as long as an individual state of consciousness, while Thomas Metzinger advances a functionalist analysis of consciousness to argue that the self is not something that exists but rather a representational construct. See Derek Parfit, *Reasons and Persons* (Oxford: Clarendon Press, 1984); Galen Strawson, *The Subject of Experience* (Oxford: Oxford University Press, 2017); Thomas Metzinger, *Being No One* (Cambridge: MIT Press, 2003).

4 Marya Schechtman, *The Constitution of Selves* (Ithaca, NY: Cornell University Press, 1996), 1.

5 The term "phenomenology" first appears as early as the eighteenth century. French thinkers in the 1920s began to consult Hegel's *Phenomenology of Spirit* for the phenomenological method, but this was after Husserl's "inauguration" of the movement. Husserl's main influence in using the term was Franz Brentano's friend, Ernst Mach. For a detailed account of the origins of phenomenology as a movement, see Dermot Moran, *Introduction to Phenomenology* (London: Routledge, 2000), 7.

6 Moran, *Introduction to Phenomenology,* 4.

7 Robert Sokolowski, *Introduction to Phenomenology* (Cambridge: Cambridge University Press, 2000), 54.

8 Sokolowski, *Introduction to Phenomenology,* 44.

9 Sokolowski, *Introduction to Phenomenology,* 49.

10 Paul Ricoeur, *Oneself as Another,* trans. Kathleen Blamey (Chicago: University of Chicago Press, 1992), 128.

11 Shaun Gallagher and Dan Zahavi put it nicely: "Accordingly, we should not think of the self, in this most basic sense, as a substance, or as some kind of ineffable transcendental precondition, or as a social construct that gets generated through time; rather it is an integral aspect of conscious life and involves this immediate experiential character." "Phenomenological Approaches to Self-Consciousness" *Stanford Encyclopedia of Philosophy* (Summer 2019 Edition), ed. Edward N. Zalta.

12 My book takes a phenomenological approach to the relationship between unselfing in a range of literary forms (from Weil's aphoristic notebooks to Valéry's "test case" short stories) whose special empirical status separates these unconventional forms from other literary genres, such as the novel. The aesthetic implications of this empirical status are discussed in more detail in the "From Experience to Narrative" section of chapter 2. For a study of the relationship between existential poetics and the novelistic form, see Yi-Ping Ong, *The Art of Being: Poetics of the Novel and Existential Philosophy* (Cambridge: Harvard University Press, 2018). One of Ong's central claims is that existentialist philosophers approach the genre of the realist novel as philosophically significant for the conception of self-knowledge it makes possible. She argues that existentialist thinkers ascribe the poetic tension between characterological freedom and (realist) novelistic form to the authority of the first-person perspective.

13 Paul Ricoeur, Martin Heidegger quoted in Dermot Moran, *Introduction to Phenomenology* (London: Routledge, 2000), 3.

14 Moran, *Introduction to Phenomenology,* 13.

15 Moran, *Introduction to Phenomenology,* 18.

16 Edmund Husserl, *Cartesian Meditations: An Introduction to Phenomenology,* trans. Dorion Cairns (The Hague: Martinus Nijhoff, 1970), 37.

17 Herbert Spiegelberg, *The Phenomenological Movement: A Historical Introduction,* second edition (Dordrecht: Springer, 1971), 434.

18 He was also first to have his works on the phenomenology of sympathy translated into French, followed by Heidegger. Spiegelberg, *The Phenomenological Movement,* 432.

19 Maurice Merleau-Ponty, *Sense and Non-Sense,* trans. Hubert L. Dreyfus and Patricia Allen Dreyfus (Evanston: Northwestern University Press, 1964), 28.

20 Spiegelberg, *The Phenomenological Movement,* 426.

21 Jean Paul Sartre, *Being and Nothingness,* trans. Hazel E. Barnes (New York: Washington Square Press, 1992), 21. "... mais c'est au sein même de l'être en son coeur, comme un ver." Jean Paul Sartre, *L'être et le néant* (Paris: Gallimard, 1943), 57.

22 Spiegelberg, *The Phenomenological Movement,* 435.

23 Spiegelberg, *The Phenomenological Movement,* 425–7.

24 Moran, *Introduction to Phenomenology,* 370.

25 Moran, *Introduction to Phenomenology,* 357.

26 Sartre, *Being and Nothingness,* 103.

27 Spiegelberg, *The Phenomenological Movement,* 538.

28 Lewis R. Gordon, *What Fanon Said: A Philosophical Introduction to His Life and Thought* (New York: Fordham University Press), 73.

29 Camille Robcis, *Disalienation: Politics, Philosophy, and Radical Psychiatry in Postwar France* (Chicago: University of Chicago Press, 2021), 48.

30 Gordon, *What Fanon Said,* 2.

31 Robcis, *Disalienation,* 56.

32 Paget Henry, "Africana Phenomenology: Its Philosophical Implications," *CLR James Journal* 11, no. 1 (2005): 79.

33 Leela Gandhi, "Theory and Practice in Postcolonial Studies," in *The Oxford Handbook for Postcolonial Studies,* ed. Graham Huggan (Oxford: Oxford University Press, 2013), 412–15.

34 Moran, *Introduction to Phenomenology,* 14. Moran calls Merleau-Ponty's claim "sloppy talk"; see his introductory chapter for more on the many philosophical uses and misuses of the term "phenomenology" and its relationship to other disciplines.

35 David Chalmers introduced the debate on the "hard problem" of consciousness in the 1990s after the work of Thomas Nagel, John Searle, Daniel Dennett, and Owen Flanagan. The "hard problem" questions whether it will be possible to link conscious states with physical (neural) phenomena.

36 Embodied approaches to cognition have been advanced by scientists and philosophers such as Francisco Varela, Evan Thompson, Eleanor Rosch, and Andy Clark.

37 Shaun Gallagher and Dan Zahavi, *The Phenomenological Mind: An Introduction to Philosophy of Mind and Cognitive Science* (New York: Routledge, 2008), 5.

38 Daniel Kahneman, *Thinking, Fast and Slow* (New York: Farrar, Straus and Giroux, 2011).

39 Kahneman, *Thinking, Fast and Slow*, 381.

40 Kahneman, *Thinking, Fast and Slow*, 406–7.

41 Kahneman, *Thinking, Fast and Slow*, 407.

42 See chapter 2 for a discussion of this issue in trauma theory.

43 Antonio Damasio, *Self Comes to Mind* (New York: Random House, 2010), 214.

44 Damasio, *Self Comes to Mind*, 222.

45 Damasio, *Self Comes to Mind*, 224.

46 Antonio Damasio, *Descartes' Error: Emotion, Reason, and the Human Brain* (New York: Putnam 1994), 240.

47 I discuss the implications of the total loss of consciousness in the next chapter, in chapter 4 on the overdose experience, and in chapter 6 on the Muselmann victims of the Nazi death camps.

48 Shaun Gallagher, quoted in Dan Zahavi, *Subjectivity and Selfhood: Investigating the First-Person Perspective* (Cambridge: MIT Press, 2005), 143–4.

49 Antoine Compagnon, *Écrire la vie: Montaigne, Stendhal, Proust*, Audio, Collège de France: Littérature française moderne et contemporaine, accessed June 15, 2015, http://podcastfichiers.college-de-france .fr/compagnon-20090224.m4a See this lecture for a discussion of the archetype of the hunting story and its relationship to narrative subjectivity.

50 Compagnon, *Écrire la vie*. Compagnon explores Montaigne, Stendhal, and Proust as three writers who produce coherence or unity of a life from repeating patterns of character, rather than a narrative with a beginning, middle and end.

51 Joshua Landy, *Philosophy as Fiction: Self, Deception, and Knowledge in Proust* (New York: Oxford University Press, 2004), 93.

52 Albert Memmi, *Racism*, trans. Steve Martinot (Minneapolis: University of Minnesota Press, 2000), 42.

53 Paul Ricoeur, *Time and Narrative*, vol. 1, trans. Kathleen McLaughlin and David Pellauer (Chicago: University of Chicago Press, 1984), 52.

54 Marya Schechtman, "The Narrative Self," *The Oxford Handbook of the Self* (Oxford: Oxford University Press, 2011), 395.

55 Alisdair C. MacIntyre, *After Virtue: A Study in Moral Theory* (Notre Dame: University of Notre Dame Press, 1984), 206.

56 Daniel Dennett, "Who's on First? Heterophenomenology Explained" *Journal of Consciousness Studies, Special Issue: Trusting the Subject?* (Part 1) 10, no. 9–10 (October 2003): 19–30. Eager to rehabilitate the classical legacy, Zahavi argues that the Husserlian model does, in fact, engage with "heterophenomenology," that is, the distinct givenness of others and the

knowledge of the other, as experienced from the first-person conscious perspective. See Dan Zahavi, *Self and Other: Exploring Subjectivity, Empathy, and Shame* (Oxford: Oxford University Press, 2014), 111.

57 Cazenave and Célérier show how Sartre's interpretive frame has both shaped and constrained the critical appraisal of Francophone African production. See Odile M. Cazenave and Patricia Célérier, *Contemporary Francophone African Writers and the Burden of Commitment* (Charlottesville: University of Virginia Press, 2011), 6.

58 Zahavi, *Self and Other*, 97.

59 Spiegelberg, *The Phenomenological Movement*, 490.

60 Emmanuel Levinas, *Totality and Infinity: An Essay on Exteriority*, trans. Alphonso Lingus (Dordrecht: Kluwer Academic, 1991), 199.

61 Levinas, *Totality and Infinity*, 203.

62 Ricoeur, *Oneself as Another*, 18.

63 Ricoeur, *Oneself as Another*, 193–4.

64 Zahavi, *Self and Other*, 189.

2. What Is Unselfing?

1 Maria Antonaccio writes, "for Murdoch the paradigmatic instance of unselfing is the recognition that 'other people exist' – that they have a reality and value irreducible to our psychic projections and manipulations ... The perception of others extends to reality in general, indeed for Murdoch it is *the* paradigmatic instance of 'the real.'" Maria Antonaccio, "Picturing the Soul: Moral Psychology and the Recovery of the Emotions," *Ethical Theory and Moral Practice* 4, no. 2, Cultivating Emotions (June 2001): 138.

2 Friedrich Nietzsche, *Beyond Good and Evil: Prelude to a Philosophy of the Future*, trans. Walter Kaufmann (New York: Vintage Books, 1989), 126.

3 The interplay between experiencing self and narrative self (explored in depth in the previous chapter) serves as a theoretical underpinning for the exploration of unordinary experiences of selfhood, as experienced during altered states of consciousness. Chapter 1 outlines the phenomenological approach to self-consciousness by presenting the transplant of the classical tradition in France in the early twentieth century and its radiation into various approaches to the *what-it-is-like* of first-person experience throughout the global French-speaking world. It highlights the literary nature of phenomenological inquiry and the resonance of the phenomenological method in French-language literature.

4 See, for example, Thomas Metzinger's claim that the self does not exist. He argues that we do not see reality as it is, but rather through a "tunnel

of consciousness." *The Ego Tunnel: The Science of the Mind and the Myth of the Self* (New York: Basic Books, 2009).

5 Iris Murdoch, *The Sovereignty of Good* (London: Routledge & Kegan Paul, 1970), 47, 52.

6 "We use our imagination not to escape the world but to join it, and this exhilarates us because of the distance between our ordinary dulled consciousness and an apprehension of the real." Murdoch, *The Sovereignty of Good*, 88.

7 Murdoch, *The Sovereignty of Good*, 63, 23.

8 Simone Weil, *Waiting for God*, trans. Emma Craufurd (New York: Harper Perennial Modern Classics, 2001), 105. Simone Weil, "Formes de l'Amour implicite de Dieu," *Œuvres*, ed. Florence de Lussy (Paris: Gallimard, 1999), 735–6.

9 Antonaccio offers a definition: "Given Murdoch's account of human egoism, what consciousness should seek is illusionless or non-egoistic knowledge of reality. This can only come about through a disciplined effort to combat our own egoism which she calls 'unselfing' – an effort to refocus psychic energy on new objects of attention." "Picturing the Soul," 137.

10 Murdoch, *The Sovereignty of Good*, 84.

11 Murdoch, *The Sovereignty of Good*, 82.

12 Murdoch, *The Sovereignty of Good*, 82.

13 Murdoch writes, "Following a hint in Plato (*Phaedrus* 250) I shall start by speaking of what is perhaps the most obvious thing in our surroundings which is an occasion for 'unselfing,' and that is what is popularly called beauty." Murdoch, *The Sovereignty of Good*, 82.

14 Murdoch argues that something is missing (both empirically and morally) from the behaviourist, existentialist, and utilitarian vision of man in their assumption that morality can only be concerned with external, public acts, and the reduction of the substantial self to a solitary will.

15 Murdoch, *The Sovereignty of Good*, 98.

16 Elaine Scarry, *On Beauty and Being Just* (Princeton: Princeton University Press, 1999), 62.

17 Arthur Schopenhauer, *The World as Will and Representation*, trans. E.F.J. Payne, vol. 1 (New York: Dover Publications, 1969), §68: 390.

18 Scarry, *On Beauty*, 32.

19 Scarry, *On Beauty*, 52.

20 Scarry, *On Beauty*, 112.

21 Scarry, *On Beauty*, 114.

22 Nietzsche, *Beyond Good and Evil*, 126.

23 Nietzsche, *Beyond Good and Evil*, 127–8.

24 Fritz Breithaupt uses this reading of Nietzschean self-loss to underscore the "dark sides" of empathetic response: "Nietzsche's thesis is that empathy engenders an asymmetry that empowers an (imaginary) other; the empathetic person is at the same time emptied out and weakened." Fritz Breithaupt, *The Dark Sides of Empathy*, trans. Andrew B.B. Hamilton (Ithaca, NY: Cornell University Press, 2019), 60.

25 See John 3:30 "He must become greater, I must become less"; or Matthew 16:24 "Then Jesus said to his disciples, 'Whoever wants to be my disciple must deny themselves and take up their cross and follow me.'" David Marno writes of "holy attention" practiced in Christian spiritual exercises as a cultivation of hollowness that allows for the presence of the divine. David Marno, *Death Be Not Proud: The Art of Holy Attention* (Chicago: University of Chicago Press, 2016).

26 "Simone Weil tells us that the exposure of the soul to God condemns the selfish part of it not to suffering but to death. The humble man perceives the difference between suffering and death." Murdoch, *The Sovereignty of Good*, 101.

27 David J. Gordon, "Iris Murdoch's Comedies of Unselfing," *Twentieth Century Literature* 36, no. 2 (1990): 121.

28 *The Connected Discourses of the Buddha: A New Translation of the Samyutta Nikaya*, trans. Bhikkhu Bodhi, vol. 1 (Somerville, MA: Wisdom Publications, 2000), 37.

29 "Bhikkhus, form is nonself. For if, bhikkus, form were self, this form would not lead to affliction, and it would be possible to have it of form: 'Let my form be thus; let my form be not thus.' But because form is nonself, form leads to affliction, and it is not possible to have it of form: 'Let my form be thus; let my form not be thus.'" "Anatta-lakkhana Sutta," *The Connected Discourses of the Buddha*, 22: 59, 901–2.

30 "Anatta-lakkhana Sutta," *The Connected Discourses of the Buddha*, 22: 59, 902.

31 Robert Wright explains this as ceasing to cling to the aggregates like personal possessions: "Liberation consists of changing the relationship between your consciousness and the things you normally think of as its 'contents' – your feelings, your thoughts, and so on. Once you realize that these things are 'not-self,' the relationship of your consciousness to them becomes more like contemplation than engagement, and your consciousness is liberated." Robert Wright, *Why Buddhism Is True: The Science and Philosophy of Meditation and Enlightenment* (New York: Simon and Schuster, 2017), 67. Miri Albahari explains further that the self in Buddhism – as a bounded, unified, enduring, happiness-seeking, and *dukkhā*-avoiding subject – "cannot be the *self* that is erased through the practice of the Noble Eightfold Path." Miri Albahari, *Analytical Buddhism: The Two-Tiered Illusion of the Self* (London: Palgrave Macmillan UK, 2006), 73.

32 Albahari, *Analytical Buddhism,* 3. Albahari describes her Buddhist-derived
    theory of as a "two-tiered illusion of selfhood," wherein a unified,
    elusive, unbroken awareness creates a non-illusory tier, which when
    infused with another tier of "mentally constructed input," creates the
    impression of a bounded self. She uses the analogy of a dreamt-of sound
    (e.g., a shrill voice) that has a non-dream component (e.g., an alarm
    clock). The dreamt-of sound is analogous to the Buddhist account of the
    self (it is illusory but involves a non-illusory component).

33 François Trotet writes of Michaux's fascination with Eastern philosophies
    and practices as a simultaneous absenting of oneself from the world in
    order to be entirely present to it. François Trotet, *Henri Michaux ou la
    sagesse du vide* (Paris: Albin Michel, 1992), 15.

34 "What is whittled away will *not* be the witnessing with its contributing
    sense of unity and unbroken presence, but only those *tanhā*-involving
    [desiring] tendencies that have the subject assuming it is a bounded
    personal owner and agent with those features." Albahari, *Analytical
    Buddhism*, 75.

35 Henri Michaux, *Œuvres complètes*, eds. Raymond Bellour and Ysé Tran,
    vol. 1 (Paris: Gallimard, 1998), 409. See note 1, p. 1154, of this work for the
    editors' notes on first translations and commentaries on these citations in
    French.

36 Hugh B. Urban, "Desire, Blood, and Power: Georges Bataille and the
    Study of Hindu Tantra in Northeastern India," *Negative Ecstasies: Georges
    Bataille and the Study of Religion,* eds. Jeremy Biles and Kent L. Brintnall
    (New York: Fordham University Press, 2015), 69.

37 Georges Bataille, *The Accursed Share*, trans. Robert Hurley, vols. 2 and 3
    (New York: Zone Books, 1991), 230. The full list is as follows: "Laughter,
    tears, poetry, tragedy and comedy – and more generally, every art form
    involving tragic, comic or poetic aspects – play, anger, intoxication,
    ecstasy, dance, music, combat, the funeral horror, the magic of childhood,
    the sacred – of which sacrifice is the most intense aspect – the divine and
    the diabolical, eroticism (individual or not, spiritual or sensual, corrupt,
    cerebral or violent, or delicate), beauty (most often linked to all the forms
    previously enumerated and whose opposite possess an equally intense
    power), crime, cruelty, fear, disgust, together represent the forms of
    effusion which classical sovereignty recognized sovereignty, undoubtably
    does not conjoin in a complete unity, but which virtual sovereignty
    would if we were to secretly attain it."

38 Bataille, *The Accursed Share*, vols. 2 and 3, 198.

39 Georges Bataille, "The Unarmed Society: Lamaism," *The Accursed Share*,
    trans. Robert Hurley, vol. 1 (New York: Zone Books, 1988), 93–114.
    Bataille bases his commentary in this section on the work of Charles Bell,

Portrait of the Dalai Lama (1946). Georges Bataille, "La société désarmée: Le lamaïsme," *La part maudite* (Paris: Éditions de Minuit, 1967), 130–50.

40 Peter Harvey, *The Selfless Mind: Personality, Consciousness and Nirvana in Early Buddhism* (New York: Routledge, 1995), 1.

41 See chapter 6 for a detailed discussion of these influences on her concept of *décréation*.

42 Simone Weil, *Œuvres complètes*, eds. André A. Devaux and Florence de Lussy, vol. 6, *Cahiers 2* (Paris: Gallimard, 1997), 87.

43 J.J. Clarke, *Oriental Enlightenment: The Encounter Between Asian and Western Thought* (New York: Routledge, 1997), 68.

44 Brook Ziporyn, *Evil and/or/as the Good: Omnicentrism, Intersubjectivity, and Value Paradox in Tiantai Buddhist Thought* (Cambridge: Harvard University Press, 2000), 43.

45 Ziporyn shows that *Laozi* features 1) the notion of value arising out of anti-value, 2) the deliberate positing of namelessness as the key to value in a practical sense, 3) the adaptation of Ruist values of unification and stability in an unseen central point (and allows for omnicentrism), 4) the double status of namelessness as one pole in the nameless-named dyad and as the transcendence of all dyads and 5) the creative use of practical paradox of counterproductivity. In *Zhuangzi* (Inner Chapters) one finds full omnicentrism; each perspective intersubjectively implies its other (its opposite). *Evil and/or/as the Good*, 98–9.

46 *Lao-Tzu: Te-Tao Ching, A New Translation Based on the Recently Discovered Ma-wang-tui Texts*, trans. Robert G. Henricks (New York: Ballantine Books, 1989), chapter 43, 108.

47 Weil, "Formes de L'Amour Implicite de Dieu," 752.

48 Michaux, *Œuvres complètes*, vol. 1, 381.

49 Abdelkebir Khatibi, *Œuvres de Abdelkébir Khatibi*, vol. 2, *Poésie de l'aimance* (Paris: la Différence, 2008), 12.

50 Abdelkebir Khatibi, *Class Warrior – Taoist Style*, trans. Matt Reeck (Middletown, CT: Wesleyan University Press, 2017), 2.

51 David Fieni, Review of Abdelkébir Khatibi's "Class Warrior – Taoist Style," *b2o*, September 12, 2018, https://www.boundary2.org/2018/09/david-fieni-review-of-abdelkebir-khatibis-class-warrior-taoist-style/.

52 *Lao-Tzu: Te-Tao Ching*, chapter 5, 196. Robert G. Henricks notes that the interpretive problem of the chapter's first four lines is not solved by the discovery of the Ma-wang-tui texts; "one must still choose between a 'tough' interpretation wherein Heaven and Earth and the Sage are ruthless in regarding people an things as pawns in a game, versus the 'soft' line, where the point is that Heaven and Earth and the Sage see each person and thing as playing a necessary role in the grand cosmic scheme."

53 Callisto Searle, "The Hermeneutics of Contentious Imagery: What Exactly the *Zhuangzi* Has to Say about the Straw Dogs in the *Laozi*," *Religions* 10, no. 6 (2019): 359.

54 Khatibi, *Œuvres*, vol. 2, 13.

55 Khatibi, *Class Warrior*, 3.

56 Khatibi, *Œuvres*, vol. 2, 24.

57 Khatibi, *Class Warrior*, 25.

58 Jenny Hung uses Galen Strawson's notion of thin selfhood in order to resolve the Zhuangzian tension between the idea of the True Lord (a substantial self that is a substance that owns but is not identical to the changing mental properties) and Oneness metaphysics (wherein everything undergoes perpetual transformation), Jenny Hung, "The Theory of the Self in the Zhuangzi: A Strawsonian Interpretation," *Philosophy East and West* 69, no. 2 (2019): 376–94.

59 *Zhuangzi: The Essential Writings,* trans. Brook Ziporyn (Indianapolis: Hackett, 2009) 2:48, 21.

60 *Zhuangzi* 6:50, 48.

61 Xiaofan Amy Li, *Comparative Encounters between Artaud, Michaux and the Zhuangzi: Rationality, Cosmology, and Ethics* (London: Taylor & Francis, 2015), 157.

62 See Bruno Thibault, "Voyager contre: la question de l'exotisme dans les journaux de voyage d'Henri Michaux," *French Review* 63, no. 3 (Feb 1990): 485–91 for an analysis of Michaux's travel writing as writing against the "illusion of exoticism."

63 See, for example: "Toute pensée indienne est magique. Il faut qu'une pensée agisse, agisse directement, sur l'être intérieur, sur les êtres extérieurs." Michaux, *OC*, vol. 1, 287.

64 Simone Weil, "Autobiographie spirituelle" in *Œuvres* ed. Florence de Lussy (Paris: Gallimard, 1999), 772. As Kapani (a commentator who generally applauds Weil's understanding of Indian texts) notes, Weil seems to deliberately ignore the dissonances between her Neoplatonic and largely Christian world view. For instance, the notion of *samsara*, which is the background for the *Upanishads* and the *Gītā*, is absent from Judeo-Christian accounts of the soul. Weil does not discuss this tension. Lakshmi Kapani, "Simone Weil, Lectrice des *Upanishad védiques* et de la *Bhagavad-Gita*: L'action sans désir et le désir sans objet, *Cahiers Simone Weil* 5, no. 2 (June 1982): 118.

65 Weil, "Formes de l'Amour implicite de Dieu," 735–6.

66 Weil, *Waiting for God*, 105.

67 Kapani, "Lectrice des *Upanishad védiques*," 112.

68 Dan Zahavi, *Self and Other: Exploring Subjectivity, Empathy, and Shame* (Oxford: Oxford University Press, 2014), 103.

69 See Zahavi, *Self and Other*, 105, for a discussion of this intellectual history.

70 Suzanne Keen, *Empathy and the Novel* (Oxford: Oxford University Press, 2010), 5. See chapter 2, "The Literary Career of Empathy" (pp. 70–97) for a detailed study of the related concepts and an intellectual history of the distinction.

71 C. Daniel Batson, David A. Lishner, and Eric L. Stocks, "The Empathy-Altruism Hypothesis," *The Oxford Handbook of Prosocial Behavior*, eds. David A. Schroeder and William G. Graziano (Oxford: Oxford University Press, 2015), 259–81.

72 Empathy has been conceived as 1) a folk concept, which involves caring, sharing mental states or knowing in pre-theoretical understandings to the topic wherein the observer and the subject feel the same emotions, as in situations of mimicry and emotional contagion (Adam Smith, Heinz Kohut); 2) sharing the mental states of the other, but excluding low forms of mimicry and contagion and does not require caring (Nancy Eisenberg and Janet Strayer, Martin Hoffman, and Alvin Goldman); 3) high-level empathic simulation processes like imaginative perspective-taking, and requires knowledge of those states, but not caring about them (Peter Goldie, Amy Coplan); and finally 4) mindreading via both theory-theory and simulation (William Ickes). Heather D. Battaly, "Is Empathy a Virtue?" *Empathy: Philosophical and Psychological Perspectives*, eds. Amy Coplan and Peter Goldie (New York: Oxford University Press, 2011), 278–301.

73 Jeremey Rifkin, *The Empathic Civilization: The Race to Global Consciousness in a World in Crisis* (New York: J.P. Tarcher/Penguin, 2009). While he mentions one "dark side" of increased Internet use – an upswing in narcissism – he does not address obvious situations wherein social media use leads to decreased empathy.

74 Rifkin, *The Empathic Civilization*, 24.

75 Barack Obama, Commencement Speech. Northwestern University, June 19, 2006. http://www.northwestern.edu/newscenter/stories/2006/06/barack.html.

76 Fritz Breithaupt, *The Dark Sides of Empathy*, 17–18.

77 Zahavi, *Self and Other*, 101.

78 Zahavi, *Self and Other*, 152.

79 Simon Baron-Cohen, *Mindblindness: An Essay on Autism and "Theory of Mind"* (Cambridge: MIT Press, 1995); Alison Gopnik and Henry M. Wellman, "Why the Child's Theory of Mind Is Really a Theory," in *Folk Psychology: The Theory of Mind Debate*, eds. Martin Davies and Tony Stone (Oxford: Blackwell, 1995), 232–58.

80 Alison Gopnik, "Theory of Mind," *The MIT Encyclopedia of the Cognitive Sciences*, eds. R. Wilson and F. Keil (Cambridge: MIT Press, 1999).

81 Andrew Meltzoff, "Origins of Social Cognition: Bidirectional Self-Other Mapping and the 'Like-Me' Hypothesis," in *Navigating the Social World: What Infants, Children, and Other Species Can Teach Us*, eds. Mahzarin R. Banaji and Susan A. Gelman (Oxford: Oxford University Press, 2014), 143. This is distinct from Lacan's theory of the mirror stage, which implicates mirrors in the ontogenesis of the self. Meltzoff argues that because mirrors are not culturally universal, social mirroring provides a better explanation of the ways in which infants develop a sense of themselves through action.

82 Alvin Goldman, "Interpretation Psychologized," in *Folk Psychology: The Theory of Mind Debate*, eds. Martin Davies and Tony Stone (Oxford: Blackwell, 1995), 74–99; Robert Gordon, "Folk Psychology as Simulation," *Mind and Language* 1, no. 2 (1986): 158–71.

83 Giacomo Rizzolatti, Luciano Fadiga, Vittorio Gallese, and Leonardo Fogassi, "Premotor Cortex and the Recognition of Motor Actions," *Cognitive Brain Research* 3 (1996): 131–41. Vittorio Gallese, Luciano Fadiga, Leonardo Fogassi, and Giacomo Rizzolatti, "Action Recognition in the Premotor Cortex," *Brain* 119 (1996): 593–609.

84 Marco Iacoboni, *Mirroring People: The New Science of How We Connect with Others* (New York: Farrar, Straus and Giroux, 2008), 126.

85 Vittorio Gallese, "Mirror Neurons, Embodied Simulation, and the Neural Basis of Social Identification," *Psychoanalytic Dialogues* 19, no. 5 (2009): 519–36.

86 In addition to Iacoboni, see Christian Keysers, *The Empathic Brain: How the Discovery of Mirror Neurons Changes Our Understanding of Human Nature* (Los Gatos, CA: Smashwords Edition, 2011).

87 Zahavi, *Self and Other*, 100–1.

88 Paul Armstrong, *Stories and the Brain: The Neuroscience of Narrative* (Baltimore: Johns Hopkins University Press, 2020), 157.

89 Zahavi, *Self and Other*, 152. Embodied simulationists like Gallese and Guerra argue that we begin to bridge these gaps by reusing our mental states and processes, represented in corporeal form, to attribute them to others. Vittorio Gallese and Michele Guerra, *The Empathic Screen: Cinema and Neuroscience* (Oxford: Oxford University Press, 2020), 2.

90 Maurice Merleau-Ponty, *Phenomenology of Perception*, trans. Donald A. Landes (New York: Routledge, 2012), 372.

91 Lisa Zunshine maps the interaction between text and reader, arguing that great literature exploits our cognitive makeup by engaging and challenging our theory of mind facilities. This theory of literature as a site for the development of mind-reading capabilities does not necessarily have a pro-social component. Lisa Zunshine, *Why We Read Fiction: Theory of Mind and the Novel* (Columbus: Ohio State University Press, 2006).

Gallese and Guerra describe the immersive experience of cinema as a form of "liberated embodied simulation," which "enables us to build other possible, parallel, and imaginary worlds." Gallese and Guerra, *The Empathic Screen*, 41.

92 Martha Nussbaum, like Murdoch, argues that fiction helps us to notice and respond justly to the world, serving as a means of improving our moral decision-making abilities. Martha Nussbaum, "'Finely Aware and Richly Responsible': Literature and the Moral Imagination," *Literature and the Question of Philosophy*, ed. Anthony J. Cascardi (Baltimore: Johns Hopkins University Press, 1987), 167–91. For a critique of the idea that fictions are morally improving, see "Chaucer: Ambiguity and Ethics" in Joshua Landy, *How to Do Things with Fictions* (Oxford: Oxford University Press, 2012), 23–39.

93 Keen, *Empathy and the Novel*, 98.

94 Armstrong, "Neuroscience and the Social Powers of Narrative," in *Stories and the Brain*, 150–198. Armstrong argues that these paradoxes of the alter ego are better understood through phenomenological categories than grammatical ones.

95 Charles T. Tart's definition focuses on the qualitative nature of the difference between ordinary and unordinary: "An altered state of consciousness for a given individual is one in which he clearly feels a *qualitative* shift in his pattern of mental functioning, that is, he feels not just a quantitative shift (more or less alert, more or less visual imagery, sharper or duller, etc.), but also that some quality or qualities of his mental processes are *different*." Introduction to *Altered States of Consciousness* (Garden City: Doubleday, 1972), 1–2.

96 Stephane Allix and Paul Bernstein, eds., *Manuel clinique des expériences extraordinaires* (InterEditions, 2009), 3. Exploring examples such as near-death experiences, lucid dreaming, transcendental mystical states, and occasions of extra sensory perception, the institute, which was founded in 2007, investigates these experiences as the "frontier zone" of the human mind.

97 I first came across the notion of "Altered Selves" at the "Altered Self/ Altered Self Experience" conference organized by Alexander Gerner and Jorge Gonçalves in at the Universidade Nova de Lisboa in 2013. The meeting brought together researchers across disciplines (philosophy, neuroscience, developmental psychology, religious studies, cinema, and literary studies) to investigate how experiences in which the self is temporarily or permanently altered pose opportunities to apply, verify, or craft new theoretical accounts of the self. See the volume that came out of this conference for the edited papers: *Altered Self and Altered Self Experience*, eds. Alexander Gerner and Jorge Gonçalves (Books on Demand, 2014).

98   John Locke, "Of Identity and Diversity," in *Personal Identity*, ed. John Perry, 2nd ed. (Berkeley: University of California Press, 2008), 39.

99   Locke, "Of Identity and Diversity," 51.

100   For further discussion of the "metaphysical criterion" in Locke's essay, see Shelley Weinberg, "Locke on Personal Identity," *Philosophy Compass* 6, no. 6 (June 2011): 398. Weinberg writes, "Locke also seems to see his theory of personal identity as complementing his moral and theological views."

101   Heidegger explores this idea in *Being and Time* in the context of the relationship between beings and equipment. Tools that are ready-to-hand (*zuhanden*) are integrated into the flow of conscious experience, while objects of conscious attention are distinguished from self-consciousness (*vorhanden*). He writes, "The peculiar and self-evident 'in-itself' of the nearest 'things' is encountered when we take care of things, using them but not paying specific attention to them, while bumping into things that are unusable." Martin Heidegger, *Being and Time*, trans. Joan Stambaugh (Albany: SUNY Press, 1996), 74–5.

102   In the carpenter illustration, the subject/object distinction is lost as the hammer becomes phenomenologically transparent through hitch-free use of objects. The carpenter's practiced hammering has a distinct phenomenological signature (*readiness-to-hand*), which makes possible a "hitch-free" relationship to the self. Michael Wheeler, *Reconstructing the Cognitive World : The Next Step* (Cambridge: MIT Press, 2005), 129.

103   Murdoch, *The Sovereignty of Good*, 55.

104   William James, *Varieties of Religious Experience, a Study in Human Nature* (New York: The Modern Library, 1936), 381.

105   Indeed, Murdoch once claimed, "we need a theology that can continue without God." Iris Murdoch, *Metaphysics as a Guide to Morals* (New York: Penguin Press, 1992), 511. See Maria Antonaccio, "Imagining the Good: Iris Murdoch's Godless Theology," *The Annual of the Society of Christian Ethics* 16, 1996, 223–42 for an analysis of Murdoch's moral philosophy as an expression of such a theology.

106   Michel de Certeau, "Mysticism," *Diacritics* 22, no. 2 (1992): 13.

107   Thomas A. Carlson, "Locating the Mystical Subject," in *Mystics: Presence and Aporia*, eds. Michael Kessler and Christian Sheppard (Chicago: University of Chicago Press, 2003), 207.

108   Thomas J.J. Altizer, *The Contemporary Jesus* (Albany: SUNY Press, 1997), 187, quoted in Carlson, "Locating the Mystical Subject," 210–11.

109   This dissolution "comes to light most notably in the all-consuming culture of technological image, where distinctions between surface and depth, exteriority and interiority, immanence and transcendence are themselves unsettled." Carlson, "Locating the Mystical Subject," 211.

110 Richard H. Jones, *Philosophy of Mysticism* (Albany: SUNY Press, 2016), 2.

111 Jones, *Philosophy of Mysticism*, 5.

112 *Lao-Tsu: Te-Tao Ching*, 218.

113 *Zhuangzi*, 4:8, 26–7.

114 Jones, *Philosophy of Mysticism*, 6.

115 Simone Weil, letter to G. Thibon, September 15, 1941, Fonds Simone Weil, NAF 28437 "Correspondance," BNF, Paris, accessed 13 December 2019.

116 William Blake, *The Marriage of Heaven and Hell* (New York: E.P. Dutton & Co., 1927), 14.

117 These inductive altered states of consciousness include states of self-experimentation, which writers like Michaux pursue in the legacy of Rimbaud, Baudelaire, and de Quincey, in addition to Huxley.

118 Leigh Gilmore, *The Limits of Autobiography: Trauma and Testimony* (Ithaca, NY: Cornell University Press, 2000).

119 Cathy Caruth, *Unclaimed Experience* (Baltimore: Johns Hopkins University Press, 1996), 91–2.

120 Cathy Caruth, introduction to *Trauma: Explorations in Memory* (Baltimore: Johns Hopkins University Press, 1995), 4, original emphasis.

121 The psychoanalyst Dori Laub has called traumatic memory "a record that has yet to be made," insisting that extreme human pain and massive psychic trauma "precludes its registration; the observing and recording mechanisms of the human mind are temporarily knocked out, malfunction." Dori Laub, "Bearing Witness or the Vicissitudes of Listening," in *The Holocaust: Theoretical Readings*, eds. Neil Levi and Michael Rothberg (New Brunswick: Rutgers University Press, 2003), 221. The physician Bessel A. van der Kolk and his co-authors also pursue this line of thought, referring to the encoding of trauma as "black hole," citing Caruth in the process. Bessel A. van der Kolk, Alexander C. McFarlane, and Lars Weisath, *Traumatic Stress: The Effects of Overwhelming Experience on Mind, Body, and Society* (New York: Guilford Press, 1996), 3.

122 Ruth Leys, *Trauma: A Genealogy* (Chicago: University of Chicago Press, 2000), 253. In particular, Leys disputes two main views that characterize the work of Caruth and van der Kolk: the empirical claim that traumatic dreams and flashbacks are veridical memories, and the epistemological-ontological claim that these symptoms are literal replicas of trauma. See chapter 7, "The Science of the Literal: The Neurobiology of Trauma," 229–65. Dominick LaCapra has also engaged with the notion of trauma as a paradox of history and memory in his various interventions on the subject, including *Representing the Holocaust* (1994), and *Writing History, Writing Trauma* (2001). In *Writing History*, LaCapra describes the paradigmatic psycho-historical account of trauma as a confusion of the structural nature of trauma with the

historical; he seeks to retain the distinction between the former as a transhistorical and potentially universal phenomenon of absence and the latter as loss as a material product of history. This distinction, he notes, would help to protect against the troubling and indiscriminate generalization by which historical trauma is conflated with wound culture whereby everyone is somehow a victim (or a survivor). Dominick LaCapra, *Writing History, Writing Memory* (Baltimore: Johns Hopkins University Press, 2001), 76–7.

123 See, for example, Daniel Schacter, *The Seven Sins of Memory: How the Mind Forgets and Remembers* (New York: Houghton Mifflin, 2001), which shows how memory's "misdeeds" (transience, absentmindedness, blocking, misattribution, suggestibility, bias, and persistence) are actually adaptive features of memory, or Anthony Wagner, "The Science of Remembering," Video, MediaX at Stanford University, Augmenting Personal Intelligence, May 16, 2006. See also Daniel L. Schacter, Scott A. Guerin, and Peggy L. St. Jacques, "Memory Distortion: An Adaptive Perspective," *Trends in Cognitive Sciences* 15, no. 10 (2011): 467–74, and Thackery I. Brown, Jesse Rissman, Tiffany E. Chow *et al*, "Differential Medial Temporal Lobe and Parietal Cortical Contributions to Real-World Autobiographical Episodic and Autobiographical Semantic Memory," *Scientific Reports* 8 (2018): 6190.

124 LaCapra, *Writing History*, 23.

125 Judith Herman, *Trauma and Recovery* (New York: Basic Books, 1992).

126 Yolande Mukagasana, *La mort ne veut pas de moi* (Paris: Fixot, 1997), 258. Original emphasis.

127 Yolande Mukagasana, *Not My Time to Die*, trans. Zoe Norridge (Kigali: Huza Press, 2019), 180.

128 Dominick LaCapra, *Representing the Holocaust* (Ithaca, NY: Cornell University Press, 1994), 193.

129 LaCapra discusses Delbo as an example of writing as an act of fidelity to trauma: "In some disconcertingly ambivalent form, trauma and one's (more or less symbolic) repetition of it may even be valorized, notably when leaving it seems to mean betraying lost loved ones who were consumed by it – as seemed to be the case for Charlotte Delbo who resisted narrative closure and engaged in hesitant post-traumatic writing as an act of fidelity to victims of the Holocaust." LaCapra, *Writing History*, 70.

130 LaCapra, *Writing History*, 71.

131 As Jared Stark writes, the links between history, trauma, and culture have emerged in a "charged field" that has become "as much a matter of scholarly inquiry as of moral (and moralistic) positioning" leading to reductive or radicalizing approaches to these questions. Jared Stark, "Traumatic Futures: A Review Article," *Comparative Literature Studies* 48, no. 3, Special Issue: Trials of Trauma (2011): 436.

132 My approach to pain and unselfing thus resonates with Roger
     Luckhurst's in *The Trauma Question* (2008), who notes that outside the
     bounds of post-structuralist trauma theory and its "trauma canon"
     there exists a wide range of compelling ways to approach the seemingly
     paradoxical nature of trauma representation: "if trauma is a crisis of
     representation, then this generates narrative possibility just as must
     as impossibility, a compulsive outpouring of attempts to formulate
     narrative knowledge." Roger Luckhurst, *The Trauma Question* (New
     York: Routledge, 2008), 83.

133 In 2008, Michael Rothberg called for the "decolonization" of trauma
     studies, given that trauma theory has remained enmired in Euro-
     American conceptual and historical frameworks. Michael Rothberg,
     "Decolonizing Trauma Studies: A Response," *Studies in the Novel* 40
     (2008): 224–34. Zoe Norridge notes that while criticism of Holocaust
     testimony (the focus of trauma theory) insists on lacuna and impossibility
     of representation, African descriptions of pain are often consumed
     as anthropological evidence. Zoe Norridge, *Perceiving Pain in African
     Literature* (New York: Palgrave Macmillan, 2013), 25. See also Irene Visser,
     "Decolonizing Trauma Theory: Retrospect and Prospects," *Humanities* 4
     (2015): 250–65.

134 Though contemporary phenomenological inquiry also branches into
     an exploration of psychopathology and other challenges to theories of
     consciousness, the phenomenological tradition attempts to explain the
     ways in which selves come about in time and in narrative under ordinary
     circumstances. Psychopathological experiences of selfhood remain
     outside the purview of my study.

135 Though Ricoeur distinguishes between the epistemological ambitions
     of historical narrative and fictional narrative in *Temps et récit*, he also
     insists on the structural similarities between these forms of narrative
     characterized by a circuit of figuration, which he calls "threefold
     mimesis." See *Time and Narrative*, vol. 1, 52–87; *Time and Narrative*, trans.
     Kathleen McLaughlin and David Pellauer, vol. 2 (Chicago: University of
     Chicago Press, 1985), 3.

136 Maurice Merleau-Ponty, *Sense and Non-Sense*, trans. Hubert L. Dreyfus
     and Patricia Allen Dreyfus (Evanston: Northwestern University Press,
     1964), 28.

137 Susan Rubin Suleiman, "Do Facts Matter in Holocaust Memoirs?
     Wilkomirski/Wiesel," *Crises of Memory and the Second World War*
     (Cambridge: Harvard University Press, 2006), 162–3.

138 Charlotte Delbo, quoted in Violaine Gelly and Paul Gradhvol, *Charlotte
     Delbo* (Paris: Fayard, 2013), 212–13. See chapter 3 for full quotation.

139 Amy Hollywood, *Sensible Ecstasy* (Chicago: University of Chicago Press, 2002), 40.

140 Hollywood, *Sensible Ecstasy*, 59.

141 William James, *Principles of Psychology*, vol. 1 (New York: Dover Books, 1950), 239.

142 Evan Thompson, "Is Consciousness a 'Stream'?" The Brains Blog, July 29, 2015. https://philosophyofbrains.com/2015/07/29/is-consciousness-a -stream.aspx

143 Charles Taylor, *Sources of the Self* (Cambridge: Cambridge University Press, 1989), 456.

144 T.S. Eliot, *The Sacred Wood* (London: Faber and Faber, 1997), 44; John Keats, *Selected Letters*, ed. Jon Mee (Oxford: Oxford University Press, 2009), 147; Marcel Proust, *Contre Saint-Beuve* (Paris: Gallimard, 1954). For more on the drive towards the impersonality of modernist literature, see Paolo Bugliani, "'Facing the Monolith': Virginia Woolf, Modernism and Impersonality," *E-rea* (online) 15, no. 2 (2018).

145 Taylor, *Sources of the Self*, 481.

146 Dora Zhang, "Stream of Consciousness," *The Oxford Handbook of Virginia Woolf*, ed. Anne E. Fernald (Oxford: Oxford University Press, 2021), 133. Zhang's chapter shows how Woolf's contribution to stream of consciousness includes at least three features: free indirect discourse which allows a fluidity between perspectives; experiments with collective streams of consciousness; and a use of analogies, which convey the feeling of being conscious.

147 Dorrit Cohn, *Transparent Minds: Narrative Modes for Presenting Consciousness in Fiction* (Princeton: Princeton University Press, 1978).

148 Alan Palmer, *Fictional Minds* (Lincoln: University of Nebraska Press, 2004). See also Brian McHale, "Transparent Minds Revisited," *Narrative* 20, no. 1 (January 2012): 115–24.

149 Armstrong makes this claim about narrative in general; he distinguishes between Cohn's method and cognitive narratology: "the grammatical categories that dominate narratological analyses of so-called fictional minds cannot by themselves do justice to the inherent contradictions and complications that the paradox of the alter ego entails." Paul Armstrong, *Stories and the Brain*, 153.

150 Ricoeur, *Time and Narrative*, vol. 1, 3.

151 Armstrong emphasizes that narrative gives form to the formlessness of experience: "Stories give intelligible form to the immediacy of our interactions with the world, embodied experiences that are already meaningful but that we many not fully comprehend." Armstrong, *Stories and the Brain*, 28.

3. Unselfing as Disruption: Self-Knowledge and Pain in Paul Valéry and Charlotte Delbo

1 Julien Teppe, quoted in Roselyne Rey, *History of Pain*, trans. Louise Elliott Wallace et al. (Cambridge: Harvard University Press, 1998), 318.

2 Rey, *History of Pain*, 318.

3 Elaine Scarry, *The Body in Pain: The Making and Unmaking of the World* (New York: Oxford University Press, 1987), 22 original emphasis.

4 Contemporary definitions of minimal self-experience points to Valéry's foresight on the nature of cognition. Antonio Damasio writes that the "core self" is responsible for consciously attending to a given object, and thereby emitting pulses of provisional subjectivity. *Self Comes to Mind: Constructing the Conscious Brain* (New York: Pantheon Books, 2010). This definition recalls Valéry's "l'homme de l'attention" in *Œuvres*, eds. Jean Hytier and Agathe Rouart-Valéry, vol. 2 (Paris: Gallimard, 1957), 25.

5 Teste's wife calls her husband a "mystique sans Dieu" in "Lettre de Madame Émile Teste." Paul Valéry, *Œuvres*, vol. 2, 34. Judith Robinson-Valéry includes Valéry on her list of "mystique(s) sans Dieu," which also includes Beckett, Bonnefoy and Patrick White. Judith Robinson-Valéry, "'TO GO TO THE LAST POINT' À la recherche d'une nouvelle définition du mysticisme," in *Paul Valéry: Musique, Mystique, Mathématique*, eds. Paul Gifford and Brian Stimpson (Lille: Presses universitaires de Lille, 1993), 15–36.

6 Michel de Certeau, "Mysticism," *Diacritics* 22, no. 2 (1992): 13. See also Robinson-Valéry, "Une nouvelle définition du mysticisme," 17.

7 Judith Robinson-Valéry, "Une nouvelle définition du mysticisme," 12. Unless otherwise attributed, translations from the French are my own.

8 Paul Valéry, *Cahiers 1894–1914*, eds. Judith Robinson-Valéry and Nicole Celeyrette-Pietri, vol. 2 (Paris: Gallimard, 1987), 61.

9 Reino Virtanen, "The Egocentric Predicament: Paul Valéry and Some Contemporaries," *Dalhousie French Studies* 3 (October 1981): 112.

10 Jacques Scherer, *Le "Livre de Mallarmé": Premières recherches sur des documents inédits* (Paris: Gallimard, 1957), 151.

11 Paul Valéry, *Cahiers*, ed. Judith Robinson-Valéry, vol. 2 (Paris: Gallimard, 1974), 366; *Cahiers*, vol. 16 (Paris: C.N.R.S., 1959), 698.

12 Paul Valéry, *Cahiers/Notebooks*, trans. Paul Gifford, eds. Paul Gifford, Brian Stimpson, Robert Pickering, and Judith Robinson-Valéry, vol. 1 (New York: P. Lang, 2000), 302, original emphasis.

13 Paul Ryan, "'L'ici est le moi de l'espace': Self Genesis and the Space of Writing in Valéry's Cahiers," *The Modern Language Review* 97, no. 3 (2002): 555.

14 Jacques Bouveresse, "Philosophy from an Antiphilosopher: Paul Valéry," trans. Christian Fournier and Sandra Laugier, *Critical Inquiry* 21, no. 2 (Winter 1995): 375.

15 Bouveresse, "Philosophy from an Antiphilosopher," 375–6.

16 Valéry, *Œuvres,* vol. 2, 64.

17 Valéry, *Œuvres,* vol. 2, 13. See pp. 1376–7 for more on the various editions and translations of the Cycle Teste.

18 Valéry, *Œuvres,* vol. 2, 18.

19 Paul Valéry, "The Evening with Monsieur Teste," *Paul Valery: An Anthology,* ed. Jackson Mathews, selected by James R. Lawler (Princeton: Princeton University Press, 1977), 7.

20 Valéry, *Œuvres,* vol. 2, 14.

21 Edmund Husserl, *Cartesian Meditations: An Introduction to Phenomenology,* trans. Dorion Cairns (The Hague: Martinus Nijhoff, 1970), 37.

22 Jed Deppman, "Re-Presenting Paul Valery's Monsieur Teste," *Symploke* 11, no. 1 (2003): 210.

23 Deppman, "Re-Presenting Paul Valery's Monsieur Teste," 209.

24 Maurice Merleau-Ponty, *Phénomenologie de la perception* (Paris: Gallimard, 1945). Paul Ryan argues that Valéry's thinking correlates to Merleau-Ponty's in this work in "L'ici est le moi de l'espace," 555.

25 Paul Valéry, *Cahiers,* vol. 9 (C.N.R.S., 1959), 494. original emphasis.

26 Paul Valéry, *Cahiers/Notebooks,* vol. 1, 398.

27 Valéry, *Œuvres,* vol. 2, 24.

28 Valéry, "The Evening with Monsieur Teste," 14.

29 Valéry, *Œuvres,* vol. 2, 24.

30 Valéry, *Œuvres,* vol. 2, 24.

31 Valéry, "The Evening with Monsieur Teste," 15.

32 Valéry, *Œuvres,* vol. 2, 25.

33 Valéry, "The Evening with Monsieur Teste," 15.

34 Scarry, *The Body in Pain,* 164.

35 Valéry, *Œuvres,* vol. 2, 25.

36 Valéry, "The Evening with Monsieur Teste," 15.

37 Valéry, *Œuvres,* vol. 2, 17.

38 Valéry, "The Evening with Monsieur Teste," 6.

39 Valéry, *Œuvres,* vol. 2, 17.

40 Valéry, "The Evening with Monsieur Teste," 6.

41 Daniel Kahneman, *Thinking, Fast and Slow* (New York: Farrar, Straus and Giroux, 2011), 406–7.

42 Valéry, *Œuvres,* vol. 2, 18.

43 Valéry, "The Evening with Monsieur Teste," 6.

44 Valéry, *Œuvres,* vol. 2, 18.

45 Valéry, "The Evening with Monsieur Teste," 7.
46 Valéry, Œuvres, vol. 2, 24.
47 Valéry, "The Evening with Monsieur Teste," 14.
48 Valéry, Œuvres, vol. 2, 24.
49 Valéry, "The Evening with Monsieur Teste," 14.
50 Valéry, Œuvres, vol. 2, 25.
51 Valéry, "The Evening with Monsieur Teste," 15.
52 Valéry, Œuvres, vol. 2, 25.
53 Valéry, "The Evening with Monsieur Teste," 15–16.
54 Valéry, Œuvres, vol. 2, 25.
55 Valéry, "The Evening with Monsieur Teste," 16.
56 Delbo's statement on her memoir is quoted in Lawrence L. Langer,
    introduction to Auschwitz and After by Charlotte Delbo, trans. Rosette
    C. Lamont (New Haven: Yale University Press, 1995), x. See Langer's
    introduction for more on the publication and reception of Delbo's works.
57 Michael Rothberg, Multidirectional Memory: Remembering the Holocaust in
    the Age of Decolonization (Stanford: Stanford University Press, 2009), 204.
    See in particular chapter 7: The Counterpublic Witness: Charlotte Delbo's
    Les belles lettres, 199–224. Rothberg's thesis in Multidirection Memory is that
    the emergence of Holocaust memory and the work of decolonization in
    the 1960s are overlapping and not separate processes (as distinct from the
    "competitive memory" model).
58 Rosette C. Lamont, Translator's Preface to Auschwitz and After (New Haven:
    Yale University Press, 1995), vii.
59 Frédéric Marteau, "Regarder, voir, savoir: Enjeux du regard et poétique
    de la lecture dans l'œuvre de Charlotte Delbo," in Charlotte Delbo: Œuvre
    et engagements, ed. Christiane Page (Rennes: PU Rennes, 2014): 166.
60 Langer, "Introduction," Auschwitz and After, xiii.
61 Charlotte Delbo, Auschwitz et après, vol. 1, Aucun de nous ne reviendra
    (Paris: Minuit, 1970), 7.
62 Charlotte Delbo, Auschwitz and After, trans. Rosette C. Lamont (New Haven:
    Yale University Press, 1995), 1.
63 Charlotte Delbo, Auschwitz et après, vol. 2, Une connaissance inutile (Paris:
    Minuit, 1970), 37.
64 Delbo, Auschwitz and After, 138.
65 Sarah Kofman, Smothered Words, trans. Madeline Dobie (Evanston:
    Northwestern University Press, 1998), 36.
66 Charlotte Delbo, Auschwitz et après, vol. 3, Mesure de nos jours (Paris: Minuit,
    1971), 12.
67 Delbo, Auschwitz and After, 236.
68 Charlotte Delbo, Mesure de nos jours, 15.
69 Debo, Auschwitz and After, 238.

70 Delbo, *Aucun de nous*, 179.
71 Delbo, *Auschwitz and After*, 111.
72 Delbo, *Aucun de nous*, 180–1.
73 Delbo, *Auschwitz and After*, 112.
74 Delbo, *Aucun de nous*, 182.
75 Delbo, *Auschwitz and After*, 113.
76 Delbo, *Aucun de nous*, 181.
77 Delbo, *Auschwitz and After*, 113.
78 Charlotte Delbo and Madeleine Chapsal, "Rien que des femmes:
    Entretien avec Charlotte Delbo," in *Les Revenantes. Charlotte Delbo: La
    Voix d'une communauté à jamais déportée*, eds. David Caron and Sharon
    Marquart (Toulouse: Presses universitaires du Mirail, 2011), 23.
79 Quoted in Violaine Gelly and Paul Gradhvol, *Charlotte Delbo* (Paris:
    Fayard, 2013), 212–13.
80 Charlotte Delbo and Madeleine Chapsal, "Rien que des femmes:
    Entretien avec Charlotte Delbo," in *Les Revenantes. Charlotte Delbo: La
    Voix d'une communauté à jamais déportée*, eds. David Caron and Sharon
    Marquart (Toulouse: Presses universitaires du Mirail, 2011), 21.
81 Lawrence L. Langer, "Hearing the Holocaust," *Poetics Today* 27, no. 2 (June 20,
    2006): 307. "Our initial witness" refers to a source quoted earlier in the article.
82 Jason D. Tougaw, "'We Slipped into a Dream State': Dreaming and
    Trauma in Charlotte Delbo's 'Auschwitz and After,'" *JAC* 24, no. 3,
    Special Issue, Part 2: Trauma and Rhetoric (2004): 584.
83 Delbo, *Aucun de nous*, 87.
84 Delbo, *Auschwitz and After*, 54.
85 Delbo, *Aucun de nous*, 88.
86 Delbo, *Auschwitz and After*, 54.
87 Delbo, *Aucun de nous*, 88–9.
88 Delbo, *Auschwitz and After*, 54–5.
89 Delbo, *Aucun de nous*, 91.
90 Delbo, *Auschwitz and After*, 56.
91 Delbo, *Aucun de nous*, 93–4; Delbo, *Auschwitz and After*, 57.
92 Kahneman, *Thinking, Fast and Slow*, 406–7.
93 Delbo, *Aucun de nous*, 45.
94 Delbo, *Auschwitz and After*, 26.
95 Delbo, *Aucun de nous*, 49.
96 Delbo, *Auschwitz and After*, 29.
97 Theodor W. Adorno, "Cultural Criticism and Society," in *Prisms*, trans.
    S. and S. Weber (Cambridge: MIT Press, 1981), 33.
98 See "In the Beginning Was the Silence" in Lawrence L. Langer, *The
    Holocaust and the Literary Imagination* (New Haven: Yale University Press,
    1975) for a discussion of Adorno's proposition and literature of atrocity.

99   Michaela Hulstyn, "Charlotte Delbo à l'écoute: Auditory Imagery in *Auschwitz et après*," *Women in French Studies* 6 (2016): 70–82.

100 Delbo, *Aucun de nous*, 21–2.

101 Charlotte Delbo and François Bott, "Je me sers de la littérature comme d'une arme: Entretien avec Charlotte Delbo," in *Les Revenantes. Charlotte Delbo: La Voix d'une communauté à jamais déportée*, eds. David Caron and Sharon Marquart (Toulouse: Presses universitaires du Mirail, 2011), 26.

102 Delbo, *Aucun de nous*, 114.

103 Delbo, *Auschwitz and After*, 70.

104 Scarry, *The Body in Pain*, 166.

105 Delbo, *Aucun de nous*, 114.

106 Delbo, *Auschwitz and After*, 70.

107 Delbo, *Aucun de nous*, 115.

108 Delbo, *Auschwitz and After*, 70.

109 Delbo, *Aucun de nous*, 115–16.

110 Delbo, *Aucun de nous*, 123.

111 Delbo, *Aucun de nous*, 118.

112 Delbo, *Auschwitz and After*, 72.

113 Delbo, *Aucun de nous*, 118.

114 Delbo, *Aucun de nous*, 118–19.

115 Delbo, *Auschwitz and After*, 72. The beginning of this citation is rendered quite differently in the English translation. [Each morning she puts herself close to me. She hopes that I will leave her a few drops at the end of my tin cup. Why would I give her my water? Especially since she is going to die soon.]

116 Antoine Compagnon, *Écrire la vie: Montaigne, Stendhal, Proust*. Audio. Collège de France: Littérature française moderne et contemporaine.

117 Charlotte Delbo, *Mesure de nos jours*, 12.

118 Delbo, *Auschwitz and After*, 236–7.

119 Delbo, *Aucun de nous*, 48.

120 Delbo, *Auschwitz and After*, 28–9.

121 Paul Gifford, "Self and Other: Valéry's Lost Object of Desire," in *Reading Paul Valéry: Universe in Mind*, eds. Paul Gifford and Brian Stimpson (Cambridge University Press, 1998), 284.

122 Quoted in Gifford, "Self and Other: Valéry's Lost Object of Desire," 285, original emphasis.

123 Gifford, "Self and Other: Valéry's Lost Object of Desire," 285.

124 Delbo, *Aucun de nous*, 56–7.

125 Delbo, *Auschwitz and After*, 33–4.

126 Emmanuel Levinas, *Totality and Infinity*, trans. Alphonso Lingus (Kluwer Academic Publishers, 1991), 199. See p. 30 for more on the "epiphany of the face."

127 Under ordinary circumstances, this could have pushed us towards the
     view that abandoning our interest in identity dissolves the conflict between
     self-interest and interest in others (that is, Derek Parfit's position in *Reasons
     and Persons*). Delbo's text cannot be used to bolster this view, either.

4. Unselfing as Mutation: Hallucination and the Remains in Henri Michaux and Yolande Mukagasana

1 While Mukagasana's work refers to the "Rwandan genocide" at the time
   of publication in 1997, I have adopted the recent language agreed upon
   by the UN and the Rwandan government and refer to these events as
   "the 1994 genocide against the Tutsi in Rwanda." Moreover, following
   Jennie Burnet's anthropological work on representations of victims
   and perpetrators in Rwanda, I use the term "genocide" to refer to the
   state-sponsored killing of eight hundred thousand Rwandans, primarily
   Tutsi and also politically moderate Hutus between April and July of
   1994. See Jennie Burnet, "Whose Genocide? Whose Truth?" in *Genocide:
   Truth, Memory, and Representation*, eds. Alexander Laban Hinton and
   Kevin Lewis O'Neill (Durham: Duke University Press, 2009), 101, for a
   justification and discussion of this terminology, these figures, and the
   controversial inclusion of Hutus in this category.
2 Alain Badiou writes, "Is the term 'conversion' appropriate to what
   happened on the road to Damascus? It was a thunderbolt, a caesura, and
   not a dialectical reversal. It was a conscription instituting a new subject."
   Saint Paul: The Foundation of Universalism (Stanford: Stanford University
   Press, 2003), 17. See chapter 2 of this volume for more on the conversion
   narrative for unselfing.
3 Henri Michaux, *Les grandes épreuves de l'esprit et les innombrables petites*
   (Paris: Gallimard, 1966), 203.
4 Henri Michaux, *Misérable miracle, la mescaline* (Paris: Gallimard, 1972), 69.
5 Henri Michaux, *Miserable Miracle: Mescaline,* trans. Louise Varèse and
   Anna Moschovakis (New York: NYRB, 2002), 65.
6 Michaux, *Misérable miracle, la mescaline*, 70.
7 Michaux, *Miserable Miracle*, 65–6.
8 "One conclusion was forced upon my mind at that time, and my
   impression of its truth has ever since remained unshaken. It is that our
   normal waking consciousness, rational consciousness as we call it, is but
   one special type of consciousness, whilst all about it, parted from it by
   the flimsiest of screens, there lie potential forms of consciousness entirely
   different. We may go through life without suspecting their existence;
   but apply the requisite stimulus, and at a touch they are there in all their
   completeness, definite types of mentality which probably somewhere

have their field of application and adaptation. No account of the universe in its totality can be final which leaves these other forms of consciousness quite disregarded. How to regard them is the question – for they are so discontinuous with ordinary consciousness. Yet they may determine attitudes though they fail to give a map. At any rate, they forbid a premature closing of our accounts with reality. Looking back on my own experiences, they all converge towards a kind of insight to which I cannot help ascribing some metaphysical significance." William James, *The Varieties of Religious Experience, a Study in Human Nature* (New York: The Modern Library, 1936), 305–6.

 9 Huston Smith attributes the paucity of such philosophical studies to "the climate of fear created by the war on drugs." *Cleansing the Doors of Perception: The Religious Significance of Entheogenic Plants and Chemicals* (New York: Jeremy P. Tarcher, 2000), xv.

10 Martin, *Henri Michaux*, 522.

11 Michaux, *Misérable miracle, la mescaline*, 170, *Miserable Miracle*, 159.

12 Rabinovitch traces the connection between secular and sacred forms of insight in nineteenth- and twentieth-century aesthetic movements, such as supernaturalism, surnaturalism, and surrealism. The term *supernaturalisme* first appears in French in 1836 in the context of German Romanticism when Gérard de Nerval translates *Faust*. In 1855, Baudelaire uses the word *surnaturalisme* to mean a heightened sensory experience and an internal state of revelation. Baudelaire's usage of the term marks a break with the traditional theological notion of *supernaturalisme*, referring rather to an excess of experience. Celia Rabinovitch, *Surrealism and the Sacred: Power, Eros, and the Occult in Modern Art* (Boulder: Westview Press, 2002), 38.

13 Richard Sieburth, "Technician of the Sacred: The Internal and External Voyages of Henri Michaux," *The Times Literary Supplement*, 8 February 2002, 6.

14 Rabinovitch, *Surrealism and the Sacred*, 8.

15 See Margaret Rigaud-Drayton, *Henri Michaux: Poetry, Painting, and the Universal Sign* (Oxford: Clarendon Press, 2005), 30.

16 Rigaud-Drayton, *Henri Michaux*, 5.

17 In his letter to Georges Izambard on May 13, 1871, Rimbaud writes, "Je veux être poète, et je travaille à me rendre *voyant:* vous ne comprendrez pas du tout, et je ne saurais presque vous expliquer. Il s'agit d'arriver à l'inconnu par le dérèglement de *tous les sens*." *Les lettres manuscrites de Rimbaud*, ed. Claude Jeancolas, vol. 1 (Paris: Textuel, 1997), 63.

18 Michaux was provided with mescaline by the Basque neurologist Julián de Ajuriaguerra; Jean Paulhan and Maurice Saillet accompanied him on some of his mescaline voyages and took notes based on their experiences together.

19 Michaux, *Misérable miracle, la mescaline*, 13, *Miserable Miracle*, 5.

20 Henri Michaux, *Connaissance par les gouffres* (Paris: Gallimard, 1967), 9.

21 Jean-Pierre Martin, *Henri Michaux* (Paris: Gallimard, 2003), 516.

22 "To see if a certain class of virtually non-addictive mind-altering chemicals – mescaline, psilocybin, and LSD – could facilitate behavior change in desirable directions." Smith, *Cleansing the Doors of Perception*, 9.

23 Nina Parish, *Henri Michaux: Experimentation with Signs* (New York: Rodolphi B.V., 2007), 111.

24 Peter Broome, *Henri Michaux* (London: Athlone Press, 1977), 1.

25 Albert Camus, *Essais* (Paris: Gallimard, 1965), 101.

26 Various Michaux critics have attributed to the writer an existential project and have "tended to pay more attention to the existentialist undertones in his writings until the mid-1960s," at which point a more psychoanalytic perspective on his work comes to the fore. Rigaud-Drayton, *Henri Michaux*, 6.

27 Henri Michaux, "Faut il vraiment une declaration," in *Œuvres complètes*, eds. Raymond Bellour and Ysé Tran, Bibliothèque de la Pléiade, vol. 2 (Paris: Gallimard, 1998), 1029.

28 Michaux, *Misérable miracle, la mescaline*, 80.

29 Michaux, *Miserable Miracle*, 80–1.

30 François Trotet, *Henri Michaux ou la sagesse du vide* (Paris: Albin Michel, 1992).

31 Michaux, *Les grandes épreuves de l'esprit*, 33.

32 Michaux, *The Major Ordeals of the Mind, and the countless minor ones*, trans. Richard Howard (New York: Harcourt Brace Joanovich, 1974), 22.

33 Michaux, *Les grandes épreuves de l'esprit*, 29.

34 Michaux, *The Major Ordeals of the Mind*, 20.

35 Michaux, *Les grandes épreuves de l'esprit*, 203.

36 Michaux, *The Major Ordeals of the Mind*, 166.

37 Trotet, *Henri Michaux ou la sagesse du vide*, 15.

38 Michaux, *Misérable miracle, la mescaline*, 124.

39 Michaux, *Miserable Miracle*, 124–5.

40 Michaux, *Misérable miracle, la mescaline*, 124.

41 Michaux, *Miserable Miracle*, 124.

42 Michaux, *Les grandes épreuves de l'esprit*, 207.

43 Michaux, *The Major Ordeals of the Mind*, 170.

44 Michaux's description of this "fond surcreusé" [profoundly hollowed depth] again recalls Valéry's writings on the inner contours of the self, understood as a "forme creuse, ou le creux d'un moule" ["hollowed form, or the hollow of a mold"]. In the *Cahiers*, he writes, "Si tu veux, ma Raison, je dirai – , (tu me laisseras dire) – que mon Âme qui est la tienne aussi se sentait comme la forme creuse d'un écrin, ou le creux

d'un moule et ce vide n'éprouvait attendre un objet admirable – une sorte d'épouse matérielle qui ne pouvait pas exister – car cette forme divine, cette absence complète, cet Être qui n'était que Non-Être, et comme l'Être de ce qui ne peut Être – exigeait justement une matière impossible, et le creux vivant de cette forme savait que cette substance manquait et manquerait à jamais au monde des corps – et des actes ... Ainsi doit le mortel convaincu de son Dieu dont il conçoit les attributs par négations successives des défauts et des maux qu'il trouve dans le monde ressentir la présence et l'absence essentielles de Celui qui lui est aussi nécessaire que le centre l'est à une sphère impénétrable, que l'on finit par reconnaître sphère à force d'en explorer la surface et de raisonner sur le liaisons de ses points ... Mon œuvre était cela." Paul Valéry, *Cahiers*, ed. Judith Robinson-Valéry, vol. 2 (Paris: Gallimard, 1974), 689.

45 Smith, *Cleansing the Doors of Perception*, 35.

46 Michaux, *Les grandes épreuves de l'esprit*, 16–17.

47 Michaux, *The Major Ordeals of the Mind*, 9.

48 Peter Broome summarizes this worry in Michaux's work: "Whatever one's thought, one's visual image of the moment, one's current obsession, it will launch it on the road to the absolute. It has no objective truth of its own to propose, apart from that of a scientific process, and will lend accidentally to any vision." *Henri Michaux*, 91.

49 For instance, despite the Rwandan Patriotic Front's (RPF) emphasis on national unity at the first national commemoration ceremony of the genocide in April of 1995, thousands of Hutu civilians were massacred by the Rwandan Patriotic Army (RPA) just three weeks later. Burnet, "Whose Genocide? Whose Truth?" 88.

50 Nicki Hitchcott, "The (Un)Believable Truth about Rwanda," *Australian Journal of French Studies (Liverpool University Press / Journals)* 56, no. 2 (July 2019): 203–4.

51 For more on the initiative, see "The Practice of Memory" in Odile M. Cazenave and Patricia Célérier, *Contemporary Francophone African Writers and the Burden of Commitment* (Charlottesville: University of Virginia Press, 2011) and Nicki Hitchcott, "A Global African Commemoration–Rwanda: Écrire par devoir de mémoire," *Forum for Modern Language Studies* 45, no. 2 (2009): 151–61.

52 Yolande Mukagasana, *La mort ne veut pas de moi* (Paris: Fixot, 1997), 13.

53 Zoe Norridge, Translator's Note to *Death Doesn't Want Me* by Yolande Mukagasana, 199. See this note for other reflections on metaphors that Mukagasana attributed to May, which Norridge later updated or changed in the English version in collaboration with Mukagasana.

54 Mukagasana, Afterward to *Not My Time to Die*, 187.

55   Alexander Laban Hinton and Kevin Lewis O'Neill, eds., *Genocide: Truth, Memory, and Representation* (Durham: Duke University Press, 2009), 5.

56   Yolande Mukagasana, *N'aie pas peur de savoir* (Paris: R. Laffont, 1999), 13.

57   Mukagasana, *N'aie pas peur de savoir*, 14.

58   For an analysis of this gap in Mukagasana's publication and shifts in her attitude towards writing, testimony, and reconciliation in Rwandan society and justice on an international scale, see Catherine Gilbert, "Writing as Reconciliation: Bearing Witness to Life after Genocide," *Rwanda since 1994*, eds. Hannah Grayson and Nicki Hitchcott (Liverpool: Liverpool University Press, 2019), 147–67.

59   Mukagasana, *N'aie pas peur de savoir*, 274.

60   Marie-Aimable Umurerwa and Patrick May, *Comme la langue entre les dents: fratricide et piège identitaire au Rwanda* (Paris: L'Harmattan, 2000); Pauline Kayitare, Patrick May, and Colette Braeckman, *Tu leur diras que tu es hutue: à 13 ans, une Tutsie au cœur du génocide rwandais* (Brussels: A. Versaille, 2011).

61   For instance, there had been little critical engagement with Mukagasana's testimony when I began working on it in 2012. Among the other anthologies, dissertations, and publications that have since appeared, Norridge's recent English translation is expected to bring renewed Anglophone attention to the work.

62   Norridge notes that Rwanda shifted from French to English as the international language of business and education "in part due to revulsion at France's role in the genocide and in part to align Rwanda with other East African Anglophone countries." The recent English translation aims to connect the text to a generation of Rwandans who no longer learn French in school. The English text also includes proverbs and terms in Kinyarwanda. Norridge, Translator's Note to Mukagasana, *Not My Time to Die*, 196.

63   Mukagasana, *La mort ne veut pas de moi*, 104.

64   Mukagasana, *Not My Time to Die*, 69.

65   Mukagasana, *La mort ne veut pas de moi*, 106, *Not My Time to Die*, 70.

66   Mukagasana, *La mort ne veut pas de moi*, 105.

67   Mukagasana, *Not My Time to Die*, 69–70.

68   Mukagasana, *La mort ne veut pas de moi*, 107.

69   Mukagasana, *Not My Time to Die*, 71.

70   Catherine Gilbert, "Mobilising Memory: Rwandan Women Genocide Survivors in the Diaspora," *Australian Journal of French Studies* 55, no. 1 (April 2018): 63. On "altruism born of suffering," see Eric Staub and Johanna Vollhardt, "Altruism Born of Suffering: The Roots of Caring and Helping after Victimization and Other Trauma," *American Journal of Orthopsychiatry* 78, no. 3 (2008): 267–80.

71 Timothy Longman, "Christian Churches and Genocide in Rwanda," in *In God's Name: Genocide and Religion in the Twentieth Century*, eds. Omer Bartov and Phyllis Mack (New York: Berghahn Books, 2001), 141. See this study for a history of the Catholic Church in both colonial and post-colonial Rwanda.

72 Justin Kalibwami, *Le Catholicisme et la société rwandaise: 1900–1962* (Paris: Présence Africaine, 1991), 14. In the 1991 census, 89.8 per cent of Rwandans claimed membership in a Christian church, with 62.6 per cent claiming to be Catholic, 18.8 per cent Protestant and 8.4 per cent Seventh Day Adventist. Longman, "Christian Churches and Genocide in Rwanda," 149; In 2009, Scott Merriman reports that 57 per cent of the population is Roman Catholic, 26 per cent Protestant, 11 per cent Adventist, 5 per cent Muslim and 1 per cent other. *Religion and the State: An International Analysis of Roles and Relationships* (Santa Barbara: ABC-CLIO, 2009), 276.

73 Carol Rittner, John K. Roth, and Wendy Whitworth, eds., *Genocide in Rwanda: Complicity of the Churches?* (St. Paul: Paragon House, 2004), 7–9.

74 *Les apparitions de Kibeho: une brève preséntation* (Gikongoro, Rwanda: Sanctuaire Notre Dame de Kibeho, 2006), 16.

75 *Les apparitions de Kibeho*, 18.

76 *Les apparitions de Kibeho*, 52.

77 Although Kayitare's Catholic upbringing influences her world view insofar as it is presented in her testimony, Mukagasana's particular engagement with the saintly model is found in this text alone. Kayitare, May, and Braeckman, *Tu leur diras que tu es hutue*.

78 Mukagasana, *La mort ne veut pas de moi*, 95.

79 Mukagasana, *Not My Time to Die*, 62.

80 Mukagasana, *La mort ne veut pas de moi*, 106.

81 Mukagasana, *Not My Time to Die*, 70.

82 Mukagasana, *La mort ne veut pas de moi*, 105.

83 Mukagasana, *Not My Time to Die*, 70.

84 Mukagasana, *La mort ne veut pas de moi* 105–6.

85 Mukagasana, *Not My Time to Die*, 69.

86 Mukagasana, *La mort ne veut pas de moi*, 258. original emphasis.

87 Mukagasana, *Not My Time to Die*, 180.

88 As Wieviorka writes, "le moment précis du témoignage nous dit beaucoup sur la société dans laquelle vit le témoin." Annette Wieviorka, *L'ère du témoin* (Paris: Plon, 1998), 173.

89 Timothy Longman argues that while the Western media presented the Genocide against the Tutsi in Rwanda as "a product of 'centuries old' intractable divisions between Hutu and Tutsi 'tribes,'" in fact, the genocide was far from "inevitable." Longman, "Christian Churches and Genocide in Rwanda," 152.

90 Longman, "Christian Churches and Genocide in Rwanda," 140.
91 Mukagasana, *N'aie pas peur de savoir*, 272.
92 Mukagasana, *N'aie pas peur de savoir*, 262.
93 *Les lettres manuscrites de Rimbaud*, vol. 1, 64.
94 Michaux, *Les grandes épreuves de l'esprit*, 87.
95 Michaux, *The Major Ordeals of the Mind*, 68.
96 André Malraux, *Lazare* (Paris: Gallimard, 1974), 238.
97 Jean François Lyotard, *Soundproof Room: Malraux's Anti-Aesthetics*, trans. Robert Harvey (Stanford: Stanford University Press, 2001), 86–90.
98 Michaux, *Les grandes épreuves de l'esprit*, 53.
99 Michaux, *Les grandes épreuves de l'esprit*, 191.
100 Michaux, *The Major Ordeals of the Mind*, 156.
101 Xiaofan Amy Li, *Comparative Encounters between Artaud, Michaux and the Zhuangzi: Rationality, Cosmology, and Ethics* (London: Taylor & Francis, 2015), 141.
102 Mukagasana, *La mort ne veut pas de moi*, 104.
103 Mukagasana, *Not My Time to Die*, 69.
104 Mukagasana, *La mort ne veut pas de moi*, 107.
105 Mukagasana, *Not My Time to Die*, 71.
106 Mukagasana, *La mort ne veut pas de moi*, 107–8.
107 Mukagasana, *N'aie pas peur de savoir*, 282.
108 Gilbert, "Writing as Reconciliation," 152.
109 Mukagasana, *La mort ne veut pas de moi*, 108.
110 Mukagasana, *Not My Time to Die*, 72.

5. Unselfing as Fragmentation: Languages of Alterity in Abdelkebir Khatibi and Hélène Cixous

1 For instance, nineteenth-century writers like Thomas De Quincey with his "Confessions of an English Opium Eater" (1821) and Charles Baudelaire in *Les Paradis artificiels* (1860) ardently expressed the desire to *escape* the artificial constraints of unified self-experience in favour of a more naturally fragmented existence. Thomas De Quincey, *Confessions of an English Opium-Eater: 1822* (Oxford: Woodstock Books, 1989); Charles Baudelaire, *Les paradis artificiels* (Paris: Gallimard et Librairie Générale Française, 1964).
2 Daniel N. Robinson, Preface to *Alterations of Personality: On Double Consciousness* by Alfred Binet, ed. Daniel N. Robinson (Washington, DC: U Publications of America, 1977), v–ix. Robinson writes, "And they [Janet and Binet], too, were not so much divorced from 'metaphysics,' as captains in the armies opposing it. The battle, which still rages, has been

fought on many fronts. One, which was judged to be decisive (although it hasn't been) was that which pitted the metaphysical 'unity of the self' against the scientific 'multiplicity of selves'" (xxiv).

3 Hippolyte Taine, quoted in Alfred Binet, *Les altérations de la personnalité* (Paris: F. Alcan, 1892), 83, http://gallica.bnf.fr/ark:/12148/bpt6k91455f.

4 Hippolyte Taine, quoted in Alfred Binet, *Alterations of Personality* trans. Helen Green Baldwin (New York: D. Appleton and Co., 1896), 92.

5 Binet, *Les altérations de la personnalité*, 83.

6 Sigmund Freud, *Beyond the Pleasure Principle*, trans. C.J.M. Hubback (London: The International Psychoanalytical Press, 1922).

7 The Royal Army Medical Corps divided war neuroses into four major categories including shell shock and hysteria, but the etiology of the categories overlapped considerably. All categories eliminated a man's effectiveness as a soldier and were considered to be "functional" rather than "organic" diseases, producing effects through the mediation of undetectable physical changes. On this point, see Young's work for more on the role Pierre Janet, Jean-Martin Charcot (and others) played in the historical development of the PTSD diagnosis. Allan Young, *The Harmony of Illusions: Inventing Post-Traumatic Stress Disorder* (Princeton: Princeton University Press, 1995).

8 Khatibi writes, "Freud explodes out the unifying idea of the origin, of the proper name, of the people, of the human and divine kingdom." Abdelkebir Khatibi, "Frontiers between Psychoanalysis and Islam," trans. P. Burcu Yalim, *Third Text* 23, no. 6 (2009): 693.

9 See Mairéad Hanrahan, "Fictional Analysis," in *Cixous's Semi-Fictions: Thinking at the Borders of Fiction* (Edinburgh: Edinburgh University Press, 2014).

10 Paget Henry, *Caliban's Reason: Introducing Afro-Caribbean Philosophy* (New York: Routledge, 2000), 93.

11 Frantz Fanon, *Œuvres* (Paris: La Découverte, 2011), 153–4.

12 Frantz Fanon, *Black Skin, White Masks*, trans. Richard Philcox (New York: Grove Press, 2008), 90.

13 Frantz Fanon, *Les damnés de la terre* (Paris: La Découverte, 2002), 209–11.

14 Fanon, *Les damnés de la terre*, 302.

15 Abdelkebir Khatibi, *Plural Maghreb: Writings on Postcolonialism*, trans. P. Burcu Yalim (New York: Bloomsbury Academic), 2019.

16 See Leigh Gilmore, *The Limits of Autobiography: Trauma and Testimony* (Ithaca, NY: Cornell University Press, 2001). For more on feminist autobiographical strategies, see Nancy K. Miller, *But Enough about Me: Why We Read Other People's Lives* (New York: Columbia University Press, 2002). Françoise Lionnet uses Glissant's term *métissage* to discuss the braiding of cultural forms in the autobiographical texts by postcolonial women writers in *Autobiographical Voices Race, Gender, Self-Portraiture*

(Ithaca, NY: Cornell University Press, 1989); *Les Nouvelles Écritures du Moi dans les Littératures française et francophone,* eds. Sylvie Camet and Noureddine Sabri (Paris: L'Harmattan, 2012); Alison Rice, *Polygraphies: Francophone Women Writing Algeria* (Charlottesville: University of Virginia Press, 2012); *This "Self" Which Is Not One: Women's Life Writing in French* eds. Natalie Edwards and Christopher Hogarth (Newcastle upon Tyne: Cambridge Scholars, 2010).

17 For more on which European traditions Khatibi rejected à la Fanon and the role of 'European' deconstruction in his thinking, see Mary Ellen Wolf, "Rethinking the Radical West: Khatibi and Deconstruction," *L'Esprit Créateur* 34, no. 2 (1994): 58–68. Alison Rice discusses Derridean *différance* in Maghrebi autobiography in *Polygraphies: Francophone Women Writing Algeria.* (See note 16.)

18 Derrida's *Le Monolinguisme de l'autre* (Paris: Galilée, 1996) (*The Monolingualism of the Other*) builds on Khatibi's *Amour bilingue,* as well as his essay, "Du Bilinguisme." For more on the relationship between the two, see Felisa V. Reynolds, "Khatibi as Derrida's Foil: Undermining the Last Defender of the French Language," *Contemporary French and Francophone Studies: Sites* 18 (2014): 199–206.

19 "If so called 'so-called poststructuralism' is the product of a single historical moment, then that moment is probably not May 1968, but rather the Algerian War of Independence – no doubt itself both a symptom and a product." Robert C. Young, *White Mythologies: Writing, History, and the West* (New York: Routledge, 1991), 1. Much ink has been spilled in evaluating this origin story. For more on this reading the relationship between poststructuralism and postcolonial theory, see Jane Hiddleston, *Poststructuralism and Postcoloniality* (Liverpool: Liverpool University Press, 2010); Alina Sajed, "The Post Always Rings Twice? The Algerian War, Poststructuralism and the Postcolonial in IR Theory," *Review of International Studies* vol. 38 (2012): 141–63; Megan C. MacDonald, "Haunting Correspondences and Elemental Scenes: Weaving Cixous after Derrida," in *Cixous: After / Depuis 2000,* eds. Elizabeth Berglund Hall, Frédérique Chevillot, Eilene Hoft-March, and Maribel Peñalver Vicea (Leiden: Brill, 2017): 36–54.

20 Jacques Derrida, "H.C. pour la vie, c'est à dire" (Paris: Galilée, 2002), and "Exergue," *Œuvres de Abdelkébir Khatibi,* vol. 1, *Romans et récits,* 7.

21 Abdelfattah Kilito, *Thou Shalt Not Speak My Language,* trans. Waïl S. Hassan (Syracuse: Syracuse University Press, 2008), 21.

22 Réda Bensmaïa, *Experimental Nations, or, the Invention of the Maghreb,* trans. Alyson Waters (Princeton: Princeton University Press, 2003), 104.

23 Abdelkebir Khatibi, *Œuvres de Abdelkébir Khatibi,* vol. 1, *Romans et récits* (Paris: la Différence, 2008), 269.

24 Abdelkebir Khatibi, *Love in Two Languages*, trans. Richard Howard (Minneapolis: University of Minnesota Press, 1990), 98.

25 Khatibi, *Œuvres*, vol. 1, 270.

26 Khatibi, *Love in Two Languages*, 98.

27 James McGuire, "Forked Tongues, Marginal Bodies: Writing as Translation in Khatibi," *Research in African Literatures* 23, no. 1 (March 1992): 110.

28 Matt Reeck, "Poetics of the Orphan in Abdelkébir Khatibi's Early Work," *Journal of French and Francophone Philosophy* 25, no.1 (2017): 133.

29 In one example, a group of Moroccan spectators fails to understand a series of plays in Classical Arabic. "Pour honorer la demande toujours grande, nous nous installâmes dans le grand théâtre de la ville. Au programme, des pièces poétiques en arabe classique. À la fin du spectacle, le public était toujours assis, il n'avait rien compris à cette langue des livres. Un acteur cria au public que c'était réellement la fin et qu'il pouvait partir." Khatibi, *Œuvres*, vol. 1, 66.

30 Khatibi, *Œuvres*, vol. 1, 40.

31 *Œuvres*, vol. 1, 207–8.

32 *Love in Two Languages*, 4. A deliberately literal translation of this passage emphasizes the shifting from French to Darija to Fusha: "He calmed down at once, as soon as the Arabic 'word' [French], 'word' [Darija] with its learned equivalent 'word' [Fusha], and the whole chain of diminutives, puns from his childhood: 'little word' [Darija] … The diglossia of the 'word' [Darija/ Fusha] returns without erasing the word 'word' [French]."

33 Tom Gijssels and Daniel Casasanto, "Conceptualizing Time in Terms of Space: Experimental Evidence," in *The Cambridge Handbook of Cognitive Linguistics*, ed. Barbara Dancygier (Cambridge: Cambridge University Press, 2017), 651–68.

34 Herbert H. Clark, "Space, Time, Semantics, and the Child," in *Cognitive Development and Acquisition of Language*, ed. Timothy E. Moore (San Diego: Academic Press, 1973): 27–63; George Lakoff and Mark Johnson, *Metaphors We Live By* (Chicago: University of Chicago Press, 1980); Lera Boroditsky, "Metaphoric Structuring: Understanding Time through Spatial Metaphors," *Cognition* 75, no. 1 (April 2000): 1–28.

35 Lera Boroditsky, "Does Language Shape Thought? Mandarin and English Speakers' Conceptions of Time," *Cognitive Psychology* 43, no. 1 (2001): 1–22; Lera Boroditsky, Orly Fuhrman, and Kelly McCormick, "Do English and Mandarin Speakers Think about Time Differently?" *Cognition* 118, no. 2 (January 2011): 123–9.

36 Clark demonstrates the relationship between internal spatial metaphors and the representation of time in 1973, and by the late 1990s, cognitive

psychologists argue that external features (such as writing direction in a language) also influence the way a person imagines time to be laid out. See note 39. For the influence of writing direction on representations of time, see for example, Tversky, Kugelmass, and Winter, "Cross-Cultural and Developmental Trends in Graphic Productions."

37 Lera Boroditsky, "How Languages Construct Time," in *Space, Time and Number in the Brain*, ed. Stanislas Dehaene and Elizabeth M. Brannon (San Diego: Academic Press, 2011), 339.

38 Orly Fuhrman and Lera Boroditsky, "Cross-Cultural Differences in Mental Representations of Time: Evidence from an Implicit Nonlinguistic Task," *Cognitive Science* 34 (2010): 1430–51.

39 Barbara Tversky, Sol Kugelmass, Atalia Winter, "Cross-Cultural and Developmental Trends in Graphic Productions," *Cognitive Psychology* 23, no. 4 (1991): 515–57.

40 Juanma de la Fuente, Julio Santiago, Antonio Román, Cristina Dumitrache, and Daniel Casasanto, "When You Think about It, Your Past Is in Front of You: How Culture Shapes Spatial Conceptions of Time," *Psychological Science* 25, no. 9 (2014): 1682–90.

41 Gijssels and Casasanto, "Conceptualizing Time in Terms of Space," 40.5.

42 This is something Roman Jakobson had already worked on in the context of linguistics and translation. See Roman Jakobson, "On Linguistic Aspects of Translation," in *On Translation*, ed. Arthur Reuben Brower (Cambridge: Harvard University Press, 1959), 232–9.

43 Boroditsky's work on time relies on sources both internal and external to language for temporal metaphors. Internal sources, or ones encoded in language, include differing but not incompatible ego-moving metaphors as in "We are coming up on Christmas" (front = future) and time-moving metaphor "Wednesday is before Friday" (front = past). For the original work on these two metaphors, see Clark, "Space, Time, Semantics, and the Child." External sources, such as left-to-right printing in French and right-to-left printing in Arabic are also considered.

44 It should be mentioned here that many linguists reject (varying degrees) of the "Sapir-Whorf hypothesis" which, against the thesis of Chomskyan Universal Grammar, suggests that the structure of individual languages affects the world views of their speakers. For a breakdown of the two views in the public sphere, see the Economist debate on Language from December 2010, in which Mark Liberman argues against Boroditsky's claims. Even when considering the opposing view, *Amour bilingue* is an ideal point of contact with this body of research in that the narrator explicitly interrogates the role multiple languages play in shaping his vertiginous world view. Khatibi's text should be understood as an elaborate translation of the "what it feels like" to be bilingual, of

swapping between these two mindsets. "Neo-Whorfianism: A Debate on Language and Thought," *The Economist*, December 13, 2010.

45 Khatibi, *Love in Two Languages*, 19.
46 Khatibi, *Œuvres*, vol. 1, 211.
47 Khatibi, *Love in Two Languages*, 7.
48 Khatibi, *Œuvres*, vol. 1, 281.
49 Khatibi, *Love in Two Languages*, 115.
50 Khatibi, *Œuvres*, vol. 1, 219.
51 Khatibi, *Love in Two Languages*, 20.
52 Khatibi, *Œuvres*, vol. 1, 225.
53 Khatibi, *Love in Two Languages*, 29–30.
54 Khatibi, *Œuvres*, vol. 1, 226.
55 Khatibi, *Love in Two Languages*, 30–31.
56 Khatibi, *Œuvres*, vol. 1, 226.
57 Khatibi, *Love in Two Languages*, 30.
58 Of course, perception of time also depends on non-linguistic features, such as maps, the direction that one's house faces, etc.
59 Khatibi, *Œuvres*, vol. 1, 226.
60 Khatibi, *Œuvres*, vol. 1, 226.
61 Khatibi, *Love in Two Languages*, 31.
62 Jakobson, "On Linguistic Aspects of Translation," 237.
63 Lera Boroditsky, Lauren A. Schmidt, and Webb Phillips, "Sex, Syntax, and Semantics," in *Language in Mind: Advances in the Study of Language and Thought*, eds. Dedre Gentner and Susan Goldin-Meadow (Cambridge: MIT Press, 2003), 63.
64 Boroditsky, Schmidt, and Phillips, "Sex, Syntax, and Semantics," 65.
65 Boroditsky, Schmidt, and Phillips, "Sex, Syntax, and Semantics," 65.
66 Khatibi, *Œuvres*, vol. 1, 208.
67 Khatibi, *Love in Two Languages*, 4.
68 Charles Trenet's 1936 song "Le soleil et la lune" illustrates the productive nature of such grammatical oppositions of gender in French. The song imagines the sun as a male suitor of the female moon. The two, tragicomically, never meet.
69 Khatibi, *Œuvres*, vol. 1, 41.
70 Michael Sells, *Approaching the Qur'án: The Early Revelations* (Ashland, OR: White Cloud Press, 2007), 84.
71 See Samia Kassab-Charfi, "Amour bilingue de Khatibi ou la mémoire palimpseste," ed. Alison Rice and Nasrin Qader, *Revue CELAAN* 9, no. 2 & 3 (2011): 120–34; Hassan Wahbi, *Abdelkébir Khatibi, La Fable de L'aimance* (Paris: L'Harmattan, 2009).
72 Abdelkebir Khatibi, *Œuvres de Abdelkébir Khatibi*, vol. 3, *Essais* (Paris: la Différence, 2008), 25.

73 Abdelkebir Khatibi, *Plural Maghreb*, 6.

74 Nasrin Qader, *Narratives of Catastrophe: Boris Diop, Ben Jelloun, Khatibi* (New York: Fordham University Press, 2009), 124.

75 Qader, *Narratives of Catastrophe,* 130.

76 Jane Hiddleston, *Understanding Postcolonialism* (Stocksfield: Routledge, 2009), 133.

77 When the first attempts were made to introduce *Ishq,* referring to "passionate love" into the discourse on the relationship between man and God, Annemarie Schimmel writes, "even most of the Sufis objected, for this root implies the concept of overflowing and passionate longing, a quality that God, the self-sufficient, could not possibly possess; nor was it permissible that man should approach the Lord with such feelings." Annemarie Schimmel, *Mystical Dimensions of Islam* (Chapel Hill: University of North Carolina Press, 2011), 137.

78 Samia Mehrez and Lawrence Venuti, "Translation and the Postcolonial Experience: The Francophone North African Text," in *Rethinking Translation: Discourse, Subjectivity, Ideology* (London: Routledge, 1992), 135.

79 Valéry writes, "l'homme communique avec – soi, par les mêmes moyens qu'il a de communiquer avec *l'autre.* / La conscience a besoin d'un autre fictif – d'une extériorité – elle se développe en développant cette *altérité.* Paul Gifford, "Self and Other: Valéry's Lost Object of Desire," in *Reading Paul Valéry: Universe in Mind*, eds. Paul Gifford and Brian Stimpson (Cambridge University Press, 1998), 285, original emphasis.

80 Gifford, "Self and Other: Valéry's Lost Object of Desire," 284.

81 Paul Ricœur, *Soi-même comme un autre* (Paris: Seuil, 1990), 28.

82 Khatibi, *Œuvres,* vol. 1, 264.

83 Khatibi, *Love in Two Languages,* 90.

84 Claire Boyle, "Writing Self-Estrangement: Possessive Knowledge and Loss in Cixous's Recent Autobiographical Work," *Dalhousie French Studies* 68 (Fall 2004): 70.

85 Hélène Cixous, "La venue à l'écriture," in *Entre l'écriture* (Paris: Des femmes, 1986), 67.

86 Hélène Cixous, "Coming to Writing," in *"Coming to Writing" and Other Essays* (Cambridge: Harvard University Press, 1991), 55.

87 This framework has divided feminist criticism. Cixous's notion of "écriture féminine" and "white ink" have been met with charges of essentialism, despite that Cixous often stresses in interviews that the terms "masculine" and "feminine" do not (exclusively or anatomically) apply to "men" and "women" in her work. See Katherine Binhammer, "Metaphor or Metonymy? The Question of Essentialism in Cixous," *Tessera* 10 (June 1991): 65–78 for a summary and analysis of the

essentialism debate, particularly within the Anglo-American feminist academy.

88 Cixous, "Coming to Writing," 30.

89 Hélène Cixous and Mireille Calle-Gruber, *Hélène Cixous, photos de racines* (Paris: Des femmes, 1994), 106.

90 Hélène Cixous and Mireille Calle-Gruber, *Rootprints: Memory and Life Writing* (New York: Routledge, 1997), 97.

91 Cixous and Calle-Gruber, *Rootprints*, 104.

92 Cixous and Calle-Gruber, *Rootprints*, 95.

93 Hélène Cixous, *The Hélène Cixous Reader*, ed. Susan Sellers (New York: Routledge, 1994), xviii.

94 Cixous, *The Hélène Cixous Reader*, xvii.

95 Cixous, *The Hélène Cixous Reader*, xv.

96 Boyle, "Writing Self-Estrangement," 70.

97 Cixous, *Coming to Writing*, 47.

98 Hélène Cixous, *Le livre de Promethea* (Paris: Gallimard, 1983), 27.

99 Teresa Brennan writes that Cixous's work has tried to circumvent the male dominance implied by Lacan's symbolic law, as well as psychical organization, which is an argument that "the symbolic is the condition of sanity." Teresa Brennan, Introduction to *Between Feminism and Psychoanalysis*, *Between Feminism and Psychoanalysis*, ed. Teresa Brennan (London: Routledge, 2002) Taylor & Francis e-Library ed.

100 See *La* (Paris: Gallimard, 1976); "La venue à l'écriture" (1976) or *Angst* (Paris: Des femmes, 1977) among others for this theme.

101 *The Hélène Cixous Reader*, 59.

102 Sal Renshaw, "The Thealogy of Helene Cixous," in *Religion in French Feminist Thought: Critical Perspectives*, eds. Morny Joy, Kathleen O'Grady, and Judith L. Poxon (New York: Routledge, 2003), 168.

103 H. Jill Scott, "Loving the Other: Subjectivities of Proximity in Hélène Cixous's *Book of Promethea*," *World Literature Today* 69, no. 1 (1995): 31.

104 Sarah Cornell, "Hélène Cixous: Le Livre de Promethea: Paradise Refound," in *Writing Differences: Readings from the Seminar of Hélène Cixous*, ed. Susan Sellers (New York: St. Martin's, 1988), 133.

105 Hélène Cixous, *Les rêveries de la femme sauvage: scènes primitives* (Paris: Galilée, 2000), 101.

106 Hélène Cixous, *Reveries of the Wild Woman: Primal Scenes*, trans. Beverley Bie Brahic (Evanston: Northwestern University Press, 2000), 59.

107 Cixous, *Rêveries*, 101.

108 Cixous, *Reveries*, 59.

109 Alison Rice, *Time Signatures: Contextualizing Contemporary Francophone Autobiographical Writing from the Maghreb* (Lanham: Lexington Books, 2006), 243–4.

110 Cixous, *Rêveries*, 9.
111 Khatibi, *Œuvres*, vol. 1, 207, *Love in Two Languages*, 3.
112 Khatibi, *Œuvres*, vol. 1, 209, *Love in Two Languages*, 5.
113 Cixous, *Rêveries*, 53.
114 Cixous, *Reveries*, 30.
115 Cixous, *Rêveries*, 142.
116 Cixous, *Reveries*, 80.
117 Cixous, *Rêveries*, 122, *Reveries*, 70.
118 Cixous, *Rêveries*, 125.
119 Cixous, *Reveries*, 71.
120 Cixous, *Rêveries*, 144.
121 Cixous, *Reveries*, 81.
122 Cixous, *Rêveries*, 145.
123 Cixous, *Reveries*, 81.
124 Cixous, *Rêveries*, 145.
125 Cixous, *Reveries*, 81.
126 Cixous, *Rêveries*, 145.
127 Cixous, *Reveries*, 81.
128 Cixous, *Rêveries*, 146.
129 Cixous, *Reveries*, 82.
130 Cixous, *Rêveries*, 125–6.
131 Cixous, *Reveries*, 71.
132 Cixous, *Rêveries*, 44–5.
133 Cixous, *Reveries*, 24.

6. Unselfing as Destruction: Decreation and Inner Experience in Simone Weil and Georges Bataille

  1 Bataille's erotic novel, *Le Bleu du ciel* (1957), follows the escapades of Henri Troppmann across Europe to Barcelona before the Spanish Civil War, where he meets Lazare, a strange political activist who closely resembles Weil. See Alexander Irwin's analysis of Troppmann's and Lazare's complicity as stand-ins for Bataille and Weil. Alexander Irwin, *Saints of the Impossible: Bataille, Weil, and the Politics of the Sacred* (Minneapolis: University of Minnesota Press, 2002).
  2 Primo Levi, *The Drowned and the Saved*, trans. Raymond Rosenthal (New York: Summit Books, 1988), 83–4.
  3 Giorgio Agamben, *Remnants of Auschwitz: The Witness and the Archive* (New York: Zone Books, 1999), 45.
  4 Simone Weil, *La pesanteur et la grâce* (Paris: Plon, 1948), 31.
  5 Simone Weil, *Gravity and Grace*, trans. Emma Crawford and Mario von der Ruhr (New York: Routledge, 2002), 28.

234 Notes to pages 159–63

6 Irwin, *Saints of the Impossible*, 172.

7 Jean-Paul Sartre, "Un nouveau mystique," in *Situations*, vol. 1 (Paris: Gallimard, 1947), 143–88.

8 I use quotation marks when referring to Bataille's usage of the term "project."

9 Simone Weil, *Œuvres complètes*, eds. André A. Devaux and Florence de Lussy, vol. 6, *Cahiers* 2 (Paris: Gallimard, 1997), 466.

10 Weil, *La pesanteur et la grâce*, 38.

11 Weil, *Gravity and Grace*, 32.

12 *Simone Weil*, eds. François L'Yvonnet and Emmanuel Gabellieri (Paris: L'Herne, 2014), 11.

13 For the translation of *Attente de Dieu*, I cite the original 1951 English translation by Emma Craufurd (using the 2001 Harper Perennial Classics edition). However, this translation is incomplete; some passages from the original French are not translated in the English version. I have in some cases supplemented the translation where necessary.

14 Simone Weil, "L'Amour de Dieu et le malheur," in *Œuvres*, ed. Florence de Lussy (Paris: Gallimard, 1999), 714.

15 For more on Weil's relationship to Judaism, see Florence de Lussy, "L'Antijudaïsme de Simone Weil," in *Œuvres*, ed. Florence de Lussy (Paris: Gallimard, 1999), 959–63.

16 Weil's later reflections on kenosis (a term she herself does not use in her writings) are principally guided by the New Testament, Plato, St. Jean of the Cross, and Alain. For more on these influences see Christine Hof, "Kénose et Histoire: La lecture de l'Hymne aux Philippiens," in *Simone Weil*, eds. Emmanuel Gabellieri and François L'Yvonnet (Paris: L'Herne, 2014), 385–96.

17 Simone Weil, "Lettre à Joë Bousquet," in *Œuvres*, ed. Florence de Lussy (Paris: Gallimard, 1999), 797.

18 Simone Weil, *Simone Weil Reader*, ed. George A. Panichas (New York: McKay, 1977), 91.

19 Simone Weil, "Lettre à Joë Bousquet," 789.

20 "And my greatest desire is to lose not only all will but all personal being." Simone Weil, *Waiting for God*, trans. Emma Craufurd (New York: Perennial Classics, 2001), 17.

21 Weil, *La pesanteur et la grâce*, 41–2.

22 Weil, *Gravity and Grace*, 36–7.

23 Weil, *La pesanteur et la grâce*, 36–7.

24 Weil, *Gravity and Grace*, 32–3.

25 Though he notes that there is "no sign in her letters or journals that Weil had ever read Luria or was aware of the Kabbalic strand of Jewish theology," Robert Zaretsky draws a parallel between Weil's theorization of *decreation* with Jewish mysticism through the Lurianic notion of

Tsimtsum, or presence through absence. For a Kabbalist, *Tsimtsum* captures the idea of the world-creating withdrawal of divine energy. See Robert Zaretsky, *The Subversive Simone Weil: A Life in Five Ideas* (Chicago: University of Chicago Press, 2021), 140.

26 Weil, *La pesanteur et la grâce,* 37.
27 Weil, *Gravity and Grace,* 33.
28 Weil, *La pesanteur et la grâce,* 29.
29 Weil, *Gravity and Grace,* 26.
30 Weil, *La pesanteur et la grâce,* 45.
31 Weil, *Gravity and Grace,* 39.
32 Lakshmi Kapani, "Simone Weil, Lectrice des *Upanishad védiques* et de la *Bhagavad-Gîtà*: L'action sans désir et le désir sans objet," *Cahiers Simone Weil* 5, no. 2 (June 1982), 101. Kapani also argues that Weil's writings on "desire without object," are actually compatible with Hindu soteriology which cannot be conceived as a torture (a "hunger without food"). For more on this theme of hunger in relationship to Weil's own asceticism, see Alec Irwin, "Devoured by God: Cannibalism, Mysticism, and Ethics in Simone Weil," *CrossCurrents* 51, no. 2 (Summer 2001): 257– 72.
33 Alyette Degrâces, Avant-Propos 2: "Du vide d'acte à l'acte vide: Une lecture du *Tao* et de la *Gītā*," in Simone Weil, *Œuvres complètes,* eds. André A. Devaux and Florence de Lussy, vol. 6, *Cahiers* 2 (Paris: Gallimard, 1997), 33.
34 Simone Weil, "Autobiographie spirituelle," *Œuvres,* ed. Florence de Lussy (Paris: Gallimard, 1999), 772.
35 Simone Weil, *Waiting for God,* 28.
36 *The Bhagavad-Gītā*, trans. Georg Feuerstein (Boston: Shambhala, 2011), 4.20, 4.23, p. 141.
37 Simone Weil, *La connaissance surnaturelle* (Paris: Gallimard, 1950), 306.
38 E. Jane Doering, *Simone Weil and the Specter of Self-Perpetuating Force* (Notre Dame: University of Notre Dame Press, 2010), 165.
39 The term "action non agissante" references R. Guénon's discussion of "activité non agissante" in *L'Homme et son devenir selon le Vedanta* (1941); see note 209 to K4 in Weil, *Œuvres completes,* vol. 6, *Cahiers* 2, 566.
40 Weil, *Œuvres completes,* vol. 6, *Cahiers* 2, 76.
41 Weil, *Œuvres completes,* vol. 6, *Cahiers* 2, 384.
42 Doering, *Simone Weil and the Specter of Self-Perpetuating Force,* 154.
43 See Alexander Irwin's chapter, "Transforming the Warrior's Soul," in *Saints of the Impossible* for a detailed analysis of the evolution of the idea of force in Weil's thinking over the course of her life.
44 Weil read Marcel Granet's *La Pensée chinoise,* Léon Wiegner's *Pères du système taoïste* and continued to be guided by R. Guénon. See Alyette Degrâces, Avant-propos 2: "L'Inde ou le passage obligé," in Simone Weil,

Œuvres completes, vol. 6, *Cahiers* 1, eds. André A. Devaux and Florence de Lussy (Paris: Gallimard, 1994), 49.

45 Simone Weil, "Formes de l'Amour implicite de Dieu," in *Œuvres* ed. Florence de Lussy, 752.

46 Weil, *Waiting for God*, 126.

47 Degrâces, "L'Inde ou le passage obligé," 51.

48 Weil, *Œuvres completes*, vol. 6, *Cahiers* 2, 394.

49 She writes the following in *Cahier 4*, with a question mark in the margins: "Non-intervention des taöistes appliquée à soi-même; en quel sens?" [Non-intervention of the Daoists applied to oneself; in what sense?]

50 Simone Weil, *Simone Weil: Seventy Letters*, trans. Richard Rees (London: Oxford University Press, 1965), letter 41, 130.

51 Lissa McCullough argues, "Any resemblance of Weil's thought to Cathar dualism is both incidental and superficial: incidental because the predominance of the good-evil opposition was patent in her writings for several years before her overt interest in Catharism emerged; superficial because the polar oppositions in Weil are essentially *dialectical* not dualistic." Lissa McCullough, *The Religious Philosophy of Simone Weil: An Introduction* (London: Bloomsbury, 2014), 214.

52 Simone Kotva, "The Occult Mind of Simone Weil," *Philosophical Investigations* 43, no. 1–2 (January–April 2020): 141.

53 Françoise Meltzer, "The Hands of Simone Weil," *Critical Inquiry* 27, no. 4 (Summer 2001), 622.

54 Irwin, *Saints of the Impossible*, 79.

55 Weil, "L'Amour de Dieu et le malheur," 701.

56 Weil, *Waiting for God*, 79.

57 Weil, "L'Amour de Dieu et le malheur," 701.

58 Weil, "L'Amour de Dieu et le malheur," 694.

59 Weil, *Waiting for God*, 68.

60 Weil, *Œuvres completes*, vol. 6, *Cahiers* 2, 242.

61 Weil, *Gravity and Grace*, 39.

62 Weil, *La pesanteur et la grâce*, 40.

63 Weil, *Gravity and Grace*, 35.

64 Weil, "L'Amour de Dieu et le malheur," 694.

65 Weil, *Waiting for God*, 68–9.

66 Weil, "L'Amour de Dieu et le malheur," 695.

67 Weil, *Waiting for God*, 70.

68 Weil, "L'Amour de Dieu et le malheur," 706.

69 Weil, "L'Amour de Dieu et le malheur," 705.

70 Weil, "L'Amour de Dieu et le malheur," 708.

71 Weil, "L'Amour de Dieu et le malheur," 708–9.

72 Weil, "L'Amour de Dieu et le malheur," 709.
73 On this point, one might also reflect on Weil's personal relationship to this question through, for example, her disappointment with the office job to which she had been assigned at the Free French headquarters in London in 1942 and her determination to join the frontlines with other nurses to administer first aid to the wounded under enemy fire. For more on this, see "Frontline Nurses" in Irwin, *Saints of the Impossible*, 183–9.
74 Weil, "L'Amour de Dieu et le malheur," 715.
75 Weil, "L'Amour de Dieu et le malheur," 695. She writes that it is "irréductible à toute autre chose, comme les sons, dont rien ne peut donner aucune idée à un sourd-muet."
76 Weil, "Lettre à Joë Bousquet," 798.
77 Weil, "Letter to Joë Bousquet," 93.
78 Weil, "L'Amour de Dieu et le malheur," 694.
79 Weil, "L'Amour de Dieu et le malheur," 694.
80 Weil, *Waiting for God*, 69.
81 Simone Weil, letter to Thibon, December 1941, Fonds Simone Weil, NAF 28437 "Correspondance," BNF, Paris, accessed 13 December 2019.
82 For more on the challenge of interpreting personal narrative in relation to religious lives and a rich discussion of the tension in Weil's "personalized depersonalization," see Mark Freeman, "Beyond the Human" in *The Priority of the Other* (Oxford: Oxford University Press, 2014).
83 Emmanuel Gabellieri and François L'Yvonnet, eds., "Compte rendu nécrologique paru en Septembre 1943 dans la presse britannique," in *Simone Weil* (Paris: L'Herne, 2014), 401.
84 Gustave Thibon, *Simone Weil as We Knew Her*, eds. Joseph M. Perrin and Gustave Thibon (London: Routledge and Kegan Paul), 104.
85 See Amy Hollywood, *Sensible Ecstasy* (Chicago: University of Chicago Press, 2002), 101–8 for more on the interplay between Bataille, Nietzsche, and the mystics. See also Michael Surya, *Georges Bataille, la mort à l'oeuvre* (Paris: Gallimard, 1992).
86 Georges Bataille, *L'expérience intérieure* (Paris: Gallimard, 1954), 15. The original manuscript reads: "J'entends par 'l'expérience intérieure' ce que d'habitude on nomme d'ordinaire 'expérience mystique': vivre les états d'extase, de ravissement, au moins d'émotion méditée" Fonds Georges Bataille, NAF 28086, Boite 8, Carnet 3, BNF, Paris, accessed 12 December 2019.
87 Georges Bataille, *Inner Experience*, trans. Leslie Anne Boldt (New York: SUNY Press, 1988), 3.
88 In his discussion of the historical moment the term "limit-experience" evokes, Hart distinguishes between Bataille's conception of the sacred and that of Blanchot. While Bataille conceives of the sacred as

a negative experience ("it is the revelation of the continuous through the sacrificial death of a discontinuous being"), Blanchot saw it as "an effulgence not of a transcendent point to which all things aspire but rather of an illusory point below the earth, as it were, which comes into being as one writes and attracts as it withdraws." *The Dark Gaze: Maurice Blanchot and the Sacred* (Chicago: University of Chicago Press, 2004), 23.

89 Hollywood, *Sensible Ecstasy*, 70.
90 Peter Tracey Connor, *Georges Bataille and the Mysticism of Sin* (Baltimore: Johns Hopkins University Press, 2000), 13. See "Mystical Ancestors" in this volume for more on these influences.
91 Kevin Hart, *The Dark Gaze*, 23.
92 Bataille, *L'expérience intérieure*, 15.
93 Bataille, *Inner Experience*, 3.
94 For more on the reception of Bataille's ideas in mid-century France, see Hart's chapter, "Art or the Mystical?" in *The Dark Gaze*, 22–49, footnote 8.
95 Hollywood, *Sensible Ecstasy*, 14. See the introduction to this chapter, "The Philosopher – Sartre – and Me," 25–35, for a detailed discussion of this exchange.
96 Bataille, *L'expérience intérieure*, 18.
97 Bataille, *Inner Experience*, 7.
98 Bataille, *L'expérience intérieure*, 59, *Inner Experience*, 46.
99 Bataille, *L'expérience intérieure*, 18.
100 Bataille, *Inner Experience*, 6.
101 Bataille, *L'expérience intérieure*, 10.
102 Bataille, *Inner Experience*, xxxi.
103 Bataille, *L'expérience intérieure*, 11.
104 Bataille, *Inner Experience*, xxxiii.
105 Bataille, *L'expérience intérieure*, 64.
106 Bataille, *Inner Experience*, 50.
107 Bataille, *L'expérience intérieure*, 68.
108 Bataille, *L'expérience intérieure*, 69.
109 Bataille, *Inner Experience*, 54.
110 Bataille, *L'expérience intérieure*, 67–8.
111 Bataille, *L'expérience intérieure*, 48.
112 Bataille, *Inner Experience*, 36.
113 Bataille, *L'expérience intérieure*, 48, *Inner Experience*, 36.
114 Bataille, *L'expérience intérieure*, 49, *Inner Experience*, 36.
115 Bataille, *L'expérience intérieure*, 49.
116 Bataille, *Inner Experience*, 37.
117 This cry, specifically in that it testifies to the interaction with the

Inhuman, bears a close resemblance to Lyotard's notion of stridulation [stridence]. Stridulation can be understood the sound-feeling of one's own voice heard through the throat (as opposed to the voice of others, which one hears through the ears). Lyotard writes, "De la voix pour l'oreille à la stridulation qui monte par la gorge, l'abîme s'avère infranchissable, comme entre moi et je-sans-moi." Jean François Lyotard, *Chambre sourde: L'antiesthétique de Malraux* (Paris: Galilée, 1998), 87.

118 Taylor writes, "Paradoxically, the pineal eye emits a cry that bursts out of a shattered life. This agonizing *cri* is not a 'fact of reason' but is an 'irreducible waste product' – something like excrement that cannot be digested." Mark C. Taylor, *Altarity* (Chicago: University of Chicago Press, 1987), 123.

119 Bataille, *L'expérience intérieuere*, 20.

120 Bataille, *Inner Experience*, 8.

121 Bataille, *L'expérience intérieure*, 138.

122 Bataille, *Inner Experience*, 118.

123 Bataille, *L'expérience intérieure*, 73.

124 Bataille, *Inner Experience*, 59.

125 Bataille, *L'expérience intérieure*, 74. Original emphasis.

126 Bataille, *Inner Experience*, 59.

127 Bataille, *L'expérience intérieure*, 74.

128 Bataille, *Inner Experience*, 59.

129 Bataille, *L'expérience intérieure*, 53. Original emphasis.

130 Bataille, *Inner Experience*, 41.

131 Bataille, *L'expérience intérieure*, 71–2.

132 Bataille, *Inner Experience*, 57.

133 Weil, "L'Amour de Dieu et le malheur," 708. See also note 16 in this chapter on the language of kenosis in Weil's writing.

134 Weil, "L'Amour de Dieu et le malheur," 694.

135 Weil, "L'Amour de Dieu et le malheur," 712.

136 For more on Ariadne's thread in Bataille, see Denis Hollier, *Against Architecture: The Writings of Georges Bataille* trans. Betsy Wing (Cambridge: MIT Press, 1992), 59. "We must, therefore, think of Ariadne's thread and the labyrinth as identical. The labyrinth will be our Ariadne's thread losing us as well as Bataille inside and outside Bataille. Bataille offers the labyrinth and Ariadne's thread both at the same time."

137 Bataille, *L'expérience intérieure*, 45–6.

138 Bataille, *Inner Experience*, 33.

139 Bataille, *L'expérience intérieure*, 20–1.

140 Bataille, *Inner Experience*, 8.

141 Bataille, *L'expérience intérieure*, 17.

142 Bataille, *Inner Experience*, 5.
143 Bataille, *L'expérience intérieure*, 41; *Inner Experience*, 29.
144 Bataille, *L'expérience intérieure*, 42.
145 Bataille, *Inner Experience*, 29.
146 Sartre is not convinced by this claim in "Discussion sur le péché": "Vous avez bien dit 'quand je parle' et vous avez beau jeu de faire retomber la faute sur le langage. Mais il y a, d'une part, l'exposé que vous faites et d'autre part, votre recherche concrète. C'est cette recherche seule qui m'interesse. Si le langage est déformant, alors vous êtes en faute." Georges Bataille, *Œuvres complètes*, vol. 6 (Paris: Gallimard, 1970), 345; For an analysis of this exchange between Sartre and Bataille, see Connor, *Georges Bataille and the Mysticism of Sin*, 126.
147 Bataille, *L'expérience intérieure*, 64.
148 Bataille, *Inner Experience*, 50.
149 Bataille, *L'expérience intérieure*, 72.
150 Bataille, *Inner Experience*, 57–8.
151 Bataille, *L'expérience intérieure*, 55.
152 Bataille, *Inner Experience*, 42.
153 Bataille, *L'expérience intérieure*, 76.
154 Bataille, *Inner Experience*, 61.
155 Connor, *Georges Bataille and the Mysticism of Sin*, 102.
156 Bataille, *L'expérience intérieure*, 76.
157 Bataille, *Inner Experience*, 61.
158 Susan Sontag, *Regarding the Pain of Others* (New York: Farrar, Straus and Giroux, 2003), 99. Bataille reportedly found the photo in Dumas's *Traité de psychologie* in the section on pain.
159 Bataille, *L'expérience intérieure*, 139.
160 Bataille, *Inner Experience*, 119–20.
161 Sontag, *Regarding the Pain of Others*, 99.
162 Bataille, *L'expérience intérieure*, 140.
163 Bataille, *Inner Experience*, 120.
164 Bataille, *Œuvres complètes*, vol. 6, 345. The conference also featured Maurice Blanchot, Simone de Beauvoir, Albert Camus, Jean Hyppolite, Michel Leiris, Gabriel Marcel, Maurice Merleau-Ponty, and Jean Paulhan.
165 Weil, *Œuvres completes*, vol. 6, *Cahiers* 2, 232.
166 Bataille, *L'expérience intérieure*, 41.

Epilogue: Unselfing and Coming Home

1 Safiya Sinclair, "The Art of Unselfing," *Poetry* 207, no. 3 (December 2015): 278.
2 Christy Wampole argues that "unstable soil precludes both rootedness and transcendence" in *Rootedness: The Ramifications of a Metaphor*

(Chicago: University of Chicago Press, 2016), 108. See this work for an analysis of Weil's theory of *enracinement*.

3 See chapter 3 for a discussion of Delbo's positioning of her memoir in relation to the Algerian War. See chapter 4 of Robert Zaretsky, *The Subversive Simone Weil* (Chicago: University of Chicago Press, 2020), 97–132, for a discussion of Weil's anticolonial thinking in relation to her understanding of rootedness.

4 Paul Valéry, "Préface aux *Lettres persanes*," *Variété*, vol. 2 (Paris: Gallimard, 1930), 66.

5 Daryl Cameron, Eliana Hadjiandreou, Stephen Anderson, and Julian A. Scheffer, "Moral Emotions During COVID-19: Examining the Role of Motivation and Choice," *Penn State Social Science Research Institute*, August 6, 2020, https://covid19.ssri.psu.edu/articles/moral-emotions-during-covid-19.

6 See Frans Vosman and Per Nortvedt, eds., *Care Ethics and Phenomenology: A Contested Kinship* (Bristol: Peeters Publishers, 2020) and Dan Zahavi, "How Can Phenomenology Help Nurses Care for Their Patients?" *Aeon*, September 24, 2019, https://aeon.co/essays/how-can-phenomenology-help-nurses-care-for-their-patients.

7 Najat Vallaud-Belkacem and Sandra Laugier, *La société des vulnérables: Leçons féministes d'une crise*, Tracts Gallimard 19 (Paris: Gallimard, 2020), 7.

Bibliography

Adorno, Theodor W. "Cultural Criticism and Society." *Prisms*, translated by Samuel and Shierry Weber, MIT Press, 1981, pp. 17–34.

Agamben, Giorgio. *Remnants of Auschwitz: The Witness and the Archive*. Zone Books, 1999.

Albahari, Miri. *Analytical Buddhism: The Two-Tiered Illusion of the Self*. Palgrave Macmillan UK, 2006.

Allix, Stéphane, et al. eds. *Manuel clinique des expériences extraordinaires*. Interéditions, 2009.

Altizer, Thomas J.J. *The Contemporary Jesus*. State University of New York Press, 1997.

Antonaccio, Maria. "Imagining the Good: Iris Murdoch's Godless Theology." *Annual of the Society of Christian Ethics*, vol. 16, 1996, pp. 223–42.

– "Picturing the Soul: Moral Psychology and the Recovery of the Emotions." *Ethical Theory and Moral Practice*, vol. 4, no. 2, 2001, pp. 127–41.

Les apparitions de Kibeho: une brève présentation. Sanctuaire Notre Dame de Kibeho, 2006.

Armstrong, Paul. *Stories and the Brain: The Neuroscience of Narrative*. Johns Hopkins University Press, 2020.

Badiou, Alain. *Saint Paul: The Foundation of Universalism*. Cultural Memory in the Present. Stanford University Press, 2009.

Baron-Cohen, Simon. *Mindblindness: An Essay on Autism and "Theory of Mind."* MIT Press, 1995.

Bataille, Georges. *The Accursed Share*. Translated by Robert Hurley, vol. 1, Zone Books, 1988.

– *The Accursed Share*. Translated by Robert Hurley, vols. 2 & 3, Zone Books, 1991.

– Carnet 3, Boîte 8, NAF 28086. Fonds Georges Bataille, BNF. Accessed December 12, 2019.

– *L'expérience intérieure*. Somme athéologique 1. Paris: Gallimard, 1954.

– *Inner Experience*. Translated by Leslie Anne Boldt, State University of New York Press, 1988.

– *Œuvres complètes*, vol. 6. Gallimard, 1973.

– *La part maudite*. Éditions de Minuit, 1967.

Batson, C. Daniel, et al. Stocks, "The Empathy-Altruism Hypothesis." *The Oxford Handbook of Prosocial Behavior*, edited by David A. Schroeder and William G. Graziano, Oxford University Press, 2015, pp. 259–81.

Battaly, Heather D. "Is Empathy a Virtue?" In *Empathy: Philosophical and Psychological Perspectives*, edited by Amy Coplan and Peter Goldie, Oxford University Press, 2011, pp. 278–301.

Baudelaire, Charles. *Les paradis artificiels*. Éditions Gallimard et Librairie Générale Française, 1964.

Bensmaïa, Réda. *Experimental Nations, or, the Invention of the Maghreb*. Translated by Alyson Waters. Princeton University Press, 2003.

Bhagavad-Gītā. Translated by Georg Feuerstein. Shambhala, 2011.

Binet, Alfred. *Alterations of Personality*. Translated by Helen Green Baldwin, D. Appleton and Co., 1896.

– *Les altérations de la personnalité*, edited by Daniel N. Robinson, F. Alcan, 1892. http://gallica.bnf.fr/ark:/12148/bpt6k91455f.

Binhammer, Katherine. "Metaphor or Metonymy? The Questions of Essentialism in Cixous." *Tessera* (June 1991), pp. 65–79.

Blake, William. *The Marriage of Heaven and Hell*. E.P. Dutton & Co., 1927.

Bouveresse, Jacques. "Philosophy from an Antiphilosopher: Paul Valéry." Translated by Christian Fournier and Sandra Laugier. *Critical Inquiry*, 21, no. 2, 1995, pp. 354–81.

Boroditsky, Lera. "Does Language Shape Thought? Mandarin and English Speakers' Conceptions of Time." *Cognitive Psychology*, 43, no. 1, 2001, pp. 1–22.

– "How Languages Construct Time." *Space, Time and Number in the Brain*, edited by Stanislas Dehaene and Elizabeth M. Brannon, Academic Press, 2011, pp. 333–41.

– "Metaphoric Structuring: Understanding Time through Spatial Metaphors." *Cognition*, 75, no. 1, 2000, pp. 1–28.

Boroditsky, Lera, et al. "Do English and Mandarin Speakers Think about Time Differently?" *Cognition*, 118, no. 1, 2011, pp. 123–9.

Boroditsky, Lera, et al. "Sex, Syntax, and Semantics." *Language in Mind: Advances in the Study of Language and Thought*, edited by Dedre Gentner and Susan Goldin-Meadow, MIT Press, 2003, pp. 61–80.

Boyle, Claire. "Writing Self-Estrangement: Possessive Knowledge and Loss in Cixous's Recent Autobiographical Work." *Dalhousie French Studies* 68, 2004: 69–77.

Breithaupt, Fritz. *The Dark Sides of Empathy*. Translated by Andrew B.B. Hamilton. Cornell University Press, 2019.

Brennan, Teresa, Introduction. *Between Feminism and Psychoanalysis,* edited by Teresa Brennan. Taylor & Francis e-Library Edition. Routledge, 2002.

Brown, Thackery I., et al. "Differential Medial Temporal Lobe and Parietal Cortical Contributions to Real-world Autobiographical Episodic and Autobiographical Semantic Memory." *Scientific Reports,* vol. 8, no. 6190, 2018. https://doi.org/10.1038/s41598-018-2459-y.

Bugliani, Paolo. "'Facing the Monolith:'' Virginia Woolf, Modernism and Impersonality." *E-rea,* vol. 15, no. 2, 2018. https://doi.org/10.4000/erea.6232.

Burnet, Jennie. "Whose Genocide? Whose Truth?" *Genocide: Truth, Memory, and Representation,* edited by Alexander Laban Hinton and Kevin Lewis O'Neill. Duke University Press, 2009, pp. 80–110.

Cameron, Daryl, et al. "Moral Emotions During COVID-19: Examining the Role of Motivation and Choice." *Penn State Social Science Research Institute,* August 6, 2020, https://covid19.ssri.psu.edu/articles/moral-emotions -during-covid-19. Accessed 4 Apr. 2022.

Camus, Albert. *Essais.* Paris: Gallimard, 1965.

Carlson, Thomas A. "Locating the Mystical Subject." *Mystics: Presence and Aporia,* edited by Michael Kessler and Christian Sheppard, University of Chicago Press, 2003, pp. 207–38.

Caruth, Cathy. *Trauma: Explorations in Memory.* Johns Hopkins University Press, 1995.

– *Unclaimed Experience.* Johns Hopkins University Press, 1996.

Cazenave, Odile M., and Patricia Célérier. *Contemporary Francophone African Writers and the Burden of Commitment.* University of Virginia Press, 2011.

Certeau, Michel de. "Mysticism." *Diacritics,* 22, no. 2 1992, pp. 26–37.

– "Mystique." *Encyclopædia Universalis,* vol. 11, 1968, pp. 521–6.

Cixous, Hélène. *Angst.* Des femmes, 1977.

– "Coming to Writing." *Hélène Cixous, "Coming to Writing" and Other Essays,* edited by Deborah Jenson, translated by Sarah Cornell, Ann Liddle, Susan Sellers, and Deborah Jenson. Harvard University Press, 1991, pp. 1–58.

– *La.* Gallimard, 1976.

– "La venue à l'écriture." *Entre l'écriture,* Des femmes, 1986, pp. 9–69.

– *Le livre de Promethea.* Gallimard, 1983.

– *Les rêveries de la femme sauvage: scènes primitives.* Galilée, 2000.

– *Reveries of the Wild Woman: Primal Scenes.* Translated by Beverley Bie Brahic. Northwestern University Press, 2006.

– *The Hélène Cixous Reader,* edited by Susan Sellers. Routledge, 1994.

Cixous, Hélène, and Mireille Calle-Gruber. *Hélène Cixous, photos de racines.* Des femmes, 1994.

– *Hélène Cixous, Rootprints: Memory and Life Writing.* Routledge, 1997.

Clark, Herbert H. "Space, Time, Semantics, and the Child." *Cognitive Development and Acquisition of Language,* edited by Timothy E. Moore, Academic Press, 1973, pp. 27–63.

Clarke, J.J. *Oriental Enlightenment: The Encounter Between Asian and Western Thought.* Routledge, 1997.

Cohn, Dorrit. *Transparent Minds: Narrative Modes for Presenting Consciousness in Fiction.* Princeton University Press, 1978.

Compagnon, Antoine. "Écrire la vie: Montaigne, Stendhal, Proust." Audio. Collège de France: Littérature française moderne et contemporaine. http://podcastfichiers.college-de-france.fr/compagnon-20090224.m4a. Accessed 15 Jun. 2015.

– "La guerre littéraire." Video. Collège de France: Littérature française moderne et contemporaine. http://www.college-de-france.fr/site/antoine-compagnon/course-2014-03-18-16h30.htm. Accessed June 1, 2015.

Connected Discourses of the Buddha: A New Translation of the Samyutta Nikaya. Translated by Bhikkhu Bodhi, vol. 1. Wisdom Publications, 2000.

Connor, Peter Tracey. *Georges Bataille and the Mysticism of Sin.* Johns Hopkins University Press, 2000.

Cornell, Sarah. "Hélène Cixous: Le Livre de Promethea: Paradise Refound." *Writing Differences: Readings from the Seminar of Hélène Cixous,* edited by Susan Sellers, St. Martin's, 1998, pp. 127–40.

Degrâces, Alyette. Avant-Propos 2: "Du vide d'acte à l'acte vide: Une lecture du *Tao* et de la *Gītā*." *Œuvres complètes,* vol. 6, *Cahiers* 2 by Simone Weil, edited by André A. Devaux and Florence de Lussy, Gallimard, 1997, pp. 33–4.

– Avant-Propos 2: "L'Inde ou le passage obligé." *Œuvres complètes,* vol. 6, *Cahiers* 1 by Simone Weil, edited by André A. Devaux and Florence de Lussy, Gallimard, 1994, pp. 35–52.

Damasio, Antonio R. *Descartes' Error: Emotion, Reason, and the Human Brain.* Putnam, 1994.

– *Self Comes to Mind: Constructing the Conscious Brain.* Pantheon Books, 2010.

de Lussy, Florence. "L'Antijudaïsme de Simone Weil." *Œuvres,* edited by Florence de Lussy, Gallimard, 1999, pp. 959–63.

De Quincey, Thomas. *Confessions of an English Opium-Eater: 1822.* Woodstock Books, 1989.

Delbo, Charlotte. *Auschwitz et après,* vol. 1, *Aucun de nous ne reviendra.* Minuit, 1970.

– *Auschwitz et après,* vol. 2, *Une connaissance inutile.* Minuit, 1970.

– *Auschwitz et après,* vol. 3, *Mesure de nos jours.* Minuit, 1971.

Delbo, Charlotte, and François Bott. "Je me sers de la littérature comme d'une arme: Entretien avec Charlotte Delbo." *Les Revenantes. Charlotte Delbo: La Voix d'une communauté à jamais déportée,* edited by David Caron and Sharon Marquart, Presses universitaires du Mirail, 2011, pp. 25–7.

Delbo, Charlotte, and Madeleine Chapsal. "Rien que des femmes: Entretien avec Charlotte Delbo." *Les Revenantes. Charlotte Delbo: La Voix d'une communauté à jamais déportée*, edited by David Caron and Sharon Marquart, Toulouse: Presses universitaires du Mirail, 2011, pp. 19–23.

Dennett, Daniel. "Who's on First? Heterophenomenology Explained." *Trusting the Subject? (Part I)*, special issue of *Journal of Consciousness Studies*, vol. 10, no. 9–10, 2003, pp. 19–30.

Deppman, Jed. "Re-Presenting Paul Valery's Monsieur Teste." *Symploke*, vol. 11, no. 1, 2003, pp. 197–211.

Derrida, Jacques. "Exergue." *Œuvres de Abdelkébir Khatibi*, vol. 1, *Romans et récits*. La Différence, 2008, p. 7.

– *H.C. pour la vie, c'est à dire … Galilée*, 2002.

– *Le Monolinguisme de l'autre, ou, La prothèse d'origine*. Galilée, 1996.

Doering, E. Jane. *Simone Weil and the Specter of Self-Perpetuating Force*. University of Notre Dame Press, 2010.

Ellen Wolf, Mary. "Rethinking the Radical West: Khatibi and Deconstruction." *L'Esprit Créateur*, vol. 34, no. 2, 1994, pp. 58–68.

Eliot, T.S. *The Sacred Wood*. Faber and Faber, 1997.

Fanon, Frantz. *Black Skin, White Masks*. Translated by Richard Philcox, Grove Press, 2008.

– *Les damnés de la terre*. La Découverte, 1985.

– *Œuvres*. La Découverte, 2011.

Fieni, David. Review of Abdelkébir Khatibi's "Class Warrior – Taoist Style." *b2o*, September 12, 2018. https://www.boundary2.org/2018/09/david-fieni-review-of-abdelkebir-khatibis-class-warrior-taoist-style/ Accessed 4 Apr. 2022.

Forsdick, Charles. "Between 'French' and 'Francophone': French Studies and the Postcolonial Turn." *French Studies*, vol. 59, no. 4, 2005, pp. 523–30.

Freeman, Mark Philip. *The Priority of the Other: Thinking and Living Beyond the Self*. Oxford University Press, 2014.

Freud, Sigmund. *Beyond the Pleasure Principle*. Translated by C.J.M. Hubback, The International Psychoanalytical Press, 1922.

Fuente, Juanma de la, et al. "When You Think about It, Your Past Is in Front of You: How Culture Shapes Spatial Conceptions of Time." *Psychological Science*, vol. 25, no. 9, 2014, pp. 1682–90.

Fuhrman, Orly, and Lera Boroditsky. "Cross-Cultural Differences in Mental Representations of Time: Evidence from an Implicit Nonlinguistic Task." *Cognitive Science*, vol. 34, 2010, pp. 1430–51.

Gabellieri, Emmanuel, and François L'Yvonnet, eds. *Simone Weil*. L'Herne, 2014.

Gallagher, Shaun, and Dan Zahavi. "Phenomenological Approaches to Self-Consciousness." *Stanford Encyclopedia of Philosophy*, edited by Edward N. Zalta, Summer Edition, 2019. https://plato.stanford.edu/archives/sum2019/entries/self-consciousness-phenomenological. Accessed 1 Aug. 2020.

– *The Phenomenological Mind: An Introduction to Philosophy of Mind and Cognitive Science*. First edition. Routledge, 2008.

Gallese, Vittorio. "Mirror Neurons, Embodied Simulation, and the Neural Basis of Social Identification." *Psychoanalytic Dialogues*, vol. 19, no. 5, 2009, pp. 519–36.

Gallese, Vittorio, and Michele Guerra. *The Empathic Screen: Cinema and Neuroscience*. Oxford University Press, 2020.

Gallese, Vittorio, et al. "Action Recognition in the Premotor Cortex." *Brain*, vol. 119, 1996, pp. 593–609.

Gandhi, Leela. "Theory and Practice in Postcolonial Studies." *The Oxford Handbook of Postcolonial Studies*, edited by Graham Huggan. First edition. Oxford University Press, 2013, pp. 412–15.

Gelly, Violaine, and Paul Gradhvol. *Charlotte Delbo*. Fayard, 2013.

Gerner, Alexander, and Jorge de Almeida Gonçalves, eds. *Altered Self and Altered Self-Experience*. Books on Demand, 2014.

Gifford, Paul. "Self and Other: Valéry's Lost Object of Desire." *Reading Paul Valéry: Universe in Mind*, edited by Paul Gifford and Brian Stimpson, Cambridge University Press, 1998, pp. 280–96.

Gijssels, Tom, and Daniel Casasanto. "Conceptualizing Time in Terms of Space: Experimental Evidence." *The Cambridge Handbook of Cognitive Linguistics*, edited by Barbara Dancygier, Cambridge University Press, 2017, pp. 651–68.

Gilbert, Catherine. "Mobilising Memory: Rwandan Women Genocide Survivors in the Diaspora." *Australian Journal of French Studies*, vol. 55, no. 1, 2018, pp. 52–64.

– "Writing as Reconciliation: Bearing Witness to Life after Genocide." *Rwanda since 1994*, edited by Hannah Grayson and Nicki Hitchcott, Liverpool University Press, 2019, pp. 147–67.

Gilmore, Leigh. *The Limits of Autobiography: Trauma and Testimony*. Cornell University Press, 2001.

Goldman, Alvin. "Interpretation Psychologized." *Folk Psychology: The Theory of Mind Debate*, edited by Martin Davies and Tony Stone, Blackwell, 1995, pp. 74–99.

Gopnik, Alison. "Theory of Mind." *The MIT Encyclopedia of the Cognitive Sciences*, edited by R. Wilson and F. Keil, MIT Press, 1999, pp. 838–40.

Gopnik, Alison, and Henry M. Wellman. "Why the Child's Theory of Mind Is Really a Theory." *Folk Psychology: The Theory of Mind Debate*, edited by Martin Davies and Tony Stone, Blackwell, 1995, pp. 232–58.

Gordon, David J. "Iris Murdoch's Comedies of Unselfing." *Twentieth Century Literature*, vol. 36, no. 2, 1990, pp. 115–36.

Gordon, Lewis R. *What Fanon Said: A Philosophical Introduction to His Life and Thought*. Fordham University Press, 2015.

Gordon, Robert. "Folk Psychology as Simulation." *Mind and Language*, vol. 1, no. 2, 1986, pp. 158–71.

Hanrahan, Mairéad. *Cixous's Semi-Fictions: Thinking at the Borders of Fiction*. Frontiers of Theory. Edinburgh University Press, 2014.

Hart, Kevin. *The Dark Gaze: Maurice Blanchot and the Sacred*. University of Chicago Press, 2004.

Harvey, Peter. *The Selfless Mind: Personality, Consciousness and Nirvana in Early Buddhism*. Routledge, 1995.

Heidegger, Martin. *Being and Time*. Translated by Joan Stambaugh, State University of New York Press, 1996.

Henry, Paget. "Africana Phenomenology: Its Philosophical Implications." *CLR James Journal*, vol. 11, no. 1, 2005, pp. 79–112.

– *Caliban's Reason: Introducing Afro-Caribbean Philosophy*. Routledge, 2000.

Herman, Judith. *Trauma and Recovery*. Basic Books, 1992.

Hiddleston, Jane. *Poststructuralism and Postcoloniality: The Anxiety of Theory*. Postcolonialism across the Disciplines 8. Liverpool University Press, 2010.

– *Understanding Postcolonialism*. Routledge, 2009.

Hinton, Alexander Laban, and Kevin Lewis O'Neill, editors. *Genocide: Truth, Memory, and Representation*. Duke University Press, 2009.

Hitchcott, Nicki. "The (Un)Believable Truth about Rwanda." *Australian Journal of French Studies*, vol. 56, no. 2, 2019, pp. 199–215.

Hof, Christine. "Kénose et Histoire: La lecture de l'Hymne aux Philippiens." *Simone Weil*, edited by Emmanuel Gabellieri and François L'Yvonnet, L'Herne, 2014, pp. 385–96.

Hollier, Denis. *Against Architecture: The Writings of Georges Bataille*. Translated by Betsy Wing, MIT Press, 1992.

Hollywood, Amy. *Sensible Ecstasy*. University of Chicago Press, 2002.

Hulstyn, Michaela. "Charlotte Delbo à l'écoute: Auditory Imagery in *Auschwitz et après*." *Women in French Studies*, vol. 6, 2016, pp. 70–82.

Hung, Jenny. "The Theory of the Self in the Zhuangzi: A Strawsonian Interpretation." *Philosophy East and West*, vol. 69, no. 2, 2019, pp. 376–94.

Husserl, Edmund. *Cartesian Meditations: An Introduction to Phenomenology*. Translated by Dorion Cairns, Martinus Nijhoff, 1970.

Iacoboni, Marco. *Mirroring People: The New Science of How We Connect with Others*. Farrar, Straus and Giroux, 2008.

Irwin, Alec. "Devoured by God: Cannibalism, Mysticism, and Ethics in Simone Weil." *CrossCurrents*, vol. 51, no. 2, 2001, pp. 257–72.

Irwin, Alexander. *Saints of the Impossible: Bataille, Weil, and the Politics of the Sacred*. University of Minnesota Press, 2002.

Jakobson, Roman. "On Linguistic Aspects of Translation." *On Translation*, edited by Arthur Reuben Brower, Harvard University Press, 1959, pp. 232–9.

James, William. *Principles of Psychology*. Dover Books, 1950.

- *The Varieties of Religious Experience, a Study in Human Nature.* The Modern Library, 1936.

Jones, Richard H. *Philosophy of Mysticism.* SUNY Press, 2016.

Kahneman, Daniel. *Thinking, Fast and Slow.* Farrar, Straus and Giroux, 2011.

Kalibwami, Justin. *Le Catholicisme et la société rwandaise: 1900–1962.* Présence africaine, 1991.

Kapani, Lakshmi. "Simone Weil, Lectrice des *Upanishad védiques* et de la *Bhagavad-Gîtâ*: L'action sans désir et le désir sans objet." *Cahiers Simone Weil,* vol. 5, no. 2, 1982, pp. 95–119.

Kassab-Charfi, Samia. "Amour bilingue de Khatibi ou la mémoire palimpseste." *Revue CELAAN,* vol. 9, nos. 2–3, 2011, pp. 120–34.

Kayitare, Pauline, et al. *Tu leur diras que tu es hutue: à 13 ans, une Tutsie au cœur du génocide rwandais.* A. Versaille, 2011.

Keats, John. *Selected Letters,* edited by Jon Mee, Oxford University Press, 2009.

Keen, Suzanne. *Empathy and the Novel.* Oxford University Press, 2010.

Keysers, Christian. *The Empathic Brain: How the Discovery of Mirror Neurons Changes Our Understanding of Human Nature.* Smashwords Editions, 2011.

Khatibi, Abdelkebir. *Class Warrior – Taoist Style.* Translated by Matt Reeck. Wesleyan University Press, 2017.

- "Frontiers between Psychoanalysis and Islam." Translated by P. Burcu Yalim. *Third Text,* vol. 23, no. 6, 2009, pp. 689–96.

- *Love in Two Languages.* Translated by Richard Howard, University of Minnesota Press, 1990.

- *Œuvres de Abdelkébir Khatibi,* vol. 1, *Romans et récits.* la Différence, 2008.

- *Œuvres de Abdelkébir Khatibi,* vol. 2, *Poésie de l'aimance.* la Différence, 2008.

- *Œuvres de Abdelkébir Khatibi,* vol. 3, *Essais.* la Différence, 2008.

- *Plural Maghreb: Writings on Postcolonialism.* Translated by P. Burcu Yalim, Bloomsbury Academic, 2019.

Kilito, Abdelfattah. *Thou Shalt Not Speak My Language.* Translated by Waïl S. Hassan. Syracuse University Press, 2008.

Kofman, Sarah. *Paroles suffoquées.* Galilée, 1987.

- *Smothered Words.* Translated by Madeleine Dobie, Northwestern University Press, 1998.

Kotva, Simone. "The Occult Mind of Simone Weil." *Philosophical Investigations,* vol. 43, nos. 1–2, 2020, pp. 122–41.

LaCapra, Dominick. *Representing the Holocaust.* Cornell University Press, 1994.

- *Writing History, Writing Memory.* Johns Hopkins University Press, 2001.

Lakoff, George and Mark Johnson. *Metaphors We Live By.* University of Chicago Press, 1973.

Landy, Joshua. *How to Do Things with Fictions.* Oxford University Press, 2012.

- *Philosophy as Fiction: Self, Deception, and Knowledge in Proust.* Oxford University Press, 2004.

Lamont, Rosette C. Translator's Preface. *Auschwitz and After,* by Charlotte Delbo, Yale University Press, 1995, pp. vii–viii.

Langer, Lawrence L. "Hearing the Holocaust." *Poetics Today,* vol. 27, no. 2, 2006, pp. 297–309.

– Introduction. *Auschwitz and After,* by Charlotte Delbo, translated by Rosette C. Lamont, Yale University Press, 1995.

– *The Holocaust and the Literary Imagination.* Yale University Press, 1975.

Lao-Tzu: Te-Tao Ching, A New Translation Based on the Recently Discovered Ma-wang-tui Texts. Translated by Robert G. Henricks, Ballantine Books, 1989.

Laub, Dori. "Bearing Witness or the Vicissitudes of Listening." *The Holocaust: Theoretical Readings,* edited by Neil Levi and Michael Rothberg, Rutgers University Press, 2003, pp. 221–6.

Levi, Primo. *The Drowned and the Saved.* Translated by Raymond Rosenthal, Summit Books, 1988.

Levinas, Emmanuel. *Totalité et infini: essai sur l'extériorité.* M. Nijhoff, 1984.

– *Totality and Infinity: An Essay on Exteriority.* Translated by Alphonso Lingus, Kluwer Academic Publishers, 1991.

Leys, Ruth. *Trauma: A Genealogy.* University of Chicago Press, 2000.

Li, Xiaofan Amy. *Comparative Encounters between Artaud, Michaux and the Zhuangzi: Rationality, Cosmology, and Ethics.* Taylor & Francis, 2015.

Lionnet, Françoise. *Autobiographical Voices: Race, Gender, Self-Portraiture.* Cornell University Press, 1989.

Locke, John. "Of Identity and Diversity." *Personal Identity,* edited by John Perry, 3rd ed., University of California Press, 2008, pp. 33–52.

Longman, Timothy. "Christian Churches and Genocide in Rwanda." *In God's Name: Genocide and Religion in the Twentieth Century,* edited by Omer Bartov and Phyllis Mack, Berghahn Books, 2001, pp. 139–60.

Luckhurst, Roger. *The Trauma Question.* Routledge, 2008.

Lyotard, Jean François. *Chambre sourde: l'antiesthétique de Malraux.* Galilée, 1998.

Lyotard, Jean-François. *Soundproof Room: Malraux's Anti-Aesthetics.* Translated by Robert Harvey, Stanford University Press, 2001.

MacDonald, Megan C. "Haunting Correspondences and Elemental Scenes: Weaving Cixous after Derrida." *Cixous after / Depuis 2000,* edited by Elizabeth Berglund Hall, Frédérique Chevillot, Eilene Hoft-March, and Maribel Penalver Vicea, Brill, 2017, pp. 36–54.

MacIntyre, Alasdair C. *After Virtue: A Study in Moral Theory.* 2nd ed., University of Notre Dame Press, 1984.

Malraux, André. *Lazare.* Gallimard, 1974.

Marno, David. *Death Be Not Proud: The Art of Holy Attention.* University of Chicago Press, 2016.

Marteau, Frédéric. "Regarder, voir, savoir: Enjeux du regard et poétique de la lecture dans l'œuvre de Charlotte Delbo." *Charlotte Delbo: Œuvre et engagements*, edited by Christiane Page, Presses universitaires de Rennes, 2014, pp. 165–77.

Martin, Jean-Pierre. *Henri Michaux*. Gallimard, 2003.

McCullough, Lissa. *The Religious Philosophy of Simone Weil: An Introduction*. Bloomsbury, 2014.

McDonald, Christie, and Susan Rubin Suleiman, editors. *French Global: A New Approach to Literary History*. Columbia University Press, 2010.

McGuire, James. "Forked Tongues, Marginal Bodies: Writing as Translation in Khatibi." *Research in African Literatures*, vol. 23, no. 1, 1992, 107–16.

McHale, Brian. "Transparent Minds Revisited." *Narrative*, vol. 20, no. 1, 2012, pp. 115–24.

Mehrez, Samia. "Translation and the Postcolonial Experience: The Francophone North African Text." *Rethinking Translation: Discourse, Subjectivity, Ideology*, edited by Lawrence Venuti. Routledge, 1992, pp. 120–38.

Meltzer, Françoise. "The Hands of Simone Weil." *Critical Inquiry*, vol. 27, no. 4, 2001, pp. 611–28.

Meltzoff, Andrew. "Origins of Social Cognition: Bidirectional Self-Other Mapping and the 'Like-Me' Hypothesis." *Navigating the Social World: What Infants, Children, and Other Species Can Teach Us*, edited by Mahzarin R. Banaji and Susan A. Gelman, Oxford University Press, 2014, pp. 139–44.

Memmi, Albert. *Racism*. Translated by Steve Martinot, University of Minnesota Press, 2000.

Merleau-Ponty, Maurice. *Phénoménologie de la perception*. Gallimard, 1945.

– *Phenomenology of Perception*. Translated by Donald A. Landes, Routledge, 2012.

– *Sense and Non-Sense*. Translated by Hubert L. Dreyfus and Patricia Allen Dreyfus, Northwestern University Press, 1964.

Merriman, Scott A. *Religion and the State: An International Analysis of Roles and Relationships*. ABC-CLIO, 2009.

Metzinger, Thomas. *Being No One*. MIT Press, 2003.

– *The Ego Tunnel: The Science of the Mind and the Myth of the Self*. Basic Books, 2009.

Michaux, Henri. *Connaissance par les gouffres*. Gallimard, 1967.

– *Les grandes épreuves de l'esprit et les innombrables petites*. Gallimard, 1966.

– *Misérable miracle, la mescaline*. Gallimard, 1972.

– *Miserable Miracle: Mescaline*. Translated by Louise Varèse and Anna Moschovakis, New York Review Books, 2002.

– *Œuvres complètes*, edited by Raymond Bellour and Ysé Tran, vol. 1. Bibliothèque de la Pléiade. Gallimard, 1998.

– *Œuvres complètes*, edited by Raymond Bellour and Ysé Tran, vol. 2. Bibliothèque de la Pléiade. Gallimard, 1998.

– *The Major Ordeals of the Mind, and the Countless Minor Ones*. Translated by Richard Howard, Harcourt Brace Joanovich, 1974.

Miller, Nancy K. *But Enough about Me: Why We Read Other People's Lives.* Columbia University Press, 2002.

Moran, Dermot. *Introduction to Phenomenology.* Routledge, 2000.

Mukagasana, Yolande. *La mort ne veut pas de moi.* Fixot, 1997.

– *Not My Time to Die.* Translated by Zoe Norridge, Huza Press, 2019.

– *N'aie pas peur de savoir.* R. Laffont, 1999.

Murdoch, Iris. *Henry and Cato.* Open Road Media, 2010.

Murdoch, Iris. *Metaphysics as a Guide to Morals.* Penguin Press, 1992.

– *The Sovereignty of Good.* Routledge & K. Paul, 1970.

Nietzsche, Friedrich. *Beyond Good and Evil: Prelude to a Philosophy of the Future.* Translated by Walter Kaufmann, Vintage Books, 1989.

"Neo-Whorfianism: A Debate on Language and Thought." *Economist,* 13 Dec. 2010, http://www.economist.com/blogs/johnson/2010/12/neo-whorfianism. Accessed 11 Mar. 2022.

Norridge, Zoe. *Perceiving Pain in African Literature.* Palgrave Macmillan, 2013.

– Translator's Note. *Not My Time to Die,* by Yolande Mukagasana, translated by Zoe Norridge, Huza Press, 2019, pp. 190–9.

Les Nouvelles Écritures du Moi dans les Littératures française et francophone, edited by Sylvie Camet and Noureddine Sabri. L'Harmattan, 2012.

Nussbaum, Martha. "'Finely Aware and Richly Responsible': Literature and the Moral Imagination." *Literature and the Question of Philosophy,* edited by Anthony J. Cascardi, Johns Hopkins University Press, 1987, pp. 167–91.

Obama, Barack. Commencement Speech. Northwestern University, June 19, 2006. http://www.northwestern.edu/newscenter/stories/2006/06/barack .html. Accessed 1 Jun. 2021.

Ong, Yi-Ping. *The Art of Being: Poetics of the Novel and Existential Philosophy.* Harvard University Press, 2018.

Palmer, Alan. *Fictional Minds.* University of Nebraska Press, 2004.

Parfit, Derek. *Reasons and Persons.* Clarendon Press, 1984.

Parish, Nina. *Henri Michaux: Experimentation with Signs.* Rodopi, 2007.

Perrin, Joseph Marie, and Gustave Thibon. *Simone Weil as We Knew Her.* Routledge, 2003.

Proust, Marcel. *Contre Saint-Beuve.* Gallimard, 1954.

Qader, Nasrin. *Narratives of Catastrophe: Boris Diop, Ben Jelloun, Khatibi.* Fordham University Press, 2009.

Rabinovitch, Celia. *Surrealism and the Sacred: Power, Eros, and the Occult in Modern Art.* Westview Press, 2002.

Reeck, Matt. "The Poetics of the Orphan in Abdelkébir Khatibi's Early Work." *Journal of French and Francophone Philosophy,* vol. 25, no. 1, 2017, pp. 132–49.

Renshaw, Sal. "The Thealogy of Helene Cixous." *Religion in French Feminist Thought: Critical Perspectives,* edited by Morny Joy, Kathleen O'Grady, and Judith L. Poxon, Routledge, 2003, pp. 162–75.

Rey, Roselyne. *History of Pain*. Translated by Louise Elliott Wallace, J.A. Cadden, and S.W. Cadden, Harvard University Press, 1993.

Reynolds, Felisa V. "Khatibi as Derrida's Foil: Undermining the Last Defender of the French Language." *Contemporary French and Francophone Studies*, vol. 18, no. 2, 2014, pp. 199–206.

Rice, Alison. *Polygraphies: Francophone Women Writing Algeria*. University of Virginia Press, 2012.

– *Time Signatures: Contextualizing Contemporary Francophone Autobiographical Writing from the Maghreb*. Lexington Books, 2006.

Ricoeur, Paul. *Oneself as Another*. Translated by Kathleen Blamey, University of Chicago Press, 2008.

– *Soi-même comme un autre*. Seuil, 1990.

– *Time and Narrative*, vol. 1. Translated by Kathleen McLaughlin and David Pellauer, University of Chicago Press, 1984.

– *Time and Narrative*, vol. 2. Translated by Kathleen McLaughlin and David Pellauer, University of Chicago Press, 1985.

Rifkin, Jeremy. *The Empathic Civilization: The Race to Global Consciousness in a World in Crisis*. J.P. Tarcher/Penguin, 2009.

Rigaud-Drayton, Margaret. *Henri Michaux: Poetry, Painting, and the Universal Sign*. Clarendon Press, 2005.

Rimbaud, Arthur. *Les lettres manuscrites de Rimbaud*, edited by Claude Jeancolas, vol 1. Textuel, 1997.

Rittner, Carol, et al., editors. *Genocide in Rwanda: Complicity of the Churches?* Paragon House, 2004.

Rizzolatti, Giacomo, et al. "Premotor Cortex and the Recognition of Motor Actions." *Cognitive Brain Research*, vol. 3, 1996, pp. 131–41.

Robcis, Camille. *Disalienation: Politics, Philosophy, and Radical Psychiatry in Postwar France*. University of Chicago Press, 2021.

Robinson, Daniel N. Preface. *Alterations of Personality: On Double Consciousness*, by Alfred Binet, edited by Daniel N. Robinson, University Publications of America, 1977, pp. v–ix.

Robinson-Valéry, Judith. "'To Go to the Last Point' A la recherche d'une nouvelle définition du mysticisme." *Paul Valéry: Musique, Mystique, Mathématique*, edited by Paul Gifford and Brian Stimpson, Presses universitaires de Lille, 1993, pp. 15–36.

Rothberg, Michael. "Decolonizing Trauma Studies: A Response." *Studies in the Novel*, vol. 40, 2008, pp. 224–34.

– *Multidirectional Memory: Remembering the Holocaust in the Age of Decolonization*. Stanford University Press, 2009.

Ryan, Paul. "'L'ici est le moi de l'espace': Self, Genesis and the Space of Writing in Valéry's Cahiers." *Modern Language Review*, vol. 97, no. 3, 2002, pp. 553–65.

Sajed, Alina. "The Post Always Rings Twice? The Algerian War, Poststructuralism and the Postcolonial in IR Theory." *Review of International Studies*, vol. 38, no. 1, 2012, pp. 141–63.

Sartre, Jean Paul. *Being and Nothingness*. Translated by Hazel E. Barnes, Washington Square Press, 1992.

– "Discussion sur le péché." *Georges Bataille: Œuvres complètes*, vol. 6. Gallimard, 1970.

– *L'être et le néant: Essai d'ontologie phénoménologique*. Gallimard, 1943.

– "Un nouveau mystique." *Situations*, vol. 1. Gallimard, 1947, pp. 143–88.

Scarry, Elaine. *On Beauty and Being Just*. Princeton University Press, 1999.

– *The Body in Pain: The Making and Unmaking of the World*. Oxford University Press, 1987.

Schacter, Daniel. *The Seven Sins of Memory: How the Mind Forgets and Remembers*. Houghton Mifflin, 2001.

Schacter, Daniel L., Scott A. Guerin, and Peggy L. St. Jacques. "Memory Distortion: An Adaptive Perspective." *Trends in Cognitive Sciences*, vol. 15, no. 10, 2011, pp. 467–74.

Schechtman, Marya. *The Constitution of Selves*. Cornell University Press, 1996.

– "The Narrative Self." *The Oxford Handbook of the Self*, edited by Shaun Gallagher, Oxford University Press, 2011, pp. 392–416.

Scherer, Jacques. *Le "Livre de Mallarmé": Premières recherches sur des documents inédits*. Gallimard, 1957.

Schimmel, Annemarie. *Mystical Dimensions of Islam*. University of North Carolina Press, 2011.

Schopenhauer, Arthur. *The World as Will and Representation*, vol. 1. Translated by E.F.J. Payne, Dover Publications, 1969.

Scott, H. Jill. "Loving the Other: Subjectivities of Proximity in Hélène Cixous's Book of Promethea." *World Literature Today*, vol. 69, no. 1, 1995, pp. 29–35.

Searle, Callisto. "The Hermeneutics of Contentious Imagery: What Exactly the *Zhuangzi* Has to Say about the Straw Dogs in the *Laozi*." *Religions*, vol. 10, no. 6, 2019, 359.

Sells, Michael Anthony. *Approaching the Qur'an: The Early Revelations*. 2nd ed. White Cloud Press, 2007.

Shantz, Colleen. *Paul in Ecstasy: The Neurobiology of the Apostle's Life and Thought*. Cambridge University Press, 2009.

Sidertis, Mark, et al., editors. *Self, No Self? Perspectives from Analytical, Phenomenological, and Indian Traditions*. Oxford University Press, 2010.

Sieburth, Richard. "Technician of the Sacred: The Internal and External Voyages of Henri Michaux." *Times Literary Supplement*, February 8, 2002.

Sinclair, Safiya. "The Art of Unselfing." *Poetry*, vol. 207, no. 3, 2015, p. 278.

Smith, Huston. *Cleansing the Doors of Perception: The Religious Significance of Entheogenic Plants and Chemicals*. Jeremy P. Tarcher, 2000.

Sokolowski, Robert. *Introduction to Phenomenology*. Cambridge University Press, 2000.

Sontag, Susan. *Regarding the Pain of Others*. Farrar, Straus and Giroux, 2003.

Spiegelberg, Herbert. *The Phenomenological Movement: A Historical Introduction*. 2nd ed. Springer, 1971.

Stark, Jared. "Traumatic Futures: A Review Article." *Trials of Trauma*, special issue of *Comparative Literature Studies*, vol. 48, no. 3, 2011, pp. 435–52.

Staub, Ervin, and Johanna Vollhardt. "Altruism Born of Suffering: The Roots of Caring and Helping after Victimization and Other Trauma." *American Journal of Orthopsychiatry*, vol. 78, no. 3, 2008, pp. 267–80.

Strawson, Galen. *The Subject of Experience*. Oxford: Oxford University Press, 2017.

Suleiman, Susan Rubin. *Crises of Memory and the Second World War*. Harvard University Press, 2006.

Surya, Michael. *Georges Bataille, la mort à l'œuvre*. Gallimard, 1992.

Tart, Charles T., Introduction. *Altered States of Consciousness*, 2nd ed., Garden City: Doubleday, 1969, pp. 1–6.

Taylor, Charles. *Sources of the Self*. Cambridge University Press, 1989.

Taylor, Mark C. *Altarity*. University of Chicago Press, 1987.

Thibault, Bruno. "Voyager contre: la question de l'exotisme dans les journaux de voyage d'Henri Michaux." *French Review*, vol. 63, no. 3, 1990, pp. 485–91.

This "Self" Which Is Not One: Women's Life Writing in French, edited by Natalie Edwards and Christopher Hogarth. Newcastle upon Tyne: Cambridge Scholars, 2010.

Thompson, Evan. "Is Consciousness a 'Stream'?" *Brains Blog*, 29 Jul. 2015. https://philosophyofbrains.com/2015/07/29/is-consciousness-a-stream.aspx.

Tougaw, Jason D. "'We Slipped into a Dream State': Dreaming and Trauma in Charlotte Delbo's 'Auschwitz and After.'" *Part 2: Trauma and Rhetoric*, special issue of *JAC*, vol. 24, no. 3, 2004, pp. 583–605.

Trotet, François. *Henri Michaux ou la sagesse du vide*. Albin Michel, 1992.

Tversky, Barbara, Sol Kugelmass, and Atalia Winter. "Cross-Cultural and Developmental Trends in Graphic Productions." *Cognitive Psychology*, vol. 23, no. 4, 1991, pp. 515–57.

Umurerwa, Marie-Aimable, and Patrick May. *Comme la langue entre les dents: fratricide et piège identitaire au Rwanda*. L'Harmattan, 2000.

Urban, Hugh B. "Desire, Blood, and Power: Georges Bataille and the Study of Hindu Tantra in Northeastern India." *Negative Ecstasies: Georges Bataille and the Study of Religion*, edited by Jeremy Biles and Kent L. Brintnall, Fordham University Press, 2015, pp. 68–80.

Valéry, Paul. *Cahiers*, vol. 9. Centre national de la recherche scientifique, 1959.

– *Cahiers*, vol. 16. Centre national de la recherche scientifique, 1959.

- *Cahiers*, vol. 2, edited by Judith Robinson-Valéry. Gallimard, 1974.
- *Cahiers 1894–1914*, vol. 2, edited by Judith Robinson-Valéry and Nicole Celeyrette-Pietri. Gallimard, 1987.
- *Cahiers/Notebooks*, vol. 1, edited by Paul Gifford, Brian Stimpson, Robert Pickering, and Judith Robinson-Valéry. P. Lang, 2000.
- *Œuvres*, vol. 2, edited by Jean Hytier and Agathe Rouart-Valéry. Gallimard, 1957.
- "Préface aux *Lettres persanes*." *Variété*, vol. 2, Gallimard, 1930, pp. 53–73.
- "The Evening with Monsieur Teste." *Paul Valéry: An Anthology*, edited by Jackson Mathews, selected by James R. Lawler, Princeton University Press, 1977, pp. 3–16.

Vallaud-Belkacem, Najat, and Sandra Laugier. *La société des vulnérables: Leçons féministes d'une crise*. Tracts Gallimard 19. Paris: Gallimard, 2020.

van der Kolk, Bessel A., et al. *Traumatic Stress: The Effects of Overwhelming Experience on Mind, Body, and Society*. Guilford Press, 1996.

Virtanen, Reino. "The Egocentric Predicament: Paul Valéry and Some Contemporaries." *Dalhousie French Studies*, vol. 3, 1981, pp. 99–117.

Visser, Irene. "Decolonizing Trauma Theory: Retrospect and Prospects." *Humanities*, vol. 4, 2015, pp. 250–65.

Vosman, Frans, and Per Nortvedt, editors. *Care Ethics and Phenomenology: A Contested Kinship*. Peeters Publishers, 2020.

Wagner, Anthony. "The Science of Remembering." Augmenting Personal Intelligence. Media X, 2006. https://mediax.stanford.edu/featured-events/anthony-wagner-mediax2016/. Accessed 1 Jun. 2020.

Wahbi, Hassan. *Abdelkébir Khatibi, la fable de l'aimance*. L'Harmattan, 2009.

Wampole, Christy. *Rootedness: The Ramifications of a Metaphor*. Chicago: University of Chicago Press, 2016.

Weil, Simone. "L'Amour de Dieu et le malheur." *Œuvres*, edited by Florence de Lussy, Gallimard, 1999, pp. 691–716.
- "Autobiographie spirituelle." *Œuvres*, edited by Florence de Lussy, Gallimard, 1999, pp. 767–80.
- *La connaissance surnaturelle*. Gallimard, 1950.
- "Formes de l'Amour implicite de Dieu." *Œuvres,* edited by Florence de Lussy, Gallimard, 1999, pp. 717–64.
- *Gravity and Grace*. Translated by Emma Crawford and Mario von der Ruhr, Routledge, 2002.
- Letter to G. Thibon, September 15, 1941. Fonds Weil, BNF.
- Letter to G. Thibon, December 1941. Correspondence, NAF 28437. Fonds Weil, BNF.
- "Lettre à Joë Bousquet." *Œuvres*, edited by Florence de Lussy, Gallimard, 1999, pp. 791–800.
- *Œuvres*, edited by Florence de Lussy. Quarto. Gallimard, 1999.

- *Œuvres complètes*, edited by André A. Devaux and Florence de Lussy, vol. 6, *Cahiers* 1. Gallimard, 1994.
- *Œuvres complètes*, edited by André A. Devaux and Florence de Lussy, vol. 6, *Cahiers* 2. Gallimard, 1997.
- *La pesanteur et la grâce*. Plon, 1948.
- *Simone Weil: Seventy Letters*. Translated by Richard Rees, Oxford University Press, 1965.
- *The Simone Weil Reader*, edited by George A. Panichas, McKay, 1977.
- *Waiting for God*. Translated by Emma Craufurd, Harper Perennial Modern Classics, 2001.

Weinberg, Shelley. "Locke on Personal Identity." *Philosophy Compass*, vol. 6, no. 6, 2011, 398–407.

Wheeler, Michael. *Reconstructing the Cognitive World: The Next Step*. MIT Press, 2007.

Wieviorka, Annette. *L'ère du témoin*. Plon, 1998.

Wolf, Mary Ellen. "Rethinking the Radical West: Khatibi and Deconstruction," *L'Esprit Créateur*, vol. 34, no. 2, 1994, pp. 58–68.

Wright, Robert. *Why Buddhism is True: The Science and Philosophy of Meditation and Enlightenment*. Simon and Schuster, 2017.

Young, Allan. *The Harmony of Illusions: Inventing Post-Traumatic Stress Disorder*. Princeton University Press, 1995.

Young, Robert C. *White Mythologies: Writing History and the West*. Routledge, 1990.

Zahavi, Dan. "How Can Phenomenology Help Nurses Care for Their Patients?" *Aeon*, September 24 2019. https://aeon.co/essays/how-can-phenomenology-help-nurses-care-for-their-patients. Accessed 11 Mar. 2022.

- *Self and Other: Exploring Subjectivity, Empathy, and Shame*. Oxford University Press, 2014.
- *Subjectivity and Selfhood: Investigating the First-Person Perspective*. MIT Press, 2005.

Zaretsky, Robert. *The Subversive Simone Weil: A Life in Five Ideas*. University of Chicago Press, 2021.

Zhang, Dora. "Stream of Consciousness." *The Oxford Handbook of Virginia Woolf*, edited by Anne E. Fernald, Oxford University Press, 2021, pp. 133–48.

Zhuangzi: The Essential Writings. Translated by Brook Ziporyn, Hackett, 2009.

Ziporyn, Brook. *Evil and/or/as the Good: Omnicentrism, Intersubjectivity, and Value Paradox in Tiantai Buddhist Thought*. Harvard University Press, 2000.

Zunshine, Lisa. *Why We Read Fiction: Theory of Mind and the Novel*. Ohio State University Press, 2006.

Index

www.ingramcontent.com/pod-product-compliance
Ingram Content Group UK Ltd.
Pitfield, Milton Keynes, MK11 3LW, UK
UKHW041648020225
454515UK00003B/110/J